India

Edited by Samuel Israel and Bikram Grewal
Directed and Designed by Hans Johannes Hoefer
Updated by Toby Sinclair

APA PUBLICATIONS

THE INSIGHT GUIDES SERIES RECEIVED SPECIAL AWARDS FOR EXCELLENCE FROM THE PACIFIC AREA TRAVEL ASSOCIATION.

INDIA

Third Edition

© 1989 APA PUBLICATIONS (HK) LTD
Printed in Singapore by APA Press Pte Ltd
Colour Separation in Singapore by Colourscan Pte Ltd

APA PUBLICATIONS

Publisher: Hans Johannes Hoefer
Managing Director: Julian Sale
General Manager: Henry Lee
Marketing Director: Aileen Lau
Editorial Director: Geoffrey Eu
Editorial Manager: Vivien Kim
Editorial Consultants: Brian Bell (Europe)
Heinz Vestner (German Editions)
Updating Coordinator: Hilary Cunningham (N. America)

Project Editors

Helen Abbott, Diana Ackland, Mohamed Amin, Ravindralal Anthonis, Roy Bailet, Louisa Cambell, Jon Carroll, Hilary Cunningham, John Eames, Janie Freeburg, Bikram Grewal, Virginia Hopkins, Samuel Israel, Jay Itzkowitz, Phil Jaratt, Tracy Johnson, Ben Kalb, Wilhelm Klein, Saul Lockhart, Sylvia Mayuga, Gordon McLauchlan, Kal Müller, Eric Oey, Daniel P. Reid, Kim Robinson, Ronn Ronck, Robert Seidenberg, Rolf Steinberg, Sriyani Tidball, Lisa Van Gruisen, Merin Wexler.

Contributing Writers

A.D. Aird, Ruth Armstrong, T. Terence Barrow, F. Lisa Beebe, Bruce Berger, Dor Bahadur Bista, Clinton V. Black, Star Black, Frena Bloomfield, John Borthwick, Roger Boschman, Tom Brosnahan, Jerry Carroll, Tom Chaffin, Nedra Chung, Tom Cole, Orman Day, Kunda Dixit, Richard Erdoes, Guillermo Gar-Oropeza, Ted Giannoulas, Barbara Gloudon, Harka Gurung, Sharifah Hamzah, Willard A. Hanna, Elizabeth Hawley, Sir Edmund Hillary, Tony Hillerman, Jerry Hopkins, Peter Hutton, Neil Jameson, Michael King, Michele Kort, Thomas Lucey, Leonard Lueras, Michael E. Macmillan, Derek Maitland, Buddy Mays, Craig McGregor, Reinhold Messner, Julie Michaels, M.R. Priya Rangsit, Al Read, Elizabeth V. Reyes, Victor Stafford Reid, Harry Rolnick, E.R. Sarachandra, Uli Schmetzer, Ilsa Sharp, Norman Sibley, Peter Spiro, Harold Stephens, Keith Stevens, Michael Stone, Desmond Tate, Colin Taylor, Deanna L. Thompson, Randy Udall, James Wade, Mallika Wanigasundara, William Warren, Cynthia Wee, Tony Wheeler, Linda White, H. Taft Wireback, Alfred A. Yuson, Paul Zach.

Contributing Photographers

Carole Allen, Ping Amranand, Tony Arruza, Marcello Bertinetti, Alberto Cassio, Pat Canova, Alain Compost, Ray Cranbourne, Alain Evrard, Ricardo Ferro, Lee Foster, Manfred Gottschalk, Werner Hahn, Dallas and John Heaton, Brent Hesselyn, Hans Hoefer, Luca Invernizzi, Ingo Jezierski, Wilhelm Klein, Dennis Lane, Max Lawrence, Lyle Lawson, Philip Little, Guy Marche, Antonio Martinelli, David Messent, Ben Nakayama, Vautier de Nanxe, Kal Müller, Günter Pfannmuller, Van Philips, Ronni Pinsler, Fitz Prenzel, G.P. Reichelt, Dan Rocovits, David Ryan, Frank Salmoiraghi, Thomas Schollhammer, Blair Seitz, David Stahl, Bill Wassman, Rendo Yap, Hisham Youssef.

Distributors

Australia and New Zealand: Prentice Hall of Australia, 7 Grosvenor Place, Brookvale, NSW 2100, Australia. **Benelux:** Utigeverij Cambium, Naarderstraat 11, 1251 AW Laren, The Netherlands. **Brazil and Portugal:** Cedibra Editora Brasileira Ltda, Rua Leonidia, 2-Rio de Janeiro, Brazil. **Denmark:** Copenhagen Book Centre Aps, Roskildevej 338, DK-2630 Tastrup, Denmark. **Germany:** RV Reise-und Verkehrsuerlag Gmbh, Neumarkter Strasse 18, 8000 Munchen 80, West Germany. **Hawaii:** Pacific Trade Group Inc., P.O. Box 1227, Kailua, Oahu, Hawaii 96734, U.S.A. **Hong Kong:** Far East Media Ltd., Vita Tower, 7th Floor, Block B, 29 Wong Chuk Hang Road, Hong Kong. **India and Nepal:** India Book Distributors, 107/108 Arcadia Building, 195 Narima Point, Bombay-400-021, India. **Indonesia:** Java Books, Box 55 J.K.C.P., Jakarta, Indonesia. **Israel:** Steimatzky Ltd., P.O. Box 628, Tel Aviv 61006, Israel (Israel title only). **Italy:** Zanfi Editori SRL. Via Ganaceto 121, 41100 Modena, Italy. **Jamaica:** Novelty Trading Co., P.O. Box 80, 53 Hanover Street, Kingston, Jamaica. **Japan:** Charles E. Tuttle Co. Inc., 2-6 Suido 1-Chome, Bunkyo-ku, Tokyo 112, Japan. **Kenya:** Camerapix Publishers International Ltd., P.O. Box 45048, Nairobi, Kenya. **Korea:** Kyobo Book Centre Co., Ltd., P.O. Box Kwang Hwa Moon 1 658, Seoul, Korea. **Philippines:** National Book Store, 701 Rizal Avenue, Manila, Philippines. **Singapore:** MPH Distributors (S) Pte. Ltd., 601 Sims Drive #03-21 Pan-I Warehouse and Office Complex, S'pore 1438, Singapore. **Switzerland:** M.P.A. Agencies-Import SA, CH. du Croset 9, CH-1024, Ecublens, Switzerland. **Taiwan:** Caves Books Ltd., 103 Chungshan N. Road, Sec. 2, Taipei, Taiwan, Republic of China. **Thailand:** Far East Publications Ltd., 117/3 Soi Samahan, Sukhumvit 4 (South Nana), Bangkok, Thailand. **United Kingdom, Ireland and Europe (others):** Harrap Ltd., 19-23 Ludgate Hill, London EC4M 7PD, England, United Kingdom. **Mainland United States and Canada:** Graphic Arts Center Publishing, 3019 N.W. Yeon, P.O. Box 10306, Portland OR 97210, U.S.A. (The Pacific Northwest title only); Prentice Hall Press, Gulf & Western Building, One Gulf & Western Plaza, New York, NY 10023, U.S.A. (all other titles).

Chinese editions: Formosan Magazine Press Ltd., 6 Fl. No. 189, Yen Pin S. Road, Taipei, Taiwan, R.O.C. **French editions:** Editions Gallimard, 5 rue Sébastien-Bottin, F-75007 Paris, France. **German editions:** Nelles Verlag GmbH, Schleissheirner Str. 371b, 8000 Munich 45, West Germany **Italian editions:** Zanfi Editori SLR. Via Ganaceto 121 41100 Modena, Italy. **Portuguese editions:** Cedibra Editora Brasileira Ltda, Rua Leonidia, 2-Rio de Janeiro, Brazil.

Advertising and Special Sales Representatives

Advertising carried in Insight Guides gives readers direct access to quality merchandise and travel-related services. These advertisements are inserted in the Guide in Brief section of each book. Advertisers are requested to contact their nearest representatives, listed below.
Special sales, for promotion purposes within the international travel industry and for educational purposes, are also available. The advertising representatives listed here also handle special sales. Alternatively, interested parties can contact Apa Publications, P.O. Box 219, Orchard Point Post Office, Singapore 9123.

Australia and New Zealand: Harve and Gullifer Pty. Ltd. 1 Fawkner St. Kilda 3181, Australia. Tel: (3) 525 3422; Tlx: 523259; Fax: (89) 4312837.
Canada: The Pacific Rim Agency, 6900 Cote Saint Luc Road, Suite 303, Montreal, Quebec, Canada H4V 2Y9. Tel: (514) 9311299; Tlx: 0525134 MTL; Fax: (514) 8615571.
Hawaii: HawaiianLMedia Sales; 1750 Kalakaua Ave., Suite 3-243, Honolulu, Hawaii 96826, U.S.A. Tel: (808) 9464483.
Hong Kong: C Cheney & Associates, 17th Floor, D'Aguilar Place, 1-30 D'Aguilar Street, Central, Hong Kong. Tel: 5-213671; Tlx: 63079 CCAL HX.
India and Nepal, Pakistan and Bangladesh: Universal Media, CHA 2/718, 719 Kantipath, Lazimpat, Kathmandu-2, Nepal. Tel: 412911/414502; Tlx: 2229 KAJI NP ATTN MEDIA.
Indonesia: Media Investment Services, Setiabudi Bldg. 2, 4th Floor, Suite 407, Jl. Hr. Rasuna Said, Kuningan, Jakarta Selatan 12920, Indonesia. Tel: 5782723/5782752; Tlx: 62418 MEDIANETIA; Mata Graphic Design, Batujimbar, Sanur, Bali, Indonesia. Tel: (0361) 8073. (for Bali only)
Korea: Kaya Ad Inc., Rm. 402 Kunshin Annex B/D, 251-1 Dohwa Dong, Mapo-Ku, Seoul, Korea (121). Tel: (2) 7196906; Tlx: K 32144 KAYAAD; Fax: (2) 7199816.
Philippines: Torres Media Sales Inc., 21 Warbler St., Greenmeadows 1, Murphy, Quezon City, Metro Manila, Philippines. Tel: 722-02-43; Tlx: 23312 RHP PH.
Taiwan: Cheney Tan & Van Associates, 7th Floor, 10 Alley 4, Lane 545 Tun Hua South Road, Taipei, Taiwan. Tel: (2) 7002963; Tlx: 11491 FOROSAN; Fax: (2) 3821270.
Thailand: Cheney, Tan & Van Outrive, 17th Fl. Rajapark Bldg., 163 Asoke Rd., Bangkok 10110, Thailand. Tel: 2583244/2583259; Tlx: 20666 RAJAPAK TH.
Singapore and Malaysia: Cheney Tan Associates, 1 Goldhill Plaza, #02-01, Newton Rd., Singapore 1130, Singapore. Tel: 2549522; Tlx: RS 35983 CTAL.
Sri Lanka: Spectrum Lanka Advertising Ltd., 56 1/2 Ward Place, Colombo 7, Sr Lanka. Tel: 5984648/596227; Tlx: 21439 SPECTRM CE.
U.K., Ireland and Europe: Brian Taplin Associates, 32 Fishery Road, Boxmoor, Hemel Hempstead, Herts HP 1ND, U.K. Tel: (2)215635; Tlx: 825454 CHARMAN.

APA PHOTO AGENCY PTE. LTD.

The Apa Photo Agency is S.E. Asia's leading stock photo archive, representing the work of professional photographers from all over the world. More than 150,000 original color transparencies are available for advertising, editorial and educational uses. We are linked with Tony Stone Worldwide, one of Europe's leading stock agencies, and their associate offices around the world:
Singapore: Apa Photo Agency Pte. Ltd., P.O. Box 219, Orchard Point Post Office, Singapore 9123, Singapore. **London:** Tony Stone Worldwide, 28 Finchley Rd., St. John's Wood, London NW8 6ES, England. **North America & Canada:** Masterfile Inc., 415 Yonge St., Suite 200, Toronto M5B 2E7, Canada. **Paris:** Fotogram-Stone Agence Photographique, 45 rue de Richelieu, 75001 Paris, France. **Barcelona:** Fototec Torre Dels Pardais, 7 Barcelona 08026, Spain. **Johannesburg:** Color Library (Pty.) Ltd., P.O. Box 1659, Johannesburg, South Africa 2000. **Sydney:** The Photographic Library of Australia Pty. Ltd., 7 Ridge Street, North Sydney, New South Wales 2050, Australia. **Tokyo:** Orion Press, 55-1 Kanda Jimbocho, Chiyoda-ku, Tokyo 101, Japan.

D E F G

The publication of *Insight Guide: India* marks a major step in Apa Productions' coverage of Asia. The result of nearly 15 months work by a sizable team of native and expatriate writers and photographers, this book has benefited from careful planning and meticulous execution.

As the *Insight Guides* series continued to expand in the first half of the 1980s, much of Apa Productions' attention was directed to the Americas. Among the many American titles that sprang to life up to and during 1985 were *Hawaii, Florida, New England, Southern California, Northern California, American Southwest, Alaska, The Pacific Northwest, Texas* and *The Rockies.* The release of *India* is a reminder that it was in Asia that the series first cut its teeth. When founder-publisher

Hoefer *Israel* *B. Grewal*

Itzkowitz *Seshan* *Mukhia*

Hans Hoefer orchestrated a photo-guidebook to Bali in 1970 (then newly arrived in Asia and armed with diplomas in printing, book production, design and photography from Krefeld, West Germany), he not only laid the foundation stone for a successful Asia-based publishing company, but simultaneously introduced a whole new style of guidebooks. The Asian series has stood the test of time well; *Burma, Nepal* and *Sri Lanka* are still popular.

Apa Productions turned to Executive Editor **Jay Itzkowitz** to help set the India book on the road. His first involvement with Apa came when he edited *Insight Guide: New England.* Itzkowitz graduated from Harvard (where he was an editor of the Harvard Lampoon) in 1982 and from Rutgers Law School in 1985. Along the way he found time to write two guidebooks to Italy, short comedy films, songs, and cartoons for Jim Henson's Muppets, and remains actively involved with Apa projects on New York, Great Britain and Italy. He has long had a personal and professional interest in India and had travelled widely there researching the legal aspects of joint venture

and investment opportunities. Itzkowitz hopes to continue his involvement with India as he pursues his legal career. In August 1984, he found himself in New Delhi searching for the perfect India team. His search ended quickly when he met two men: **Samuel Israel,** doyen of Indian book-publishing editors, and former Director of the National Book Trust, India; and **Bikram Grewal,** Managing Director, Dass Media, an Indo-British publishing enterprise.

A major problem, both for the editors, writers and photographers, was how to compress all there is to say and illustrate about India into a single volume — in short, how to do justice to an entire subcontinent. A decision was made to be selective — to assess priorities and present them to the reader. *India* has succeeded in both covering all the major and many of the secondary places of interest and placing them in their proper cultural and historical perspective.

Israel and Grewal, working in close association with **Vivien Loo,** Apa Assistant Editor in Singapore, brought together an outstanding team of writers and photographers that benefits from substantial native expertise. Fresh perspectives are also supplied by non-Indian contributors whose knowledge is no less authoritative.

Dr Kamala Seshan, geographer and Lecturer at the National Council of Educational Research and Training, New Delhi, uses her experience of writing video scripts on geography to follow the trail of the monsoon across India. **Professor Harbans Mukhia,** who takes us in a wide sweep through Indian history, from ancient times to independence, teaches the subject at Jawaharlal Nehru University, New Delhi, a center of advanced learning in India. He is the author of two books and a number of learned papers on medieval Indian history. India Today, as is appropriate, is covered by one of India's leading economic and political commentators, **Prem Shankar**

Jha, Senior Asst. Editor, *The Times of India,* one of India's foremost and oldest national dailies. His book, *India, A Political Economy of Stagnation,* received wide and positive comment.

A broad picture of the peoples of India and their ways is presented by **Radhika Chopra,** who is currently working on her Ph.D. thesis in sociology. Chopra has supplemented her formal sociological research by spending a year in a Punjab village. The complex subject of religion in India has been covered in a perceptive essay by **Professor V. S. Naravané,** former Professor of Philosophy, Puné University (earlier Asst. Professor at Allahabad University). Dr. Naravané now divides his time between writing in India and teaching as a Visiting Professor for a quarter or a semester at a U.S. university or college each year. He is the author of six books and numerous articles on Indian thought, literature and culture.

Turning to Part Two of this Guide, covering places, we have a fresh mix of writers and approaches.

M. C. Joshi, as a professional archeologist (he is a Director in the Archeological Survey of India), and, as a leading expert on Islamic monuments in northern India, covers Delhi and Uttar Pradesh, the heartland of ancient Hinduism and Buddhism and also that of the great medieval Islamic empires. The mountain state of Himachal Pradesh is covered by **Vijay Parmar,** a young Asst. Director in the Centre for Cultural Resources and Training, New Delhi. He has made a special study of folklore and has been active in documentation of traditional arts. He has travelled extensively in and made a special study of Himachal Pradesh, both out of personal interest and as part of his official duties.

Jammu and Kashmir are covered by **Jeffrey Young Campbell,** a young American who was born in India and has spent most of his working life there, achieving in the areas of travel, photography, authorship and nature study, in his 30-odd years, more than others could manage in a lifetime. He first visited Kashmir when he was 7 weeks old and has gone back practically every year since. Term-time, Campbell teaches at the American Embassy School in New Delhi.

Punjab and Haryana are covered by a distinguished son of the soil, **Sardar Khushwant Singh,** M.P., one of India's seniormost editors and today one of India's most widely syndicated political commentators. His two-volume study, *History and Religion of the Sikhs,* is the standard work on the subject. He is also author of the novel, *Train to Pakistan,* set among the tragic events following the parti-

tion of the Indian subcontinent in 1947, and many other books published in India, Britain and the USA.

Covering the whole of eastern and northeastern India and the Andamans is a young Frenchman, **Michel Vatin,** who has previously contributed to the APA guide to Indonesia. Vatin has travelled widely in South-East Asia and India, especially, Bengal, Bihar, Assam and Orissa. Lack of space prevents the presentation of all the interesting things he has found out about the places he has visited, but the sampling we have been able to include will indicate a traveller who is not satisfied with re-

Chopra

Naravané

Parmar

Campbell

Khushwant Singh

Wacziarg

Nath

Dharkar

Albuquerque

maining on the beaten track.

For Rajasthan, we also turned to a sensitive Frenchman, **Francis Wacziarg,** this time in collaboration with graphic designer, photographer and advertising copywriter and executive, **Aman Nath,** who also co-authored and illustrated their book, *Rajasthan, The Painted Walls of Shekhavati.* Aman is also the author of the profusely illustrated work, *Goa.* Rajasthan enthusiasts are not difficult to find, but few have the intimate knowledge and understanding of the state that Wacziarg and Aman Nath display.

M. M. Buch, who covers Madhya Pradesh, was a senior civil servant till a few years ago, when he resigned to devote himself entirely to ecological studies and the organization of environmental conservation and the conservation of the cultural heritage of Madhya Pradesh. His knowledge of the state is intimate and his concern for it personal. He is currently Chairman, National Centre for Human Settlements & Environment.

The Bombay piece is the joint contribution of Bikram Grewal, Associate Project Editor, who explored Bombay and came to love the city when he lived and worked there for a few years, and Project Editor, Samuel Israel, for whom Bombay is home ground. Grewal has also contributed the article on Madras, where

Jaitly

Soundararajan

Kamath

Noble

R. Grewal

Samson

Sen

Sinclair

Tyabji

he has also lived and which he visits frequently.

Maharashtra is covered by **Anil Dharkar**, editor of the sophisticated Bombay magazine, *Debonair*. Dharkar also contributes the article on Indian Film in Part III of this volume. His years as member of the Film Censor Board and as a senior executive in the National Film Development Corporation, and his continuing role as film critic, make him an eminently suitable writer for this topic.

Usha Albuquerque who contributes with great feeling on Goa again has the advantage of being an insider and an outsider at the same time. She was born of Goan parents in north India, and while she has lived in the east, west and south of India, she has never

been a regular resident of Goa. She has been the next best thing: regular visitor since childhood, spending her holidays there with her grandparents in one of Goa's stately homes. Albuquerque is active in many areas of the media — journalism, radio (talks and western music), and television documentaries.

Jaya Jaitly has come to her subject through her love for and concern with the handicrafts of Gujarat. She is a Consultant on Handicraft Development to the Gujarat State Handicraft and Handloom Development Corporation. While she operates from Delhi, Jaitly makes frequent trips to Gujarat, visiting handicraft centers, often remote from the main towns, in all regions of the state. She has written extensively on travel and craft subjects.

For Tamil Nadu and Andhra Pradesh, as in the case of Delhi and Uttar Pradesh, the editors turned to a distinguished archeologist and art historian, **Dr. K. V. Soundararajan**, Retired Additional Director General, Archeological Survey of India. Author of a dozen learned books and more than 400 research papers, he has been a Visiting Professor at the Universities of Chicago and of California (at Los Angeles) and has held high office in learned societies related to his profession. To the temples and sculptures of South India there could be no better guide.

M. V. Kamath, veteran journalist and editor has covered his home state of Karnataka with great affection. For the Press Trust of India, he was United Nations correspondent for three years; later, for *The Times of India* group, he was European and subsequently, for four years, Washington correspondent. He is the author of a dozen books and his articles regularly appear in several Indian journals and magazines.

A rather unconventional contributor is **Pepita Noble**, a young Englishwoman, who believes the only way to really understand a people and their ways is to become, in a real sense, one of them, and to partake of their innermost feelings and beliefs. Noble's presentation of Kerala is based on perceptions growing out of this endeavor. Besides being a scholar and writer, Noble is a talented photographer who has done much to document religious ritual in Kerala.

After covering places, this guide is rounded off in Part III with seven feature articles. **Royina Grewal**, a writer on travel and cultural subjects, very appropriately deals both with some of India's numerous festivals and, in a separate contribution, with the wide variety of food Indians eat, and serve to their guests, especially during festivals. She is also the compiler of the Guide in Brief at the end of this

Continue on page 359

TABLE OF CONTENTS

TABLE OF CONTENTS

OTHER INSIGHT GUIDES TITLES

COUNTRY/REGION

ASIA
Bali
Burma
Hong Kong
India
Indonesia
Korea
Malaysia
Nepal
Philippines
Rajasthan
Singapore
Sri Lanka
Taiwan
Thailand
Turkey

PACIFIC
Hawaii
New Zealand

NORTH AMERICA
Alaska
American Southwest
Northern California
Southern California
Florida
Mexico
New England
New York State
The Pacific Northwest
The Rockies
Texas

SOUTH AMERICA
Brazil
Argentina

CARIBBEAN
Bahamas
Barbados
Jamaica
Puerto Rico
Trinidad and Tobago

EUROPE
Channel Islands
France
Germany
Great Britain
Greece
Ireland
Italy
Portugal
Scotland
Spain

MIDDLE EAST
Egypt
Israel

AFRICA
Kenya

GRAND TOURS
Australia
California
Canada
Continental Europe
Crossing America
East Asia
South Asia

GREAT ADVENTURE
Indian Wildlife

CITYGUIDES
Bangkok
Berlin
Buenos Aires
Dublin
Istanbul
Lisbon
London
Paris
Rio de Janeiro
Rome
San Francisco
Venice
Vienna

INTRODUCTION TO A SUBCONTINENT

India, since time immemorial, has beckoned and welcomed the traveller, intrigued the visitor, and often held him in her embrace forever. Many came never to return and became one with the others in this ancient melting-pot of peoples; many returned with India in their hearts. In a very literal sense, this is what has made India what it is today, and what will make it what it is going to be tomorrow.

There is evidence, from earliest historical times, of great movements of peoples across the subcontinent, sometimes replacing existing populations, sometimes integrating with them. The Indo-Aryans themselves came in massive sweeps through the lofty passes in the northwest, bringing with them the rudiments of the Hindu faith, later to be developed on Indian soil into one of the most philosophically subtle and complex of all religions.

While it is only in recent years that Hinduism is again having a major influence outside the Indian subcontinent, Buddhism, which grew out of Hinduism, is a major world religion. But India has also received the gifts of Islam, Christianity, Zoroastrianism, and, on a very small scale but very significantly, Judaism. India has been the proverbial sponge, and not only in matters religious. In fact, overarching religious differences is a steady process of assimilation and synthesis.

With various races and religions came a variety of ethnic types, their art, architecture, culture, languages, customs, literature, style of music and dance, administrative structures, systems of thought, science, technology and medicine. Few of these have entirely lost their identity, all have had their influence, and many have found a permanent place in the mosaic that India is.

While it is this variety and complexity that makes India attractive for the traveller, it is also the source of many of India's difficulties, past and contemporary. It is just this heterogeneity that makes it, perhaps, one of the most difficult of countries to govern; especially since the people of India have freely and clearly demonstrated, time and again, that only a democratic system of government is acceptable to them and that this is the only system that can keep them together. As the late Prime Minister of Pakistan, Zulfikar Ali Bhutto, as shrewd and knowledgeable an observer as one could get, said, "India has been kept in one piece by the noise and chaos of her democracy."

To understand India, one must observe her closely and in the perspective of her history, ancient and modern. Sympathy and interest will grow with understanding.

India, divided by the Tropic of Cancer, extends from the lofty Himalaya across the broad Ganga plain and peninsular plateau which dips to the shores of the vast Indian Ocean. The greatest deserts of the world — the Mexican desert, the Sahara and the Arabian desert — lie between 8° and 36° north of the Equator. Though India is in this zone and has its share of desert, it also has rain forests and even alpine meadows.

India's summer, which runs from March to May, is hot and dry, with flurries of wind raising a dusty curtain over the northern plain and temperatures averaging 104°F (40°C). Tempered by the sea breezes, South India is sultry and hot but temperatures are bearable, between 80.5°F (27°C) and 84°F (29°C).

A cool rainy season follows the monsoon trail from June to September, and when these winds retreat in October a fierce heat follows. The eastern and southeastern coasts, however, get rain and cyclonic squalls. In November, when the sun crosses south of the Equator, the winter season starts in the northern plain. Till February the weather remains cold (below 41°F) in the Himalaya and its foothills, where skiing is possible, pleasant in the plains (between 59°F and 68°F) and warm (above 68°F) in South India, except in the Nilgiri Hills and the Ghats.

Come June, the intense heat of the northern plain causes the upper air currents to move north of the Himalaya and draws the monsoon across the entire country. Starting from the southwestern coast it branches eastward and northward, crossing the plateau, and on reaching the Ganga delta follows the wide river valleys bounded by the Himalaya with its heavily forested foothills.

The most luxuriant rain forests, however, lie on the southwest coast, in Kerala, where the interconnected lagoons are canopied by coconut trees. The coast stretches north to the estuarine plains of Goa with its wide sunny beaches lapped by the gentle waves of the Arabian Sea. The rest of the coast is mostly rocky, rising to the low red lateritic plateaus and then steeply to the black, forest-covered slopes of the Western Ghats. Farther north, in Kathiawar, the coast becomes dry and salt-encrusted with marshy lowlands which are the sanctuary of the flamingo.

Inland, the open country covered with cotton and sunflower fields merges into the rocky desert. From the Rann (saline marshlands) of Kaccha in the west to the Luni River is the Great Desert, and farther north between Jaisalmer and Jodhpur is the Little Desert. Here is open scrub country with rocky hills often capped by the forts of the Rajput kings. This yellow and red desert landscape stretches east to meet the eroded flanks of the Aravalli ranges. Wandering herds of sheep and goats, and camels carrying cotton and marble, are seen in this area.

Separating the desert from the Gangetic plain and the Deccan lava tableland are the rugged plateaus of Malwa, Bundelkhand and Rewa. Stony, harsh and covered with only a thin layer of soil, the plateau is drained by the Chambal, Ken and Betwa Rivers. The grand fort of the Scindias at Gwalior and the temples of Khajuraho are in this region. In the ravines made by the rivers, are scattered hamlets surrounded by fields of mustard and wheat forming a patchwork of green and gold.

On the west, steeply rising from the plain to the lava plateau, is the Vindhya range. The Narmada, flowing through a narrow gorge, and the Tapi, through a broad valley, are separated by the Satpura range. South of the Tapi are the hills where Buddhist monks carved and painted in the caves at Ajanta and Ellora. At the mouth of the Tapi is the ancient port city of Surat, famous for its gold and silver brocade (zari). It was here that the British East India Company set up its first "factory," as its trading centers were then called, since their "factors" (commercial agents) were based in them.

By the 15th of June, the eastward moving monsoon winds reach the Chhotanagpur plateau which is drained by the Damodar. It is a wide plateau with conical and dome-shaped hills which look like gigantic bubbles that have solidified. During the three long monsoon months the brown forests of sal, bamboo and teak turn green and the tribesmen collect lac (the secretion of a forest insect) and mahua flowers since lumbering is suspended during these months. The upper slopes of the hills are cultivated and the Santhal tribes graze their buffaloes in the low valleys. The steel city of Jamshedpur and the coal and iron-ore mines introduce a veneer of urban culture here. The plateau is flanked by the Rajmahal Hills which descend steeply to the Ganga plain where the river takes a sharp bend to the sea.

Distinct from these plateaus is the black lava-covered Deccan where streams meander among hills that seem to have had their tops neatly sliced off. It was on the "table-tops" of steep-sided hills of this type that the Marathas built a series of impregnable fortresses.

Deccan Peninsula

South Deccan is the dry heartland of the peninsula, the Telengana and Karnataka plateaus. Cut across by the Krishna, Godavari and Kaveri flowing east, the wet Karnataka plateau has dense sandal, teak and sisoo forests, where elephants roam wild. The Telengana plateau, just adjacent, has in contrast a thin cover of red lateritic soils with

rocky humps between. Thorny scrub and wild Indian date palms grow on this soil. The landscape has a scarred and wounded appearance because of the dried river channels in which are seen bunded tanks that have been built to hold water when the rivers are briefly in flood. Here is the erstwhile princely state of Hyderabad, the pearl city, surrounded by vineyards.

Preceding pages: Kathakali dancer; Himalayan landscape; Ladakh Valley; camel fair at Pushkar, Rajasthan; Hawa Mahal, Jaipur; Rajasthani elder; a common sight on Indian roads. Above, *The Monsoon,* an 18th Century artistic representation from Bundi, Rajasthan.

Southwest of the plateau, separated from Kerala by the blue Nilgiris, with its coffee plantations and the cloud-covered Palni Hills, in the rain shadow, is the Coimbatore plateau which extends east to the coast near Madras. The Kaveri which rises here flows into the Tamilnad plains. The Kaveri delta is the ricebowl of Tamil Nadu, its prosperity reflected in the lofty temple towers of Thanjavur.

India's stony east coast, with vast bare spaces scattered over with aloes and palm trees and swampy alluvial shores, merges northwards into the fertile deltaic lowlands of the Krishna, Godavari and Mahanadi Rivers. Wooded forests replace the open fields of sugarcane and tobacco in places reached by the summer monsoon.

Replenishing itself in its passage over the Bay of Bengal, the southwest monsoon continues westwards along the wide Ganga plain and eastward along the Brahmaputra gorge.

Eastwards, the Brahmaputra Valley cuts across the Shillong plateau, by the Garo, Khasi and Jaintia Hills, through the Assam-Burma range. The Brahmaputra swings across its wide valley which is encased in an immense rocky corridor. On the rises and levees of the river tiny hamlets are surrounded by rice fields and tea plantations. On the slopes tussar silkworms are bred on the mulberry trees, and pineapple plantations are seen.

Alluvial Rice Basins

The Brahmaputra reaches the wet Ganga delta which is dominated by the port of Calcutta. Criss-crossed by the distributaries of an ever-growing delta, the mangrove forests offer excellent opportunities for boating among their roots. Farther inland, patches of jungle have been cleared to grow barley and pulses.

Following the monsoon winds westwards comes the Middle Ganga plain in which tract the annual rainfall decreases from 55 inches (140 cm) to 31 inches (80 cm) near Delhi. North of this plain are the foothills of the Himalaya across which the tributaries of the Ganga flow, through steep reed-filled courses in sal forests. Here, as in the Duars of Bengal, the Terai has jungles of sisoo and tamarisk which afford excellent hideouts for tigers.

When the now comparatively dry monsoon winds reach the upper course of the Ganga, the fields are ready for sowing wheat, barley and gram. The canal-irrigated wheat plains of Punjab merge into the dry land of Haryana to the southwest. Delhi, the gateway to the Ganga plain and the junction of the routes from the Deccan and Gujarat, is located here.

North of this varied and interesting plain, the foothill ridges of the Shiwaliks and the gravel vales rise to successive ridges and valleys and finally to the snowcapped peaks of the Himalaya. The ascent is from some 980–1,960 feet (300–600 meters) above the plain to 15,750 feet (4,800 meters) in the middle Himalaya in which are Nanda Devi and Annapurna peaks rising up to 22,970 feet (7,000 meters).

The Tista Valley in the Eastern Himalaya lies opposite the Ganga delta at the head of which is Sikkim. Orchids and rhododendrons grow wild here and the musk deer and rhinoceros are found in these dense forests. The valleys are a patchwork of green paddy fields, and seen on the terraced slopes are yellow maize and millet fields.

Largely deforested, but excellent for trekking and fishing, the Central Himalaya lies wholly in the state of Himachal Pradesh. The golden, snowcapped Dhola Dhar ranges of the lesser Himalaya separate the river Beas from the Ravi. At the head of the Beas is apple-land and the Kulu Valley. The most striking feature of this area is the Sutlej River which emerges suddenly from the earth, some 19 miles (30 km) from the Mansarowar Lake in Tibet, and descends across the mighty Himalaya. The chir and deodar jungles of the upper slopes enclose broad sloping river terraces which are covered with fields of potato and rice enclosed by thick hedges. From the Kulu Valley traditional routes of the Bhotiya shepherds enter the upland pastures of Ladakh, with its Buddhist monasteries and serene beauty.

From the lofty glacier-garlanded heights of Badrinath, the Alakananda and Baghirathi, tributaries of the Ganga, flow across the Kumaon Himalaya.

The lowest valleys of the Himalayan foothills, the Terai, are hot and sultry in summer and get heavy rainfall in July. The nomadic ways of the Bhotiyas are replaced by a settled pastoral economy on the forest edge, and farming is done in the valleys.

The lofty Himalaya of the north, dipping to the vast Ganga-Yamuna plain which is hemmed in by the rocky massif of the plateau in the south, suggest powerful and conflicting forces beneath the earth which have molded the features of this unique subcontinent. Across this the monsoon winds travel, weaving a pattern of brown and green vegetation. In this setting are India's fields and villages.

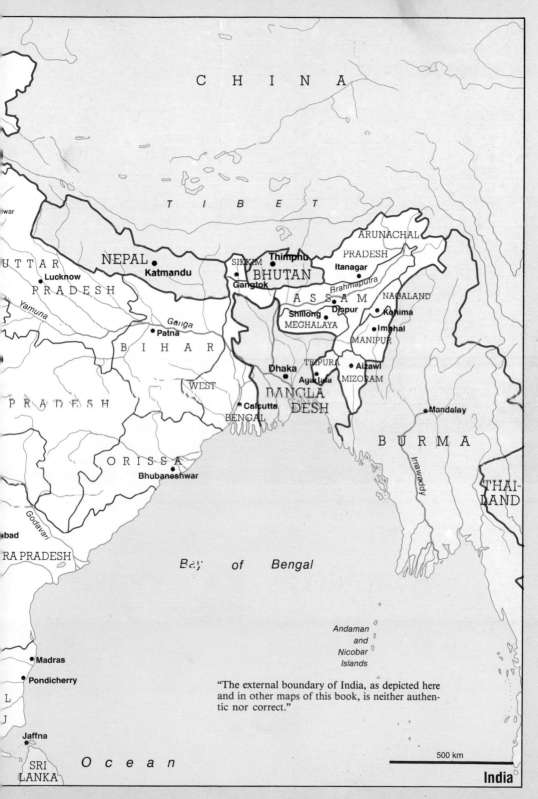

C H I N A

T I B E T

war

UTTAR
Lucknow
P R A D E S H

NEPAL
Katmandu

Yamuna

Ganga

Patna

B I H A R

ARUNACHAL
PRADESH
Itanagar

SIKKIM
Thimphu
BHUTAN
Gangtok

A S S A M

Brahmaputra

NAGALAND
Dispur
Shillong
MEGHALAYA
Kohima

Imphal
MANIPUR

WEST
PRADESH
BENGAL

Dhaka
TRIPURA
Agartala
Aizawl
MIZORAM

BANGLA
DESH

Calcutta

Mandalay

O R I S S A
Bhubaneshwar

B U R M A

Godavari

bad

Irrawaddy

THAI-
LAND

RA PRADESH

Bay   of   Bengal

Andaman
and
Nicobar
Islands

Madras

Pondicherry

L
J

"The external boundary of India, as depicted here
and in other maps of this book, is neither authentic nor correct."

Jaffna

SRI
LANKA

O c e a n

500 km

India

Ancient Land, Young Nation

The strikingly complex society that today comprises India, Pakistan and Bangladesh, but was until 1947 a single unit, India, evokes the vision of a very long process of evolution. Many facets of human existence indeed contributed to this process: ecology, human skills and labor, social divisions and the ensuing frictions, and not least culture and religion. Interaction among these facets was at times silent and discernible only over long stretches of time; at other times it was marked by violent eruptions. Either way things never remained the same. It is the story of this evolution that the following pages seek to tell, though in a mere outline.

Basic Factors

A cardinal feature of the Indian ecology, which exercised a considerable influence on the historical development of the subcontinent, was the very high fertility of its land. The topsoil in the river basins was renewed annually with the inundations caused by the summer monsoons which deposited enormous quantities of fertile silt from the mountains. The Indus and Ganga alone are estimated to bring down a million tons of suspended matter daily. Understandably, cultivation began and came to be densely concentrated in the valleys of the great rivers, and most Indian soils yielded an average of two crops a year.

The tropical climate allowed the peasant in most Indian regions to make do with a mud house and clothe himself with a brief piece of coarse cotton cloth wrapped around the loins. Peasant women would similarly attire themselves with a somewhat longer unstitched wrap-around. The contrast between the high agricultural yield and the dismal level of consumption by the bulk of the population made large surpluses available, quite early in Indian history, maintaining a substantial number of towns at an impressive level of civilization.

The Beginnings

The earliest known civilization in India, the starting point of Indian history, was a highly developed urban one; it went back to about

Preceding pages, fishermen preparing to go out to sea at Puri, Orissa. Left, the Lion Capital of an Ashokan pillar, now the emblem of the Government of India.

2500 B.C. Discovered in the 1920s, it was initially thought to have been confined to the valley of the Indus, hence its early identification as the Indus Valley Civilization. Of its towns, two earned great renown, for they represented the high-water mark of that civilization. These were Mohenjodaro and Harappa, both now in Pakistan. Subsequent archeological excavations, however, established the contours of this civilization to a widespread area in northwestern and western India, far beyond the valley of the Indus; hence 'Harappa culture' is the more recent label put on these discoveries. Among the Indian sites are the ones at Ropar in Punjab, and Lothal and Kalibangan in Gujarat and Rajasthan.

The towns at Mohenjodaro and Harappa were well planned, with streets criss-crossing one another at right angles, a system of sewage and a fairly clear division of localities and types of houses earmarked for the upper and the lower strata of society. There were also public buildings, the most famous being the Great Bath at Mohenjodaro, meant perhaps for ritual bathing, and the granaries. Production of several metals such as copper, bronze, lead and tin was also undertaken and some remnants of furnaces have survived to bear evidence. There were two kilns to make the burnt bricks used extensively in domestic as well as public buildings. The Harappa culture had developed its own pictographic script; unfortunately, its definitive decipherment still remains to be achieved.

Among the discoveries at Harappa sites are a couple of thousand seals in various quandrangular shapes and sizes, each with a human or an animal figure carved on it. It is not unlikely that these seals served as the trademarks of merchants, for Harappa culture had extensive trade relations with the neighboring regions within India and with distant lands in the Persian Gulf and Sumer (in Iraq).

That the Harappa society was divided between rich and poor, traders, artisans and peasants is clear from the evidence pointing to different professions as well as from the standardized sizes of residential buildings characteristic of different localities. That such an advanced social and economic organization should have had an organized government can be safely assumed, even if we know little about its form or actual working. We know, however, that the Harappans worshipped gods and goddesses represented in male and female forms; they might also have held some trees sacred. They had perhaps evolved some ritual ceremonies. But we know little else for certain about their religious life.

By about 1700 B.C. the Harappa culture was on the decline, partly due to repeated flooding of towns located on river banks and partly to ecological changes which forced agriculture to yield to the spreading desert. When the initial migrations of the Aryan people into India, probably from northeastern Iran and the region around the Caspian Sea, began about 1500 B.C., the developed Harappa culture had already been practically wiped out.

Deriving its name from the four *Vedas,* the earliest Hindu scriptures comprising hymns in chaste Sanskrit, the Vedic Age was spread over several centuries; it was consequently not of bottle-gourd and sugarcane.

The Harappa culture too had used the plow and was known to have grown rice, wheat and cotton besides sesamum and peas, but the early Vedic literature makes no reference to the first three of these crops, though they do attain prominence in the later *Vedas.* Cattle were understandably highly valued, and beef-eating was reserved for very honored guests.

Aryan Society

The Aryans were organized into tribes which had settled down in separate regions in northwestern India. Tribal chiefship gradually became hereditary, though the chief operated with advice from either a committee or the entire tribe, depending on the occasion and,

one piece. The Aryan immigrants were a pastoral people who gradually familiarized themselves with agriculture. Cattle-breeding and agriculture perfectly complemented each other. The notion of individual landholdings and perhaps individual cultivation was slow to grow; indeed, in early Vedic literature, cattle and enslaved women are the only movable forms of property mentioned — land was not yet a commodity. The local inhabitants whom the Aryans had defeated and enslaved might have been employed in the fields. The plow drawn by oxen was the primary agricultural implement; the Indian bull had mercifully been provided with a hump by nature, making the yoking of the plow so much easier. The crops cultivated were barley, sesamum, cucumber, in time, the giving or taking of advice was institutionalized. With work specialization, the internal division of Aryan society developed along caste lines. The early division was between the fair-skinned Aryans and the dark-skinned slaves; hence caste was formerly known as the *varna* (color) division. It was not long before the Aryans themselves came to be grouped into the Brahmana (priests), Kshatriya (warriors), Vaishya (agriculturalists) and Shudra (menial workers). It was, at the outset, a division of occupations; as such it was open and flexible. Much later, caste-status and the corresponding occupation came to depend on birth, and change from one caste or occupation to another became far more difficult.

The Aryans were rather fond of intoxicating

drinks, gambling and horse-chariot racing. They worshipped many gods, most of them nature's elements such as the sun, the wind, water and fire.

Culture and the Leisure Class

The prosperity generated by agriculture and cattle breeding and the employment of enslaved labor gave the Aryans adequate leisure to meditate and seek answers to fundamental questions about the origin of the universe and life. Their language, Sanskrit, spoken with a musical intonation, was highly conducive to speculative thinking.

The relationship of one's life with the universe too was a subject of speculation and the notion of a cycle of lives in various forms

Even though the Aryans had developed a sophisticated language, they were slow to evolve a script. Imparting of knowledge was therefore done orally and through repetitive memorizing.

Iron and Development

Around 1000 B.C. iron was discovered in India, a discovery that was to lead to several changes in society. Since iron axes made clearing of forests much easier, a considerable extent of forest land gave way to the plow; agricultural expansion was also facilitated by an iron plowshare, sickle and hoe. One could perhaps assume that extension of the cultivated area led to growth of population, a greater degree of specialization of functions

through which the soul had to pass was hinted at, if not yet fully developed. This was later to grow into the doctrine of *Karma* (one's deeds), according to which, one's next status in or even form of life depended on one's deeds in the present life. This doctrine served as a major deterrent to protest against oppression, for a person's current misery would be easily attributed to his or her past misdeeds, for which the person must undergo appropriate punishment in order to ensure a better life next time.

Left, a prehistoric cave painting from Central India. Right, Lothal, Gujarat, where a proto-historic city (2000 B.C.) has been excavated.

and more trade; it certainly led to a second urbanization. With land gaining prominence as a form of individual property and with the demand for it growing faster than could be met through primitive techniques of forest clearing, society came to be divided into the rich and the poor.

Poverty and misery in contrast with gross luxuries in the 6th Century B.C led two sensitive persons, Mahavira and the Buddha, both *Kshatriyas,* to seek answers to the question: Why is there so much suffering in life? Clearly, they were not satisfied with Vedic solutions.

Mahavira and the Buddha separately meditated for many years and in the end came upon simple truths as answers to their query: a moderate, balanced life based upon non-violence, abstinence, truthfulness and meditation would free one of greed and therefore of suffering. These teachings won immediate popular acceptance owing to their simplicity and practicality; the sermons of both were preached in commonly spoken languages. Both sects, Jainism and Buddhism, were essentially atheistic and therefore a challenge to Brahmanical orthodoxy.

Rise Of The State

With land becoming property and society being divided, conflicts and disorders were bound to arise. Organized power to resolve those conflicts and suppress disorders therefore emerged, giving rise to full-fledged state systems, including vast empires. The vastest

devoted himself to spreading its message. His son and daughter became missionaries.

The Mauryan economy was essentially agrarian. Huge state-owned and private farms were cultivated by a variety of forms of labor. While the state mobilized slaves, laborers and prisoners to work its lands, private fields were tilled by bonded or wage laborers and perhaps sharecroppers. The mighty Mauryan state also had amongst its sources of income gambling houses and brothels; but of course the chief source was taxes collected on land, trade and manufacture of handicrafts.

Pre-Mauryan and Mauryan India had become familiar with the Hellenistic civilization. The Greeks became familiar with India in the 6th and 5th centuries B.C., through their conflict with the Persian Empire, which

and also the best known of these was the Magadha Empire with its capital near modern-day Patna in Bihar ruled by the Maurya dynasty. Emperor Ashoka was its most famous ruler; he ruled from 269 B.C. to 232 B.C.

Ashoka inherited from his father an empire that covered practically the entire subcontinent, save Kalinga, modern-day Orissa. This too Ashoka conquered; but the sight of the battlefield, with thousands of dead and wounded bodies strewn all over it, shook the emperor. He too asked the question: Whàt was the end result of worldly ambition? And the answer that satisfied him was the one that the Buddha had given. From then onwards he turned to the Buddhist way of life, and

bordered northwestern India.

In 327 B.C. Alexander of Macedon crossed into northwest India. When his armies seemed to have lost heart on the banks of the fifth river of Punjab and forced their chief to turn homewards, Alexander left behind Greek governors to rule over the territories conquered by him. Over time, these territories lost out to Indian states through conflict as well as slow absorption. But there was another sphere where contact between the two cultures left a far more lasting impact: art. Sculpture, especially of the region bears a marked Greek influence.

The Mauryan empire did not long survive Ashoka. Its disintegration was an open invitation to invaders, mainly from Central Asia, to seek their fortunes in India. Among them were the Bactrian Greeks, survivors of Alexander's men who had settled in Iran and Afghanistan, the Parthians, the Shakas and the Kushanas. They established kingdoms in the northwestern and northern regions that lasted for varying lengths of time. Over the decades they were submerged in the mainstream of Indian life, just as happened with several earlier and later groups of invaders.

South India at this time was divided into several states, all of them continually at war among themselves. But a more durable aspect of South Indian society was then evolving: its culture, particularly a collective literature, was beginning to emerge in the form of poems composed in assemblies of wandering minstrels and bards. Three such assemblies were

Asian regions of Java, Sumatra and Bali. The Roman empire imported spices, textiles, precious stones and birds like the peacock from India and paid for them mainly in gold. Understandably, therefore, the merchant community of this region has a long history behind it. It was in Malabar, in present-day Kerala, that India first came into contact with Christianity and later on, Islam.

The Gupta Age

The second great empire in Indian history emerged in the 4th Century A.D. It too covered a large part of the subcontinent, though not as much as the Mauryan empire had done, nor was its administration as highly centralized. This was the Gupta Empire which

held at Madurai, then capital of Tamil Nadu (the country of the Tamils). At the third of these assemblies, over 2,000 poems were collectively composed: these are known as the Sangam literature, an invaluable source of information about early Tamil society, culture and polity.

The control over the eastern and western coasts of the Indian peninsula also facilitated establishment of trade relations between the Chola kingdom of the Tamil Nadu region and the Roman empire as well as the Southeast-

Lift, figurines found at Mohenjodaro: representations of the Mother Goddess (far end) and a dancer. Above, series of enlightened beings at Gwalior.

lasted more than two centuries. Alternately waging war and entering into matrimonial alliances with the smaller kingdoms in its neighborhood, the empire's boundaries kept fluctuating with each ruler.

In the Gupta Age, orthodox Hinduism reasserted itself against the heretical sects that had sprung up. This was facilitated by the patronage the rulers extended to the Hindu religious tradition. However, there is little evidence of the use of violence to re-establish the supremacy of Hinduism; indeed, we have the evidence of the Chinese traveller, Fa Hsien, who came to India in the beginning of the 5th Century, that the Buddhists and the Brahmins lived in peaceful coexistence. The Buddhist monastery at Ajanta, cut into hillocks and decorated with breathtaking murals, was a creation of this period. The caste system, however, became far more rigid in this period, and a group of people, the untouchables, below the rank of even the lowest caste, came to be treated at subhuman levels; even the sight of them was sufficient to pollute the upper castes.

Yet this age registered considerable progress in literature and science, particularly in astronomy and mathematics. The most outstanding literary figure of the Gupta period was Kalidasa whose choice of words and imagery brought Sanskrit drama to new heights. Aryabhatta, the astronomer, had argued that it was the earth that moved round the sun but he was completely ignored, though not persecuted. An iron pillar erected at Delhi during the reign of one Gupta ruler still stands there in the open to this day, upright and without a trace of rust, evidence of an advanced knowledge of metallurgy.

Post-Gupta India witnessed many significant changes. Indian economy had always been predominantly agrarian, though supplemented by national and international trade and handicraft production. But with the end of the Gupta Age, both external and internal trade declined dramatically and this led to a greater ruralization of the economy. The amount of money in circulation also contracted; this led to a localization of economic and administrative units, for the states had to alienate the revenue of their territories by way of payment of salaries to civil and military officials as well as grants of charity to temples and Brahmins. Land became the primary, almost the exclusive source of state as well as private income.

Nevertheless, in many ways the centuries following the decline of the Gupta Empire witnessed a great deal of economic progress, especially in agricultural production.

Agricultural Expansion and Social Change

The high fertility of Indian soils has already been mentioned. For the realization of this fertility water was the prime need. The early medieval centuries, the 8th to the 12th of the Christian era, witnessed an impressive progress in the provision of irrigation to the fields. In northwestern and northern India various kinds of wheels were developed to draw water from ponds or wells. These were initially manually operated; later on, from about the 13th Century, a geared wheel was drawn by a pair of oxen — this was the Persian wheel, which still caters to the irrigation needs of much of the region today, although electricity or diesel operated pumps are fast displacing it.

In South India, tanks provided the chief source of irrigation. Small tanks were constructed by the individual farmer, the bigger ones by the village as a whole, or by the state. Canals and water channels also marked the rural landscape.

The availability of irrigation water greatly facilitated expansion as well as intensification of agriculture. New lands were brought under cultivation and new crops began to be experimented with.

But this economic advance was also creating a society far more complex than the earlier one, for it was creating greater social and economic disparities. While the Persian wheel could ensure water supply and thereby agricultural improvement, its installation was a costly affair. Only the upper stratum of peasants could make the investment and reap the benefit, leaving behind their less fortunate brethren. The same applies to other agricultural implements and superior cash crops. Thus, the agricultural advance benefitted farmers with different levels of resources differentially.

As noted earlier, one of the developments of this period was the development of a greater degree of rigidity in the caste system. One's caste status and profession came to be determined by one's birth, and it was not easy, though not impossible, to overcome it. It is possible that the demand for labor for agricultural production bore some relationship to this development. As agriculture expanded, labor became scarce. The operation of caste laws therefore excluded some of the lower castes from holding land of their own; it was *their* labor that came to be used by the entire community of cultivators, irrespective of its own stratification. This also introduced a paradox: a class of landless agricultural laborers was created in the context of an abundance of land. This was a peculiarly Indian solution to the problem of labor scarcity; medieval Europe had solved the same problem through the system of serfdom.

Greater agricultural production also meant greater resources for the rulers, who began to appropriate a large part of the produce, at times as much as a half of it, in the form of land revenue. This in turn necessitated a greater perfection of and centralized control over the system of revenue collection. On a small scale, such developments had, indeed, already taken place in the regional kingdoms of the 11th and 12th centuries all over the subcontinent.

Right, Yakshi (tree spirit) sculpture from Barhut, Madhya Pradesh, 2nd Century B.C.

At the outset of the 13th Century, a new wave of invaders, again from Central Asia, made its way to north India. This time the invaders had come to stay. They professed a different religion, Islam. A new state was established in 1206 with Delhi as its capital. This came to be known as the Delhi Sultanate. By the first quarter of the 13th Century it had brought under its direct or indirect control the greater part of the subcontinent, although the territorial boundaries of the Sultanate kept fluctuating with each ruler. During the 320 years of its existence, the throne of the Delhi Sultanate changed hands among six dynasties.

The process of centralization of administrative control over revenue collection that had begun in the early medieval centuries reached its climax under the sultans of Delhi. Land revenue was legally fixed at half the produce; soldiers and officers were assigned territories to collect revenue that equalled their annual salary. Other high officials were given charge of large territories from which they were to collect the revenue, maintain an army and, of course, themselves, and look after law and order. About 6 percent of the state revenue was given away in charity to religious institutions and pious individuals.

While this picture might suggest a considerable resemblance to feudal Europe, it is important to keep in mind some crucial differences. The assignees had no right over the land, which belonged to the peasants; they had the right merely to collect the revenue due to the state. Secondly, the officials (or assignees) were actually transferred from one territory to another every three or four years. This was to preempt their sinking local roots and gaining personal control over the administrative apparatus. It is thus that the growth of a permanent landed aristocracy, with its power based on control over land, was prevented down to the 19th Century. It is only under the aegis of colonial rule that such a class took root in India.

The Revenue System

Although a large majority of the administrative officials of the Sultanate were Muslims, the bulk of the revenue collection machinery was still run by Hindus. Often the tensions generated by conflicts of interests between the two sections were portrayed as being religious in nature. Inevitably, the establishment of the new state and its subsequent reinforcement

and expansion created manifold tensions. There were several forms in which these tensions manifested themselves; at times they were inter-regional, at times religious, and at times sectarian.

The increased produce from the land was beginning to find its way into an expanding network of markets. This process was accelerated when the Sultanate began to show its preference for the collection of revenue in cash. With a large number of officials, who were fairly mobile, and who were attuned to urban rather than rural life, cash collection

certainly made more sense than collecting foodgrains and carting them around. Once liquid cash came into their hands, they could spend it at the centers of their residence, which were also their administrative centers, in urban or semi-urban locales. This necessarily gave a spurt to the growth of urban centers, as well as to markets.

The Sultanate also introduced several new crafts and promoted or changed old ones. The Persian wheel with its gearing already mentioned was a West-Asian machine brought to India in the late 12th or early 13th Century. The spinning wheel, though of uncertain origin, is first encountered in India in the 14th Century; its productivity compared to that of the distaff was five to six times higher. This led to a greater production of coarse cotton textiles, worn by the poor. Paper also came to India at this time, as did gun-powder, both perhaps from China. In the building industry, new styles were introduced: the Qutb Minar has no predecessor in India, though minarets were common in Central Asia; similarly, the perfect round dome sitting on top of a square or rectangular base, which marks all monuments of this and the subsequent Mughal period, surely required new construction techniques. The building industry also witnessed the introduction of the true (arcuate) arch.

However, in some regions, in periods when they had not yet been subjugated to the authority of the Delhi Sultanate, altogether different styles of architecture were creating some of the most exquisite pieces, especially

in temple architecture. The temples at Konarak in Orissa and Khajuraho in Madhya Pradesh are expressions of architectural grandeur and sculptural finesse that is hard to excel. The preoccupation with dance and Eros in the sculptures is perhaps reflective of the adoption of tribal symbolisms from the neighborhood. Magnificent temples and sculptures were also created in South India — at Madurai, Rameshwaram and Thanjavur.

The break-up of the Delhi Sultanate began in the second quarter of the 14th Century,

Left, Mughal Emperor Jahangir at Fatehpur Sikri, the town built by his father Akbar; and right, Sher Singh, a Sikh chieftain.

during the reign of Mohammad bin Tughlaq. Tughlaq was an intellectual *par excellence,* enamored of the force of reason, possessing a powerful imagination, impatient with those who failed to keep pace with his ideas, and completely out of touch with the realities of life. His reign of 26 years was marked by 15 rebellions of his nobles spread out in almost every corner of the empire. Among the parts of the Sultanate that broke away were two southern regions, each harboring an independent dynasty, one Hindu, the other Muslim. Both these, the Vijayanagar Empire and the Bahmani Kingdom waged constant war with each other; both have left behind some of the most magnificent architectural monuments, though in ruins.

The much-contracted empire of the Sultans of Delhi lingered on as several of its regions went on detaching themselves and establishing independent kingdoms; the remainder of the 'empire,' much weakened, provided an irresistible temptation to any Central Asian adventurer with a strong army to reach out here for plunder. The most devastating of these plundering raids was led by Timur in 1398; among the prized loot that Timur carried home were numerous Indian artisans.

The Mughal Empire

A descendant of Timur as well as Changez Khan, an Uzbek prince who had failed to protect his kingdom against his cousins' intrigues and battles, was to follow the old invaders' route of northwestern mountain passes into India in 1526. This was Zahiruddin Mohammad Babur, founder of the Mughal Empire in India. It was during the reign of his grandson Akbar, who ruled over practically the whole of north India and parts of the south from 1556 to 1605, that the basic institutions and policies of the empire were framed.

Ascending the throne at the age of 13, Akbar began to take interest in the affairs of state only after spending another four years in adolescent playfulness. However, at the age of 17 he took full charge of the situation and never looked back.

Akbar realized that if the empire was to attain stability, it must grow local roots in that it should seek support from the local ruling groups. He thus began altering the predominantly alien character of the nobility by recruiting groups of indigenous rulers from various regions. The most powerful amongst these were the Rajputs of Rajasthan. He took the daughters of several of the Rajput houses as his wives, gave respect to their customs and religion, bestowed upon them some of the highest imperial offices, but dealt ruthlessly with those who refused to surrender. Gradually he reduced every group in the higher nobility to a small minority, including his own Mughal brethren. This was aimed at eliminating the chance of any one group becoming dominant. Each group had to learn to tolerate the others.

The administrative institutions of the Delhi Sultanate were modified and a new bureaucratic framework was evolved. Under this, every official of state was placed on the army rolls, irrespective of his duties, and every official, from the lowest to the highest, was recruited and paid by the imperial department of the army. This greatly tightened central control both over the bureaucracy and the army. The system of transfer of officials was rigorously implemented. Payment of salaries was first made in cash; gradually, however, the old system of revenue assignment came back into vogue. But then a person might be posted in Gujarat and yet his revenue assignment might be located in Bengal. This necessitated revenue collection in cash.

Land was classified into four categories according to productivity and a graduated land tax was imposed on peasants, going by the period for which their land had remained fallow. The ideal was of course two regular crops each year from every field. Revenue was fixed on the basis of the previous 10 years' productivity on each holding and was converted into cash on the basis of prices prevailing in the neighboring market over the past decade; this revenue demand was valid until later revision which would take into account any rise in productivity or prices. Peasants were accordingly given documents stating their liabilities.

Akbar the Great

Himself illiterate, Akbar took great interest in intellectual discussions on matters of religion and metaphysics; he called assemblies of theologians professing various religions, including Christians, and engaged in an exchange of ideas with them, refusing to accept the primacy of Islam. He also patronized the writing of history and a monumental historical work was compiled during his reign: the *Akbar Nama* (the 'Book of Akbar'). In his numerous and massive buildings at Fatehpur Sikri and Agra, where he had established his capital, there is an exquisite assimilation of elements and motifs from both the Islamic and the Hindu architectural styles.

The structure of the Mughal Empire was strong enough to sustain utter mediocrities as rulers and an almost unbroken tradition of princes revolting against their fathers and fighting it out among themselves. Akbar's son and grandson, Jahangir and Shah Jahan, had little of the grandeur of their ancestors in them. There was, however, an impressive record of diverse cultural activities during their regimes.

Predilection towards cultural sophistication was a characteristic of the Mughal Empire from its inception to its terminal point. Both its founder and his last descendant were eminent poets; several of the emperors and princes were deeply concerned with problems of metaphysics, some others were writers of superb memoirs. Jahangir, besides leaving behind one such book of memoirs, was a connoisseur and patron of the art of painting; Shah Jahan's fame rests on the creation of the Taj Mahal in memory of his queen who had died giving birth to his 14th child.

The Austere Emperor

There were, too, prosaic puritans in the line of Babur's descendants. Aurangzeb, the third of Shah Jahan's four surviving sons, was one such. Cold to freezing point, ambitious like other princes, and zealous on behalf of pristine Islamic purity, Aurangzeb fought a bloody war of succession with his brothers while their father was still alive, killed his brothers one by one without mercy, and kept his father in prison for seven years in an octagonal room in the Agra Fort where he died watching the reflection of the distant Taj Mahal in a small piece of glass. Keen on establishing an "Islamic" state in India, much in opposition to the Mughal tradition, Aurangzeb had no time for the finer things of life. Music, painting, architecture, even history-writing were for him occupations on which no energy or money need be squandered. Denied imperial patronage, these pursuits began to wither. In a desperate bid to make an appeal to the emperor's heart about their plight, some musicians of the capital (now Delhi) took out a funeral procession of music with loud wails that could not miss imperial ears. Aurangzeb looked out of the window of his palace and inquired about the goings-on. "Your Majesty," replied the mourners, "we are musicians, going out to bury our music for lack of appreciation." "Bury it so deep," said Aurangzeb, "that it never surfaces again."

The only time Aurangzeb betrayed some emotion was on his death-bed when he confessed to his failure in doing almost everything he had set out to do, particularly in ameliorating the conditions of life of the hardworking but grossly exploited peasants. He died in 1707 after a reign of 50 years.

Europe Comes to India

During the 17th Century, India had also been host to a very large number of West European travellers; among them were Italians, Englishmen, Frenchmen and Dutchmen. Some of them had come to India for reasons of commerce, others in pursuit of knowledge, and still others bitten by the travel bug. Some, like the French doctor Francois Bernier, rose high in the confidence of princes and other high nobles; others went around on their own, observing things and noting down impressions to be published later in their travelogs.

Beside individual travellers, organized European intervention in India's commerce took place during the 17th Century as several

in Goa; but their territorial and commercial hold in India remained rather limited. During the late 16th and the 17th Century they remained unrivalled as pirates on the high seas; but inland the other European companies were making their presence felt, though entirely in commercial terms.

The companies were trading in a sellers' market, competing with one another to purchase finished Indian goods. Of their own countries' products there was little that could be sold in India. They had brought with them woolen cloths and garments, but these commanded a rather limited market, given India's temperate climate. At any rate, woolens were produced in India too and it was difficult to break the established patterns of demand. Among other things Europeans had brought

countries floated East India Companies: England, France, the Netherlands and Denmark. Chartered as trading companies by their respective governments, they sought chiefly Indian textiles, both silk and cotton, indigo and, at times, sundry other things. The spices of Malabar (in Kerala) had attracted the Portuguese as early as the end of the 15th Century when, in 1498, Vasco da Gama had landed at Calicut, sailing via the Cape of Good Hope. Early in the 16th Century, the Portuguese had already established their colony

Qutb Minar (13th Century), a monument built by pre-Mughal Delhi Sultans.

with them were knives and clocks. Knives after all could hardly be transported and sold on a scale to balance the purchase of textiles and indigo; and clocks did not make for a great success because the measurement of time in India was done on an altogether different pattern. The European companies therefore had to make their purchases in India by paying mostly in gold and silver.

The Prosperous Years

Valuable as the European Companies' trade was for Indian economy, it still formed a very small fraction even of commerce, leaving aside agriculture. Trade carried on by Indian merchants was far higher in value in comparison.

One great Indian merchant of the 17th Century in Surat, Abdul Ghaffoor, had greater assets at his disposal than the Indian assets of all the East India Companies together. There were very many other merchants scattered in Surat and elsewhere in the country, not as great as Ghaffoor, but nonetheless important. Indeed the companies had often to depend upon individual merchants and brokers for loans to pay for their transactions.

India in the 17th Century thus presented a picture of prosperity and dynamism. Even the fertile lands of the river valleys had not been fully brought under cultivation; there was yet scope for expansion of agriculture and of population. The economy was essentially agrarian; yet trade and money had penetrated to almost every village. The currency was trimetallic, with gold, silver and bronze being molded into coins in a large number of imperial mints. Besides, anyone who had gold or silver in his possession could walk into a mint and have his metals coined for a nominal commission. There was considerable standardization of coins in the empire, though, in the regions, both inside and outside the empire, local currencies continued to remain in circulation. All these monetary transactions had given rise to a highly skilled professional class of money-changers and moneylenders. Insurance and bills of exchange had also reached a degree of sophistication that earned the uniform admiration of European observers.

If Indian economy was predominantly agrarian, there was yet a strong urban streak in it. One writer at the end of the 16th Century had enumerated 3,200 cities and towns in the Mughal empire. There were also plenty of them outside the empire, especially in the south; and about 15 percent of the population dwelled in urban centers, a percentage that was a shade higher than in contemporary Europe. Undoubtedly, most of these urban centers would be no better than townships; but it was commonly observed by 17th Century travellers that several Indian cities compared favorably with London or Paris in terms of physical dimensions and the size of the population.

The degree of centralization of control over the administration of the vast empire was unparalleled in the contemporary world; this was combined with a high degree of centralized control over the empire's resources. It has been estimated that a bare 73 individuals (or 0.9 percent of the nobles) had under their command 37.6 percent of the revenues of the empire in the middle of the 17th Century and they did not include the emperor himself. The magnitude of such control over the economy and the administration alone can explain the grandeur which has almost become synonymous with

the word "Mughal." But then the collapse of such authority also usually occurs in comparable enormity; as it certainly did in this case.

Religion and Literature

If impressive progress in the sphere of music, painting and, above all, architecture occurred under the aegis of the emperor or his nobles or under their indirect patronage, literature developed outside the imperial precincts. Sanskrit and Tamil were of course classical languages with highly sophisticated poetry antedating all empires by several centuries; but many regional languages, such as Hindi, Urdu, Gujarati, Marathi, Bengali etc., had begun to take shape from around the 15th Century. By the 17th Century, each had acquired a distinct identity with its own developed literature. The languages that are spoken today in most parts of India are the ones that evolved and grew to maturity in this medieval period.

By the 17th Century India had also learnt to live with a number of religious communities. Hindus still constituted the preponderant part of the population. There were of course the Muslims at different social planes from the highest to the lowest. Amongst Muslims the Sunnis predominated, though the Shias too had pockets of large population and two small but very powerful states in the northern part of South India. In South India, in Kerala in particular, Indian Christians too were a familiar sight. Among the older sects, the Jains continued to dominate trade in western India. Buddhism had, however, practically ceased to exist in any significant magnitude. On the other hand, the medieval period, especially from the late 15th to the 17th Century witnessed the evolution of a new sect in Punjab, then stretching across the current international border between India and Pakistan: the Sikhs. This sect, commanding the support of hardy peasants, cultivating the most fertile of Indian plains, denounced the caste system and emphasized social equality and devotion to God and the word of their Guru (teacher). Founded by a gentle and compassionate Guru, Nanak by name, the sect came into violent clash with the Mughals who executed two of its ten Gurus. In self-defence, it transformed itself into a truly militant religion under the guidance of its tenth Guru late in the 17th and early 18th Century. Hospitable and generous to a fault, the Sikhs have adhered to a tradition of militancy whenever their religious institutions or symbols have been tampered with.

Even as clashes occurred between the Mughal state and various groups that were to form regional kingdoms in the 17th and 18th centuries — and these groups comprised Hindus in Maharashtra, Sikhs in Punjab and Muslims in several other regions — medieval Indian society was almost completely devoid of tensions between religious communities. Indeed, through the five-and-half centuries when most regions in India were under the rule of Muslim dynasties, there was just one single incident of communal rioting where Hindus and Muslims clashed over the slaughter of a cow, held sacred by the Hindus since the later Vedic period. This was equally true of territories under the rule of Hindu dynasties but with substantial populations of other religious denominations. If we compare this single incident with the 400-odd incidents of communal clashes involving common members of

An Empire Crumbles

The 18th Century was to witness a sea change in the overall scene in India. After 1707, the mighty Mughal Empire began to crumble and give way to smaller regional kingdoms. Such of the empire as survived was riven with such friction and intrigue that the flight of a playwright's imagination could not have matched. The ever-expanding class of officials was beginning to find the resources at its disposal utterly unequal to the demand; this led to intense struggles amongst officials at every level to grab whatever they could and strive to hold on to whatever others were seeking to wrest from them. The consequent loss of control over the delicate system of checks and balances within the administrative set-up

different religious groups that have become an annual feature of Indian life today, we should be able to appreciate the absence of communal tensions at the social level in medieval India. The numerous European travellers in the 17th Century were indeed able to appreciate the harmonious relationship in which various religious communities lived in India. This struck them as remarkable in the context of the history of massive clashes between the various sects of Christians in contemporary Europe.

An Indian artist's impression at the beginning of British rule.

gave free rein to officials to fleece the peasants; the peasants in turn resisted this by taking to arms. Individual and factional ambitions further intensified the prevailing conflict and chaos; it became a no-holds-barred situation for everyone.

The regional states which inherited the Mughal Empire were not of uniform character. Some of them had been established by eminent Mughal nobles who had broken away from the empire: among these were Bengal, Awadh and the newly founded state of Hyderabad; others had come into existence following popular rebellions against the imperial authority — these included the Maratha kingdom in Maharashtra and the state of an Afghan tribe called Rohillas who had settled in Uttar

Pradesh. Inevitably, the Mughal model continued to exercise overwhelming influence on the evolution of regional polities in these states, although some of them stuck to the model more closely than others. However, the fact that the regions to be administered were much smaller units than the empire introduced a degree of efficiency and cohesion. Of the states that had been erected on the debris of the Mughal empire, Hyderabad maintained its existence down to 1952; the others went through several metamorphoses before freedom came to India.

The Maratha Empire

The power that came closest to imperial pretensions was that of the Marathas. Starting from scratch, the non-Brahmin castes in the Maharashtra region had been organized into a fighting force by their legendary leader, Shivaji. Diminutive in height, clever beyond his enemy's imagination, Shivaji led every day of his life like a drama in which he was always a step ahead of his adversaries. In the 18th Century the Marathas moved like lightning and suddenly appeared in areas where least expected, at times hundreds of miles away from their home. They always went back with their hands full of plunder, looting both Muslims and their Hindu co-religionists. Gradually, states began to pay them vast amounts in "protection money," insurance against their plundering raids. By the third quarter of the 18th Century the Marathas had under their direct administration or indirect subjection enough Indian territory to justify use of the term "the Maratha Empire," though it never came near the dimensions of the Mughal Empire. The Marathas also never sought to formally substitute themselves for the Mughals; they often kept the emperor under their thumb but paid him formal obeisance.

Pillage and Slaughter

The disintegration of the Mughal Empire was also an invitation to foreign invasions — a scenario so common in Indian history. Nadir Shah, Iranian ruler, led an attack in 1739, massacred several hundred thousand inhabitants of Delhi, his whole army plundering the capital at will; in the loot he carried home were the Koh-i-Noor diamond and the Peacock Throne. This throne had been crafted in the shape of a peacock, studded with gems and diamonds, for Shah Jahan. It continued to be Iran's imperial throne until the establishment of the Islamic Republic there a few years ago.

The second invasion in the 18th Century, under the command of the ruler of Afghanistan, led to more permanent consequences. In 1761, the Afghan armies met the Marathas in battle near Delhi; the decisive defeat of the Marathas put an end to their imperial ambitions for all time and eliminated any chance of an indigenous power filling the vacuum created by the decline of the Mughal Empire. The road was now wide open to the British to move in and colonize India. Several Maratha houses continued to rule over small or large territories after 1761; but none of them had the capacity to rise to imperial stature.

East India Companies

Some of the intrigues that had characterized the imperial polity at Delhi had also found imitators in the successor states in the 18th Century. In pursuit of factional or personal ambitions, overtures were at times made to the Europeans present there.

The European companies had organized their trade around the "factories" they had established in several towns; these "factories" were in reality mere warehouses for the commodities they had purchased. As the power of the Mughal Empire to protect them declined, they began to fend for themselves, recruiting their own miniature armies and using European weapons which were often superior to the Indian weapons. This provided an irresistible temptation to the groups engaged in ousting each other from positions of power in the states. The Europeans too were eager to sell their services to the highest bidder. Bit by bit they came to acquire a foothold in the political and administrative set-up in several of these states. Inevitably, different European groups often stood in opposite Indian camps; their own rivalries, operating through their Indian patrons, contributed to the prevailing friction in no small measure.

Of the European East India Companies which had come to trade in India, the Dutch had shifted their attention to Indonesia in search of spices long ago and did not have much of a presence on the Indian subcontinent in the 18th Century; the Portuguese held on to Goa and two other small territories, but were no contenders for imperial status; the Danes were never a significant factor anyway. The real contest was therefore between the English and the French. The English ultimately outwitted the French through a variety of maneuvers to become masters of India for nearly two centuries.

The Taj Mahal, Agra memorial to an empress.

It was in Bengal that the English made the first successful bid for establishing their rule in India. In 1757 and again in 1765 they defeated the Bengal ruler and, during the intervening years, engaged in the most unscrupulous intrigues at the court. The battle of 1765 was followed by an atrocious division of authority: while the local ruler was responsible for the administration, the British took charge of the revenues. The chaos that resulted is not difficult to imagine; the battle led, in the words of a Bengali poet, to "a night of eternal gloom for India."

creating a class of landed aristocracy akin to the feudal aristocracy of Europe. In Mughal India, as has been noted, while officials and other intermediate groups were entitled to a part or whole of the revenue due to the state, the land belonged to the peasants. The British devised "Permanent Settlement," which altered this situation and created a class that held its vast lands permanently so long as it paid revenues to the state. The peasants were placed entirely at the mercy of this class. The first experiment of this sort was made in Bengal, but the system was extended to many of the other

The English East India Company continued its commercial activities of course; but it no longer needed to import gold and silver into Bengal to purchase textiles for export to Britain and thence to Europe; it could make the purchases with the fabulous Bengal revenues. There was, besides, private trade carried on by private British citizens as well as the Company's servants who were never reluctant to use for themselves the concessions that had been granted to the Company. Nor was there any lack of financial corruption on the part of British officials, including governors.

Towards the end of the 18th Century, the Company started planning for a long stay in the country. For this purpose it required a degree of local support. This was obtained by

areas subsequently conquered by the British. Grateful that they had been granted unfettered rights on the land and its cultivators, members of this class were to remain loyal to the British cause for a long time to come. The increasing demand for revenue by the British government on this class was passed on to the peasants who ultimately had to bear the burden.

In the first half of the 19th Century the British extended their hold over many Indian territories. A large part of the subcontinent was brought under the Company's direct administration; in some parts local rulers were retained as subsidiaries of the Company, militarily and administratively completely at its mercy and yielding to it an overwhelming portion of the revenues. By 1857, "the British empire *in* India had become the British empire *of* India." The means employed to achieve this were unrestrained and no scruple was allowed to interfere with the imperial ambition.

Vested Interests

Although the activities of the Company were regularly and closely supervised by the British Parliament, there was little possibility of placing any real restraints on the Company's functioning, for the revenues drained from India in money and in trade brought prosperity on a large enough scale in Britian to create a widespread vested interest in the colonization of India. This was apart from the personal landed aristocracy, the artisan could still sell his goods to the Company, for which the demand had not contracted. This was particularly true of silk and cotton textiles, though the market for indigo was shrinking, for a better quality indigo was being manufactured in the West Indies. The superior quality of Indian textiles, however, posed a threat to the development of the English textile industry throughout the 18th Century and heavy duties and fines were imposed on the import and use of these cloths. In 1760, one English lady had to pay £200 as fine for using an Indian handkerchief. Yet the demand for these textiles did not decline. The decisive shift came with the industrialization of cloth manufacture in Britain. The very scale of its production and low price brought it into distant markets and

benefit that many Members of Parliament derived from direct involvement in the Company's enterprises; indeed, not infrequently the Company or its retired employees invested money to purchase seats in the House of Commons for its agents. Among its patrons the Company could count even the sovereign.

The British hold over the Indian economy and society too underwent a substantial change in the first half of the 19th Century. If the peasant was carrying the ever-rising burden of supporting the government and the indigenous

Left, Indian troops under British officers pose for picture (c. 1878, in the course of the 2nd Afghan War); right, the Rajputs are what the British used to call a martial race.

began to drive out the handloom-manufactured textiles. The rising class of textile manufacturers in Lancashire and Manchester too began to make its presence felt in the British Parliament which enacted laws requiring the Company to export British goods to India on a prescribed scale. In 1794 the value of British cotton manufactures sold in India amounted to £156; in 1813 it had risen to £110,000. Under pressure of the manufacturers' lobby, Parliament in 1833 abolished the Company's monopoly over the Indian trade and opened the floodgates to British goods, the custom duties for which were fixed at nominal levels. By 1856 British manufactures imported into India were valued at £6,300,000.

Inevitably, the Indian textile industry, based on craft production, was ruined. Instead, Indian raw cotton was exported to Britain to be turned into finished goods and then sent back to the Indian market. Another commodity exported from India by the British was opium, but this was taken to China and forced into the Chinese market in spite of the Chinese government's ban on it. The British, however, meticulously observed their own government's ban on the import of opium into their own country.

For capturing the vast Indian market it was necessary to develop the means of transport and communication. Steamships started navigating the network of Indian rivers; old roads were repaired and improved; but, above all, railways were introduced in India in 1853. In that year, the telegraph was also introduced.

reformers who had had the opportunity to compare traditional Indian with modern European educational and social systems. Clearly, these changes were only the first step towards a transformation of Indian society; the overwhelming part of it still remained steeped in tradition, not all of which was admirable.

The progress of British rule in India had understandably generated varied kinds of resentment in different locales. Such of the princely houses which had been deprived of their territories and power could hardly relish the goings-on; the Company's high civil and military officials seldom adhered to their own declared principles, for it was after all not easy to sacrifice the prospect of territorial expansion for the sake of a scruple. Impoverishment of ruling houses brought in its train misery on

Along with these modern means of transport and communications came certain modern concepts of social organization. A separation of civil administrative functions from those of the army and the police, and the notion of the rule of law and equality before the law were all major departures from the then existing forms of social functioning. So also was the attempt at rooting out some of the social customs such as a widow burning herself at the funeral pyre of her husband, or the infanticide of female children. Western sciences and philosophy taught through the medium of English were also first experimented with in 1835, in Bengal. There was considerable support for these measures amongst many Indian intellectuals and social

vast numbers of those directly or indirectly dependent on court patronage for their livelihood — courtiers, soldiers, servants, merchants, artisans. Artisans, especially textile weavers, suffered directly too when the Company, newly ensconced in levers of political and administrative power, first sought to depress the wages of labor and prices of goods and later flooded Indian markets with British goods. Several towns, centers of textile production, were ruined. In the countryside, peasants were being subjected to an ever-rising demand for revenue either by the Company's government directly or on its behalf by the indigenous landed aristocracy. Even the government's benign measures, such as the ban on widow burning, were viewed in some sections as unwarranted interference with age old Indian customs.

The Rebellion of 1857

The British hold on India and the unfolding of its political and economic policies were marked by sporadic and local-level uprisings in some regions. What happened in 1857, however, was a concerted effort on a grand scale in large parts of India to be rid of alien rule. This was an endeavor in which the Mughal "emperor," a number of princely states in the regions, artisans and peasants and Indian sepoys of the Company's army joined hands. "Mughal" was still a hallowed name, although the "emperor" was an aged and

A rumor began to spread that the cartridges were greased with the fat of cows and pigs. Since cows were held sacred by the Hindus and there were few sins greater than eating beef, this order greatly hurt their sentiment. The Muslims were on the other hand hurt by the utter indifference to their religious sentiment which forbade them even to touch pork, held unclean by them. Thus, irrespective of the truth of the rumor, both Hindu and Muslim sepoys were alienated at one go; but then the fact that the rumor was easily believed pointed to the general level of alienation of the government from the people. The rumor clearly served as a spark to set the growing forest of discontent on fire.

On May 10, 1857, many sepoys stationed at Meerut, near Delhi, mutinied. This was the

decrepit man, whose "empire" did not extend beyond the walls of the Red Fort in Delhi which housed his palace and whose "revenue" was a pension settled on him by the Company. Yet this old man became the center and the symbol of the massive rebellion.

The immediate cause of the rebellion was an order issued by the Company's army commanders to the Indian sepoys to bite the cartridges before putting them into their rifles.

Left, rajas of the period. Some resisted British domination and were destroyed; these others became British vassals and their states survived till after Indian independence. Right, Western India Turf Club, Poona (c. 1900).

beginning of the rebellion. From Meerut the sepoys marched to Delhi where they were joined by the local infantry who killed their British officers and carried off the "emperor" to "lead" them. From Delhi the revolt spread to the whole of northern and central India; it also spread downwards into the ranks of townsmen and peasants. However, the class of landed aristocracy that the British had created through the Permanent Settlement stood by its master in that moment of trial.

It was a fight to the end on both sides with all the accompanying bloodshed, violence and hatred; but the end did not favor India. While vast numbers of Indians rose in revolt, many groups and regions stood by silently; there were others who joined hands with the British.

The British were also better armed and had more efficient and quicker means of communication, the railways and telegraph among them. The "emperor" at any rate did not possess the capacity of leadership in a situation in which leadership was of critical importance.

The Rebellion lasted a year and a half; by the end of 1859 the "emperor" had been deported to Burma where he died a lonely death, bringing to a formal end the grand era of Mughal rule in India. Many of his sons were executed in Delhi and their bodies were left hanging for several days to drive the point home.

The Rebellion, even in its failure, produced many heroes and heroines of epic character and the folklore around this event has produc-

Parliament. The Crown's viceroy in India was to be the chief executive. The army was reorganized with a far greater number of British officers than had been the case hitherto. No Indian was allowed to rise to an officer's position until the second decade of the 20th Century. Although Indians could compete for high civil service jobs, the number of those successful remained too meagre to be of any significance. The higher posts in most administrative departments were reserved for the British subjects of the Crown.

The new government also sought to accommodate some of the princely states which had stood by the British in 1857; they were to be the bulwark of Britain's Indian Empire. But of course this accommodation was to be allowed within the overall framework of complete

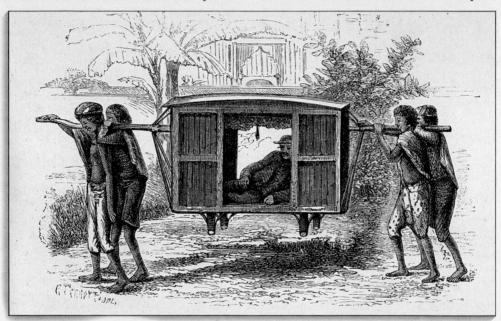

ed some masterpieces of popular literature. Above all, it produced a sense of unity between the Hindus and the Muslims of India that was only to be witnessed in later years.

For one of the chief lessons the government was to draw from 1857 was that such unity must be preempted. Immediately following the Rebellion the government pursued discriminatory policies against the Muslims: they were denied opportunities of employment in the government as well as modern education to ensure that they remained backward compared to the Hindus and thus for ever in contention with them.

The Rebellion saw the end of the Company's rule in India. Power was transferred to the British Crown in 1858 by an Act of British

subordination to imperial authority. Given this subordination, their territories were declared proof against any further annexation.

Gone too was the zeal for social reform; the government began carefully to refrain from interfering with any of the social customs of Indians, however backward-looking. Enthusiasm for imparting modern education to Indians too began to wane and university education remained confined for a long time to three cities — Calcutta, Bombay and Madras — where universities had been established in 1857. A most dramatic expansion took place in the army, on which as much as 52 percent of the Indian revenues were spent in 1904. This army was used not only to suppress any form of popular protest either against the British government or the princely states, but also in aggressive compaigns in countries in India's neighborhood: thus were Burma and Afghanistan subordiated to the British rulers of India.

Industrialization

The Indian contact with Britain's growing industrialization had initially undermined the market for the products of India's artisans. The effect on the weavers had been particularly disastrous, as already mentioned. Gradually, however, this contact also brought modern industry to India. The first textile mill began operating in Bombay in 1853 and the first jute mill in Bengal two years later. By 1905, more than 200 cotton textile mills and 36 jute mills

preneurs. Expectedly, the government extended all patronage to British-owned industries (and plantations such as tea, indigo and coffee) and discriminated against Indian capital.

There was too a remarkable degree of social awakening in various regions of India in the second half of the 19th Century; apparent were the growth of modern ideas and realization of the need for removing social evils. At times it took on a religious garb so that religious reform movements were often covers for protest against evils like the stigma on widow remarriage, or the practice of child marriage. Complicated religious rituals also came under attack, as they had several times earlier.

Above all, there was a growing political consciousness that encompassed all other spheres

were functioning. A large iron and steel plant was established in Bihar which continues to operate to this day. Some of these mills and factories were established by Indians, among them the iron and steel plant just mentioned. But most were under the control of British capital, which saw enormous profits in the cheap raw materials and labor and a vast market in India and abroad. The introduction of modern industry brought with it incipient conflict between British and Indian entre-

Left, a Sahib riding in a palanquin, c. early 18th Century. Right, young Queen Victoria, first Sovereign Empress of India, from a painting at Fort St. George Museum (Madras).

of activity. The violent uprising of 1857 had ended in failure; new methods of protest against alien rule had to be adopted if protest were to be effective. The crucial new method was to be based on organized strength, challenging the government on its own ground, within the framework of the British government's laws and policies. This clearly required a class of highly educated Indians, especially lawyers. British-trained Indian lawyers were indeed to play the crucial leadership role in the movement for India's liberation, the Indian National Movement.

Experiments had already been made at forming local and regional level organizations of educated Indians here and there. In 1885, a national-level organization was formed which

was to play a decisive role in the country's subsequent history until and after independence: this was the Indian National Congress. The initial thrust for its creation came indeed from a retired English civil servant, A. O. Hume, who collected eminent educated Indians in Bombay and held the first session of the organization. He had conceived of it as a "safety valve" against the spread of popular discontent. In his own words, "A safety valve for the escape of great and growing forces generated by our own action was urgently needed."

To begin with, the Congress sought to air reservations against the government's laws and political and administrative measures. Gradually, various strands began to appear within the organization, not all of which were committed to mild expressions of views. The "moderate" and the "extremist" wings began to make their appearance by the beginning of the 20th Century. While the Moderates sought gradual reform within the structure of law and government and expressed their aspirations through speeches and petitions, the Extremists were basically hostile to the very notion of an alien government and were prepared to use violence to achieve their objective. However, in either case, political activity remained confined to the highly educated Indians.

"Boycott British Goods"

A major departure in the growth of Indian nationalism occurred in 1905. In that year an order was issued for the partition of the province of Bengal into two units. The public justification for this order was that this would make the two provinces administratively more viable; privately, officials at various levels admitted that the objective was to stem the tide of nationalism then on the rise among Bengalis, by separating east and west Bengal and isolating them from the people of other linguistic regions (Assam, Bihar and Orissa) which together constituted a single province. Leaders of the National Movement understood the purpose of this move and prepared to oppose it tooth and nail. If nothing else had mobilized the masses of Indian people into opposition to the government, the proposed partition of Bengal did. There were hunger strikes, general strikes, marches, demonstrations, public meetings, in all of which milling crowds participated. Above all,

Left, Bahadur Shah Zafar, the last Mughal, deported to Burma on the fall of Delhi; right, Bhagat Singh, who belonged to one of a number of revolutionary groups active in the 1930s, was hanged by the British.

a brand new weapon, likely to touch the British where it hurt most, was adopted: boycott of British goods and use of India-made commodities. This gave an enormous spurt to Indian industry in various sectors. The movement, with its nerve center in Calcutta, began to spread all over the country in diverse forms, from peaceful strikes and slogan shouting and protest marches to acts of terrorism.

The government countered with unprecedented repression and police violence was unleashed on even the most peaceful of protestors. Imprisonment was, of course, the least of the government's repressive acts. But a political maneuver on government's part at this moment was to have a far more lasting impact on India's future: calculated steps were taken to create dissensions between the predominant-

ly Muslim east Bengal (now Bangladesh) and predominantly Hindu west Bengal. The degree of government's success is indicative of the easy receptivity to provocation of dissension between the two communities. This was increasingly to become a central question in the National Movement and to lead to far-reaching consequences. Several attempts were made to find a solution of this problem. None succeeded.

Divide and Rule

The British policy of weakening the National Movement by creating dissensions within it bore its first fruit in 1906 when the All India Muslim League was founded. It stood up in support of the partition of Bengal and demanded special concessions from the government for the Muslims, such as proportionate reservation of government jobs for them. However, the League's claim to be the representative of all the Muslims of India was challenged by a large number of Muslim leaders who had pledged their support to the Congress. Even so, two political entities, one representing the Muslims exclusively, the other the Hindus predominantly, began to operate on the Indian scene. At times they entered into agreements with one another, at others they adopted mutually antagonistic postures. In either case their separate identities persisted.

While the government responded to the growing Movement by resorting to repression

thereby paralyse the functioning of the legislatures.

Gandhi Arrives

It was in 1917 that a new phase began in the developing struggle for India's freedom. In 1915, Mohandas Karamchand Gandhi returned to India from South Africa where he had experimented with new forms of resistance to the apartheid regime. He had gone to South Africa to practice as a lawyer after his training as barrister-at-law in England. In South Africa he witnessed and experienced humiliation because of the color of his skin. In protest he began to organize the Indian victims of apartheid to wage a completely non-violent protest. The victims were to violate the unjust

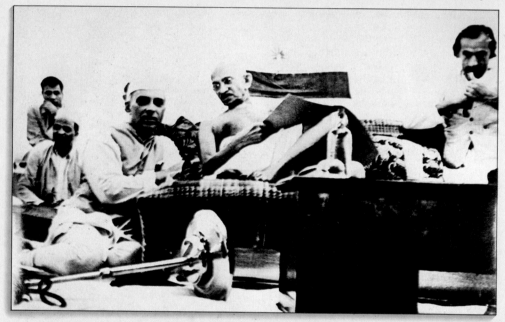

as well as divisive tactics, it also sought to appease public opinion by amending its legal structure. It began to visualize legislatures with elected as well as nominated members and with some control over a few of the departments of administration. Voting rights were, however, severely restricted. Such measures were wide of the mark that the National Movement had set for itself. Most of the leaders of the Movement were lawyers who had had their legal training in England and had familiarized themselves with the working of the parliamentary system there. These leaders, while participating in these legislatures were forever dissatisfied with the severe limitations placed on them. Consequently they were ever willing to tender their resignations collectively and

law publicly and take the punishment willingly, without even an expression of pain. The strategy was to appeal to the conscience of the oppressors; it also aroused the latent moral protest among the victims, and unleashed the energy and power of the vast multitudes without incurring any expense on arms.

The story of Gandhi's experiments had reached India, his homeland. When, therefore, he returned in 1915 he was already a well-known figure.

Before launching himself into the struggle Gandhi sought to familiarize himself with conditions in India, from where he had been gone for a long time. He undertook extensive tours of various regions of India and saw for himself the immense poverty and degradation suffered by the masses of Indian people at the hands of both their Indian and foreign masters. The misery of the lower castes, perpetrated by the upper castes, the inhuman treatment of bonded agricultural laborers in several regions, the deprivation from which Indian women suffered everywhere — all these facets of inhuman existence came alive to him as he travelled in crowded trains, bullock-carts and on foot. Gandhi also came to realize that most of India still lived in villages; that it was there that India's real strength lay. But this resource could be tapped only if relief were brought to Indian peasants from exploitation both at the hands of Indian landlords as well as the British government and planters.

Gandhi reached a similar conclusion about the industrial workers; their living conditions

Gandhi, however, always imposed one inviolable condition: defiance of law, or "civil disobedience" as it came to be called, must always be completely peaceful.

The government had been familiar with the passing of resolutions at annual Congress sessions; it was familiar too with demonstrations, public meetings and terrorist activity; but this was altogether a new form of protest which it did not know how to handle. Consequently, it reacted clumsily. If it imprisoned the leaders, as it often did, multitudes of Indians would line up for filling the jails; they had to be released because prisons could no longer hold them. If it opened fire on unarmed and peaceful protestors, as it did in 1919 in Punjab, its own pretensions to civilized behavior would be exposed and its legitimacy question-

must improve and Indian millowners must sacrifice a part of their profit for this purpose.

From the beginning, Gandhi waged a moral protest against oppression by defying unjust laws and willingly taking punishment. He would often undertake fasts lasting several weeks until his demands had been conceded. Defying laws frequently led him into prison. Following him, other leaders went to jail for the same offence; then masses of people, moved by his inspiring leadership, followed suit.

Gandhi and Nehru at a Congress Meeting, left; and right, the closing negotiations, where Mountbatten, Nehru, Jinnah and other leaders discuss the details.

ed. It was willing to give some concessions, but these fell far short of the demand.

Late in 1920 a massive "Non-Cooperation Movement" was launched. The government was asked to atone for the utterly unwarranted killings in Punjab and for going back on the British government's assurance given to Turkey during the First World War. The British prime minister, Lloyd George, had declared that Turkey would not be deprived of "the rich and renowned lands of Asia Minor and Thrace which are predominantly Turkish in race" once the war was over; yet Thrace was detached from Turkey just as the war concluded. The British treatment of the Turkish Caliph also hurt Muslims in many lands who treated him as the head of the Muslim world.

In India, the Muslims had launched a movement in protest; the Congress joined this movement to win the Muslims over for joint struggles against the British Indian government.

In 1921 and 1922 unprecedented scenes of mass participation in the Non-Cooperation Movement were witnessed throughout India. People of all communities, regions and ages responded to the call by giving up their studies, jobs, everything. Women joined the movement in massive numbers. Boycott of European cloth became a public cry and bonfires of such cloths were made. Hindus and Muslims forgot all about their differences. A surge of human bonds, breaking all barriers, united the diverse people in this hour of magnificent struggle.

This was an anticlimax which was not appreciated by most of the leaders of the National Movement, both old and young. Among the latter was Jawaharlal Nehru. The Movement began to drift without much force and without a clear aim. But this mood was not to last long.

Late in the 1920s a new strand of leadership was beginning to emerge both within the Congress and outside. This strand comprised a younger group of men and women inspired by the socialist ideas of Marx and Lenin and moved by the experiment of socialist revolution in the U.S.S.R. In 1925 the Communist Party of India had been formed; its membership remained rather small, but its influence, particularly among workers, peasants and the intelligentsia, was quite disproportionate to its

The government reacted as usual with imprisonment and use of gunfire, which only helped to bring ever more people into the movement.

But the government was saved by Gandhi himself at a time when the movement was attaining ever higher peaks: he suddenly withdrew the struggle because in an obscure village in eastern Uttar Pradesh some policeman had fired upon a procession of 3,000 peasants and the peasants had, in a moment of rage, burnt down the police station and caused the death of 22 policemen. Gandhi's basic condition of non-violence had been violated by the protestors; he would have nothing to do with any protest which carried even a suggestion of violence.

numerical strength. Within the Congress, leadership was beginning to pass into the hands of younger men, who also carried distinctly socialist sympathies: men like Subhash Chandra Bose and Jawaharlal Nehru, among others.

There were, besides, young men and women who together constituted a stream of revolutionary terrorists. They were moved by a commitment to the vision of remolding Indian society as much as by anti-imperialist sentiment. The most outstanding of these was Bhagat Singh who courted death for throwing a bomb into the central legislative assembly hall during a session. He was still studying the writings of socialist thinkers when he was called out to the gallows.

The influence of socialist ideas brought the concern with economic issues to the center of the Movement's thinking. The shape of things after British rule was terminated began to emerge in the minds of leaders; it also found expression in their writings and speeches. This concern in turn brought even larger numbers of India's poor masses into the struggle; the struggle itself became more fervent.

The Demand for Independence

It was this mood that was reflected in the resolution of the Congress passed at its annual session in 1929: the resolution demanded complete independence for India. Jawaharlal Nehru was the young president of the session, succeeding his father. January 26, 1930, the

day the resolution was adopted, was designated Independence Day, the anniversary of which was to be observed by all Indians every year by unfurling a new tricolored flag and taking the independence pledge which declared that it was "a crime against man and God" to submit to British rule.

A second movement of civil disobedience was launched early in 1930; this was to defy laws that were considered unjust. Gandhi chose to dramatize this defiance by taking up an item that touched the poorest of Indian

Left, Nehru's address at Red Fort on August 15, 1947; and right, a December 1946 report in the *Illustrated London News*.

households. The government had a monopoly of manufacture of salt from which it derived a large revenue. Gandhi decided symbolically to "manufacture" salt on the Gujarat coast without paying any tax. After declaring his intention of doing so, he set out on foot to march to the coast about 150 miles (250 km) away, accompanied by a handful of supporters. He was then 60 years old. As he walked people joined him in the thousands, a substantial number of them women.

Once again, mass participation in this movement eliminated differences of community, region, language and sex and brought out the noblest in the humblest of men and women.

The government's response was predictable: imprisonment and firing on unarmed people. It also called a Round Table Conference in London where representatives of various groups would confer on the future of India. The Congress demanded preparatory steps towards complete independence, but that was unthinkable for the British. The negotiations broke down; the Civil Disobedience Movement was resumed, but it had to give way in the face of the intense terror and repression unleashed by the government.

In 1935, the Government of India Act was passed by the British Parliament. This proposed a bicameral legislature at the center in which the princes would nominate their representatives and about 14 percent of the people of India, who had been given the right to vote, would elect the others. Even with this balance between people's representatives and the government's allies, the legislature had extremely limited powers. In the provinces, however, the elected assemblies had much greater, though not full control over the various departments of administration. The Congress opposed the Act but nonetheless decided to contest elections under it and form governments. Except in Bengal and Punjab, the Congress swept the polls.

The Fascist Threat

Between 1935 when the Act was passed and implemented and the Second World War, the whole world was in a ferment. The growth of Nazism in Germany and Fascism in Italy and Japan was threatening the very existence of humanity; on the other hand the colonial people's struggles for liberation were getting more determined. India's sympathy clearly lay with these struggles all over the world, even as she was willing to side with her own imperialist master and its allies in the fight against Nazism. More than ever before this brief period placed India's National Movement in the context of the developing global situation and established linkages between local and international issues.

However, India's support to Britain in the war was not unconditional. If India were to help Britain retain its freedom against possible enslavement by Hitler, surely this could not be done by India herself remaining enslaved. A free India, in fact if not in form, would be able to render much more effective assistance in resisting the Nazi onslaught than an India in bondage. The government would not even consider such a proposition; it was appalled by the fact that the Indian leaders should attach any conditions to their offer of support in fighting such an unmixed evil as Nazism.

Things came to a head in 1942. The Congress gave a call to Indians to ensure that the British "Quit India"; Indians were called upon

strength. Britain certainly was no longer a great power, economically and militarily. The new great powers, the U.S.A. and the U.S.S.R., were both in favor of seeing India a free nation. Indeed, there was growing support for India's demand for independence even in Britain; many sections of the Labour Party were in sympathy with the demand. As a result, things moved fast in that direction when the Labour Party came to power in Britain after the war. If Churchill's government had been adamant in retaining India — which had once been described as "the brightest jewel in the British Crown" — and if the Prime Minister had declared that he had not been elected to that office "to preside over the liquidation of the empire," the new government headed by Attlee was less moved by considera-

to 'do or die' in this endeavor. Once again, a massive movement was under way to achieve freedom; once again it was matched by massive repression. In several regions the rebels were able briefly to establish their own administration; but all these victories were shortlived. Subhash Chandra Bose, who had quit the Congress earlier, organized Indians in southeast Asia into a powerful armed force called the Indian National Army. He sought Japanese help to lead this Army into India and free it from British control. The defeat of Japan in the war, however, put an end to this dream.

The Allies had won the war but the effort had left several of them with much depleted

tions of past imperial glory than by the visible writing on the wall.

It was becoming quite clear that the spirit of rebellion against the alien government was spreading and that the government could not long depend on this spirit keeping within the bounds of non-violence. There had been a strong tradition of terrorism in the Indian National Movement at the best of times and terrorists commanded as much respect with the people of India as the non-violent agitators; now, with the government's unbending at-

The Mountbattens say farewell.

titude on the basic question of India's independence, non-violent methods would be increasingly discredited. Also, the government's grip over the mainstay of its authority, the army and the bureaucracy, was beginning to loosen. Sympathy for Bose's Indian National Army was often visible in the ranks of the Indian armed forces. In 1946, the ratings of the Indian Navy burst into a revolt in Bombay and waged a pitched battle with British forces; they were prepared to go on, if they had not been persuaded by the nationalist leaders to surrender. There were widespread strikes too in the Indian Air Force, the Signals Corps and the police in some cities. All this was in tandem with widespread strikes by the common people everywhere. Industrial workers, by now a sizeable force, were waging particularly militant strikes; the peasants too were getting ready for a last-ditch action. Attlee's government was sensitive to these developments as also to the weakness of Britain's position and, for the first time, independence for India became negotiable.

The Muslim League

There was, however, one major development that was to embitter the taste of independence for millions of Indians. The Muslim League, which always enjoyed government's patronage, sought guarantees from the government as well as the Congress that the rights of the Muslim minority (about 10 percent of the population) would be safeguarded. The Congress was willing to give them oral assurances, but it was argued that the fact that the Congress itself had a strong wing of leaders who were staunch Hindu communalists ever justified a degree of skepticism concerning these assurances. Since the Congress commanded the support of the majority community, the Hindus, it could always camouflage its own communalism under the slogan of nationalism as well as democracy, it was said. No one doubted the personal integrity of leaders like Gandhi and Nehru when they spoke of Muslims as their brothers: but much more was at stake than the promise of honest persons. How could the Muslims be certain that the future too would produce leaders of the same calibre and integrity?

A solution that the British government had worked out was to establish separate electorates for the Hindus and the Muslims, each community electing its representatives. This was tantamount to validating the theory that the League had begun to propound, namely that the Hindus and the Muslims were two separate nations, thus equating religion with nation. The Congress had never accepted this theory, for it implied that the Congress could not enrol Muslims as members, nor represent them. Some of the most illustrious presidents of the Congress had been Muslims and not all Muslims sympathized with the League anyway. Yet, the Congress contested elections on the basis of separate electorates while never giving up its reservations concerning them.

Separate electorates could only have reinforced the communal division. The paths of the Congress and the League began to diverge more sharply than ever. In 1940 the League raised the demand for a separate independent state for the Muslims, and frequently reiterated it subsequently. The state was to be called Pakistan.

The New State of Pakistan

The tension that this demand created led to widespread communal rioting of the most inhuman kind as the prospect of independence began to take shape. Both Hindus and Muslims participated in the mass butchery in 1946, each blaming the other community for the first killing. There were, too, heroic people on both sides who laid down their lives in defence of brethren of the other community; but in a situation of such large-scale turbulence their effort was too feeble to bridge the wide chasm of hatred.

By early 1947 the decision to grant freedom to India had been taken; but this freedom would be accompanied by the partition of the country to create the new state of Pakistan. Not all the effort on the part of leaders of the Congress and the Muslim League could resolve the communal problem. Pakistan was to comprise two regions, one in the west and the other, separated by nearly 1,300 miles (2,000 km) of Indian territory, far out in East Bengal, now Bangladesh. Large numbers of Hindus from the regions that were to constitute Pakistan, and Muslims from India began to emigrate. Millions, often with no more than the clothes they were wearing, moved in opposite directions. Not all of them reached their destinations.

Thus it was that freedom came to India on August 15, 1947, in the midst of stupendous tragedy, a most senseless shedding of human blood. As the dividing hour between August 14 and 15 approached, and people burst into the joy of breathing free air after two centuries of slavery, Gandhi lay forlorn on a thin jute mattress spread out on the floor of an unlit house in Calcutta, silently weeping over the loss of all that he had held closest to his heart: non-violence, humanity, compassion and love for fellow human beings, irrespective of color or of skin, religion or creed.

INDIA TODAY

India's political and economic development in the nearly four decades since she attained her independence is an enigma that has fascinated two generations of social scientists both at home and abroad. To begin with, India is a democracy in the most orthodox sense of the term. While the democratic experiment has failed almost without exception in the countries of the third world, India's democratic institutions have grown perceptibly stronger from one general election to the next.

The enigma grows deeper when one considers the kind of country that India is. No other country in the developing world — not even China — is as heterogeneous as this one. India has 14 major languages, and at least 200 dialects or closely related subsidiary languages. It has six major religious groups — the Hindus, the Muslims, Christians of various churches, Sikhs, Parsis (Zoroastrians) and Jains.

But perhaps the greatest cause of diversity is the caste system. Hindu society is divided into anywhere between 200 to 300 *jati* (the Indian word for caste). In addition, the country has some 60 million tribal people, of whom some tribes predate the earliest immigration of Caucasians from Central Asia, which took place around 8,000 years ago. Lastly, the country has Hindus who fall outside the fold of orthodox Hinduism — the Harijans, who were once called the untouchables, until Mahatma Gandhi renamed them "the people of God."

Between religion, language, caste and tribe, the country is splintered into a million self-contained, often socially isolated fragments. How could 750 million people of such bewildering diversity ever fulfill the preconditions of nationhood — the creation of a common national psyche, a common set of cultural and ethnic values, and a common desire to project these, while rejecting the values imposed on the country from outside?

Why did internal conflicts and contradictions not frustrate the birth of incipient nationalism at its outset? And since the society was by no means free of conflicts — political, economic, religious and linguistic — what was the binding force that converted India not only into a viable nation, but a vibrant democracy?

These are questions that do not plague only the academics. Till very recently they tormented, and perhaps still torment, most thinking Indians. The Indian intelligentsia has passed through several periods of acute self-doubt in which its belief in itself has been severely tested. In 1962, when the Chinese in-

Control room at one of India's atomic power stations.

flicted a humiliating defeat on India in their Himalayan border war; in 1964 when Pandit Nehru, India's first Prime Minister died; and in 1966 and 1967 when two successive, crippling droughts brought the economy close to ruin. These doubts had arisen even earlier. For instance, when Pandit Nehru sanctioned the reorganization of the Indian states (India has a federal democracy) to bring their borders in line with linguistic divisions, many intellectuals looked on with horror and predicted that this was the beginning of the disintegration of the country.

"Dangerous Decade"

But the years of self-doubt have now been left behind. From the mid-70s onwards a series of political events have conclusively demonstrated that Indians take their democracy very seriously indeed, and will not allow any event, nation, or individual to rob them of it. The first occasion on which the electorate showed its power was during the 1977 elections. These were held after 19 months of "emergency" rule in which the Congress government led by Mrs. Indira Gandhi severely curtailed democratic freedoms, jailed a number of leading members of the opposition and an estimated 100,000 political activists, imposed censorship on the press, and ruled virtually by presidential decree.

Mrs. Gandhi probably did not consider the declaration of the emergency as more than a temporary expedient. But the people of India were not prepared to take any chances. In the elections that followed the emergency in March 1977, they threw the Congress out of power and elected a coalition of the very same opposition parties whose leaders had spent the previous 19 months in jail.

The second time that the electorate unambiguously demonstrated its deepening commitment to national unity and democracy, was in the December 1984 elections to the central parliament. On this occasion, made traumatic by the assassination of Prime Minister Indira Gandhi on October 31 by Sikh extremist members of her bodyguard, an unprecedented 49.2 percent of a record electoral turnout voted for the Congress and swept it back to power with 401 out of 508 seats. If there was one lesson to be learned from the election it was that the Indian people were not prepared to allow any shock — whether internal or external — to destabilize their political system and threaten the unity of the nation. As if to drive the lesson home, the very same electorate elected opposition parties to the state assemblies in two major southern states a bare two months later, because they were headed

by popular and incorruptible chief ministers. Clearly it has learned to discriminate between national and state issues, and is capable of choosing the best option in each case.

For those who have watched the political evolution of the country from the earliest post-independence years, and shared both the hopes and the doubts of the past three decades, the coming of age of India's democracy remains by far the most outstanding achievement of the country.

What are the ingredients of India's unexpected, and still somewhat bewildering success? Many explanations can be given — the country's ancient history, the lack of natural, geographic divisions within it, the strength and pervasiveness, yet flexibility, of its Hindu ethos, and so on. But above all it can be traced to two factors: the gradual evolution of India's freedom movement, and the unique character that was imparted to it by Mahatma Gandhi.

Democratic Roots

When India obtained her independence in 1947, the Congress party, which spearheaded the freedom movement, had been in existence for a full 61 years! It was established in 1885 and was then a small party of middle-class, western-educated professionals who had banded themselves together to press the British government for a larger measure of self-government. Till the first decade of the 20th Century, the class composition of the Congress remained broadly unchanged, and nine tenths of the members of the All-India Congress Committee were lawyers, doctors and other professionals, with lawyers predominating.

The Congress acquired a mass base in two stages in the first two decades of the 20th Century. With this, its outlook became more militant. The first major expansion came when Bal Gangadhar Tilak harnessed the forces of resurgent Hinduism to the nationalist cause. But since, Hindu India had been subjugated not only by the British for a hundred years, but by a succession of Muslim dynasties which had ruled for seven hundred years prior to that, the harnessing of Hindu nationalism also sowed the seeds of Muslim separatism. The British were quick to perceive this and from 1909, when they began to give niggardly doses of self-government, they insisted that each expansion of self-rule — in 1923, and 1935 — be accompanied by separate electorates for Hindus and Muslims, and special treatment for certain other favored minorities. Under this dual impulse, Muslim nationalism in India gradually began to chart a different course from Hindu nationalism.

The second major widening of the Congress movement occurred after Mahatma Gandhi rose to preeminence within the party in the early 20s. Mahatma Gandhi broadened the base of the Congress by accommodating under its umbrella a host of local movements for self-determination that had sprung up not only in different parts of British India but also in the 400-odd princely states which occupied one-third of the Indian subcontinent and over whom the British exercised paramountcy. At the same time he deepened the appeal to the religious sentiments of the majority Hindu population by preaching a doctrine of non-violent struggle that drew its inspiration from one of the most revered of Hindu scriptures — the Bhagavad Gita. By January 26, 1930, when the Congress gave its first call to the British

invaluable experience in government. Thus, by the time India attained its freedom, the Congress party had a mass base, a strong internal constitution with elections to each level of the party hierarchy, and a galaxy of charismatic leaders drawn from all over the country.

Federal Policy

The second, more important cause of India's success was the decision of its pre-independence leadership to actually turn the country's breathtaking diversity into an asset in the struggle for democracy. They did this by adopting a federal constitution which would give full scope for the development of the country's diverse ethnic and linguistic groups within the overall framework of a

to "Quit India," the party consisted of leaders drawn from all parts of the country, united by a common desire to both free and *modernize* India, supported by a large mass base of common people aroused at the deepest levels of religious and patriotic awareness.

As the power of the Congress grew, the British followed a grudging policy of accommodation. By constitutional reforms in 1923 and 1935, they devolved increasing powers of self-rule to elected governments in the provinces. These experiments in partial self-rule proved short-lived because they fell short of the Congress demands, and because the division of powers envisaged in them between the legislatures and the Crown proved unworkable. But they did give the Congress party

single nation. This was achieved in two stages — the adoption of a federal constitution on January 26, 1950, and the redrawing of the boundaries of the states, which had remained unchanged since British days, to fit major linguistic or ethnic divisions.

Such a re-alignment was already implicit in the technique Mahatma Gandhi had adopted to widen the base of the Congress party. But Mahatma Gandhi's more important contribution to India's political evolution was the technique of political mobilization to secure change that he introduced in the country, a technique that has been assiduously employed for six decades. Labelled *satyagraha* by him (literally, the urging of truth), it consisted essentially of demonstrating the potential for violence, without ever actually unleashing it.

Satyagraha has often been described as a doctrine of non-violent political action. This is not only an over simplification of what Mahatma Gandhi practiced, but a distortion of it. *Satyagraha* drew its inspiration from the commitment to *ahimsa* (literally the abjuring of violence) but it was not by itself non-violent. Instead, the power at the command of the agitators to press for change was shown through immense mobilizations of demonstrators. The demonstrations were peaceful, which meant that the option of resorting to outright violence was left to the government. But implicit always in the mass mobilization of *satyagraha* was the threat that if the government did resort to violence first, it would be responsible for the consequences.

Crisis Management

After independence, the same techniques of mass mobilization and *satyagraha* have continued to be deployed by every political group seeking its place in the Indian political sun. When Potti Sriramulu led the demand for a distinct Andhra State within the Indian Union, he chose to fast to death. His death in 1952 virtually destroyed the resistance within political and administrative circles in New Delhi to what became, in 1956, the linguistic reorganization of the states. When Sant Fateh Singh pressed the demand for a smaller Punjab in which the Sikhs would form a majority, he threatened to immolate himself. The Center, much the wiser from experience, conceded the demand in 1964. Most recently, the

An equally important objective of this strategy, which Mahatma Gandhi also justified by referring to the Bhagavad Gita, was to gain a moral victory over one's opponents. He who resorted to violence first automatically suffered moral defeat. Thus every act of violence against one's opponents strengthened them and multiplied their ranks. Before this wholly new political weapon, backed by the threat of the sheer numbers of India, the British were powerless and gave ground steadily.

Left, a rural political meeting; right, a hangover from the 'Raj,' the Hunt at Ooty, South India.

seven-year-long agitation in the eastern state of Assam to check the inflow of illegal immigrants from Bangladesh, and of people from other parts of India, which was rapidly reducing the Assamese to a minority in their own state, has been almost completely non-violent.

This does not mean that there is no violence in India. One has only to open the pages of a newspaper to see that this is not so. But the violence is individual, highly localized, and usually traceable to specific local feuds and grievances between groups of people. The relationship between organized political movements and the state has almost always been non-violent and accommodation fairly easily achieved.

Economic Enigma

The evolution of the Indian economy is almost as much of an enigma as that of its political system. For more than three decades India's national income has grown by no more than 3.6 percent a year, one of the slowest growth rates in the developing world. Its per capita income of around US$240 is also among the lowest in the world. But it is a nuclear power, has launched satellites into space, produces its own steel, and builds its own warships and many of its aircraft. It has an impressive heavy-engineering base, and is one of the few developing countries that is able to bid successfully for heavy engineering turnkey contracts in other developing countries. Its progress in agriculture is equally impressive.

What is even more impressive than the overall management of debt is the fact that India is among the very few oil-importing developing countries today that does not have a balance of payments problem.

India has managed to avoid the debt trap mainly because, unlike most developing countries, it has relied almost exclusively on its own domestic savings to finance its industrialization. Of the roughly $800 billion (in current prices) that has been invested in the economy in the last third of a century, foreign aid has accounted for only 6 percent.

The doctrine of self-reliance, long the guiding philosophy of India's economic development, is radically at odds with the one that was in fashion throughout the 1960s and and 1970s in the third world, and which had

But its most impressive achievement is that, at a time when nearly all the developing countries, and many industrialized ones, feel that they are increasingly at the mercy of outside forces over which they have little control, the Indian economy is stable and healthy.

Nothing illustrates the contrast between India and even the most dynamic countries in the third world more vividly than its external payments position. In the middle of 1984, when the combined debt of the oil-importing developing countries touched $700 billion, and that of Brazil, Argentina and Mexico $90 billion, $45 billion and $80 billion respectively, the total external debt of India, which has two-fifths of the population of the third world (excluding China) was only $19 billion.

received the endorsement of development economists and international lending institutions like the World Bank and the IMF.

Industrial Policy

Put succinctly, while the developing countries aimed at maximizing the rate of growth of their national product, and indeed identified economic development with increases in the gross national product, India's planners adhered steadfastly to an older and increasingly less fashionable notion of development.

This was the building up of an all-round capacity to produce the goods and services needed by an industrial society. Thus, for Indian planners *what* was produced and *by whom* was as important as *how much* was produced. In concrete terms, this preoccupation was reflected in an unswerving determination to achieve self-reliance by minimizing the country's dependence on imports. And this in turn involved the setting up of heavy industries from the very start, even if they locked up large sums of capital and reduced the increase in national product yielded by every rupee of investment.

The planners were also determined that production in the modern sector would be dominated by Indian entrepreneurs. The creation of a powerful entrepreneurial class was almost as important an objective as securing all-round industrial development. This was fostered by heavy protection against imported goods and a reluctance to let foreign investors

gain a toehold in the Indian economy, except as minority shareholders in new ventures.

Losses and Gains

Thus, for almost three decades, India remained out of step with the prevailing economic wisdom in the rest of the world. For this it paid a price. The emphasis on heavy industry made capital inefficient and lowered the annual rate of growth of GNP to about 3.6 percent between 1950 and 1975. An obsession

Left, graffiti in Calcutta depict assassination of Mrs Indira Gandhi (artist in foreground). Right, giant billboard portrait of Prime Minister Rajiv Gandhi.

with self-reliance also made much of Indian industry technologically obsolete. Lastly, excessive protection made the Indian entrepreneurial class complacent.

But the strategy did yield fruit. By the mid-1970s India had a well-developed industrial base that could produce almost anything that the country needed and a scientific and technical infrastructure capable of responding to new needs. With the second phase of the green revolution which began in 1975, mainly in rice, India also became self-sufficient in foodgrains. Thus by the mid-1970s, the inward-oriented growth strategy had succeeded in largely insulating the economy from the external shocks that nearly brought even the most rapidly growing countries like Brazil and Yugoslavia to their knees in the early 80s. The worst of these have been the rise in oil prices and the debts crisis brought on by the rise in American interest rates from 1980 onwards.

By 1978, the planners had realized that the first phase of industrialization was largely over. India now had not only a heavy industrial base, but also an entrepreneurial class that was increasingly taking on the multinationals in the world market for products and turnkey engineering contracts. As a result, just when other countries began to increase protection, the Indian government began to lower protective barriers, invite global tenders for its major investment projects, and encourage industry to secure the most up-to-date technology from abroad.

The policy of liberalization has worked. The resulting increase in the industrial growth rate and the second spurt of the green revolution have raised the long-term growth rate of the economy from 3.6 percent to over 4 percent. More importantly, since like that of the United States, the Indian economy responds very largely to domestic impulses, this growth rate has been maintained with no let-up right through the global recession of 1979—82. Nor have India's exports been seriously affected. These continued to grow in rupee terms by about 8 percent a year and in dollar terms by 4 percent, throughout the depression years of 1979—83. Lastly, what is perhaps most important of all is that, thanks to its insulation from external shocks, the Indian government has been able to keep its domestic budget on a fairly tight leash. The overall budget deficit has never exceeded 3 percent of the GNP against 5 percent of the United States in 1983, and 18 percent for Mexico, and 30 percent for Brazil for 1982. As a result, inflation has throughout been moderate by third world standards, at around 7 percent a year.

To reflect upon the Indian people is to behold a variegated multitude, brown, black or yellow, sinewy and lean, square and stocky, or softly rounded with good living and heredity, whom nothing could bind but the claim that they are, they truly are, the Indian people.

Flux is the essence in India, flux unfolding against a background of invasions and migrations which brought to the country people of varied looks and habits. Bounded by mountain and ocean, the subcontinent was a vast cul-de-sac, enticing streams of people through passes in its northern mountains but deterring major southward movement through uncharted waters.

Four major racial groups met and merged in India, producing men of different hue and stature. The pale-skinned Europoid entered from the western mountain passes, encountering settled populations of *Dasyu,* the dark-skinned ones of Rig Vedic description. Proof of initial fusion is evident in *lingam* (phallus) worship, a symbol of fertility traced to Dravidian culture, in Aryan rite as well as in the presence of people with Europoid features but dark skins in southern India where the *Dasyu* were eventually pushed.

The Aryans dominated the northwest and the Gangetic plain, but the Himalayan region and the highlands of the northeast were the home of populations of Mongoloid descent. Their affinity with the southeast Asian world was strongly marked and emerges today in the motifs woven on their sarongs and in their small-statured, slant-eyed offspring.

Though the Mongoloid people influenced the racial pattern of tribes in Orissa and Bihar, by and large they stayed within central India. Splay-nosed southerners in peninsula India might have had a link with Negroid racial elements, as deduced from contemporary populations with dark skins and tightly curled hair. But the only true Negrito are isolated in the Andaman Islands, who have few links with the mainland.

The dovetailing and mingling of races did as much to looks as it did to the way of life. One must move then, from observing the physically different people to understanding the traditions each race brought. Language

Preceding pages; Bhil tribal from Madhya Pradesh; a typical Rajasthani elder; beauties at Spring festival procession, Jaipur; young girl of Jaisalmer. Left, Muslim hawker selling satchels in Bombay.

encompassed diverse culture and identity, but geography and environment encouraged coexistence; the result was an ethnic and linguistic pattern of unparalleled complexity. The folk regions of Madhyadesh (the middle kingdoms), Chattisgarh and Bundelkhand in north and central India developed distinct literary traditions, giving focus to regional identity. The territory of Madhyadesh is today associated with the languages of eastern and western Hindi, Punjabi, Pahari and Rajasthani. Language welded together what is today a political region, the Hindi-speaking heartland whose uniform voting pattern can support or destroy the political ambitions of vote-seeking politicians.

Political regions sometimes overlook internal differences of speech which mark off groups from each other. In the Hindi zone, speech separates upper castes and untouchables, signalling social separation. In South India, omnipresent caste divorces Brahmin dialect from non-Brahmin and both from Untouchables.

For all the confusion, the 225 dialects identified by the linguistic expert, Grierson, in 1928, trace their origin to four major language families.

Major Languages

The Indo European group, particularly the sub-branch of Indic languages, concentrated as dialects of northwest India and the Gangetic plains, share a linguistic pool with modern French, English, Greek and Iranian, indicative of migrations of Europoid people.

The Dravidian language family consists of 23 languages, but only the four major ones form the basis of the southern states of India. Tamil is spoken in Tamil Nadu, Telugu in Andhra Pradesh, Kannada in Karnataka and Malayalam in Kerala. All four possess independent scripts and literary histories dating from the pre-Christian era, a lineage which is jealously guarded against intrusions from the Hindi-speaking north.

Scattered through the highlands of eastern and central India are the languages of the Austro-Asiatic family spoken largely by tribal groups of Ho, Oraon, Munda and Santhal. But many of the dialects with only oral traditions were lost to the intrusions of more dominant non-tribals, who hegemonized the speech of the tribals. In Orissa some tribes now address all "superior" beings, whether gods or administrators, not in their own tongue but in Oriya, the mainstream language. The presence of these languages in isolated mountain and jungle havens reflects a long history of retreat in the face of intruders. It is rare to find tribes like the Birhor of Bihar who might still steal away into their diminished forest refuge at the first sign of a motorcar.

Less than 1 percent of modern India's population speak languages of the Tibeto-Burman family. But the protection that geography and, later, political policy, afforded to the Mizo, Nagal, Lushia and Khasi, to name a few tribes, strengthened their sense of identity and sustained their ethnological and linguistic links with Tibet and Southeast Asia. Even Christian missionaries contributed. The lexicography, grammar and spelling of Khasi was standardized when the missionaries translated and published the Bible. Standardization gave an impetus to the growth of a written literary tradition which culminated in Khasi being officially recognized at the university level, complete with the beneficence of state grants.

Conquests and conversions, migrations and resettlements, generated divergences within the same language family. Twenty-three major and minor dialects evolved from the Dravidian pool. But other processes reduced structural dissonance between languages of different families, in phonology, syntax and grammar, creating a situation where modern north-Indian languages are more similar to Dravidian languages than to Indo-Aryan languages outside the subcontinent. Marathi (Indo Aryan) and Kannada (Dravidian) switch codes with an ease born of long practice and intimate contact.

The modern-day Dravidian languages have adapted to economic, social and political changes; all of them are used for basic courses in science and the arts. The new technological terminology is based either on indigenous linguistic material in Tamil or coined from Sanskrit models.

The Caste System

Sanskrit not only provided a literary model but also a pan-Indian cultural one. The early Sanskrit text, the *Rig Veda,* expounded the hierarchical division of society into four *varna* (castes). The *varna* scheme conceived society as originating from a single source, the living body of a gigantic primordial "Code Man" who was possessed of the most powerful of coded substances, the words of the Veda. After producing a set of male and female genera by dividing himself in half, the Code Man generated four named and ranked classes or *varna,* each ascribed with a particular occupation and code of conduct. Brahmins (the priestly caste) were generated from his mouth, Kshatriyas (the warrior caste) from his arms, Vaishyas from his loins and Shudras from his feet. Implicitly, the legend conceives of the four as interdependent; the well-being of the whole rests on the occupational exchanges made among the *varna.* The Vaishyas's code, inherent in the generative loins, enjoins him to produce and accumulate wealth by trade, cultivation and rearing livestock. Unlike the three higher *varna,* the Shudra was not encoded with distinct occupational substances. His code, born of his lowly origin, was to render bodily service to the higher castes in exchange for maintenance.

While the *varna* scheme is the formal model of reference, and of legend, the social units of everyday life are the *jati,* defined as collectivities which reproduce their own kind. The *jati* scheme encompassed diversities of culture and religion, race and language, allowing their coexistence, and encouraging their interdependence. It affords a dynamic and mobile society of proliferating social groups which formed in response to a variety of circumstances. Each group had an occupation and a social milieu; and each found a niche within the order. But the order was not the static structure of *varna;* it is the living flux of *jati,* where power and wealth jostle with myth and text.

The legitimacy of regarding a barber and sweeper as inferior rests upon the cultural notions of *dharma,* the prescribed code of conduct that ranks the groups along a scale of polluted to pure.

Powerful notions of pure and impure underlie interactions between *jati,* carefully governing exchanges of food, restricting marriages to within the group and regulating occupations of individuals, lest they affect the *dharma* of the *jati.*

The selection of a marriage partner is of immense concern for it is an event when two lineage groups merge. The alliance enhances the status of each or, conversely, degrades it. In village and city the caste of a possible partner is the first to be ascertained; only subsequently do astrology and gifts, temperament and looks, play a role in making the perfect union.

An individual, then, can be a real threat to the group, for the *jati* will share the shame of incorrect behavior or improper sexual alliance by the individual. Thus the most important moments of an individual's life cycle are birth and marriage, events which incorporate people into groups, and these are strictly regulated by rite and prescription. The most urbanized of people will forbid their daughters to be wed in anything other than a red sari, an age-old attire mentioned in 7th Century Tamil texts.

Assimilation

The stress at every level is upon inclusion and incorporation of individuals into groups identified by *jati,* language or, crucially, by religion. India has for centuries given shelter to most of the major religions of the world, accommodating their proliferating sects through its ever-elastic caste system.

Hindus, themselves not given to proselytizing, were quite willing to overlook the alien origins of people who might have wanted to graft themselves on Hindu society so long as such grafting took place over a sufficiently long period of time and was enmeshed with complicate matters. But it is necessary to distinguish between religions which came from the 'outside' and those which grew as movements within the overall order of Hinduism.

Buddhism and Jainism were early religious and social movements which revolted against a rigid caste structure and against Brahminical predominance within it. Buddhism was perceived as an assertion of Kshatriya power against Brahmin supremacy. Pali, the widely spoken language of the masses became a vehicle of protest against elitist, Brahminic Sanskrit. Jainism found support among the trading caste. Neither movements severed their links with Hinduism; rather they espoused some of its central principles.

More modern movements such as the Brahmo Samaj and Arya Samaj were cast in

caste. Converts to different religions often continue to maintain their caste links and sometimes never entirely relinquish their Hindu beliefs. Modern-day Mazbhis of Punjab, who are adherents of the Sikh faith, recognize the primacy of their caste origin (sweeper) in intermarriages with sweepers who converted to Christianity. Though the bride wears white, a vermilion spot on her forehead symbolizes her married status in a traditionally Hindu way.

Schisms and sects combine with caste to

Above left, Parsi (Zoroastrian) portrayed in stained glass, Bombay; right, venerable Muslim gentleman.

similar reform-seeking molds. The rationalist philosophy of the Brahmo Samaj and the evangelical fervor of the Arya Samaj's *shuddi* conversions were western, Christian accretions; but explanation was sought from within Hindu philosophy as well. The bile of revolt was absorbed as reform, not expelled as rivalry.

In sharp contrast came the proselytizing religions of the outside, particularly Islam and Christianity. Both were backed by highly articulate traditions and rich and varied civilizations which rivalled Hindu society and culture. More crucially, both were associated with ruling powers of long tenure.

In Punjab, the entrance hall of invasions, the impact of Islam was strong and deep.

Here, Hindu dress disappeared even among women, who are thought to be the repositories of tradition. The sari was dropped in favor of the Islamic *salwar-kameez*. The competition for favor between the stitched clothing of the Muslim and the unstitched draped garments of the Hindu was an expression in daily life of competing notions of civilized propriety. For many years Hindu tailors were a rare species and even today some of the most skilful in north India are Muslims.

A Mingling of Cultures

With the rivalry, however, there were also strong undercurrents of interaction. Two cultures mingled to evolve a new identity epitomized in the emergence of Hindustani,

does not speak the same tongue. They both understand the intricacies of soil, seed and weather and the urgency of crop cycles; the rest is not for them.

The rhythms of the agricultural cycle sustain the community of peasants both materially and morally. Because food is thought to make up the physical and moral fiber of an individual, its production and consumption are classified and ritualized. The physical processes of sowing, nurturing and harvesting food crops which occur through the agricultural year are inextricably linked with the calendar of social and ceremonial activity of the community.

The act of harvesting is imbued with notions of prosperity and increase, and life-cycle rites like marriage, which augment the household,

a language based on Hindi and Urdu, which is spoken in much of north India.

The principle of accommodation, of finding common ground, is most evident in rural society in which 80 percent of India's population lives. Agriculture and the growing of food provide a set of common experiences for a majority of rural folk. Overloaded trains with people clinging to roofs and doorways moving from Bihar in the east to Punjab and Haryana in the west bear testimony to the fact that Indians still find major outlets for employment in agriculture. The maintenance of separate identities receives a jolt in the face of an overwhelming demand for labor. It matters naught to a man of Ahir *jati* from eastern Uttar Pradesh that his Punjabi Jat employer

are arranged in this monetarily lush and ritually auspicious period.

Conversely, all ceremonies and ventures whose *raison d'être* is future increase are prohibited in the liminal period of a seed's gestation, when the future prosperity inherent in the seed is unconfirmed.

Inter-caste Cooperation

The other face of caste which rests not only on hierarchy and separation but also on co-operation reveals itself in village society. Because occupations are specific to groups and prohibited for others, an exchange of services is the fulcrum of society. The *jajmani* of rural India is such a system. It links households of artisans with households of patrons in relations which are hereditary but alienable and which extend beyond the merely economic. The barber cuts his patron's hair, and acts as a marriage go-between for the patron's daughter. The sobbing wail of the barber's wife is the first public announcement of death in the patron's household. In return the patron is obligated to pay the barber in money and in a share of grain and fodder at each harvest, assist the barber in conducting marriage and death rituals in his household, and share food with him on ritual occasions in acknowledgement of the barber's inclusion in the ongoing cycle of the patron's life.

The power of the patron to command the services and loyalties of his clients accrues as much from his ritual status as member of a

higher caste, as from his control over secular sources of dominance. In agrarian society, control of land supports dominance and can even be a lever up the ritual ladder. Hierarchies are propagated on an interplay between ritual status and secular power. Merely a higher caste status is insufficient for heading the hierarchy. In Punjabi, the Bhaman (Brahmin) is a figure of ridicule; deference is displayed to the real powerholders, the landholding Jats.

Far left, gipsy from Western India; left, tribal from the northeast; and, above, a Brahmin.

For decades, the Brahmins of South India, the Iyers and Iyengars of Tamil Nadu, Nambudris of Kerala, and the Madhawas of Mysore, deftly manipulated the bureaucracy, politics and education to reinforce their ritual status, achieving a virtual stranglehold on society. People of lower *jati* adopted Brahminical ways in a bid to climb the ladder, for it was Brahmins who set the mores by which rank was judged. *Jati* beginning the arduous climb upwards shun meat, prohibit widowed daughters from remarrying and try to gain entrance into temples. The nearer they are allowed to approach the *sanctum sanctorum,* the purer they are considered to be. An enormous movement among non-Brahmin castes, protesting against Brahmin dominance in Tamil Nadu, focused upon the issue of temple entry, arousing passions on both sides to fever pitch.

The Kammas and the Reddis, peasant castes of Andhra, could more easily claim ritual purity, for few could resist their power. But the very low caste of Adi Dravidas in Tamil Nadu, with virtually no resources, faced a brutal backlash when they tried to adopt high-caste practices.

The attempts to prove status are of great concern for an individual's circle of interaction and the doors that readily open for him depend upon the group to which he belongs. The British census officials opened a virtual Pandora's box by trying to record the caste status of each group; claims and counter-claims clogged the courts of local magistrates, caste myths and genealogies were speedily requisitioned and Brahmins bribed to preside over life-cycle rites as proof of purity.

"Placing" the Stranger

Over the years the concern has not vanished. It is difficult for a newcomer to be accepted until he has been "placed" and identified with a group. The perennial question, "From where you are, please?", "What is your native place?", and so on through a gamut of extraordinary constructions are not mere gambits to keep a conversation from flagging. They are of intense interest, for the name of a man's village, town or locality reveals a great deal to the knowledgeable. Wonderfully elaborate names, Thirumalai Kunnavakam Annantanpillai are an encyclopedia of information on a man's region, village, *jati,* lineage, father's name and of course his own identity.

Placing the newcomer will elicit the proper response because people's behavior towards each other depends upon their respective positions in the social hierarchy. Less than proper conduct towards a guest signals a deliberate insult towards his group, and the onus is upon the insulted to fathom the reason for their fall.

Towns and cities stir up men's lives, accelerating the pace of change, and do a great deal to break down barriers. Who knows the caste of co-passengers in overcrowded Bombay buses? Distances are maintained when people are known quantities; amorphous urban contact undermines strictly defined relations.

But custom does not easily dissipate. A Keralite's mania for cleanliness travels with him. A Tamilian will not only wash himself but douse his home and shop with meticulous thoroughness every evening. Neither do identities disappear. India's minority religious groups tend to be highly urbanized, reflecting tradition with its roots in history. The pattern of Muslim rule was to control the countryside from cities and forts. The present-day urban Muslim reflects a political tradition as well as the fact that many urban Muslims were, and are, craftsmen concentrated in old political centers. Since they have for centuries lived an urban life the city Muslim, especially the literati, adhere to traditional form-bound lives rather than tension-filled ones. Jains and Parsis, enriched through commerce, are extremely important communities in the cities of Gujarat and Maharashtra. The pale-skinned Parsis, who sought sanctuary in India from the 10th Century onwards, though distinct in looks and speech, found parallels at various levels with Hindu ideology. The cult of fire worship, beliefs in the protective powers of spirits *(pitarah,* the Parsi guardian spirit, and *Pitr,* the benevolent ancestor of Hindu thought) were the source of tolerant acceptance of each other.

Acceptance and tolerance do not dissolve the need to belong. Urban space reflects the need in its clustered ghettos; in Delhi, the largerly Muslim Jama Masjid lies cheek by jowl with Hindu Chandni Chowk. Refugees displaced from Sind or East Bengal settled together in suburban colonies.

The knots of tradition are loosened but do not slip away. Newspaper columns replace aunts and barbers as marriage go-betweens; the medium is new, the form as old as memory. Only a handful of matrimonial advertisements carry the magic phrases "Caste no bar," "No dowry required." The children of mixed marriage cull looks and habits from both groups but formally acknowledge one.

Norms and traditions are more consciously attacked by modern politics. The patron — client link is challenged by institutions of secret ballots and 'reserved constituencies,' where, by constitutional decree, candidates must belong to lower castes. They encourage attempts to overthrow or displace the right of patrons to bank upon the unquestioned support of dependent castes. But the challenge is Janus-faced. While in the political arena, vertical caste links have lost some vitality, the horizontal links have gained in strength and significance with *biradari* (brotherhood) confronting *jajmani* (the traditional hierarchical interdependence between castes).

Demographic pressures encourage movement and migration where different faces, skins, food and speech mark the incoming stranger from the "native." Political issues of space and jobs simmer beneath aggressively couched cultural movements of 'sons of the soil' or vernacular chauvinism. Traditional authority patterns which equate age with wisdom confront a demographic expansion of

under 25-year-olds, reflected in the changing face of voters and their wrinkle-free political leaders.

Women and Untouchables

Two groups in India symbolize both the stability of tradition and the processes of change within the social structure: women and the untouchables.

Traditionally, both groups were ranked below men of the three "pure" *varna.* Neither could directly approach God but worshipped their *swami* (lord), the "twice-born" male who mediated their access to God.

But for all their impurities, or perhaps because of them, in dangerous, liminal periods women and untouchables act as bridges between two well-defined states of being.

In the early days after death, the funeral rites are presided over by lower caste men who assist in the incorporation of the lonely, wandering ghost in the realm of benevolent ancestors, meanwhile staving off the harm that liminal ghosts can unleash upon the living. All over India, women transplant rice, when the plant is neither in its clearly defined state of seed nor in the fully matured plant, but is instead a seedling tended through its liminal passage by women.

Yet neither group is untouched by change. The caste of leatherworkers reviewed their low status when prosperity encompassed their ranks. The fervor for reform ignited the *Ad dharmi* (true religion) movement, transfor-

dowry demands of their in-laws, is forced, by sari-clad agitators burning with their own passion for justice, to face the fact of its own brutality.

The influence of women is largely ignored, for it is scarcely conscious. But the child's first world-view is imparted to him by the females of his home, and encompasses a dynamic tradition. Amazement is often expressed at the simultaneous participation of Indians in highly technological society and their involvement with traditional values and forms of living. A man educated in the United States will still seek an Indian bride through traditional channels. But in the Indian context one's whole socialization makes one adept at switching between contexts without any apparent disjunction. The modern Indian is not a rootless

ming a diffuse group into a demanding, cohesive entity which was not easily ignored.

Mahila Mandals, the women's wing of political parties, are no longer token gestures toward the second sex. Urban activists agitating against confining notions of womanhood gather support in tenements and suburbs, among housewives and tellers in banks, washerwomen and weavers. A social order which still, from time to time, witnesses the smothering of new-born girls and the burning of young brides unable to satisfy the illegal

person; he is firmly anchored in the culture of his daily life.

Constant flux with endless levels and unending divisions. But there is also the power of Tirupati, a pilgrim center in South India, and Vaishno Devi, in the far north, to excite and energize pilgrims from all over India; or Punjabi farmers throwing their political weight behind a leader from Maharashtra. The whole notion of *sangam,* confluence, merging, meeting, reverberates through Indian cultural perception.

A delightful legend points the way: every year the Ganga, in the guise of a black cow, takes a dip in the Kaveri, the holy river of South India, and, thus renewed, wends her way back to her proper place.

Far left, Gharwali; above left, woman from Tamil Nadu; and above right, Jain nuns.

Religion is an integral part of the total Indian tradition. Four of the world's major faiths have met on Indian soil: Hinduism, Buddhism, Christianity and Islam. The first two of these were born in India. In addition, India gave birth to Jainism, Sikhism and countless minor cults and regional sects. India has also played host to Jews and Zoroastrians who have become part of Indian life. All these religions have acted and reacted upon each other for centuries. Even religions which came from outside have assimilated the subtle, indefinable shades of mood, attitude and lifestyle that are distinctively Indian and a survey of Indian religions provides fascinating glimpses of the colorful, variegated pattern of Indian life and culture.

In Prehistoric Times

There was a time when historians looked upon the Aryans, who came to India in the second millennium B.C., as the founders of the Indian cultural tradition. But recent archeological studies have changed the picture. It is now realized that pre-Aryan elements have played an important part in shaping religious attitudes and practices. The term "pre-Aryan" denotes the indigenous inhabitants of India, usually referred to as Dravidians, and the people of the Indus Valley, to whom the Dravidians were probably related.

Little is known about the religion of the Dravidians who lived mostly in central and southern India. They worshipped images of the Mother Goddess, and of several animal deities. Their fertility and funerary rites seem to have been similar to those performed in other Middle Eastern civilizations.

We are on surer ground when we turn to the Indus Valley culture which flourished between 3500 and 2500 B.C. This was a predominantly urban civilization, the two main cities being Harappa and Mohenjo-daro. As many of the important archeological finds came from Harappa, the Indus Valley culture is also known as Harappan culture.

Excavations have yielded a large number of terra-cotta figurines and clay seals bearing inscriptions. A few steatite and metal statuettes have also been found. The inscriptions have not yet been deciphered, but enough evidence

The annual Rath (chariot) Festival at Puri, Orissa.

has been gathered to suggest that many features of later Hinduism were anticipated by the Harappans. One of the statuettes shows a man meditating in a typically yogic posture. Figures of ascetics, standing rigidly, point to a world-negating attitude. The worship of images, probably in temples, seems to have been popular. One of the images, which appears on many clay seals, is that of a god carrying a three-pronged weapon, surrounded by an elephant, a tiger and other animals. This figure has been described as "proto-Shiva" because it anticipates many features of Pashupati (Lord of the Beasts), a form of Shiva still worshipped several centuries later in many Hindu temples. The extreme conservatism of the Indus Valley culture suggests a theocratic state in which the temple dominated the court.

Historians differ regarding the causes which led to the decline of the Indus civilization, but it can hardly be doubted that the final blow was delivered by invaders belonging to the Aryan tribes whose migrations from their original home, perhaps somewhere in southern Russia, were destined to alter the face of the civilized world. The arrival of the Aryans — or rather the Indo-Aryans, as distinct from other branches of the Aryan family — marks the beginning of the religious tradition known historically as Hinduism.

Hinduism

"A museum of religions": that seems to be the only way to describe Hinduism. No other religious tradition is so eclectic, so diversified in its theoretical premises, as well as its practical expressions. It is the only major religion which has not been traced to a specific founder, and the only one which does not have a "holy book" as the one and only scriptural authority. One may regard the *Rig Veda* as one's personal "Bible," or one may turn to the *Upanishads,* or the *Bhagavad Gita;* or one may dispense with all sacred texts and still claim to be a good Hindu. One may worship Vishnu or Shiva or some other gods or goddesses; or one may not worship any deity and meditate on the Supreme Spirit dwelling within one's own heart. Some Hindus visit temples for prayer, worship or devotional music; others prefer sacrificial ritual, or bathe in holy rivers, or go on pilgrimages; still others regard all rituals as redundant. The same flexibility can be seen in Hindu theories concerning creation or the nature of God.

Hinduism thrives on contrasts. At one end is the most abstruse metaphysical speculation about Ultimate Reality; at the other there are popular cults based on the propitiation of tree-spirits and animal deities. Absolute monism goes hand in hand with extreme pluralism. On the one hand, Hinduism accepts the validity of many paths leading to the same goal, and is willing to recognize the divinity of the prophets of other religions. But along with this tolerance one sees rigid adherence to caste distinctions and custom-ridden practices.

This pluralistic approach, while hampering precision and homogeneity, gives Hinduism its amazing popular appeal and makes the Hindu tradition rich and colorful. The Hindu temple, which became increasingly elaborate

heroes but also with the sun and the moon, stars and planets, rivers, lakes, oceans, animals, trees and flowers. On all these occasions, fairs and festivals and bazaars spring up, street-shows are put up by itinerant entertainers, ancient and medieval ballads are sung, leaders of different Hindu sects are taken out in procession.

An interesting feature of Indian religious life is the presence of large numbers of *sadhus* (wandering hermits). They are ubiquitous and can be seen in cities and villages, in the forests, on the banks of rivers and, of course, in the Himalaya. Usually dressed in yellow or ochre robes, with their bodies smeared with ash and foreheads anointed with sandal-paste, the *sadhus* carry all their worldly possessions with them: a bowl, a staff, a blanket. Some move

with the passage of centuries, serves as the nucleus of the social and aesthetic, no less than the religious life of the community. Temple walls are adorned with sculptures, often painted. In the courtyards, sacred poems are recited, hymns are chanted, dances are performed. All these show infinite variety of style, mood, theme and atmosphere.

Hindu Festivals and Ceremonies

A foreign visitor once asked how many Hindu festivals there are in a year. The answer was 360, an average of a festival a day. (The Hindu calendar is lunar, with 30 days in each month.) There are festivals and ceremonies associated not only with gods, goddesses and

alone, others in small groups. Some have taken vows of silence, others preach or chant hymns, sometimes bursting suddenly into songs of religious ecstasy. One is not supposed to ask questions about their homes or destinations. They are simply eternal wanderers.

The continuity and variety of Hinduism can be best appreciated by tracing the main stages through which this unique religious tradition has passed.

The Vedic Age

The Indus Civilization was on its last legs when the Aryans came into India. They brought with them a new language, Sanskrit, which they molded into a remarkably versatile medium for the expression of sublime thoughts and rich images. Thrilled by the grandeur of the Himalaya and by the luxuriance of Indian forests and river valleys, the Aryans poured out their joy, their sense of mystery, their reverence for the Divine, in beautiful hymns and prayers. These have been collected in the four *Vedas* (from the Sanskrit root *vid,* "to know"). The most important among these is the *Rig Veda.*

The Vedic hymns, composed between 1600 and 1000 B.C., were addressed to gods and goddesses who were regarded as personifications of the powers of nature: Indra, god of rain and thunder; Prajapati, "Lord of the Creatures"; Agni, god of the sacred fire; the Maruts, gods of winds and storms; Savitr, the sun god; Ushas, goddess of dawn; and

were worshipped, they were increasingly seen as manifestations of a single Divine Principle. The Vedic concept of *rita* (cosmic law) points to a single rhythmic force animating the entire universe. This led to a deep feeling for the close kinship between man and nature which has always characterized Indian life. Also, by combining religion with philosophy and poetry the Vedas initiated a typical Hindu concept of perfection, the concept that the man of wisdom must combine the intellectual clarity of the philosopher with the faith of the sage and the aestheticism of the artist.

Lighting the Sacred Flame

On its practical side, Vedic religion consisted mainly of sacrificial ritual. The sacred flame

Varuna, god of the sea and upholder of the moral law. The hymns are believed to have been composed by *rishis* (sages) who were divincly inspired. Hence they are known as *shruti* ("heard"), as distinguished from later religious texts referred to as *smriti* ("remembered").

The Vedas are regarded as the fountainhead of Hinduism. They contain ideas and suggestions that have shaped the entire Hindu tradition and show a tendency to move from pluralism to monism. Although different gods

Left, images of Hindu deities placed on rocks in the sacred River Ganga at Hardwar. Right, Hindu ascetic at peace — coins and flowers presented in homage.

was kindled in the center of a raised platform. The sacrificer offered oblations to the flame while the priest chanted hymns and invocations. In the centuries that followed, the mystical and symbolic meaning of the *yajna* (sacrifice) receded into the background. The ritual became all-important and increasingly conventional. Every detail had to be meticulously followed: the kindling of the fuel, the shape of the vessel containing the holy water, the exact intonation of the words. The Brahmins, who had the expertise for performing this complicated ritual, became the dominant class in society.

The *Upanishads* (800 to 400 B.C.) represent a reaction against this decline in values. They are dialogues between teachers and disciples and are regarded as a continuation of the *Vedas* and hence a part of *shruti.* The monistic trend in the Vedas is developed to the point where Reality, in its essential nature, is declared to be absolutely one. By implication, multiplicity is illusory. The human soul is identical with the Absolute. Viewed objectively, as pure, all-pervasive Being, Reality is described as *Brahman.* Viewed subjectively, as the essence of our own existence, it is called *Atman.* The Absolute (Brahman-Atman) cannot be known through reason. It can only be experienced through intuition, though reason can prepare us for the supreme vision.

The most popular text in the Vedic tradition is the *Bhagavad Gita* ("Song of God"). Although it is a part of the *Mahabharata,* an epic poem which belongs to a much later period, the *Bhagavad Gita* (usually shortened to the *Gita*) is strongly influenced by the *Upanishads.* "The Upanishads are the cows," says a famous Sanskrit couplet, "and the Gita is the sweet, nourishing milk which the cows yield." Mahatma Gandhi once described the Gita as his "spiritual dictionary."

The *Mahabharata* revolves around the conflict between the five Pandava brothers and their cousins, the Kauravas, who had wrongly usurped the kingdom. Krishna, an incarnation of God, became the advisor of Arjuna, the commander of the Pandava army. On the eve of battle Arjuna was beset with doubt and refused to fight against his kith and kin. In this dramatic setting, Krishna gave him a discourse on the immortality of the soul and his obligation to fulfil his *dharma* (sacred duty).

Krishna's discourse, with occasional questions from Arjuna, covers almost every aspect of human life. The Gita's tremendous appeal derives from its earnestness, optimism and tolerance. There is something in it for everyone. The Gita accepts the validity of three different paths leading to the common goal of self-realization: the path of *Jnana* (Knowledge), the path of *Bhakti* (Devotion and Love), and the path of *Karma* (Work). These correspond to the intellectual, the emotional and the practical sides of human nature. In addition, the "special path," the path of Yoga, is also recognized. For 2,000 years, millions of people have derived hope and consolation from the Gita's simple message: Work without attachment, dedicating the fruit of your work to the Divine. Krishna says to Arjuna: "Whichever path you tread, you can reach me. Offer me but a flower, a fruit, even a leaf, or a little water. I will accept it if you come to me with a pure and loving heart."

Hindu Mythology

In India, mythology has always been very close to the actual life of the people. It has performed the important function of transforming abstract philosophical concepts and ethical ideals into concrete realities, strengthened by the sanction of religion. There are hundreds of myths about gods, goddesses, heroes, sages, demons, and natural phenomena like the sun and the moon, lakes, rivers, mountains, trees, flowers and animals. These myths are picked up and remembered even by people who have had no formal education. They are kept alive through fairs and festivals, and the daily round of religious ritual, during which myths are celebrated in folk songs, folk plays and dances. In classical Indian music and dance,

too, mythology provides the main motifs.

Hindu mythology begins with the Vedas, but Vedic deities gradually lost some of their importance — not that the Vedic gods like Indra and Varuna were forgotten, but other gods, Rama and Krishna in particular, became more popular. Vishnu and Shiva, who were minor deities in the Vedas, became predominant in the later Hindu pantheon.

The two great epic poems, *Ramayana* and *Mahabharata,* constitute a veritable treasure-house of mythology. Stories from these epics, and other myths derived from various sources, were later elaborated in a vast body of literature known as the *Puranas.* Of these, the *Shiva Purana,* the *Vishnu Purana* and the *Bhagavata* are specially important since they contain myths of Shiva, Vishnu and Krishna respectively.

The *Ramayana,* whose author, Valmiki, is a legendary figure, has exerted a deep influence on the religious and cultural life of India and Southeast Asia. The story of the *Ramayana* is simple enough. Rama, eldest son of King Dasharatha of Ayodhya, was banished for 14 years through the machinations of his stepmother. He went into the forest, accompanied by his wife, Sita, and younger brother, Lakshmana. Sita was kidnapped and taken to Sri Lanka on the orders of the demon-king, Ravana. Rama, supported by an army of monkeys led by Hanumana, defeated Ravana and rescued his wife. Rama, an incarnation of Vishnu, emerges from the narrative as *Purushottama* ("Perfect Man").

state of dissolution. When he wakes up, the universe evolves. The cycles goes on. Periodically, Vishnu descends on earth to protect truth and virtue and to destroy evil. His earlier *avataras* (descents) were in animal forms. In his seventh, eighth and ninth incarnations, Vishnu appeared as Rama, Krishna and the Buddha respectively. Vishnu's wife is Lakshmi, the Goddess of Prosperity.

Shiva has many roles. He is the Great Yogi meditating on Mount Kailasa. He is Nataraja (Lord of Dance), creating and destroying. In another aspect he is the seed of life and his phallic symbol is worshipped in many temples. Shiva's spouse is Shakti (Energy). In her beneficent form she is Parvati, while in her terrifying form she appears as Kali.

He is the ideal king, the ideal brother, the ideal son. Stories of Rama's devotion to his parents and teachers, his courage, generosity and compassion, have been woven into the poem. There are vivid descriptions of the life and landscape of the various regions through which Rama passed.

Who's who in the Hindu Pantheon

Vishnu, or Narayana is the highest of the gods. When he is asleep, the universe is in a

Left, "Sati stone" (Jodhpur Fort) marks spot of self-immolation by women whose husbands died in battle; right, a funeral pyre.

Of all the Hindu gods, Krishna is the most human. We see him as a child, stealing butter and, though he is God incarnate, enjoying the punishment he receives from his mother. Then we see him as a handsome youth, wearing a crown of peacock feathers, dressed in yellow silk, with a garland of jasmine-buds around his neck. Cows stop grazing and listen spellbound when Krishna plays his flute. All the *gopis* (cowherd girls) are in love with him. Among them, Radha is his favorite. The romantic love of Radha and Krishna is interpreted symbolically as the relationship of the human soul with the Divine Spirit. In his mature years, Krishna appears as the wise philosopher whose teaching is embodied in the *Bhagavad Gita.*

Hindu Ideas and Practices

The Hindu epics were probably composed in the 1st Century A.D., and the later Puranas were completed by 500 A.D. The basic principles of Hinduism had by then been firmly established. Hinduism received fresh support from the Vedanta philosophy. Based on the Upanishads, Vedanta was brilliantly systematized by Shankaracharya in the 8th Century. In the Vedanta it was asserted that, from the transcendental viewpoint, Brahman is the sole Reality and everything else is a mere appearance. But from the empirical viewpoint, the reality of the world and the values and distinctions of human life must be accepted. This distinction between perspectives enabled Hinduism to reconcile diverse, and even seemingly contradictory ideas within a single, broad framework.

The fundamentals of the traditional Hindu world-view may now be summarized.

The Goal and the Paths: The ultimate goal is *moksha,* liberation from the cycle of existence. There are many paths leading to this goal.

Karma and Rebirth: Until *moksha* is attained, all human beings are subject to rebirth. The conditions of life in each birth are determined by the cumulative results of the *karma* (deeds) performed in previous lifetimes.

Four Objectives: In addition to the final objective *(moksha),* three proximate ends are recognized as legitimate — *kama* (pleasure, including sex), *artha* (prosperity, fame), and *dharma* (truth, righteousness). The first two must be subordinated to the third.

Four Stages in Life: The normal rhythm of life takes us through four stages — the stage of the learner, demanding self-control and abstinence; the stage of the householder, when *kama* and *artha* are valid ends; the stage of detachment or gradual turning away from worldly concerns; and the stage of renunciation, when one leads a wholly spiritual life, preparing for *moksha.*

Four Castes: Differences in aptitudes and temperaments are reflected in the division of society into four castes — the *Brahmins* (priests, teachers); *Kshatriyas* (warriors, rulers); *Vaishyas* (traders, merchants); and *Shudras* (unskilled workers). Caste is partly determined by *karma.*

Yoga: Through *yoga* (inner integration) one can proceed from physical control, through mental control, to the recognition of one's own reality as Pure Spirit. Through self-recognition, tranquility can be attained. For *yoga,* as for spiritual progress in general, the guidance of a qualified *guru* (teacher) is essential.

Hinduism in the Middle Ages

The coming of Islam to India in the 12th Century was a turning point in the evolution of Hinduism. The Sikh religion, founded by Guru Nanak in the 15th Century, played an important part in bringing the two faiths (Islam and Hinduism) together. In the 16th Century, Catholic missionaries came to India and Hinduism began to feel the impact of Christianity. However, in spite of these influences, and conversion of many Hindus to new faiths, Hinduism remained the dominant religion of India, and its essential assumptions remained unchanged.

In the Middle Ages, poetry, rather than philosophy or mythology, was the chief medium of religious expression. And religious poetry was now composed in regional languages rather than Sanskrit. This was the age of the great poet-saints whose songs are still on the lips of millions of Hindus. Great emphasis was placed on devotion to a personal God. Religion was simplified. Metaphysical speculation about the nature of Absolute Reality no longer received much attention. Hinduism became humanistic and democratic. Some of the greatest poets belonged to the lower castes. A great wave of *bhakti* (devotion and love) swept over India.

The cult of Shiva claimed many adherents. But the Vaishnavas, worshippers of Vishnu in his incarnations as Rama and Krishna, had a stronger emotional appeal for the common man. Chaitanya and his followers in Bengal, Surdas in northern India, and Mirabai in Rajasthan, represented the Krishna cult. Among the devotees of Rama, Tulsidasa was the most distinguished poet. The popularity of his poem *Rama-charita-manasa* ("Holy Lake of Rama's Deeds") remains undiminished after four centuries.

Whether the deity eulogized was Shiva, Rama or Krishna, the essential message of all the poets was the same. "Love" was the common watchword of them all. Medieval Indian poetry shows that the concept of *Avatara* can make Hinduism an extremely tolerant religion. Many Hindus are willing to accept Jesus, Muhammad and the Buddha as incarnations of the same Divine Power that is manifested in Rama and Krishna. This partly explains the absence of proselytization in the Hindu tradition.

Hinduism in Modern India

The consolidation of British rule in India at the end of the 18th Century exposed India to new influences from the West: western liberalism and humanism, Christianity, scientific thought and technology. In the new situation, Hinduism once again showed its diversity and its power to assimilate elements from other traditions while retaining its own basic values.

Hinduism reacted to the West in two divergent ways. There was a strong movement for reform, led by Raja Ram Mohan Roy, with a positive approach to western thought and culture. But there was also a revivalist trend represented by Dayanand Sarasvati, the founder of the Arya Samaj, and others who felt that the West had nothing valuable to offer. They urged Hindus to go back to the wisdom of the Vedic sages. Surprisingly, the Theosophical Movement, which was introduced into India by foreigners, threw its weight on the side of revivalism. In the 19th

tion yet modern in his outlook. He was the first to carry the message of Hinduism to Europe and America. The Ramakrishna Mission and the Vedanta Society, founded by Vivekananda, continue to present Hinduism in a rational, non-dogmatic manner.

In the 20th Century, the finest exponents of Hinduism were Gandhi and the poet, Rabindranath Tagore. Gandhi described himself as an orthodox Hindu, but he believed firmly that the essential message of all religions is the same. He was inspired as much by the New Testament as by the *Bhagavad Gita*. His ancestors were Jainas, and some of his closest friends were Muslims. In interpreting Hinduism he gave primacy to Truth and Non-violence. While Gandhi represented the moral aspect of Hinduism, Tagore focused his atten-

Century two extraordinary men infused new vigor into Hinduism: Ramakrishna Paramahansa and his disciple Swami Vivekananda.

Ramakrishna, though devoid of any formal education, had an amazing grasp of the best that Hinduism could offer. He showed, by his personal example, that the ideas of unity, tolerance and universal love had to be *lived,* not just understood or expounded. He communicated the ancient wisdom of India through beautiful poetic metaphors. Vivekananda was a scholar, a man of strong convictions, wholly committed to the Hindu tradi-

Namaz at Jami Masjid, Delhi.

tion on its creative and aesthetic achievements. Tagore and Gandhi supplemented each other. Together they expressed the deepest truths of the ancient Hindu tradition in the context of the modern age.

Buddhism

The Light of Asia is the expressive title of Sir Edwin Arnold's poetical account of the Buddha's life. Indeed, the personality and teaching of the Buddha has illumined the lives and thoughts of millions of people in Asia. It was in India that the light was first kindled. The Buddha was born in India. He lived and died there. His teaching was imparted in the context of his Indian heritage. A thousand years after his death, he was accepted as an incarnation of Vishnu, the highest god in the Hindu pantheon. Buddhism remained an Indian religion for many centuries before it became an Asian one.

Life of the Buddha

Siddhartha, who was later known as the Buddha, the Enlightened One, was the son of King Shuddhodana of Kapilavastu and his queen, Maya. He was born at Lumbini in the Himalayan foothills, in what is now Nepal but was then a part of India. His family name was Gautama and he belonged to the Shakya clan. Hence he is sometimes called Shakyamuni (Shakya Sage) or Shakyasimha (Shakya Lion). Among his other epithets are Amitabha (Infinite Light) and Tathagata (He Who Has Arrived At Perfection).

Queen Maya died a week after delivering the prince. At Siddhartha's birth, the royal astrologer prophesied that he would one day become disillusioned with worldly pleasures and go forth as a mendicant in search of the wisdom that can overcome suffering. Siddhartha grew up into a handsome youth, gentle and compassionate, skilled in all the arts. The king, remembering the astrologer's prophecy, tried to save his son from unpleasant sights. He was lodged in a beautiful palace and surrounded by every conceivable luxury. The king found for him a lovely wife, Yashodhara, princess of a neighboring kingdom. Yashodhara bore him a son. But the seeds of disenchantment had already sprouted in Siddhartha's heart. He named his son Rahula (Impediment).

As prophesied, Siddhartha saw the three signs of suffering: sickness, old age and death. On the night of the full moon in the month of Vaishakha, corresponding with April–May in the western calendar, Siddhartha prepared for the Great Renunciation. He stood at the door of his bedchamber, looked at his sleeping wife and son for a few moments, and left the palace.

He sat at the feet of famous masters, but none of them could explain to him the cause of sorrow. For a while he joined a group of ascetics and performed severe austerities. He became extremely weak in body and mind, and realized that wisdom could not be attained through self-mortification. At last, meditating under a tree near Gaya, he attained *Bodhi* (Illumination). Prince Siddhartha had become the Buddha, the Fully Awakened One. And the tree which had sheltered him came to be known as the Bodhi Tree.

After becoming enlightened, Gautama the Buddha could have immediately released himself from the cycle of rebirths and attained Nirvana, Supreme Liberation. But the compassionate side of his nature prevented him from tasting the fruit of liberation so long as a single living creature was in pain. He decided to postpone his Nirvana and share his wisdom with others. His first sermon was preached in the Deer Park at Sarnath, near the ancient holy city of Banaras. The ascetics from whom he had parted company a few months earlier became his first audience. According to legend, deer from the forest came and listened enraptured, to the Buddha's first sermon, sensing that his message was for all living beings.

As the number of his followers increased, the *Bhikshusangha* (Order of Monks) was formed. At first, only men were admitted. But later, urged by his foster-mother Gotami, the Buddha admitted women and an Order of Nuns was formed. After a few months the Buddha visited Kapilavastu and met his father, wife and son. He had left as a prince: he returned as a mendicant. He was hailed as a hero, a conqueror in the spiritual realm. During the remaining 40 years of his life the Buddha travelled from village to village, except during the rainy season, preaching the message of love, compassion, tolerance, self-restraint. Sometimes he spent a few days in the cities of Shravasti and Vaishali. Mingling with ordinary people, and speaking their language in preference to Sanskrit, the Buddha led the life of a humble mendicant, bringing solace and hope to countless human beings. He died in 483 B.C., in his 80th year at Kusinara, not far from the place of his birth. Just before his death, when his favorite disciple, Ananda, started weeping, the Buddha said: "All component things must dissolve. A Buddha can only point the way. Become a lamp unto yourself. Work out your own salvation diligently." These were his last words.

The Buddha's Teachings

While Hindu thought was preoccupied with the essential nature of Absolute Reality, the Buddha avoided metaphysical controversies. "The arising of sorrow, the termination of sorrow, that is all I teach," he once said. Nevertheless, two philosophical principles are implicit in his teaching. First, there is the Law of Impermanence. Everything in the phenomenal world is subject to change, though obviously some things are more enduring than others. The second assumption is the Law of Causation. Nothing happens by chance. Apart from natural causes, we are subject to the operation of our *karma*. As a corollary to the Laws of Impermanence and Causation, it follows that the popular notion of a "soul" which somehow survives the body is illusory. The Buddha urges us to discard this illusion. He did not, however, reject the Universal Spirit or Self *(Atman)* of the Upanishads.

The Buddha's first sermon contains an excellent summary of his teaching. It is called the Sermon of the Middle Way, in which the Buddha offers a balanced, harmonious view of life, steering between two sets of extremes: on the ethical plane, the extremes of self-indulgence and asceticism; and on the philosophical plane, the extremes of naive acceptance of everything as real and the total denial of everything as unreal.

The Buddhist religion rests upon the Four Noble Truths enunciated in the first sermon. These truths are: (i) suffering is universal,

(ii) suffering is caused and sustained by *trishna* ("thirst," craving), (iii) suffering *can* be prevented and overcome, (iv) there is a *way* leading to the removal of suffering. The fourth "noble truth" spells out the practical side of the Buddha's ethical and religious teaching. The Middle Way now becomes the "Eightfold Path of the good life," consisting of right conduct, right motive, right resolve, right speech, right livelihood, right attention, right effort and right meditation.

By following this path of many-sided

Sikh priest reading the *Guru Granth,* the Sikh scripture.

restraint and self-perfection, one can conquer craving. Then one is within sight of Nirvana, the transcendental state of complete emancipation. Being by its very nature beyond the sphere of phenomenal experience, Nirvana cannot be defined or described. Asked what Nirvana was like, the Buddha merely smiled — suggesting, perhaps, that it was blissful. And when pressed hard for an answer, he only said, *"Shantam Nirvanam:* Nirvana is peace, silence."

Buddhism is thus not the gloomy, pessimistic creed that its critics make it out to be. The Buddha begins with suffering but proceeds to the conquest of suffering. Nirvana is not an "afterthought" introduced to mitigate a sorrow-centered world-view. It is basic to Buddhism. "Just as, O Ananda," the Buddha once said, "every drop in the ocean has the taste of salt, so does every word that I have uttered carry the flavor of Nirvana."

Buddhism after the Buddha

Shortly after the Buddha's death, his oldest disciple, Kashyapa, convened a Council at Rajagriha. The Master's teachings were classified into three main sections, known as *Tripitaka* (Three Baskets). These, along with later commentaries, became the scriptures of Buddhism. A century later, another council was convened at Vaishali to sort out the differences that had arisen. In the 3rd Century B.C. the great Mauryan emperor, Ashoka, saddened by the bloodshed of war, became a Buddhist. Ashoka's conversion marked the beginning of the expansion of Buddhism. Ashoka set up inscriptions throughout the vast Indian subcontinent exhorting his subjects to follow the Buddha's message of compassion and tolerance.

Differences between the two main trends in Buddhist thought, later resulting in a schism between Hinayana and Mahayana, first surfaced at the third Council convened by Ashoka at Pataliputra (modern Patna). In Hinayana ("Little Vehicle") the psychological and ethical aspects of the Buddha's teachings are emphasized. Hinayana is also known as Theravada ("Doctrine of the Elders") because its followers claimed that their views had the support of the Buddha's immediate followers. The Mahayana ("Large Vehicle") was more philosophical in its approach. To the Hinayana, the Buddha was the supreme teacher, the man who unraveled the cause of suffering, the man of absolute self-control, the *Arhat* (Conqueror). The followers of Mahayana looked upon the Buddha not merely as a teacher but as a savior, a Bodhisattva ("Wisdom-Essence") who, not content with attaining enlightenment through insight and self-mastery, dedicated himself to the service of all living beings.

The difference between Hinayana and Mahayana is largely a matter of emphasis. They both claim conformity to the Buddha's teachings. Both accept the basic principles of Impermanence and Causation. They also accept Nirvana as the ultimate goal, and craving as the main obstacle. They derive their inspiration from two different sides of the Buddha's personality. While the Hinayanist glorifies the Buddha's insight and moral perfection, the Mahayanist is stirred by his compassion, love, joy, tranquility and sensitivity to beauty. The profound influence of Buddhism on India's religious consciousness arose from a combination of the two approaches.

Buddhism and Hinduism Compared

Buddhism has played a decisive role in molding India's values and ideas. Yet at one time it was seen as being opposed to Hinduism and as signifying a break in the Indian religious tradition. Actually, the two faiths supplemented each other. The Buddha rejected the infallibility of the Vedas, the supremacy of the Brahmins and some of the external features of Hinduism. But he accepted the basic structure of Hindu thought as expressed in the Law of Karma and Rebirth. Buddhism, like Hinduism, gives priority to experience over thought, and sees a universal rhythmic principle uniting man with nature.

In the first phase of the development of Buddhism, these similarities were overshadowed by the differences in emphasis. But a few centuries after the Buddha's death, the two faiths came close to each other. The Mahayana evolved a concept of Absolute Reality very similar to that in the Upanishads. The Buddha was venerated as a god. Buddhism produced its own mythology. Buddhists adopted Sanskrit in preference to Pali, the dialect in which the Buddha himself had delivered his discourses. It is significant that the great epoch of Brahmanical revival, such as the golden age of the Gupta dynasty (4th and 5th centuries A.D.), coincided with a splendid blossoming of Buddhist philosophy, art and poetry.

Even in its heyday, Buddhism was not the religion of the majority of Indian people. In the Middle Ages, Buddhism remained dormant in India while it became the dominant religion of Thailand, Cambodia and some other Asian countries. In modern India, there has been a revival of interest in Buddhism.

Yet, Buddhists constitute a very small proportion of the Indian population. This has led some people to assert that India "repudiated" and "banished" Buddhism. But something which has been assimilated until it flows through the very bloodstream of Indian culture cannot be said to have been rejected simply because we cannot see it on the surface. Even when there was an ideological conflict between Hinduism and Buddhism, the Buddha's personality and character attracted the admiration of Hindus and Buddhists alike. The Buddha's emphasis on compassion, love and non-violence has become a permanent part of India's spiritual heritage.

Buddhism has inspired some of the finest masterpieces of architecture, sculpture and painting. The stupas of Sanchi and Amaravati, the frescos of Ajanta, the remains of the university of Nalanda, the monasteries of Buddha-gaya and Rajagriha and, above all, the Buddha images of the Mathura and Sarnath schools — all these bear witness to the fact that the influence of Buddhism has been much more enduring than its numerical strength might lead one to expect.

Jainism

About the same time as the Buddha was preaching his *dharma,* and in the same region, another religious tradition was being established. Vardhamana, better known by his title Mahavira ("Great Hero") was an elder contemporary of the Buddha. The two teachers had much in common: both were *Kshatriyas* of royal descent and went through prolonged and rigorous discipline after renouncing the worldly life; both rejected caste barriers and questioned the sacredness of the Vedas. Mahavira's fame has been eclipsed by the Buddha's; yet Jainism, the religion preached by Mahavira, counts more than 2 million adherents in India today, whereas the Buddha's faith has very few followers in the land of its birth.

The theme of self-conquest, common to all religions, is supremely important to the Jainas. The very word Jaina is derived from *jina,* conqueror. Carrying the idea of self-conquest to its extreme limit, Jainism has become the world's most rigorously ascetic faith. God has no place in this system. The popular gods of Hinduism are accepted, but they are placed lower than the Jinas, who are regarded as the true recipients of worship. Mahavira, though usually accepted as the founder of the faith in the context of history, is said to be the last of a line of 24 Jinas. All of them are said to have attained perfect wisdom *(Kaivalya)* by vanquishing their desires and breaking their bonds with the material world. The Jinas are also known as Tirthankaras ("crossing-makers"). The "crossing" refers to the passage from the material to the spiritual realm, from bondage to freedom.

Jainism not only rejects the notion of a Personal God which is assumed by most religions, but also the ideas of a single impersonal Absolute Reality. It regards each living being as an independent *jiva* (soul). In its mundane condition, the soul is permeated by material particles through the working of *karma*. To attain liberation, a double process is necessary: the incursion of new karma-particles must be stopped; and those that have already tainted the soul must be expelled. This is possible only through right faith, right knowledge and right conduct: the *tri-ratna*

(three jewels) of Jainism:

Right conduct is spelled out negatively as the rejection of falsehood, theft, lust, greed and violence. Of these five sins violence is the most heinous. The highest virtue is the total abjuration of any thought or action which can hurt a living being. *Ahimsa paramo dharmah:* "Nonviolence is the supreme religion" — this Jain motto was adopted by Mahatma Gandhi in the modern age. Sometimes, however, the Jainas carry their nonviolence, like their asceticism, to extreme limits. For instance, Jaina monks are often seen with their nose and

Navjote, the initiation ceremony for young Parsis.

mouth covered by a fine cloth mask to ensure that they do not involuntarily "kill" germs while breathing.

Jainas have made valuable contributions in many areas of Indian culture: philosophy, literature, painting, sculpture and architecture. Their poetry is often excessively didactic. Their sculpture is of a very high quality, and some of the images of Tirthankaras are technically perfect. Their faces are, however, devoid of any expression, as they are supposed to have transcended all human emotions. The greatest glory of Jaina religious art lies in temple architecture, particularly at Girnar, Palitana and Mount Abu. These temples reveal a breadth of aesthetic sensitivity and a feeling for ornamentation reminiscent of the finest specimens of classical Hindu and Buddhist architecture. It is fortunate that, while building their temples, the Jainas forgot to be solemn!

Hinduism and Islam Meet in India

No two religions in the world appear on the surface to be as dissimilar as Hinduism and Islam. Unlike Hinduism, Islam was founded by a historical person and has a specific scripture, the Quran. Hinduism is eclectic and pluralistic; Islam is homogeneous and has a definite concept of God. Hinduism has the luxuriance of the tropical forests and river valleys; Islam has the simplicity and austerity of the desert. The Hindu temple is enclosed on three sides, and there is an air of mystery in the dark inner sanctum; the Muslim mosque is open on all sides, exposed to light and air. The Hindu worships sculptured images of deities; to the Muslim, idol-worship is the most grievous of sins. Hinduism shuns proselytization; Islam regards conversion of non-Muslims as a meritorious deed.

Yet these two faiths met in India, influenced each other and, after an initial period of confrontation and conflict, accommodated and enriched each other. Within a few decades of their arrival in India, Muslims began to consider India as their home. Between the 13th and the 18th centuries, northern India witnessed a fruitful synthesis of Hindu and Islamic elements in almost every sphere of life and culture.

Muhammad and His Creed

Muhammad was born at Makka (popularly spelt, "Mecca") in 570 A.D., a posthumous child. His mother died when he was four. Muhammad's childhood was not a happy one. As a boy, he earned a paltry living doing odd jobs for traders in caravans. He was 25 when he married Khadijah, a wealthy widow who had employed him. Arabia was at that time a battleground for warring tribes. Religion was ridden with superstitions. People worshipped stone images of innumerable gods. Muhammad, introspective and sensitive by nature, was distressed by this. He often sought solitude in the desert and the mountains.

He had his first mystical experience at the age of 40. The archangel Gabriel appeared before him in a vision, hailed him as the *Rasul* (Messenger) of God and called upon him to proclaim the glory of Allah, the one true God. Gabriel repeated his message in several dreams. Muhammad was disturbed by the visions. A period of depression followed. Khadijah, the first to believe in the genuineness of the revelations, urged him to proclaim his message publicly. Meanwhile, Gabriel had again appeared in a vision and shown Muhammad a written text which later became a part of the Quran.

As the number of his followers increased, Muhammad became bolder in his denunciation of idolatry. The tribesmen harassed and threatened him. In 622 A.D. Muhammad left Makka and went to Medina, a town 200 miles to the north, at the invitation of some merchants. The Islamic calendar is dated from this migration *(hijrah)*. In Medina, Muhammad consolidated his new religion, Islam ("Submission to God"). His followers, the Muslims ("Those Who Have Submitted") now numbered several thousand. Eight years later the Prophet returned to Makka and defeated his opponents in battle. He died in 632 A.D.

Within two decades the Muslims had conquered Iraq, Syria, Egypt and Turkey. By 670 the Arabs were masters of Iran and the whole of northern Africa. In 710 they invaded Spain and penetrated into the south of France. Their success was the result of their faith in the Prophet and the holy book, their strong sense of brotherhood and equality of all Muslims, and the precision and simplicity of their creed. Its success cannot be attributed to force alone. Muhammad himself was a man of deep generosity and wisdom. The God of Islam is Compassionate and Merciful *(Rahman* and *Rahim)*. He is not the God of Vengeance.

The basic injunctions of Islam are summed up in the "Five Pillars": a good Muslim is to assert that "There is no God but Allah, and Muhammad is his Prophet"; to pray, preferably five times a day; to perform acts of charity; to observe a fast from dawn to dusk throughout the month of Ramazan (this is a holy month for Muslims because the Prophet received his divine revelation in this month); and to go on a pilgrimage to Makka at least once during one's lifetime.

Islam in India

Arab traders came to India as early as the 7th Century. After that, Muslim invaders made sporadic raids into India from time to time until, at the end of the 12th Century, the first Muslim kingdom was established at Delhi. The Muslims gradually extended their rule eastwards and southwards. In the reign of Alauddin Khilji only the southern tip of India remained outside the sphere of Muslim power. The Mughal Empire was founded by Babur in 1506. The greatest among the Mughal emperors was Akbar (1556–1605) whose policy of religious tolerance brought Hindus and Muslims together.

In its first phase, Islamic rule in India was aggressive. But the mystics of Islam, known as Sufis, played an important part in spreading the message of universal love and toning down the aggressive trends in Islam. This message was conveyed most effectively by the classical Persian poets, particularly by Rumi who expressed the spirit of Sufism through beautiful symbols and images. Persian, not Arabic, was the court language during Muslim rule. The Sufi poets were very popular in India throughout the Middle Ages.

Renowned Sufi saints came and settled in India. Among these, Moinuddin Chishti of Ajmer and Nizamuddin Aulia of Delhi were the most influential. Even today festivals in their honor are celebrated annually. Amir Khusrau, poet, musician and historian, was a disciple of Nizamuddin. Khusrau was famous as a poet in the classical Persian tradition, but he also wrote religious poetry in Hindi and was one of the makers of the Urdu language. The prevalent spirit of Hindu–Muslim integration was reflected admirably in Khusrau's work.

This process of bringing Hinduism and Islam close to each other was continued by two remarkable men: Kabir and Nanak. Born in a Brahmin family, Kabir was brought up by Muslim foster-parents. He was a disciple of Ramananda, a famous Hindu saint, but he was also deeply influenced by Sufism and used Sufi terminology in many of his poems. Inspired by Kabir, Guru Nanak founded the Sikh religion with the avowed purpose of synthesizing Hinduism and Islam.

Islam's spirit of brotherhood helped in loosening the rigidity of the caste system. The simplicity and directness of Islam led many Hindus to question the value of conventional rituals. The interaction of the two faiths found aesthetic expression in poetry, music and architecture.

Sikhism

Nanak (1469–1539), the founder of the Sikh faith, belonged to the Punjab, a region where Hindus and Muslims had come in closer contact than in any other part of India. Nanak was attracted, from his childhood, towards Hindu as well as Muslim saints and poets. He visited the sacred places of Hinduism and also made the pilgrimage to Makka. A Hindu by birth and training, his closest companion was a Muslim musician. Inspired by his discovery that the essential teaching of both religions was the same, Nanak began to preach his message of unity. He attracted many followers and soon came to be known as Guru Nanak. His disciples came together, and a new religious tradition was born. The term *Sikh* is derived

It is known as *Adi Granth* ("The First Book") or *Granth Sahib* ("Book of the Lord").

The spread of the Sikh faith alarmed orthodox Muslims. The Sikhs were persecuted. Guru Arjun was put to death on a charge of sedition in 1606. Arjun's martyrdom convinced his successors that Sikhs must have military training to defend themselves. The 10th Guru, Govind Singh, transformed the pacifist Sikh sect into a martial community. He introduced rites of initiation into a well-organized Sikh army known as the *Khalsa*. Govind Singh also decided to terminate the succession of gurus. He asked his followers to look upon the Granth Sahib as the sole object of veneration. The Holy Book became the symbol of God for Sikhs.

Roman Catholic procession in Kerala.

from the Sanskrit word *shishya* (disciple).

Angad, who succeeded Nanak as the Guru of the Sikhs, started compiling the master's writings. He also introduced a script which was already being used by some Punjabis. He called it *Gurmukhi* and made it the official script of the Sikhs. Guru Arjun, the fifth in succession, started building the temple at Amritsar which later became the holiest of Sikh shrines. Arjun also systematized the collection of sacred hymns and poems by Nanak, Kabir and some other saints. This collection became the scripture of the Sikhs.

Sikhism is strongly monotheistic. It is opposed to the caste system, and all Sikh men carry the last name "Singh." Idol worship is also rejected. These features show the influence of Islam. But the ideas of *karma* and rebirth are accepted. In their actual religious life and ritual, Sikhs are very close to the Hindus. It is not uncommon for a Hindu householder to bring up one of his sons as a Sikh. There are frequent intermarriages between Hindus and Sikhs. In spite of these similarities, the Sikh community has evolved its own unmistakable identity. Even their physical appearance and dress mark them out. They are tall and well-built; the men all grow beards and wear turbans over their long hair which is never cut. Every Sikh considers it a religious obligation to wear a *kara* (steel bangle) on his right wrist. There are other religious injunctions, like abstaining from tobacco, which are obeyed rigorously. Although they constitute less than 2 percent of India's population, the Sikhs have become a distinct element in the configuration of Indian religions.

Christianity

According to a strong tradition prevalent in South India, Christianity in India is as old as Saint Thomas, one of the Apostles of Jesus Christ. The saint is said to have spent a few years near Madras and to have died there. Other legends describe Saint Bartholomew as the first Christian missionary in India. Latin

Christianity began to play a constructive role in India through the labors of two remarkable men: William Carey and Alexander Duff. Carey founded the Seminary at Serampore and was closely associated with the Fort William College at Calcutta. He established the first printing press and the first newspaper in Bengali. Alexander Duff came to India in 1830 and continued Carey's educational and social work. Throughout the 19th Century, Catholic as well as Protestant missionaries, besides preaching Christian doctrines, made contributions to education and scholarship.

Indian social reformers, like Keshab Chandra Sen of the Brahma Samaj, realized that Christianity had enriched India's religious life in many ways. Ramakrishna lived as a Christian for several months. A Christian

historians in the Middle Ages have made frequent references to Christian settlements in India. Historically, however, Christian missionary activity can be said to have begun with the arrival of Saint Francis Xavier in 1542. His tomb in Goa is still visited by thousands of Catholics every year.

Saint Francis Xavier was succeeded by Portuguese missionaries. Some of them visited Akbar's court, and even entertained the hope of converting the emperor. Other Catholic countries soon began to send missionaries to India. In the 18th Century, Protestant missionaries, especially from Denmark, Holland and Germany, started their work in India. The British conquest naturally gave the Anglican Church an advantage over others.

poet, Michael Madhusudan-Dutt, is regarded as one of the pioneers of modern Bengali poetry. Significantly, he selected a theme from the Ramayana for his most important poem. Later, Tagore paid homage to Jesus Christ in several poems. Mahatma Gandhi was deeply influenced by Christianity. His writings and speeches are full of excerpts from the New Testament. Indian Christians, who now number nearly 25 million, represent almost every denomination: Roman Catholic, Methodist, Baptist, Presbyterian, Maronite, Seventh-Day Adventist, and many others.

Interior of 16th Century synagogue at Cochin, the oldest in India.

The Parsis

Parsis are the descendants of Persians, who emigrated to India in the 8th Century after the Arab conquest of Iran. They brought with them the ancient Persian religion founded by Zoroaster in the 6th Century B.C. This religion is based on the worship of Ahura Mazda ("Wise Lord") who is eternally in conflict with Ahriman, the Evil Force. The *Avesta,* which is the scripture of the Parsis, includes the *Gathas* (songs) composed by Zoroaster.

The Parsis settled down on the western coast of India and adopted the Gujarati language. They have always adhered strictly to their ancient faith. In their agiaries (fire temples) the sacred flame is always kept burning. The Parsis still retain their Iranian physical features: a light olive complexion, an aquiline nose, bright black eyes. They are a rather exclusive community and do not allow non-Parsis inside their temples. The office of *dastur* (priest) is hereditary. The dasturs are dressed entirely in white, and they are held in great esteem. Although the Parsis are conservative in their religion, they have identified themselves with their fellow-countrymen in other areas. They have contributed to the educational, scientific and industrial progress of India; and in the early phase of Indian nationalism, the Parsi community produced great leaders like Dadabhai Naoroji.

Jews in India

Though their number never exceeded 30,000 in the vast ocean of India's hundreds of millions, India has two ancient indigenous Jewish communities — the Malayalam-speaking Cochinis and the Marathi-speaking Bene Israel (children of Israel). While, obviously, these miniscule groups could hardly influence Indian religious thought even on a local scale, they merit mention as a living illustration of the spirit of accommodation of the Hindus and Muslims among whom these groups have lived for more than a thousand years. Today, migration to Israel, England, the United States and Canada, has reduced the Indian Jewish population to about 5,000, who continue to live in the security and peace they have always enjoyed.

Religion in Contemporary India

Religion has always had a tremendous hold on the Indian mind. Even today, in spite of the impact of science, technology and materialistic ideologies, religion is a powerful force in Indian life. Mahatma Gandhi, who led India to national independence, was a deeply religious man. In the 20th Century, many famous religious leaders established spiritual centers which continue to attract thousands of people. Prominent among them were Sri Aurobindo of Pondicherry, Ramana Maharshi of Tiruvannamalai, Swami Shivananda of Hardwar and Sai Baba of Shirdi. Satya Sai Baba of Puttapuriti in Andhra is perhaps the most popular among living Hindu religious leaders.

In the West, India is often wrongly regarded as the land of the Hindus. We have seen that India has been a meeting ground for all the major religions of the world. Even today, Muslim Sufi saints are venerated all over India. Meher Baba, the "silent sage" of Maharashtra, was a Parsi. There has been a great revival of interest in Buddhism. Themes from the Buddha's life have inspired modern poets and artists. And Mother Teresa, a devout Catholic, became an Indian citizen many years ago. Yoga has transcended credal affiliations. Every town has a yoga center and Hindus are not the only ones who come to learn yoga. Religious movements of Indian origin have gained thousands of followers outside India — Krishna-Consciousness Movement, Transcendental Meditation, Center for Self-Realization and many others.

In 1947 India became an independent nation after two centuries of foreign rule. India is a secular republic. The state has no connection with any particular religion. But the protection of religious minorities is recognized as one of the obligations of the state. The constitution of India guarantees the right of religious freedom to all citizens. By and large, barring incidents of religious conflicts when fanatical elements temporarily gained the upper hand, adherents of different religions have been living together peacefully.

Important festivals of all religions have been recognized as national holidays: Diwali and Holi; Christmas and Easter; I'd and Muharram; and the birthdays of the Buddha, Mahavira and Nanak. The three colors of the Indian national flag have religious significance. Orange represents Hinduism, green the color of Islam, and white represents all the other faiths. And in the beautiful national anthem, composed by Rabindranath Tagore, a tribute is paid to the different religions of India. Addressing the Divine Power as *Bharata-bhagya-vidhata* (the "dispenser of India's destiny"), the poet says: "Your call goes out to the Hindus, the Buddhists, the Sikhs, the Jainas, the Parsis, the Muslims and the Christians. They all come, gather around your throne, and weave a garland of love for your worship."

THE INDIAN KALEIDOSCOPE

The Indian Union comprises 22 States and nine Union Territories. There are wide variations in terms of area and population among the states, ranging from the giant Uttar Pradesh with a population of more than 100 million to Nagaland in the northeast with a population of less than a million. Much more relevant for the visitor to the country is the wide variety of scene, atmosphere, custom, costume, culture, topography and climate, art and architecture, and facilities that the country offers. In Uttar Pradesh alone are to be found a profusion of ancient Hindu and Buddhist monuments, the mighty Islamic structures built by the medieval Sultans and the Mughals, pilgrim centers on the holy Ganga, dense jungle sanctuaries for tiger and elephant, some of the most charming hill resorts in the Himalayan foothills, with endless opportunities for trekking and climbing, and mighty Himalayan peaks challenging the adventurous and the expert.

Widen the field, and even the *GRAND TOUR* featured in this book must be split up to cover regions rather than the whole country, unless one has weeks to spare. Each will pursue his or her special interests — trekking in the Himalayan foothills, scaling Himalayan peaks, studying and photographing wildlife in the sanctuaries, making the rounds of medieval forts and palaces in Rajasthan, sun and sea bathing on the golden sands of Goa or Kovalam, spending a quiet week walking and enjoying the scenery in one of India's numerous hill resorts, touring the exquisite sculptured temples of South India, studying the erotic and other sculptures at Khajuraho or Konarak, getting acquainted with Indian music, dance and painting, or just wandering around, absorbing the atmosphere, sampling the food, and getting to know the people.

The following pages will help the traveller make his choice to best meet his interest. They are also intended to provide a glimpse of places he is unable immediately to visit, so that, even if his travels were limited, his view of the country and its people is a rounded one.

DELHI, A
LIVING HISTORY

History lives in Delhi, the capital of India. The ancient and the modern, the old and the new are in constant juxtaposition here, not only in the remains of a succession of empires, but equally in present social structure and lifestyles.

The name Delhi, Dehali or Dilli is derived from *Dhillika,* the name of the first medieval township of Delhi, located on the southwestern border of the present Union Territory of Delhi, in Mehrauli. This was the first in the series of seven medieval cities. It was also known as Yoginipura, that is, the fortress of the *yoginis* (female divinities).

There was, however, an ancient urban settlement in Delhi known as Indraprastha on the banks of the Yamuna which is traditionally believed to have been founded by the Pandava brothers, the mythical heroes of the *Mahabharata,* the national epic of India. Excavations at the site of the township inside Purana Qila suggest that the date of the oldest habitation in the Delhi area is around the 3rd or 4th Century B.C.

A more significant phase of development of Delhi, however, commenced around the 8-9th Century A.D. with the foundation of Dhillika, the first of the seven medieval cities under the Tomars, a local line of Rajput chieftains. Dhillika, which was protected by a stone fortification, now known as **Lalkot,** had beautiful temples, tanks and other buildings. Around the middle of the 12th Century, the Tomar kingdom of Delhi was conquered by the Chahamanas (Chauhans) of Central Rajasthan. Prithviraja Chauhan III extended the area of the town by constructing a second defence wall with gates, now called **Qila Rai Pithora,** on three sides of the Tomar fortification.

The authority of Prithviraja did not last long. In 1192-93, Muhammad-bin-Sam, the Turkish invader from Ghor (Central Asia), defeated and killed Prithviraja. With this, Hindu rule came to an end and a new epoch of Islamic ascendancy began.

Gradually, the invaders got Indianized and developed a unique composite culture, the reflection of which can be observed in the Indian way of life even today. From this cultural fusion came a unique style of architecture termed Indo-

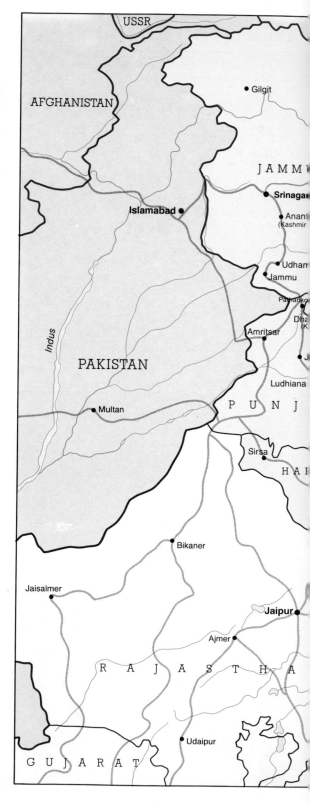

Northern India

200 km

India

KASHMIR

Leh
(Ladakh)

CHINA

Kyelang
(Lahul and Spiti)

Manali

Kulu

IMACHAL PRADESH

Mandi

TIBET

Shimla

Chandigarh

Uttarkashi

Mussoorie

Gangotri

Badrinath

Ambala

Dehra Dun

Gopeshwar
(Chamoli)

Yarlung Zang bo or Tsangpo

Saharanpur

Chamoli

Hardwar

Almora

Muzaffarnagar

Naini Tal

Dailekh

Meerut

DELHI

Moradabad

Rampur

Ganga

Bareilly

Sarda

N E P A L

Tansen

Aligarh

Shahjahanpur

Ghaghara

Katmandu

Mathura

UTTAR PRADESH

Agra

Lucknow

Gorakhpur

Kanpur

Faizabad

Gomati

Shivpuri

Jhansi

Orcha

Yamuna

Allahabad

Varanasi

Patna

B I H A R

Mirzapur

Sasaram

Lalitpur

MADHYA PRADESH

Islamic, the poetic language of Urdu and forms and styles of music, dance, dress and cuisine. Delhi, as the main Indo-Islamic city, played a significant role in the process.

The Khalji Sultanate came to power in Delhi in 1290 and it was Alau'd-Din Khalji (1296-1316) who built **Siri,** the second Delhi northeast of the original Tomar township.

The Khaljis were followed by the Tughluqs as the masters of the Delhi Sultanate. The founder of the new royal house, Ghiyasu'd-Din, within his short reign (1321-25), raised the third city of Delhi called **Tughlaqabad,** five miles (eight km) to the south of Lal-kot. His successor, Muhammad Tughluq (1325-51), transferred his capital to the south, but soon shifted it back to Delhi where he founded the fourth city, **Jahanpanah** between Siri Fort and Qila Rai Pithora (the first city).

The third Tughluq, Firuz Shah (1351-88) constructed the fifth city of Delhi under his own name, **Firuzabad,** away from the hills on the banks of the Yamuna. The citadel area of Firuz's town and the remains there is still called **Firuz Shah Kotla** and is a city landmark.

The Tughluq line continued till 1414 when it was replaced by the Saiyads, who were followed by the Lodis from 1451 onwards. Under the Saiyad and Lodi Sultans, the seal of construction was modest in the Delhi area. The last of the Lodis, Ibrahim, was defeated and killed by Babur, the Mughal conqueror from Kabul in 1526.

Babur, during his short rule of about five years, introduced the formal Persian garden in India. He had his capital at Agra and did not enrich Delhi. In 1530, Humayun, the second Mughal emperor, laid the foundation of the sixth capital city of Delhi under the name **Din Panah** on the bank of the Yamuna to the south of Firuzabad, around the ancient site of Indraprastha. It comprised a citadel (Purana Qila) and city.

Akbar, son and successor to Humayun, spent his childhood in Delhi but later moved to Agra. It was his grandson, Shah Jahan (1628-58) who, finding Agra too congested, selected a site north of Firuzabad and constructed the seventh Delhi, a well planned township which he called **Shahjahanabad.** The famous Red Fort was its citadel on the river bank.

Preceding pages, dusk in Pushkar, Rajasthan; Dilwara Temple, Mount Abu; Gujarat, after a day in the fields; Gurkha troops at Republic Day Parade, Delhi. Below, Tuglaqabad Fort, citadel of early Delhi.

Shahjahanabad functioned as the Mughal capital till as late as 1857, although the Mughal rulers, after 1707, gradually lost their power and prestige and functioned merely as nominal heads of the state. The British East India Company, became the supreme controller of the affairs of most Indian states and the Mughal State was no exception.

In 1857, the last attempt to restore the authority of the Mughal emperor failed and the old Mughal ruler was dethroned and for the next 50 years Delhi was just an ordinary provincial town.

The historic city once again became the capital of India under the British in December 1911. It was at this time that the then British Government transferred the viceregal headquarters there from Calcutta, in view of Delhi's secure and central location in relation to the vast territories of undivided India, and its strong traditional association as a royal seat of power. Simultaneously, a decision to build a new Indian metropolis, befitting the glory of the British Crown, was also taken. After much thought and exploration, a site to the south of Shahjahanabad, covering a part of the Ridge on the west was selected.

Two architects, Edwin Lutyens and Herbert Baker, were assigned the task of designing and building the new capital of British India, styled as New Delhi, which was formally inaugurated for occupation in January 1931.

Some of the landmarks of the Lutyens-Baker Delhi are **Rashtrapati Bhavan,** official residence of India's President (the former Viceregal Lodge) built in a commanding position on Raisina Hill with adjoining administrative North and South Blocks and the **Parliament House** on one side, beside the Memorial Arch of the First World War called **India Gate,** and a circular marketing center with double-storied blocks around a park known as **Connaught Circus.**

The principal aim of the builders of New Delhi, often described as a city of gardens, was to serve the administration and to provide comfortable living to the colonial rulers and their associates. This is, perhaps, why little provision for its future expansion was made.

Yet, with the Second World War and the change of the political situation, especially after independence in 1947, New Delhi had to grow under the pressure of increasing population and new re-

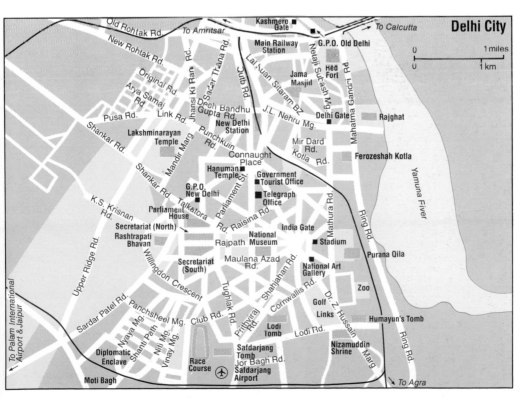

quirements. In the decades since independence, despite difficulties, Delhi has grown steadily, both horizontally and vertically, on modern lines, covering a much greater area than all its predecessor seven cities put together. The city and its population continue to grow.

Monuments and Historical Ruins

Almost paradoxically, this rapidly changing and growing city is also a city of monuments and historical ruins. Mostly, such remains are medieval in origin and are Islamic in character.

The tourists intending to see pre-Islamic ancient remains may visit the site of the Rock Edict of the Buddhist Emperor Ashoka (273-236 B.C.) near Srinivasapuri (South Delhi) which contains the appeal of the great humanitarian monarch to his people to follow the path of righteousness. Further elaboration of the same theme is also available in his inscriptions on two pillars, one in Kotla Firuz Shah and the other on the ridge in north Delhi.

The architecture of Delhi of the medieval period is Islamic in nature. Standard Indo-Islamic architecture with deve-

loped techniques and refined features, like the pointed true arch, low dome and geometric decoration, emerged during the Khalji period. Of the extant structural specimens of the Khalji period, **Alai Darwaza** in the Qutb complex is the finest.

Tughluq architecture is characterized by battered (sloping) walls, plain exteriors, pointed arches and arcuate doorways with lintels. During the periods of the Saiyads and Lodis, some of the structural features of Tughluq monuments underwent modification; the octagonal type of tombs with a veranda around it and kiosks above became popular.

Edifices raised during the Mughal period, however, represent the best of Delhi's structural style.

The Mughal monuments also possess traditional Hindu and late sultanate traits. Shahjahanabad has some fine examples of architecture of the time of Shah Jahan and later kings.

The main attraction among the remains of the first four cities is the ruined **Quwwatu'l Islam** (Might of Islam) **Mosque** complex inside the Tomar Fortress. Built originally by Qutbu'd-Din during 1192-98, out of demolished Hindu temples, as a congregational mosque, it con-

Left, gateway to Purana Qila, the Old Fort; right, Jantar Mantar, one of Raja Jai Singh's observatories.

sists of a courtyard, cloisters and a prayer hall. To enhance its elevational grace, a lofty arched-screen was erected facing the prayer hall. A fascinating aspect of the edifice is the enclosing wall and corridor of reutilized Hindu carved pillars. In the courtyard of the mosque stands a rust-free iron pillar, raised originally as a standard of Lord Vishnu, by Chandra Gupta, a ruler of the 4th century A.D.

Qutbu'd Din started building the **Qutb Minar** in 1199 as a memorial of victory and also as an accessory to the adjoining mosque, to call the faithful to prayer. The Minar is a tapering tower of five tiers (72.5 meters high).

Alai Darwaza is the southern entrance to the enlarged enclosure of the Qutb complex, added by Alau'd Din in 1311. Its well-finished form using the principle of the arch and treatment and decorations in a mixture of red sandstone and marble illustrates a maturity in structural experience. Amongst other remains of the complex is the rather ornate tomb of Sultan Iltutamish.

A little west of Qutb Minar is the township of **Mehrauli**, conspicuous on account of its narrow conventional bazaar. It has two notable shrines: the temple of goddess Jogmaya and the tomb of Muslim divine Khwaja Bakhtyar Kaki (1336) visited by local pilgrims.

Other interesting monuments in Mehrauli include **Adham Khan's tomb, Shamsi Tank, Jahaz-Mahal** and **Jamali's Tomb** with its colored ceiling.

Built by the first Tughlaq ruler on rocky ground with high rubble walls, Tughlaqabad (perimeter 6.5 km) was a well-planned city with a citadel and a vast reservoir to its south. The most well-preserved monument here is the mausoleum of Ghiyasu'd-Din Tughlaq. It is a red-stone edifice with sloping walls and a marble dome enclosed within a mini fortress, with bastions and battlements.

On his way back from Tughlaqabad a visitor may see within the ruined Jahanpanah (fourth Delhi) some notable Tughluq (14th Century) buildings like **Khirki Mosque** modelled like a tiny fortress, **Begampuri Mosque** with its extensive facade, and the damaged mansion called **Bijay-Mandal.**

Tombs, Mosques and Mausoleums

Leaving the Siri (second Delhi) fortifications on one side, past newly constructed localities in a northerly direction

is the sacred tomb of the Muslim saint Nizamuddin Aulia. This saint, who died in 1325, had numerous followers during his lifetime. He was well-known for his miracles and learning. His tomb is regarded as a holy shrine and many visit the place to pray for the fulfilment of their desires. Close by stand the **Jamaat-khana Mosque** (1315) and other historical ruins.

To the east of Nizamuddin, lies **Humayun's Mausoleum** raised by his spouse in 1565. Exemplifying early Mughal architecture, it is a garden-sepulchre with an irregular octagonal plan and double-domed elevation and was to serve as the model for the Taj Mahal.

Further north, on Mathura Road, are remains of Humayun's Dinpanah township. On the right are visible ruins of a market, a city gate and a mosque built by Akbar's wet-nurse (1561) and opposite are ramparts, a moat and portals of **Purana Qila** (Old Fort), Humayun's citadel. Inside stand a beautiful mosque and a double-storied octagonal pavilion (**Sher Mandal**) of the 16th Century.

At a short distance from Purana Qila, to the north is the **Kotla** (fort of) **Firuz-shah,** built of rubble. The inscribed Asokan column is installed into one of its buildings.

Adjacent to the south wall of Purana Qila is the **Delhi Zoo,** famous for its white tigers and others varieties of animals and birds, many of them migratory.

A little westward from Purana Qila lie **India Gate,** the memorial of the First World War, with spacious lawns and shallow tanks, and the **Presidential Palace,** with its 340 rooms and extensive grounds. The drive between the Memorial Arch and President's Palace serves as the arena for the colorful spectacle of India's Republic Day Celebrations on 26 January each year.

Just southeast of the India Gate lawns is the **Gallery of Modern Art** housing specimens of paintings and sculptures of the artists of modern India. It also exhibits a number of paintings of the world-famous Indian poet Rabindranath Tagore, Amrita Shergil and Jamini Roy.

On the southern side of the lawns is the **National Museum of India,** which contains representative collections of Indian art and archeology besides several Central Asian murals and antiquities.

Specimens of traditional crafts of India in different mediums are displayed at the **Crafts Museum,** northeast of India Gate on Mathura Road.

Indo-Muslim sepulchres are to be seen at the **Lodi Gardens.** The structural harmony of the medium-sized tombs of Saiyad and Lodi rulers and other remains is set off by the beautifully laid-out garden which surrounds them.

Further west is another mausoleum of Safdarjung, a Mughal noble of the early 18th Century, built in the characteristic Mughal garden-tomb style.

Connaught Place

A drive along Aurobindo Marg, past **Vijay Chauk** (Victory Square) and Parliament Street leads to **Connaught Place** with its big and small shops, hotels and restaurants. Of special interest are the rows of small shops along Janpath, especially those of Tibetan refugees selling all kinds of curios and oriental objects. The official emporiums dealing in regional handicrafts and textiles are on Baba Kharak Singh Marg, which runs off Connaught Place.

A curious structure, not to be missed, near the junction of Parliament Street and Connaught Circus is Mughal grandee Jaisingh's (1699-1743) observatory, **Jantar Mantar** with huge astronomical "instruments" built in rubble masonry. Its main purpose was standardization of almanacs.

However, more significant structurally is another shrine to the west on the Lower Ridge, the **Lakshmi-Narayana Temple** built some decades ago by the Birlas, a famous family of Indian Industrialists. It is a large picturesque complex with a central shrine dedicated to Narayana or Vishnu and his spouse Lakshmi, the goddess of wealth.

Planned as a quadrant (of a circle), Shahjahanabad, the last historic city of Delhi, had several gates, some of which are still standing — the Delhi, Ajmeri, Turkman and Kashmiri Gates, for example. Its narrow lanes, flanked by houses with traditional central courtyards, are usually crowded, for Shahjahanabad still continues to be a major business center.

The **Red Fort** stands along the eastern edge of the walled city, on the west bank of the Yamuna River. It was planned as an irregular oblong (2.41 km perimeter) and was built as the royal residential and official complex by Shah Jahan. Entry is through the **Lahori** and **Delhi Gates,** via the **Naubat Khana,** the middle portal.

View of Old Delhi from Jami Masjid minaret.

The fort has also a market known as the **Chhata Bazaar** (covered market) between Lahori Gate and the Naubat Khana. The palaces, mostly in marble, are along the river front. Notable amongst the edifices inside are the **Halls of Public and Private Audience;** the royal baths with inlaid floors; the **Moti Masjid** (Pearl Mosque); the private palace of the king, **Rang-Mahal**; and the ornamental canal, **Nahr-i-Bahisht,** beside the gardens. Some of the finest aspects of Mughal art can be seen in the *pietra dura* panels in the royal mansions.

Opposite Red Fort is the principal marketing street of Shahjahanabad, **Chandni Chauk** (Silver Square), which had, originally, a canal dividing the central thoroughfare. During the British period the canal was covered and a church, a fountain and a clock tower were added. The area is the commercial heart of Old Delhi, with many wholesale markets. It is especially noted as a market for traditional silver jewelry, handicrafts and sweetmeats.

On the left of the road to Chandni Chauk from the Red Fort are three important religious buildings. These are the **Lal Mandir** of the Jains, **Gauri-Sankar Temple** dedicated to Lord Shiva and his family, and a Sikh Gurdwara built at the site of the martyrdom of the ninth Sikh preceptor, Guru Tegh Bahadur. He was killed under the orders of the Emperor Aurangzeb (1656-1707) because he refused to embrace Islam.

The **Jami Masjid** (Congregational Mosque) was constructed on a natural elevation by Shah Jahan about a mile west of Red Fort during 1651-56. It is one of the largest mosques in India and is most impressive structurally.

To the north of Red Fort, beyond Kashmiri Gate, are **St. James's Church** (1824), with its artistic sculptures; **Metcalfe House** built as the home of the British Resident in 1835; an Ashokan pillar brought to Delhi by Firuz Tughluq; and the **tomb of Princess Roshanara** placed in what was originally her pleasure garden. In fact, the area between Kashmiri Gate and the Ridge on the north was developed by the British before the construction of New Delhi and the area is still known as **Civil Lines. Delhi University** and its various institutions are located in this area around the old Viceregal Residence.

Parliament House.

UTTAR PRADESH: FUSION OF CULTURES

Uttar Pradesh, literally "northern province," one of India's most densely populated states, is popularly styled U.P. The state's population comprises diverse religious, cultural and ethnic elements and, over its vast territory, even displays sociocultural differences amongst themselves. Through the centuries these elements have lived together in cordiality and have been accommodating to strangers. This is why U.P. is often spoken of as "everyone's home."

Uttar Pradesh occupies an area of about 113,500 sq miles (294,000 sq km). It shares borders with Tibet (China) and Nepal on the north and northeast; borders on five other Indian states, viz. Himachal Pradesh, Haryana, Delhi, Rajasthan and Madhya Pradesh, on the west and south; and Bihar on the east. The whole territory can be divided into three distinct physiographical regions: the Himalayan region on the north, the vast Gangetic plain in the center, and the Vindhya Range and plateau on the south.

The Himalayan region, with valleys and hills of varying altitudes and colder climate than the plains, is the area where most of the rivers of U.P. rise. The Himalayan forests with cedars, oaks, pines, rhododendrons and other varieties of trees and flowers, together with charming streams and high mountains make excellent scenic surroundings. The prominent Himalayan peaks within Uttar Pradesh are: Kamet (25,446 feet/7,756 meters), Nandadevi (25,646 feet/7,817 meters), Trisul (23,340 feet/7,120 meters), Dunagiri (23,182 feet/7,066 meters), Badrinath (23,418 feet/7,138 meters), Kedarnath (22,778 feet/6,943 meters), and Bandarpunchi (20,718 feet/6,315 meters).

The central part of the state, the Gangetic plain, is alluvial and fertile. It is watered by mighty rivers like the Yamuna, Ganga, Ghagra, Gandak, Gomati, Ramganga and Chambal, and their tributaries. Almost all the important towns and trading centers of Central U.P. are located on these rivers. The confluence of the Ganga and the Yamuna, the two most sacred rivers of India, at Allahabad has been a popular place of pilgrimage through millennia.

The southern fringe of the Gangetic

Sunrise and sunset enhance the aura of peace at the Taj.

plain is marked by the low Vindhyan hills and the adjoining plateau has a variety of soils, including black cotton soil. Two important rivers of the area are the Betwa and the Ken which flow into the Yamuna.

Uttar Pradesh is India's most populous state, with over 110 million people, roughly, a sixth of the total population of the country. Of diverse ethnic origins and varied socio-cultural complexion, distributed mostly on a regional basis, the people of the state consist of Hindus, Muslims, Christians and others, besides tribal and aboriginal communities in relatively isolated pockets.

Archeology and History

Hindu myths and legends claim a hoary antiquity for Uttar Pradesh but archeological data reveal a different picture. The beginning of human cultures in the state, according to archeologists, can be traced back to the prehistoric age, as attested by the discovery of stone tools like hand-axes, choppers, scrapers and cleavers in the southeastern area of the state, around Mirzapur in the Vindhyan tracts.

By about the beginning of the first millennium B.C. iron has begun to replace copper technology in north India, including Uttar Pradesh. In the ensuing centuries the new technology brought about remarkable socio-economic changes with greater colonization of the forested Gangetic plain, increase of population and improvement of agriculture due to the growing use of iron implements like pickaxes, saws, axes, sickles and plowshares. A surplus in agricultural production brought about trade, which was initially based on barter, but, by 600 or 500 B.C., was transformed into money-based exchange, with the introduction of "punch-marked" coins issued by trade guilds. Increased commercial activity made for the emergence of urbanism and many important townships came into existence. In fact, the history of some of the well-known cities of modern Uttar Pradesh like Varanasi, Saket (Ayodhya) and Mathura can be traced back to this period.

Around the 6th Century B.C., the territory today covered by U.P. consisted of some eight semi-independent or independent principalities which were either monarchical or oligarchical. Amongst these were Kashi (Varanasi), Kosala (in the area of modern Avadh or Oudh — capital: Shravasti in Gonda-Bahraich District),

Fatehpur Sikri, Akbar's deserted city.

Vatsa (region of Allahabad — capital: Kausambi on the Yamuna), Malla (Deoria District in eastern U.P. — capitals: Kusinagar and Pawa), Chedi (Bundelkhand region), Surasena (Mathura area), Panchala (capitals: Ahichchhatra and Kampilya respectively in Bareilly and Farrukhabad Districts) and Kuru (capital: Hastinapura, Meerut District) in western U.P.

A Birthplace of New Faiths

What is more interesting in the context of the early history of Uttar Pradesh during the 6th and 5th Century B.C. is its association with Buddhism and Jainism, the two anti-orthodox religious movements professing *ahimsa,* non-injury to living beings. The site of the Buddha's native city, Kapilavastu, has been recently identified by some scholars with a village called Piparhawa (Basti District) in eastern U.P. (It has, so far, been traditionally located in Nepal.) The Buddha first preached his doctrines at Sarnath (near Varanasi) in his 35th year. He and his elder contemporary, Mahavira, the founder of historical Jainism, preached in several areas included in Uttar Pradesh, and both of them passed away in the two capitals of the Malla principality, viz. Kusinagar and Pawa. Amongst politically notable personalities of the period associated with the Buddha were Prasenjit, ruler of Kosala, and Udayana, king of Vatsa and a hero of later Indian romances.

Gradually, the major and minor states of ancient Uttar Pradesh were annexed into the growing empire of Magadha, now located in the neighboring state of Bihar, and, by about the 4th Century B.C., virtually the whole of U.P. became a part of the Magadhan kingdom under the Nanda dynasty. The Nandas were followed by the Mauryas who unified India into a strong and vast empire. U.P. still preserves several archeological vestiges of the Mauryan epoch, including pillars and epigraphs of Ashoka, the great Mauryan monarch (272-236 B.C.).

The Maurya dynasty was succeeded by that of the Sungas in a major part of north India. The founder of the dynasty, Pusyamitra Sunga, a former commander of the Mauryan army, successfully repulsed the invading armies of the Indo-Greeks then occupying the northwestern regions of the subcontinent. The post-Sunga period was marked by the rise of local kingdoms in U.P. which even issued their own coinage. It seems there was a general improvement in trade and artistic activity. This was also the time when Mathura and Kausambi emerged as important centers of art.

Towards the end of 1st Century B.C., the Sakas, a foreign tribe, established themselves at Mathura. They were succeeded by another line of Central Asian adventurers, the Kushans. They extended their kingdom up to Varanasi and even beyond in the further east under one of their noted rulers, Kanishka I. Under the Saka-Kushan monarchs, northern India enjoyed prosperity, and great achievements were made in the field of culture, literature and art, with the fusion of many new and even foreign ideas into the cultural fabric. The city of Mathura, one of the capitals of the extensive Kushan Empire, became the epicenter of growing cultural activity under its newly acquired cosmopolitanism.

After the downfall of the Kushans, about the 3rd Century A.D., their north-Indian empire got divided into small states which were again unified in the 4th Century A.D. into a strong kingdom under the Guptas who had their capital at Pataliputra (modern Patna in Bihar). Uttar Pradesh which formed a constituent of the Gupta empire was one of the main centers of cultural activity of the Gupta kings and played an important role in the growth of art and literature in the period. It still has many notable archeological remains of the Gupta period (4th to 6th Century A.D.), including highly graceful sculptures like the Sarnath and Mathura images of the Buddha.

With the disintegration of the Gupta empire, the Maukharis captured political authority in Uttar Pradesh and a part of Bihar. Their capital was Kanauj (Farrukhabad District) which in the 7th Century A.D. passed on to Harsha, originally a prince of Thaneshwar in Haryana. Harsha was a successful ruler who is known for his patronage of Buddhism and for holding quinquennial assemblies at the confluence of Ganga and Yamuna at Allahabad.

Encounter with a New Culture

In the post-Harsha period, the kingdom of Kanauj continued to play an important role in the political and cultural life of the Gangetic plain and neighboring regions. The throne of Kanauj was occupied in almost a direct succession by Yasovarman, the Ayudhas, the Pratiharas and the Gahadwalas, till the beginning of the 13th Century, when nearly the whole of U.P., with the exception of some border areas in the Himalayan and Vindhyan belts, was annexed into the Sultanate of Delhi, under its Mameluke rulers.

The Mamelukes were followed in succession by the other Delhi Sultanate rulers belonging to the houses of the Khaljis, Tughlaqs, Saiyyids and Lodis who, generally, controlled U.P. till 1526, partly or fully, through their governors or fief-holders, depending on their own administrative organization and personal capacities. On some occasions, the local chiefs or governors of U.P. revolted against the central authority at Delhi. Towards the end of the 14th Century, Malik Sarwar, a Tughlaq noble, established an independent kingdom with Jaunpur (eastern U.P.) as its capital. Sarwar's successors were known as Sharqis (easterners). The house came to an end with the defeat of Husain Shah Sharqi at the hands of Bahlul of the Lodi dynasty in 1458.

Under the Sharqi sultans, Jaunpur became a seat of learning and a center of arts — the "Shiraz of the East." The Jaunpur rulers developed a unique variety of Indo-Islamic architecture with ornamental qualities and high and impressive facades which can be observed in their extant edifices.

Cultural Synthesis

During the early Sultanate rule, the Hindu population of U.P., after initial resistance, adjusted themselves in the changed situation and discarded their earlier hostile attitude towards the Islamic rulers. Consequently, some new cultural elements, with composite ideas and practices, related to both Hinduism and Islam, developed. The best products of this cultural synthesis were the Urdu language, which was essentially a variation on Hindi, written in Arabic script; the graceful styles of medieval Indian architecture; and the medieval Hindu reformation movements.

With the foundation of Mughal rule by Babur in 1526, Agra, his capital, rose to prominence. Even earlier it had been the capital of Sikandar Lodi (1489 — 1517). Yet the real glory of Agra belongs to the periods of Akbar (1556 — 1605), Jahangir (1605 — 27) and Shah Jahan (1628 — 58). During the time of Akbar,

both Agra and the nearby Fatehpur Sikri not only served as imperial capitals, but also turned into renowned centers of trade and commerce, and culture and learning, with their celebrated architectural wealth and material riches. In fact, Agra achieved international fame for its grandeur during early Mughal rule. Other towns of the Ganga plain like Mathura, Allahabad and Varanasi also attained considerable importance during the Mughal epoch.

Throughout the early Mughal age, Uttar Pradesh prospered with its urban centers, producing and selling a number of commodities, including textiles. These cities also witnessed the growth of literature, art, architecture, crafts, music and dance, all of which received generous patronage from the court and the nobility. They developed a composite city culture which was widely imitated in other regions of India.

During later Mughal rule, following the death of Aurangzeb in 1707, the sixth of the Great Mughals, the process of internal dissension and disintegration of the empire set in. The kingdom was raided by Afghans, Iranians, Jats and Marathas, and most provincial governors, including the Nawab of Lucknow, declared their independence. Gradually, the well-organized British East India Company captured the administrative power, which ultimately resulted in the overthrow of the Mughal authority and that of other local rulers like the Nawab of Lucknow and Rani of Jhansi in U.P., and elsewhere, by 1857, when the popular rising against the British East India Company was crushed. In 1858, the British crown took over from the Company.

Not Just the Taj

Uttar Pradesh presents a variety of attractions for the traveller. The state is well-covered by a network of motorable roads, railway lines and airports. Delhi or any of the main U.P. cities is a convenient starting point for a tour of the state. Southwest U.P. is right next to Delhi, the usual point of entry to north India. Agra, Fatehpur Sikri and Mathura lie in this region.

The main part of **Agra** city, on the right bank of the Yamuna, continues to be medieval in structure, with narrow, crowded streets and lanes, full of colorful shops selling all kind of goods, especially

Left, terraced farming on the Kumaun Hills, Uttar Pradesh; right, the Imambara complex, Lucknow.

local handicrafts, including gold and silver embroidery and imitation Mughal inlay on marble and fine leather goods. The place is also known for its pumpkin sweet *(petha)* and *dalmoth* (savory fried chickpeas) and delicious non-vegetarian dishes of Mughal origin.

Among the monuments is, needless to say, the world-famous Taj Mahal. But there are also matchless gems to be seen in the Agra Fort and at the mausoleums of Akbar and Itimadu'd-Daula, and the remains of the abandoned town of Fateh-pur Sikri.

Agra Fort lies on the bend of the River Yamuna, almost in the heart of the town. It was built by Akbar as his citadel over the years 1565-73 in the finest architectural style. It has imposing gates and walls of red sandstone and a moat. The fort, approachable through its two lofty main portals on the west and south, besides a private gate on the east, was successively occupied by three great Mughals — Akbar, Jahangir and Shah Jahan, each of whom made significant structural contributions to this complex.

Of the conspicuous edifices inside the fort, mention must be made of **Jahangiri Mahal; Khas Mahal** (Private Palace) with its attached vineyard called **Anguri Bagh,** and the ornamental bath called **Shish Mahal;** the ornate **Musamman Burj,** where Shah Jahan died as captive of his son, passing his last days gazing at the Taj Mahal (the tomb of his beloved wife), the **Diwan-i-Khas** (Hall of Private Audience) and **Diwan-i-Am** (Hall of Public Audience), **Machchhi Bhawan** (palace with fish-tanks), and **Moti Masjid.** Most of these were built during the reign of Shah Jahan. Shah Jahan's architectural creations are mostly in marble and display great refinement in contrast to the building style of his grandfather, Akbar, which is bold, original and virile.

The Diwan-i-Khas and Diwan-i-Am in royal Mughal complexes are halls intended for closed official meetings and public assemblies *(or durbars)* respectively and state functions in which the emperor was seated on a throne placed under a raised canopy built into the back of the hall.

"A Dream in Marble"

Not far from the historic fort is the **Taj Mahal,** the mausoleum of Empress Mumtaz Mahal, the beloved spouse of Shah Jahan, who died in 1630. The Taj complex comprises a forecourt, a lofty entrance, a charming formal Mughal garden with canals and a central tank with a series of fountains, the tomb proper, and an attached mosque on the west, and its symmetrical counterpart on the east. The main mausoleum, where Shah Jahan also lies, is a domed two-storied building, irregular octagon in plan, with four tall minarets at the corners — all built of brick and encased in marble. The actual graves are in the crypt.

The Taj is remarkable for its perfect proportions and rich *pietra dura,* with minute details executed with great skill. The building, often styled "a dream in marble," is said to have taken at least 18 years (1631 — 48) to build. It marks the most developed stage of Mughal architecture. The designer of this grand sepulchre is believed to be Ustad Ahmad Lahori, a master architect of the age. The calligraphic ornamentation on the Taj Mahal was authored by Amanat Khan Shirazi, a great writer of the 17th Century.

According to popular belief, Shah Jahan wanted to build another mausoleum in black marble for himself opposite the Taj Mahal, but, for reasons unknown, could not do so

Across the river from Agra Fort, lies the small but beautiful sepulchre of Mirza Ghayas Beg, called Itimadu'd Daula, who was the father of Jahangir's most beloved consort, Nurjahan. Mirza was elevated, due to his daughter's influence, to the rank of high chamberlain and prime minister to the emperor. The edifice also enshrines the mortal remains of the empress' mother. It was built between 1622 and 1628, and has an unusual structural character in relation to other Mughal tombs. It is a square building with four corner towers and a crowning pavilion with a canopy-shaped roof and floor inlaid with an arabesque pattern. It has a well-decorated marble exterior notable for its bold inlaid design in semi-precious stones. The interior is painted.

To the northwest of Agra proper, some 7½ miles (12 km) away, is **Sikandara,** the locality named after Sikandar Lodi. Here stands the mighty tomb of Emperor Akbar, within a spacious garden enclosed by high walls on the Agra-Delhi road. It has on the southern side a high gate with four towering *minars* rising above its roof and the false gates placed, for the sake of symmetry, at each of the other three sides of the walled enclosure. The gate is further distinguished by bold and thick ornamental mosaic patterns. The mausoleum, which is centrally located, was begun by Akbar himself, but was completed in 1613, in the reign of Jahangir. Jahangir made some modification in its original design and added the top terrace with marble cloisters containing a false grave of the emperor. The real grave lies in the crypt-like sepulchral chamber.

Close to Akbar's tomb, on the road to the southeast, is a realistic stone figure of Akbar's war horse, and a little to the southwest is the tomb of his Christian wife, Mariam Zamani, mother of Jahangir.

Other significant edifices in Agra include the unfinished marble memorial *(samadhi)* to the 19th Century founder of the Hindu Radha Swami order; the remains of an old Roman Catholic cemetery belonging to the Mughal period; Raja Jaswant Singh's Chhatri (memorial canopy); and Chini-ka-Rauza, a ruined tomb of the period of Shah Jahan, known for its colored-tile decoration.

Fatehpur Sikri

About 20 miles (35 km) southwest of Agra lie the imperial ruins of the Mughal city of **Fatehpur Sikri,** Akbar's capital for a short 12 years. It occupies a sandstone ridge and the area around it, within a circumference of nearly nine miles (11 km), enclosed within a wall. The royal residences and offices were located on the ridge itself and important markets on the slope. Emperor Akbar is said to have selected Sikri as the seat of his government believing it to be auspicious for himself as prophesied by the saint, Shaikh Salim Cheshti, who lived there. Actually, Fatehpur Sikri was raised by the great emperor as a city expressing his ideals and vision, where he carried out his experiments in art and architecture.

The red-stone mansions of Sikri exhibit a robust stability combined with originality. Their design combines several regional elements of Indian architectural styles with that of Central Asia and Iran. Each of the important edifices here represents a type by itself. The finest monuments are the cloistered **Diwan-i-Am;** the single-pillared **Diwan-i-Khas;** the astrologer's kiosk; the Turkish sultana's house with minute carvings; the storied pavilion called **Panch Mahal; Mariyam's house** with its interesting paintings; the ornate **house of Birbal; Jodhabai's grand palace;** and the **Jami Masjid** complex, with its pillared hall, monumental portal **(Buland Darwaza)** and charming **tomb of Saint Shaikh Salim Chishti** which is visited by many seeking fulfilment of their wishes.

Krishna Country

About 30 miles (50 km) from Agra, on the highway to Delhi, is **Mathura** on the right bank of the Yamuna. It is a great center of Hindu pilgrimage, being regarded as the birthplace of Lord Krishna. Mathura has several temples dedicated to this deity, of which the most outstanding are the **Dwarkadhish shrine** in the crowded marketplaces, the temple at the birthplace of Krishna, and **Gita Mandir** on the way to Vrindavan, where Krishna grazed his cattle during his childhood. Mathura's bazaars are known for their sweets and ritualistic objects associated with the Hindu system of worship.

Mathura has an excellent museum, famous for its collection of ancient red sandstone sculptures of Buddhist, Brahmanical and Jain association, produced by the artists of Mathura between the 2nd Century B.C. and the 6th Century A.D. During the early centuries A.D., Mathura was a fortified town of international importance.

Vrindavan, six miles (10 km) north of Mathura, is also a pilgrim center. It abounds in medieval and modern Hindu temples. Significant among them are the **Govind-deo Temple** (1590); the **Jugal Kishore, Radha-Vallabh** and **Madan-Mohan Temples** (17th Century); **Rangji's and Shahji's temples** (19th Century); the famous **Bihariji shrine;** the **temple of Pagal Baba** and the recently built temple of the International Society for Krishna Consciousness (ISKON). Mathura also has a large number of monasteries, with almost every Hindu sect and sub-sect being represented. Free meals are offered to the pilgrims at these monasteries. Lost in devotion to Krishna, pilgrims sometimes dance in ecstasy *(Ram Liala),* imploring the love of Lord Krishna.

Central U. P.

Kanpur, the main industrial center of U. P., stands on the right bank of the Ganga. It produces mainly leather and textile goods of fine quality. It has amongst its historic remains the **Memorial Church,** built in 1875 in romanesque style, which contains tablets bearing the names of British citizens who died during the great Indian revolt of 1857 against the East

India Company. There is also a fine brick temple (16th Century A.D.) at **Bhitgargaon,** a village close to Ghatampur in the vicinity of Kanpur.

Lucknow, the capital of Uttar Pradesh, straddles both banks of the River Gomati, a tributary of the Ganga. It rose to importance during the Indo-Islamic (medieval) period, especially under the Mughals and, subsequently, under the Nawabs of Oudh and, still later, the British. The city is famous for its cultivated manners and refined urban culture. Fine *bidri* (silverinlaid black metalware), jewelry, cotton embroidery (*chikan* work) and toys are produced in Lucknow by traditional craftsmen.

Lucknow developed its own style of architecture during the 18th and 19th centuries. It began as a rather ornate, modified form of Mughal prototypes, but built in brick and stucco. Later, it incorporated many European traits, like triangular pediments, Corinthian capitals and round arches. The buildings of the Nawabs of Oudh are very often embossed with a pair of fish, their royal emblem.

Imported historical sites in the city include **Nadan Mahal,** a Mughal tomb; **Bara Imambara** (1784), containing the tombs of the builder, Nawab Asifu'd-Daula, and his family; the ruins of the **British Residency,** of Mutiny fame; the **Husanabad Imambara;** the **Chhatar Manzil;** the **Qaisarbagh** quadrangle; the **tombs of Saadt Ali** and his wife; **Dilkusha Palace;** and Constantania, now **La Martiniere School,** built by Claude Martin, a Frenchman, in the 18th Century. The Bara Imambara stands in a large enclosure, with an attached mosque and a great ornamental gate, the **Rumi Darwaza.** A point to be noted about this monument is its charming arcuate labyrinth, supporting the roof of the edifice, which is locally called the *bhul-bhulaiya.*

Other attractions of Lucknow are its picture gallery displaying portraits of the Oudh Nawabs, the state museum mainly displaying ancient sculptures from various parts of U.P., and the zoo with a variety of animals and birds. The city is the home of light classical Hindustani (North-Indian) music and Kathak, a traditional school of dance.

Sravasti and Kusinagara

Located respectively in Gonda-Bahraich and Deoria Districts of U.P., Sra-

The Bara Imambara, Lucknow.

vasti and **Kusinagara** were ancient cities associated with the Buddha. The sites are visited by Buddhist pilgrims from all over the world. Sravasti is also sacred to the Jain community. As a result of archeological operations in the last and present century, remains of ancient structures were exposed in these sites and interesting antiquities were recovered. At Kusinagara, a sculpture showing the dying Buddha is of great value as it was here that he passed away.

Ayodhya is a popular place of Hindu pilgrimage as it is traditionally considered to be the birthplace of Lord Rama, mythological hero and an incarnation of God Vishnu much earlier than the Krishna incarnation. At Ayodhya, the performance of the rituals of orthodox Hinduism can be observed in the scores of old and new temples, and especially in **Kanak Bhawan** and **Hanumangarhi.**

At **Faizabad,** a town of medieval origin five miles (eight km) from Ayodhya, are the tombs of Nawab Shujau'd-Daula of Oudh (1754-75) and his wife, and a small museum.

Allahabad, Varanasi and Jaunpur are the historically significant towns of Eastern U. P. **Allahabad,** also known as

Prayag in Hindu tradition, is a peaceful city where life usually moves at a slow pace. But being regarded as one of the holiest places in the country, it springs to life during religious festivals and fairs. In particular the massive Kumbha Mela, meeting ground of various Hindu sects and their ascetic orders, is held every 12 years and attracts hundreds of thousands of pilgrims.

In Allahabad stands one of Ashoka's stone pillars carrying his own epigraph and those of the Gupta king Samadragupta (335-75 A.D.), and later rulers. Allahabad's Mughal legacy includes a historic **Akbar Fort and Palace** and **Khushrobagh,** garden containing the impressive tomb of Mughal Prince Khushro and his family. The town has a fine museum housing mainly ancient sculptures and paintings.

Mirzapur, a small district town between Allahabad and Varanasi, is famous for its excellent woollen carpets with fast colors prepared by traditional Indian craftsmen.

On the left bank of the Ganga is **Varanasi** (Banaras), also known as Kashi. Like Rome, it is traditionally regarded as "an eternal city," surviving through the

Two sacred rivers meet at Deoprayag in the Himalayan foothills.

ages. Lord Shiva, under his name Vishvanath or the Overlord of the World, is believed to be the presiding deity of the town. According to a common belief, those who die here will be close to God in the other world, and many orthodox Hindus come to Varanasi to pass their last days.

The antiquity of Varanasi can be traced back to at least the middle of first millennium B.C. Since time immemorial, it has served not merely as a holy center of pilgrimage but also as a great seat of traditional Hindu learning and culture. Despite modernization, it still preserves some of the carefree and colorful aspects of the traditional Hindu way of life.

Amongst the handicrafts of Varanasi are silks, shawls, brocades and embroideries, ornamental brassware, modern brass idols of Hindu deities, and toys.

An interesting spectacle in the city is its long series of *ghats* (stepped landings) on the river front linked with crowded streets at the back, which are always full of travellers, devotees and pilgrims. A good sampling of Varanasi's almost countless temples is provided by visits to the **Visvanath Temple, Durga Kund, Sankat Mochan** (shrine of the monkey god, Hanuman), and the **Annapurna** and **Kal-Bhairava** Temples.

Conspicuous in the Varanasi skyline is the historic **mosque of Aurangzeb.** In the 18th Century, Raja Jaisingh built one of his celebrated observatories in this town. A good museum in the Banaras Hindu University called **Bharat Kala Bhawan** contains a rich collection of ancient and medieval sculptures, paintings, manuscripts and textiles. The old palace of the Raja of Varanasi, within the **Ramnagar Fort,** has a private museum housing objects of personal use, and other materials belonging to the erstwhile ruling family.

To the north of Varanasi, about four miles (six km) away, are the Buddhist remains of **Sarnath** or the ancient **Mrigadava** (Deer Park) where the Buddha delivered his first sermon after attaining enlightenment. Among the remains at Sarnath are the **Dhamekh Stupa,** the main shrine, and an Ashokan pillar. The local archeological museum has good specimens of sculpture recovered from the site. Outstanding among these are the superb seated Buddha (6th Century A.D.) and the Lion Capital of Ashoka (3rd Century B.C.), now the emblem of the Government of India.

Jaunpur has medieval historical associations. Akbar built a stone bridge over the Gomti here which is still standing. Surviving the Sharqi period are a **Tughlaq fort** and the **Atala** and **Jami Mosques.** Fine perfumed oils and scents are made by traditional methods in this town.

Southern and Western U.P.

In south U.P. are the strong medieval fort at Kalinjar (Banda District), Chandella dynasty tanks at Mahoba, a fort at Jhansi and ancient temples at Deogarh (Lalitpur District). Jhansi also has a museum of regional antiquities. A well-known scenic spot in the area is Chitrakuta, which is also regarded as a holy place because of its association with the story of Lord Rama.

Western Uttar Pradesh has a number of commercial towns like **Bareilly, Muradabad, Meerut** and **Saharanpur** which manufacture mainly furniture, ornamental brassware, sports goods and carved woodwork, respectively.

Hardwar where the River Ganga descends to the plains, and **Rishikesh** and **Dehradun** nearby are places rich in natural beauty. Hardwar is amongst the holiest places of pilgrimage in India.

The Himalayan belt runs along the whole northern border of U.P. It consists of several ranges, of which the outermost on the side of the plains is the **Shivaliks.** The area has several hill resorts: **Mussorie, Landsdowne** and **Joshimath** in Garhwal, and **Nainital, Mukteshwar, Ranikhet, Almora** and **Kausani** in Kumaun.

The Himalaya are rich in scenic beauty. The best spots to visit are **Pindari** and **Milam glaciers** in Kumaun; the eternal Hindu shrines of **Kedarnath** and **Badarinath; Ganogotri** and **Yamanotri,** sources of the Ganga and Yamuna; the enchanting **Valley of Flowers,** which is in full bloom during August and September; and the Sikh shrine of **Hemkund Sahib** in Garhwal.

Ancient temples are to be seen at **Baijnath, Jageshwar, Katarmal, Champavat** and **Dwarahat** in Kumaun and Lakhamandal, **Deoprayag, Ranihat** (Srinagar), **Adibadri, Gopeshwar, Joshimath** and **Pandukeshwar** in Garhwal.

Close to the foothills, near Ramnagar (Nainital District), is **Corbett National Park,** a wildlife sanctuary spread over an area of 125 sq miles (324 sq km). Elephants, tigers, leopards, hyenas and varieties of deer inhabit the sanctuary.

HIMACHAL PRADESH

Himachal Pradesh, nestling in the north-western lap of the Himalayan range, abounds in exotic valleys, glorious green hill-slopes, snowcapped mountains, and gushing streams. In this mountain wonderland, the pace of life is measured and tranquil.

Himachal Pradesh straddles the Himalaya from the foothills, over peaks, to the valleys of Lahaul and Spiti beyond. Its capital, Shimla (Simla), had the distinction of serving as the summer capital of India in the days of the British viceroys, a refuge for the sahibs from the heat of the plains. Not only the viceroy, but a substantial part of the secretariat of the Government of India, from members of the Viceroy's Executive Council down to clerks ("babus," the British called them) and "peons," with boxes of files and red tape, made the journey to the hills, mostly by toy-train. It is Shimla that is the scene of many of Rudyard Kipling's stories, his *Plain Tales from the Hills.*

In summer, the fragrance of fresh flowers pervades these enchanting hills and the coolness of the melting snow tempers the heat. The monsoon brings a spectacle of lush greenery and cascading waterfalls. Autumn is marked by pleasant sunny days ending in gorgeous sunsets. Winter brings snow and lots of fun and frolic. For those keen on winter sports, Himachal Pradesh has all they need and much more.

Himachal is accessible by road from Pathankot (Punjab) in the west, Chandigarh in the south, and Dehra Dun in the east. There is also a rail link between Kalka and Shimla, and one between Pathankot and Jogindernagar. An air service to Kulu is also available from Delhi and Chandigarh.

A large majority of Himachalis are Hindus, but Buddhism is also a major influence and is the religion of the Lahaul and Spiti valleys. The Buddhist existence has become particularly marked with the presence of the exiled Dalai Lama and his entourage at Dharamsala and the large settlements of Tibetan refugees in the state.

As many as six thousand temples are spread all over the area of this comparatively small state. Each year the people

Himalayan panorama.

of these hills and valleys live through a cycle of rituals and ceremonies. Gay and colorful fairs and festivals are often associated with them, along with the folk dancing which is often a part of the celebrations.

Himachal Pradesh is essentially rural. Its towns are small. The traditional village house is of special interest. It is usually three-storied. The lowest story is occupied by the household cattle; the middle provides space for storing grain and other things, but also for sleeping in winter; the top floor *(dafi)* provides living space.

Folk Songs and Dances

The folk songs of Himachal Pradesh are very melodious and rhythmic. People sing on various occasions and also while doing their daily work. *Naati* is the most popular folk dance of Himachal Pradesh. It is danced in chain formation with hands linked by dancers wearing appropriate masks. In Kinnaur and Lahaul-Spiti, the folk dances depict the perpetual strife between gods and demons. In the lower regions, the dances are more sophisticated and similar to those of the plains.

Shimla (Simla) is situated at a height of 6,900 feet (2,100 meters). The town is spread over seven miles (12 km) along a ridge. Around Shimla are excellent walks through rustling woods. At each turn, a fantastic new panorama unfolds. The green slopes are covered with fir, rhododendron, pine and the Himalayan oak. Nestling among the foliage are traditional homesteads. The level ground at the ridge is the favorite evening rendezvous, with Scandal Point at the end of it and the Mall for shopping.

Shimla's mood changes with the seasons, each with its own charm. Perhaps the best time of the year is autumn, when the days are warm and bright and the nights crisp and cool. The spring brings colorful flowers. The monsoon provides an opportunity to see some of the most magnificent sunsets in the world. Winter is known as the season of "long moon nights" in Shimla. The city glistens with frost and icy winds sweep across the city.

In spite of changes and considerable growth since India became independent, Shimla, perhaps more than any other spot in India, still presents substantial evidence of an attempt by the sahibs to build an English town in India. Relics of styles of

A Himachal village.

building long forgotten in Britain are still evident here.

Narkanda, at a height of about 8,850 feet (2,700 meters) and 40 miles (64 km) from Shimla on the Hindustan–Tibet road, is famous for its apple orchards and its beautiful scenery, especially during summer. It is a convenient starting point for visits to many places in the heart of Himachal Pradesh: Bagi, Khandrala, Rampur and Kalpa on the Hindustan–Tibet Road (the last is not very far from the Skipki-La Pass to Tibet); the apple-growing Kotgarh area and Kulu. This area, along the valley of the River Sutlej, is called **Kinnaur.**

The Valley of the Gods

Rampur Bushahr, on the bank of the Sutlej, is 90 miles (140 km) from Shimla. It provides a night halt for visitors and trekkers to Kinnaur. It is one of the biggest commercial towns of Himachal Pradesh and is famous for its three-day market fair, Lavi, which is held in November. Traders from Kinnaur, Spiti and Lahaul participate in it. While the days are spent in making bargains, the evenings are given to song and dance.

Kulu Valley on the banks of the Beas is at an altitude of about 3,900 feet (1,200 meters). It is famous for its apple orchards, its beautiful women, its old wooden temples and its folk music and dances. It offers ample scope for trekking, climbing and angling, and big and small game are plentiful in its forests.

The best time to visit the Kulu Valley is October, when the Dussera festival is celebrated. The statue of Raghunathji, the presiding deity of the valley, is ceremonially brought down to the valley from the mountains. The god stays in state in the valley for a week, along with other gods who are also present in their festive palanquins. The highlight of the fair is the dance competition held every evening.

The most remarkable temple of the valley is that of **Bijli Mahadeva** which is located a few miles away from Kulu. The temple is built of large blocks of stone without the use of cement and its 65-foot-tall (20-meter) tall flagstaff is reputed to attract lightning which, according to the local legend, is an expression of divine blessing. Every time the flagstaff is struck by lightning, the Shiva *lingam* (phallic symbol) inside the temple is shattered. It is put together each time by the priest and

Bus stop, Dharamsala.

covered with *sattoo* (a paste of roasted gram and wheat powder) and butter. The image, thus restored, stands till another similar flash repeats "the miracle."

The well-known **hot springs of Manikaran** are just 30 miles (45 km) from Kulu town, in the heart of the valley.

The road from Kulu to Manali runs along the swift and rushing torrents of the Beas. It is flanked by lofty mountains and spreading forests. On this road is **Katrain,** famous for its fruit orchards and its trout hatchery. Near Katrain, across the river, is a small town **Naggar,** where the medieval world still survives, untouched by time. The town has been made famous by the Russian painter, Nicholas Roerich, a gallery of whose paintings can be seen there.

Manali, another major resort, is circled by beautiful glades of deodars and flowering horse chestnuts. It is an ideal place for walks, climbs, treks and picnics. It is also an important trade center. The **Dhoongri Temple** at Manali, dedicated to the goddess Hidimba, is believed to be over a thousand years old.

Two miles (three km) from Manali are the **sulfur springs of Bashishta** and a little higher up is the small **Bhrigu Lake,** named after a sage. The Kulu Valley ends as the road winds up through rocky ranges to the Rohtang Pass, the gateway to the enchanting Lahaul and Spiti valleys.

Lahaul and Spiti

In the northeast of Himachal Pradesh, across the 13,200-foot-high (4,020-meter) **Rohtang Pass** lie the two valleys of **Lahaul** and **Spiti** at a height of 9,800 to 15,700 feet (3,000 to 4,800 meters). Both valleys remain cut off from the rest of the world for much of the year. The Rohtang Pass remains open only from May to October, and it is only during this period that one may cross the still' higher **Kunzam Pass** at an altitude of 14,800 feet (4,500 meters) to enter Spiti Valley. Otherwise, one has to reach Spiti by trekking up along the Sutlej and Spiti river valleys from Kinnaur.

Among the valleys, mountains, glaciers, rivers and pastures of Lahaul and Spiti are forts, *gompas* (monasteries) and ancient buildings with frescos on the walls and ceilings.

The people of these two valleys have a distinct culture of their own. Their songs and dances are as pure as the snow that glitters around them. Their *gompas* are repositories of Buddhist art treasures.

The Valley of Milk and Honey

The romantic valley of **Chamba,** a former princely state, has few rivals for scenic beauty. Its valleys, meadows, rivers, lakes, springs and streams have a unique charm. The altitude of this valley ranges from 2,000 to 20,600 feet (600 to 6,300 meters). **Chamba town** is situated on the right bank of the River Ravi at an altitude of 2,950 feet (900 meters). It can be reached from Pathankot (Punjab) by a 75-mile (120-km) road which passes through lush green forests. There is also a 100-mile-long (30-km) foot-track from Dalhousie to Chamba, through dense forests. The town is noted for its ancient Shiva and Vishnu temples, some of which date back to the 10th Century.

The **Bhuri Singh Museum** in Chamba is a veritable treasurehouse of exquisite paintings of the famous Kangra and Basohli schools and a mass of epigraphical material relating to the history of the region.

Among the innumerable fairs and festivals celebrated in Himachal Pradesh, the most important is the **Minjar Fair** of Chamba, held around August to celebrate the coming of the rains and the flowering of maize. A procession of decorated horses and banners marks the beginning of the week-long fair.

Dalhousie, Bharmaur and **Nurpur** are other places of interest around Chamba town. Dalhousie is a quiet hill-station located on five little hills. Bharmaur, the ancient capital of Chamba, is famous for the Pahari architecture of its ancient temple, and Nurpur for its handmade textiles.

The Kangra District

Kangra is one of the most beautiful and charming valleys in the Himalaya. **Dharamsala,** the headquarters of the Kangra District, is located at the foot of the Dhauladhar Range. The town consists of a lower and an upper Dharamsala, its altitude varying from 3,280 to 6,560 feet (1,000 to 2,000 meters). Upper Dharamsala is where His Holiness, the Dalai Lama, now lives. The ancient town of Kangra is famous for its historic temples, the most popular being the one dedicated to the goddess Vajreshwari. The valley is also famous for the distinct school of painting which grew and flourished there.

Near Dharamsala, there are a number of picturesque picnic spots — the waterfalls of **Bhagsunath,** whose tank and spring are considered sacred; the beautiful **Dal Lake; Dharamkat,** nearly 6,900 feet high (2,100 meters); **Triund** and the **Kareri Lakes** nearly 10,200 feet (3,000 meters) above sea level.

Dharamsala is a convenient base for to and fro trips to other places worth seeing in the Kangra Valley, such as **Kangra city** (30 miles)/48 km), **Palampur** (164 miles/263 km), **Baijnath** (220 miles/352 km) and **Jawalamukhi** (180 miles/288 km).

Mandi

Mandi offers varied climates as its height ranges from 1,970 to 13,120 feet (600 to 4,000 meters) above sea level. The town of Mandi is situated on the left bank of the River Beas at an altitude of 2,460 feet (750 meters). It is 130 miles (210 km) from Pathankot and 102 miles (165 km) from Shimla via Bilaspur.

The town has several striking stone temples with beautiful carvings, among which **Bhootnath, Triloknath, Panchvaktra** and **Tarna** are the more famous.

For the Shivaratri Fair, the town is tastefully decorated. Devotees put the *rathas* (carriages) of their village family gods and goddesses on their shoulders and go in procession to Mandi town on Shivaratri day. They present themselves at the **Raj Madhan Temple** and later pay homage to Lord Shiva at Bhootnath Temple. On this day, a week-long fair, a feast of fun, music and dance begins.

Bilaspur is 56 miles (90 km) from Shimla. Among the town's major attractions are **Vyas Gufa** (cave) and the **Lakshmi Narayan** and **Radheshyam Temples.** The **Shri Naina Devi Temple,** which attracts thousands of pilgrims during its many fairs, is situated at the top of a triangular hillock just 35 miles (57 km) from Bilaspur. This sacred place provides an unparalleled view of the holy **Anandpur Sahib,** the birthplace of a Sikh guru, on one side, and Govind Sagar (named after the Sikh guru) on the other.

Holiday Resorts and Lake Towns

Nahan is a small holiday resort tucked away on an isolated ridge in the Shiwaliks. Its proximity to the plains and its low altitude make most of the area specially attractive during autumn. Nahan has several famous temples and tanks. This town's special attraction is its lovely and lonely walks.

Poanta Sahib, 30 miles (45 km) from Nahan on the Nahan–Dehra-Dun Road, is an important pilgrimage center for the Sikhs. Its impressive gurdwara on the bank of the River Yamuna is thronged by thousands of pilgrims during the Hola festival in the month of March.

Renuka is a picturesque lake town about 30 miles (45 km) from Nahan. The sacred **Parshuram Tal** (tank) is located near Renuka Lake which appears shaped in the profile of a goddess. It is said that Rishi Jamdagni, displeased with his wife Renuka, instructed his son Parshuram to chop off her head. The son promptly carried out the order. The *rishi,* pleased with his son, offered him a boon. Parshuram instantly asked for the restoration of his mother to life. Renuka was brought back to life and, thereafter, her reunion with the family has been commemorated by a large fair held in her honor every year. People from far and near pay their homage and pray to the goddess for her blessings for a happy and prosperous family life.

Winter Sports

The little hamlet of **Kufri,** 10 miles (16 km) from Shimla, is the center for winter sports. The ice skating rink there is the only one of its kind in this part of the world. The skiing season starts in the last week of December and lasts up to about the end of February, depending on the weather. Skiing opportunities are also available at **Narkanda** (40 miles/64 km from Shimla) and **Solang** (six miles/10 km from Manali).

Naldera, 14 miles (23 km) from Shimla, has one of the oldest golf courses in the country. The nine-hole course is very popular with enthusiasts since it is perhaps the most "sporting" one east of Suez.

Chail, a small town 39 miles (63 km) from Shimla, is at a height of 7,000 feet (2,150 meters). It was once the summer capital of the Maharaja of Patiala and is now a lovely tourist resort. It boasts a cricket pitch reputed to be the highest in the world and certainly the most scenic. The town and its environs provide excellent facilities for fishing, tennis, squash and golf, in most beautiful surroundings. Bird-watchers and wildlife enthusiasts will find the forests around Chail alive with hundreds of species.

Trekking Possibilities

There is no end to the trekking possibilities in Himachal Pradesh, but for those who prefer to keep on the beaten track, there are a number of established routes of great interest.

Manali-Chandrakhani-Malana is a seven-day trek. The stages en route are Ramsu, 6,760 feet (15 miles); Chandrakhani, 11,980 feet (five miles); Malana, 6,890 feet (four miles); Kasol, 5,180 feet (five miles); Jari, 5,120 feet (nine miles); and Bhuntar, 2,950 feet (seven miles).

Manali-Chandratal involves 11 days trekking. It covers Chikka, 9,700 feet (eight miles); Chhatru, 11,020 feet (10 miles); Chhota Dara 12,270 feet (10 miles); Batal 13,000 feet (10 miles); Chandratal, 14,010 feet (11 miles); Topko Yongma, 14,170 feet (seven miles); Topko Gongma, 15,520 feet (six miles); Baralacha, 1,600 feet (six miles); Patseo 12,530 feet (12 miles); Jispa, 10,890 feet

(nine miles) and Keyong, 10,960 feet (13 miles).

Manali-Deo-Tibba, a seven-day trek, covers Khanul, 6,630 feet (six miles); Chikka, 9,840 feet (six miles); Seri, 14,990 feet (three miles); Chandratal, 14,990 feet (six miles) and back to Manali.

Manali-Solang Valley is again a seven-day trek and covers Solang, 8,140 feet (seven miles); Dhundi, 9,320 feet; Beas Kund, 11,610 feet and back (six miles); Dhundhi-Shigara Dugh, 5 miles; Marrhi, 11,090 feet (six miles).

Dharamsala-Chamba via Lakagot and Bharmaur is an eight-day trek. Lakagot is at the foot of Indrahar Pass at 18,600 feet (5,660 meters) on the majestic Dhauladhar range.

There are ample opportunities for trekking in the Chamba District. The Pangi Valley and the Manimahesh range of mountains are attractive areas.

A number of treks can be undertaken from Shimla: **Shimla to Kulu via Jalori Pass; Shimla to Mussoorie via Tuini;** and **Shimla to Churdhar via Fagu.**

Most of the peaks in Himachal Pradesh are still unscaled. However, easily accessible mountains provide a good training ground for mountaineers.

Buddhists at prayer, Dharamsala.

JAMMU AND KASHMIR

The storybook scenery of the vale of Kashmir has been legendary throughout history, but few outside the Indian subcontinent are aware that the state of Jammu and Kashmir combines three distinct areas, each unique physically, culturally and aesthetically. Not only do people in Jammu, Kashmir and Ladakh live in radically different environments; they also speak different languages, worship different gods and think along separate cultural lines. This rich diversity enhances the mystery of remote mountain valleys and flavors the cultural complexities of busy urban centers.

Jammu

Jammu is the home of the handsome Dogras, Hindus and Sikhs whose warlike forefathers rode north out of their foothill villages to conquer the disparate kingdoms of the high Himalaya. These were united under Maharaja Gulab Singh in the early 19th Century. Most Dogras today are small farmers eking out an existence on the dry sandstone slopes of the Shiwalik range, the lowest and youngest mountains in the Himalaya. The countryside is rolling, broken here and there by sudden escarpments where visible layers of the earth's crust fold up at incongruous angles. At lower elevations, cattle and goats graze between large flowering cactuses, and spreading fig trees provide shade to village men wearing loose turbans and cotton pyjamas.

The city of Jammu is a big, sprawling entrêpot town situated at the interface of the plains and the hills. It is difficult to enjoy Jammu in the terrific heat of the summer, which is when most people pass through on their way to the cool mountains of Kashmir and Ladakh, but the old part of the city has a number of unusual attractions.

There are two major temple complexes: the **Ranbireshwar Temple,** with a towering 246-foot (75-meter) tower, is dedicated to Lord Shiva and is renowned for its large crystal *lingams* (the phallic symbols of Lord Shiva); and the **Raghunath Temple,** which is surrounded by one of the largest temple complexes in northern India. Its interiors covered with gold

Houseboats in winter, Srinagar.

leaf, the temple is dedicated to Rama, the eighth incarnation of Lord Vishnu and hero of the *Ramayana* epic.

The **Dogra Art Gallery** contains over 500 paintings in the delicate miniature style which was sponsored by the royal families of neighboring hill kingdoms like Basohli and Kangra. The rough stone-cut **Bahu Fort** on the opposite bank of the Tawi River is undoubtedly the oldest monument in Jammu while the **Amar Mahal Palace** claims first prize as the oddest. Designed for an eccentric maharaja by a French architect, the Amar Mahal resembles a medieval chateau, complete with turrets. Converted into a museum, the building now houses a library, portrait gallery and more beautiful miniature paintings.

A number of interesting excursions can be made from Jammu to small lakes and temples in the surrounding hills. The **Mansar Lake,** with its shrine to a local goddess, is a wonderful oasis in the dry hills. Bordering the southern edge of the sacred lake are a tourist bungalow and a small enclosure for deer.

By far the most important shrine to north India's Hindus, is the **cave temple of Vaishno Devi,** 37 miles (60 km) northwest of Jammu city. Thousands of devout Hindus make the pilgrimage to this temple every year, many of them fulfilling vows that they would cover the distance on foot or bicycle.

The Kashmir Valley

For the visitor, the first view of Kashmir is unforgettable whether it is seen from the air or the ground. In the verdant summer the valley is a sea of deepest green rice fields, intersected by rigid avenues of tall poplar, dotted with neatly planted orchards of apple, plum and almond trees. Interspersed are villages of tall, double-story farmhouses made of wood and brick. The Mughal emperors who came here in the summer months coined a word for the valley: "Paradise." And no one would dispute that, no one who has seen the valley in its correct perspective — shaded by magnificent chinars (the oriental plane trees), surrounded on all sides by a ring of mountains and its innumerable rushing streams, and blessed with the scent of wild briar roses.

This beautiful land has been settled since very early times. Excavations have unearthed circular residential pits and stone implements dating from 2,500 B.C. Much more recently, in 250 B.C. the Emperor Ashoka is credited with having introduced Buddhism into Kashmir. On gently terraced slopes above the village of **Harwan,** just north of Shalimar, the ruins of an ancient Buddhist settlement have been found. A marvelous circular patio of fitted and decorated terra-cotta tiles was found surrounding a building made of pebbles and boulders which may have housed a temple. Curiously, Buddhism faded out in the Kashmir Valley to be replaced by Hinduism, and later, largely, by Islam.

The glorious age of Hindu rule reached its apex under King Lalitaditya who lived in the beginning of the 8th Century A.D. His memory is immortalized in the remains of his massive temple of hewn stone at **Martand,** near the modern village of Mattan on the road to Pahalgam, and in the ruins of his extensive city of **Parihasapura,** three miles (five km) off the road to Baramullah, beyond the Gulmarg turnoff.

The Kashmiri valley is sprinkled with hundreds of other ancient temples, including the famous **Avantiswami Temple** in Awantipura on the Pahalgam tourist route.

Srinagar City

The lush greenery of the valley with its terraced rice fields, fruit orchards and swirling waterways spills into the city of **Srinagar** via the Dal Lake and great avenues of poplar and chinar trees. This fresh natural atmosphere combined with the commercial clamor of the old city's twisting medieval streets gives Srinagar a distinctive and vitalizing flavor.

The water world of the Dal and Nagin lakes in Srinagar can be explored in the almost decadent comfort of *shikaras,* hand-paddled water taxis. In the mountains, sturdy hill ponies are available for riding or as pack animals to carry trekking supplies on a number of beautiful trekking routes.

Srinagar is connected by air with Delhi, Chandigarh, Amritsar, Jammu, and Leh in Ladakh. The Srinagar-Leh flight is operated twice a week and is one of the most spectacular short plane-rides in the world. Buses and taxis ply between Jammu and Srinagar and between Srinagar and Leh, though the latter route closes between late October and early May because of snow.

Life on the Lake

Most visitors begin their tour of Jammu and Kashmir in Srinagar, with a stay on a legendary houseboat. Houseboats have been a part of Kashmir's aquatic culture for centuries and a number of lake people continue to live off the bounty of their watery world on the small prototype *doonga* boats of the past. It was only with the advent of the British that houseboats began to develop as a form of tourist lodging.

Houseboats of all sizes and costs range the banks of the busy Dal Lake and the quieter, cleaner Nagin. Itinerant water-borne merchants cruise the lakes and are often eccentric characters with names like Mr. Crocodile or Mr. Marvellous the flowerman, occasionally as devious as they are colorful.

From houseboats the world of the water people can be observed firsthand. A visit to the early morning vegetable market by *shikara* is well-worth the extra effort. Farmers emerge from the maze of floating gardens and canals with their little flat-bottom skiffs loaded with vegetables, to gather in an open waterway to trade and barter from boat to boat. The first light of early morning tinges the wild gardens of lotus flowers with a delicate pink light; kingfishers dart about, flashing their azure wings and day breaks over the lake.

Mughal Gardens

The famous Boulevard Road circles the Dal Lake and leads out towards the magnificent **Mughal Gardens.** The first two gardens — **Chashma Shahi** and **Pari Mahal** — are to the right of the Boulevard, set into the slope of the circling hills. Chashma Shahi, attributed to Shah Jehan, is named after a gushing mountain spring that feeds it, while Pari Mahal is set up within a series of enclosed terraces and buildings which were once a Sufi garden college. Both are small and command beautiful views over the lakes.

The two larger gardens, **Nishat** and **Shalimar,** are located much farther down the boulevard. They are built on a symmetrical plan of a central waterway with fountains dividing a series of gardened terraces. Nishat is the larger of the two and has an impressive plantation of huge chinar trees on the highest terrace, planted perhaps by the great Mughals

themselves. The Shalimar is the more famous garden because of the celebrated romance between its builder, Emperor Jahangir, and his queen, Nur Mahal. An audiovisual in English and Urdu retells this love story every evening. The center-piece on the upper terrace is the *baradari* or summer house of Jehangir, where the emperor and his bride reclined on warm summer afternoons — surrounded by the heady bouquets of a million roses, strained through a fine spray of cool spring water.

Nagin Lake and Hari Parbat

A beautiful circular drive through apple orchards and rice fields connects Shalimar with the Nagin Lake and the old city of Srinagar. Visitors take this drive to visit the shimmering white marble mosque of **Hazratbal,** which possesses a hair of Prophet Mohammed. On the lake margin a short distance from the mosque is the tomb of Sheikh Mohammed Abdullah, the "Lion of Kashmir." Sheikh Abdullah, who died in 1982, was the undisputed leader of the people of the valley of Kashsmir and its chief minister for the last years of his long political life.

Just beyond Hazratbal and separated from the Dal Lake by a causeway, is the **Nagin Lake.** Much cleaner than the Dal, the Nagin is popular with tourists searching for a quiet vacation. Four swimming boats anchored in the deepest part of the lake offer facilities for swimming, water skiing and surf-board riding. (Swimming is not recommended from similar boats in the more polluted Dal Lake.)

Behind the Nagin Lake looms the **Hari Parbat** fortress, atop a small hill. The walls that surround the base of this 19th-Century fort were built 300 years earlier by the Mughal Emperor Akbar. Across the combined lakes from Hari Parbat, atop the Takht-e-Suleiman (throne of Solomon) hill is the temple of **Sankaracharya** which dominates the surrounding landscape. A motor road leads up the hill to this ancient Shiva temple. From the boulevard there are several nice foot trails to the top. The view from the fort or the temple is superb — the lakes and their houseboats, waterways and gardens stretch out to the north, while the old city and its seven original bridges spanning the serpentine Jhelum River stretch out to the south.

Kashmir Mosques

Foremost among the mosques in the valley is the **Jami Masjid,** a massive congregational mosque. Originally built in 1402, the mosque has been completely reconstructed twice after severe fires destroyed it. The mosque is laid out on a square, symmetrical plan, and is remarkable for its colonnades of lofty deodar (cedar) columns.

The wonderful **Mosque of Shah Hamadan** is built on the banks of the muddy Jhelum River. Made entirely of wood, the mosque is named after a great saint who is credited with the peaceful conversion of millions of Hindus to Islam during the 14th Century. Non-believers are not allowed into the mosque but may look through the door at its intricately painted papier-maché ceiling and walls. As with many mosques in Kashmir, a screened verandah running around it is used by women for their prayers, as they cannot enter the central hall.

Farther upstream, near the Zero Bridge is the **Bund,** a long promenade that runs along the river lined with a number of buildings dating from the turn of the century. This was the fashionable district for visitors in the days of the British Empire. The General Post Office, the Srinagar Club, the Residency building, which now houses the Government Arts Emporium, and some of the old shops like Suffering Moses's House of Handicrafts (run by the charming and eccentric Suffering Moses himself), are located along the Bund.

Famed Craftsmen

Kashmir boasts an unrivalled tradition of craftsmanship which flourishes to this day in the villages and back alleys of the valley. Drives through the countryside reveal hundreds of carpet looms hidden in crumbling village homes, the hand knotted Persian rugs being washed amidst clucking chickens on open courtyards. Patient and delicate wool embroidery on shawls is often the work of village men stitching away under the apple boughs. The finest quality shawls are made of pashmina wool from small Ladakhi goats, and can cost thousands of rupees. The royal shawl (shahtoosh) can be passed through a ring. A more traditional village craft is the pounded felt rug or namda, which is often decorated with appliqué

Gulmarg, Kashmir.

work in simple designs.

Finely painted papier-maché boxes, ashtrays, writing sets and other articles have long been a specialty of Srinagar's artisans — the skills being passed from father to son over the generations.

Woodcarving, and in particular, the making of beautiful walnut furniture, is another craft in which the Kashmiris excel. The walnut and its incredible grain makes each piece a unique work of art.

Kashmir's Islamic culture is a lively one, with something going on all of the time. Influenced by their Hindu forefathers, the Kashmiris have modified their customs and observances in noticeable ways. The worship of wayside shrines dedicated to *rishis* (holy men) can be observed throughout the valley. Important days of the Muslim calendar are celebrated with great festivity, and there is considerable variation in the observance of the month-long, sunrise to sunset fasts of Ramadan. Lively religious and folk music enjoys widespread popularity. During the wedding season, women link their arms and sing while the groom departs for the bride's home. *Shikara* drivers croon as they paddle along, and village women sing when they are trans-

planting rice. One of the most easily appreciated cultural forms is the distinctive Kashmiri cuisine, popularly served as part of a feast called a *wazwan*. Consisting of up to 36 different meat preparations eaten with rice, the wonders of the *waza* chef are incredible.

Hill Resorts

Pahalgam, Gulmarg and Sonamarg, the three most popular hill resorts in Kashmir, each offers a different experience of wild alpine beauty. **Pahalgam,** at the confluence of two wooded valleys at 6,890 feet (2,100 meters), lies 60 miles (90 km) northeast of Srinagar. The actual town is little more than a single street running along the bank of the Liddar River, fronted by provision stores and a variety of hotels and guesthouses. Dotted around the town are clusters of government-owned tourist huts, tented camps, and private lodges nestled amongst stands of blue pine and fir.

Pahalgam is very popular with Indian tourists as the staging point for the famous pilgrimage to the sacred ice *lingam* in the **Amarnath Cave,** four days walk to the east. A growing number of

Left, Ladakhi woman; right, Kashmiri shopkeeper with hookah.

foreign tourists go to Pahalgam to relax in surroundings that compare favorably with the Swiss alps, to play golf on the rough little nine-hole course, or to start off on a number of treks into the high altitude meadows beyond. Tents and pack ponies can be hired in Pahalgam for treks to the 11,800-foot (3,600-meter) **Kolahoi glacier,** which can be done in three days, or for the arduous 10-day walk into **Ladakh,** across the main Himalayan range.

In the summer, trekking routes and camping sites may be shared with the nomadic Bakkarval shepherds who bring herds of sheep, goats and buffaloes to graze on high pastures. They are tall handsome people, the men bearded and turbaned, the women with their hair plaited into hundreds of tiny braids, their children tied on the backs of pack ponies along with pots, pans and puppies.

Gulmarg with its famous 18-hole golf course attracts sportsmen in the summer just as its ski runs make it India's premier skiing center in the winter. The small market and a number of lodges and hotels are scattered around a broad bowl of sloping meadows at 8,860 feet (2,700 meters). Several short trekking routes and numerous day walks can be taken from Gulmarg which is only 32 miles (52 km) from Srinagar, to the southwest. Both Pahalgam and Gulmarg have a number of trout-stocked streams where fly fishing is allowed on the basis of a permit issued in Srinagar.

Sonamarg is the smallest of the hill resorts. It is located on the road to Ladakh and has grown in recent years to accommodate travellers breakfasting on their way to the Zoji La pass. At an altitude of 8,860 feet (2,700 meters), Sonamarg is 52 miles (84 km) from Srinagar. It has a Government tourist bungalow and is the staging area for the popular **Gangabal Lake** trek. Many local day visitors ride ponies to the nearby Thajiwas meadow.

Ladakh

Crossing the 11,480-foot (3,500-meter) Zoji La pass into Ladakh is like stepping into another planet. From the verdant, forested hillsides above Sonamarg, through the hair-raising twists and turns of the Zoji La climb, still carpeted with wild flowers, one passes into an immense landscape of jagged barren rock. It is as if the Himalaya was suddenly stripped of all its flesh, leaving a rare old sk\ of majestic barren bones. The m\ Himalayan range forces its rain sha\ on the lands to the north, isolating them from the influences of the south. This barrier, effective from the cultural as well as the geographical perspective, has ensured that the various people of Ladakh — the animist Dards, the Shia Baltis, and the Buddhist Ladakhis — have retained their traditions unchanged over the centuries.

In Dras, which is the first major town in this western side of Ladakh, the houses are single storied mud-brick structures. In front of them women of the Shia Muslim Balti population, dressed in heavy black woolen robes and red scarves, work in golden fields of buckwheat. Old, gnarled Bati men, with creased faces that look like topographical maps, pass, driving donkeys loaded with dung and dried thistle. The Baltis have Central Asian features. The Dards, who also inhabit Dras and a number of secluded villages to the northeast are distinctly Caucasian in their features. This extraordinary people speak a language quite unrelated to their neighbors in either direction. Dards are neither Muslim nor Buddhist, but seem to observe festivals and practices of either group in addition to their own customs.

District headquarters **Kargil,** at 8,700 feet (2,650 meters), is one of the lowest towns in Ladakh. It was once a trading town on the route between Central Asia and the Indian plains. Now buses and trucks crowd its one main street, their occupants packing into the little hotels and restaurants which have sprung up to cater to the town's new position as a night halt on the Leh road. Another road leads south from Kargil past the towering peaks of **Nun,** 23,300 feet (7,100 meters), and **Kun,** 23,200 feet (7,070 meters), to Padum, the capital of Zanskar. This road is negotiable by truck or jeep if the Pensi La pass is open. Some of Ladakh's finest and most rugged trekking routes branch off from this road to lead into the rock-hewn wilderness. Trekkers in Ladakh need to be better equipped and better organized than on the Kashmir side, because the environment is more extreme, and human habitations are sparse.

Monasteries and Monks

Wherever there is a good water supply in Ladakh, there is usually a small cluster of mud-brick homes; earth colored if their owners are Muslims and whitewashed if they are Buddhist dwellings. Carefully tended willows and poplars give each little oasis a brilliant dash of color in a landscape dominated by the brown earth and the blue sky.

As one begins to pass from predominantly Muslim to Buddhist villages, other landmarks appear, replacing the small tin-covered domes of the Muslim mosques. Multistoried monasteries in all shapes and sizes, fluttering with prayer flags, dot the semi-desert countryside. *Chortens,* or whitewashed stupas, often line the road, as do long walls covered with *mani* (prayer) stones, carved with Buddhist prayers. Dressing attire changes too; the bright maroon and saffron robes of monks and nuns mingle with the peculiar jaunty Ladakhi cap and the turquoise and coral jewelry of the women.

In the town of **Mulbekh,** a giant statue of the Maitreya, the Buddha to come, looks over the passing tourist buses from a rock pinnacle on which it was carved in ancient times. Over the 13,430-foot (4,094-meter) **Fatu La pass,** the road reaches the incredible **Monastery of Lamayuru,** looming like a Hollywood movie backdrop of Shangri La. Lamayuru is venerated as one of the oldest monasteries in Ladakh as it houses a cave where one of Tibet's great teachers, Naropa, is said to have meditated for several years in the 10th Century. Like all monasteries in Ladakh, the complex includes a number of different buildings, each with shrines to different gods and incarnations of the Buddha.

A form of Tibetan Mahayana Buddhism is practiced in Ladakh in which the pantheon incorporates a number of pre-Buddhist deities. In Ladakh, monasteries are traditional centers of religious as well as cultural activity. They are also the largest landowners and have, over the centuries, concentrated much of the wealth of the land in their coffers. Traditionally dependent on donations, the monasteries have switched to charging visitors admission fees, ranging from Rs. 5 to 15 (US 50c to $1.50).

Leh Town

After Lamayuru the road finally joins the Indus River at Khaltsi and more or less follows this famous waterway to the wide valley of **Leh.**

The drive from Srinagar to Leh by bus or taxi takes two gruelling days, but it is an unforgettable experience. In marked contrast, the flight takes only 25 minutes. On a clear day, the route goes right over the peaks of Nun and Kun, while stretching across the horizon to the north is the mighty Karakoram range, which at 28,250 feet (8,611 meters), is the second highest mountain in the world. The view is so breathtaking that the flight seems to last only a few minutes.

Leh is a rapidly growing town, spreading in all directions from its original position beneath the long abandoned **Namgyal Palace.** While the town has come a long way from the days when polo was played on its main street, Leh still retains a pleasant, traditional quality. Maybe it is the lovely vegetable sellers, dressed in their coral necklaces and turquoise-encrusted headgear and seated comfortably behind baskets of huge vegetables. Leh has over 80 registered hotels and guesthouses (many of which may contain only a couple of rooms in a family home), that vary in price and services. Newcomers are advised to find some lodging and take it easy for the first day. A stroll through the main street of the town is more than enough exercise to begin with; this minimizes problems related to exertion at high altitude and gives one time to acclimatize. After this prescribed day of rest, the monastery tours may begin.

Shey, Thikse and Hemis

Among the most visited monasteries are Shey, Thikse and Hemis, all spread along the Indus River. These can be visited in a half-day tour, but midday is not a good time to visit monasteries as very little goes on at that time. It's better to go in the early morning and late evening, when the monks say their prayers, and when the mystical chanting, the ringing of bells, the clashing of cymbals, and the blowing of long brass horns lend magic to the visit.

Shey is the oldest of these three monasteries and is not in regular use, so it is open only until nine in the morning. The monastery contains a two-story high statue of the Buddha seated in meditation. Above and below are the crumbling walls of the old summer capital of Ladakh.

Thikse is a very large monastery built

on a triangular spur of a mountain 11 miles (17 km) from Leh. A series of outbuildings work up the side of this hill culminating in the main red-colored monastery building at the top. Thikse is especially noteworthy for its new wing which houses a gigantic seated statue of the Maitreya. As in other monasteries, Thikse's main prayer hall houses hundreds of rectangular prayer books — loose sheets of printed prayers stacked between wooden covers and bound in silk cloth. Religious *thanka* paintings hang from the rafters and giant urns containing melted yak butter and water line the altars.

Hemis is the richest of the monasteries but the least hospitable. Unfortunately, some pilferages have occurred with the advent of tourism and many precious statues and relics which were once displayed openly have been hidden away. Hemis is famous for its great three-day festival which usually takes place in June.

There are dozens of other large and well endowed monasteries in Ladakh. Many can be approached in the local jeep taxis from Leh. Among these, **Alchi** on the Indus, 1½ hours drive from Leh, is the oldest and contains the most remarkable wall paintings.

A Happy People

The Ladakhi Buddhists are a happy people and their native greeting, *juley,* is spontaneous and friendly. They enjoy dancing, archery, polo, and their strong barley beer, known as *chang*. Most Ladakhis are farmers, and they can be seen plowing their small dry plots with their hardy *dzos,* cattle crossbred from yaks and hill cows. People living in remote villages subsist on a simple staple diet of roasted barley or buckwheat flour, called *tsampa,* and green salt tea mixed with butter. A strong and vibrant culture survives in the harsh and imposing landscape of Ladakh, and unusual desert flowers bloom amongst barren rock.

The state of Jammu and Kashmir is a wide open place full of untapped mountain torrents, densely wooded mountain slopes and rugged moonscapes. Its great variety of people and the depth of its varied history and culture reflect the natural bounty of the Himalaya mountains which cradle the state in their nurturing folds.

Monastery, Ladakh.

PUNJAB AND HARYANA

It is a sunburnt land, flat as a pancake, sloping imperceptibly down from the Himalayan foothills towards the deserts of Rajasthan on the one side and the extensive plains of Hindustan on the other. At one time Punjab extended northwestward up to the River Indus and beyond. The entire terrain was known to the Greeks as Pentopotamia because of the five rivers that ran through it. The Persians named it *Panj* (five) *aab* (waters) – a name which has stuck. In 1947 when India was partitioned, the larger half of Punjab went to Pakistan. Nevertheless, both Pakistan and India retained the name "Punjab" since the Punjabi language is spoken on both sides of the border. In 1966 the Indian smaller half was further divided into three: Punjab, Haryana and Himachal Pradesh.

The people of Punjab (both Indian and Pakistani) and Haryana are of the same racial stock. The peasantry are largely Jatt (to rhyme with gut) or, in Haryana, Jaat (to rhyme with part). Tall, brawny and rugged, they are renowned for their pugnacity and fierce attachment to the soil. Townsmen, though not so well-built, are equally go-ahead as traders and entrepreneurs. While Pakistan Punjabis are Muslims, Indian Punjabis are Sikhs or Hindus. Haryana is predominantly Hindu and its language, Haryanvi is a dialect of Hindi.

The climate of both Punjab and Haryana ranges from bracing cold in winter to scorching heat in summer; they also have the winter and summer monsoons. These seasonal changes consequently bring about a diversity of landscape at large. The spring comes with Basant Panchmi, a festival in early February when "all is seemly; the woodlands are in flower and loud with humming of bumble bees" (Guru Nanak). The countryside becomes an ocean of mustard yellow broken by green squares of sugarcane with its fluffy pampas plumes. As the mustard is harvested, wheat and barley take its place. Springtime sounds that pervade the Punjab and Haryana countryside are brown partridges calling to each other and the monotonous *kooh kooh* of flourmills.

Below, Golden Temple, Amritsar; right, the temple interior.

Birds and Blossoms

The short spring gives way to a long summer. Trees shed their leaves and come to life again with blossoms and new foliage. Silk cotton, coral, flame of the forest and the flamboyant are a scarlet red; laburnum which flowers in late May is like burnished gold. The partridges are silent; instead the incessant screaming of koels in mango groves and the metallic call of barbets are heard. By the time wheat is harvested the summer is full on. In the words of Guru Nanak (1469–1539 A.D.), founder of the Sikh faith, "the sun scorches, the earth burns like an oven. Waters give up their vapours, yet it burns and scorches relentlessly." The parched earth becomes a vast stretch of mud-colored plain with dust devils spiralling like dancing dervishes across the wastes. Fierce dust-laden winds sweep across. The blazing inferno lasts from April to the end of June. By mid-July, the summer monsoon comes and within a few days the heavy downpour turns the land into a vast swamp. Life begins anew with new leaves on trees and green grass everywhere.

By the time the monsoon is over, it is cool again. A new crop of rice, maize, millet and pulses is sown. Peasants adorn themselves in brightly colored starched turbans, embroidered waistcoats, and dance the *bhangra* to the beat of drums. Through October to the festival of lamps (Diwali), usually in November, there is a succession of fairs and festivals. Then once more it is wintertime, when nights are cold, the days full of blue skies and bright sunshine. And all is seemly once again.

There are several Mughal monuments in Haryana of which the most popular is **Pinjore gardens** at the base of the Shiwalik hills on the road to Simla. Inside the Mughal battlements is a beautifully laid out garden with fountains and cascades running below open balconies. It has for good reason become a favorite spot for lovers and honeymooners.

The state government has exploited its scenic spots to their best advantage. Close to Delhi is **Suraj Kund**, an 8th-Century Hindu sun temple, and beyond it the **Badkhal Lake** with a resthouse overlooking its stretch of water. A few miles southwards is **Sultanpur bird sanctuary**, and beyond it the hot spring at **Sohna**.

Punjab and Haryana were the cradles of Indian civilization. Archeologists have

found implements made of quartzite fashioned over 300,000 years ago. Agricultural tools made of copper and bronze prove the existence of rural communities around the 25th Century B.C. Later excavations have unearthed whole cities built around that period with market-places, marble baths and drainage systems and intricately carved seals with hieroglyphics. The Indus valley civilization, as it came to be known, was among the oldest in the world. Relics of these olden times continue to be unearthed in different parts of both states.

Both Punjab and Haryana have more history than historical monuments, more facilities for tourists than places of touristic interest. It is through these two states that invaders from the northwest — Greeks, Turks, Mongols, Persians and Afghans — entered India, and where many battles which decided the fate of India were fought. Their sites are still marked with commemorative stones and mausoleums of kings and commanders who fell in action. The most famous of these are at Panipat and Karnal in Haryana. There are innumerable forts, too many to be named, scattered all over the countryside of the two states.

As if to compensate for the paucity of truly great historical monuments, both states have developed wildlife sanctuaries along lakes, swamps and rivers with attractive tourist bungalows from where visitors can see a wide variety of wild fowl and herds of deer. Along all major highways are chains of milk-bars and cafes named after birds of the region: Blue Jay, Dabchick, Hoopoe, Magpie, Myna, Parakeet, etc.

Le Corbusier's City

There are many things that Punjab and Haryana have in common; the most important of these is a common capital, **Chandigarh.** Since both states have laid claims to the city, it is administered by the Central Government as a Union Territory till a final decision regarding its future is made. However, in the same city reside governors of the two states; in the same office buildings but on different floors are their separate secretariats and their respective High Courts. For the visitor, more interesting than the wrangle over its future is the city itself, which is beautifully located below the Shiwalik range of hills. Two hill torrents were canalized to form a large lake with a most attractive

boulevard, along which the citizens take the morning and evening air and watch waterfowl which have made **Sukhna Lake** a halting place on their migrations from Central Asia to India and vice versa.

The layout of the city was designed by the famous French architect, Le Corbusier assisted by his cousin, Jeanneret, and an English man-and-wife team, Maxwell Fry and Jane Drew. Corbusier himself designed most of its important public buildings, including the Secretariat, the Legislative Assembly and the High Court. Many of these buildings are on "stilts," an architectural style copied by many private institutions and homes.

Chandigarh is a very green city with a large variety of flowering trees specially chosen for their beauty by Dr. M. S. Randhawa, a renowned civil servant and botanist. It also has an extensive Rose Garden named after the first Muslim President of India, Dr. Zakir Husain. There is also a "park" with statuary made out of broken pieces of cups and saucers of which the Chandigarhians are very proud.

Punjab

Amritsar is Punjab's largest city and has Punjab's chief tourist attraction — its **Golden Temple,** the holiest of holy Sikh shrines. As Indian cities go, Amritsar is not very old; it was founded a little over 400 years ago by Guru Ram Das, the fourth of the 10 Sikh Gurus. His son and successor, the fifth guru, Arjun, raised a temple in the midst of a pool, sanctified its waters and installed the Sikhs' holy scripture, the *Granth Sahib,* in its inner sanctum. The city takes its name from the sacred pool — *amrit* (nectar) *sar* (pool). In 1803, the Sikh ruler, Maharaja Ranjit Singh (1780–1839 A.D.) rebuilt the temple in marble and gold (its domes took 400 kg of gold leaf to be covered). Ever since, it has been known as the Golden Temple. The Sikhs usually refer to it as the *Harimandir* (the temple of God) or *Darbar Sahib* (the court of the Lord). It is well worthwhile to spend an hour or two in the temple complex (be sure to have your head covered and feet bare), listening to the hymn-singing which goes on non-stop from the early hours of the morning till late into the night and watching the thousands of pilgrims at worship.

The Golden Temple complex has a number of shrines of historical importance, notably the **Akal Takht** (the throne of the timeless God) facing the Golden Temple where arms of the warrior gurus, their dresses and emblems can be seen, and the eight-storied **Baba-Atal** tower.

Besides the Golden Temple, there is its Hindu counterpart, the **Durgiana Temple**, built in recent times; and **Jallianwala Bagh** where, on 13 April 1919, General Dyer fired on an unarmed crowd and killed over 300 people. The garden has a monument commemorating the event and has become a place of pilgrimage.

There are many other Sikh temples in Punjab which are both historic and beautiful. On the foothills of the Himalaya is **Anandpur** where in 1699 A.D. the last of the Sikh gurus, Gobind Singh, baptized the first five Sikhs into the militant fraternity he called the *Khalsa* or the pure. Here are several temples as well as a fortress, Kesgarh. Every spring at the Holi festival (Sikhs celebrate it a day later as *hola mohalla*) hundreds of thousands of Sikhs, notably the Nihangs, descendants of two orders of warriors, gather and indulge in displays of mock combat on horseback and on foot.

An equally large complex of temples, palaces and forts is to be seen at **Sirhind** near Patiala. Besides these there are also remains of a Mughal and pre-Mughal city and the mausoleum of a famous divine, Hazrat Mujaddad-ud-din Altaf Sheikh Ahmed (d.1624 A.D.), popularly known as Sirhindi. Muslims from all over the world come to Sirhind to pay homage

Haryana

This state could rightly claim to be the birthplace of the most sacred religious scripture of Hinduism. At Kurukshetra (not far from Panipat) was fought the famous battle between two Aryan tribes, the Kurus and the Pandavas. On the eve of the battle, Sri Krishna, a reincarnation of God Vishnu, persuaded Arjuna, the very reluctant commander of the Pandava army, to wage the battle for righteousness. This sermon known as the *Bhagavad Gita* emphasizes the moral principle of doing one's duty without consideration of reward, victory or defeat and is regarded as the essence of the teachings of the *Vedas* and the *Upanishads*. Kurukshetra is full of temples and tanks where pilgrims come to bathe on auspicious days.

Le Corbusier's Chandigarh.

RAJASTHAN, DESERT STATE

Conjuring up images of a desert state, it is a place no one would think of palaces shimmering on idyllic lakes; or imagine, in its blazing heat, temples and forts of stunning artistry carved from stone that is honey or rose, marble-white or sandstone-red; nor would anyone fill their mind with painted streets where pageantry and color walk out of life-size frescos, producing crowds of brightly turbaned men with proud moustaches and women whose beauty is lethal, though, alas, veiled. But this is exactly what the desert state of Rajasthan is. The past flavor lingers on, and visitors can still ride painted and caparisoned elephants that recall the regalia of the royal courts or live in fantasy palace hotels built by descendants of the sun and the moon.

More than a half of Rajasthan is desert or semi-arid, a continuation of the sand belt that girdles the world. This desert belt is separated from the Indian peninsula by the Aravalli Ranges, geologically the oldest mountains in India.

Both the Thar Desert and the Aravalli Ranges lend their distinct personalities to the landscape of Rajasthan. It is interesting that this picture of a rocky, rugged skyline over the soft-staired dunes where camels plod, is only one of the two clichés which represent Rajasthan. The other, diametrically opposed, is a refreshing contrast: placid blue lakes with island palaces, gardens with pillared pavilions and kiosks — always with a few dancing peacocks.

The First Dwellers

Not many places in the world can boast an ancestry dating beyond 2500 B.C. It has now been proven that the very ancient civilization of the Indus Valley had its precursors in north Rajasthan. It seems that the local Bhil and Mina tribes inhabited this area. Around 1400 B.C. the Aryans wheeled their fast equestrian chariots into Rajasthan, shooting strong arrows from taut bows. The local people were overawed and dispersed eastwards and south. The Aryans had come to stay and father the future generations of Rajasthan.

It is not possible to trace back the mingling of blood in the prehistory of the 2nd millennium B.C. with any precision, but history has continued unabated in this land which first featured in the active campaign to spread the message of Buddhism (around the 2nd and 3rd centuries B.C.). The rest is a story of blood and battle, battle and blood. Afghans, Turks, Persians, Mughals followed, mixing their blood, first in war then in peace. Such a past is what gave a martial ancestry to the Rajputs. From the reign of Harsha (7th Century A.D.) to the time when the Delhi Sultanate was founded by the Muslims (1206 A.D.), Rajasthan was fragmented in competing kingdoms. Perhaps it was during this period that, by their wealth and power, the Rajputs, "sons of rajas," were able to persuade the Brahmin priests to provide them with genealogies that invented links with the sun, the moon, the fire god.

The mixed bunch of warriors who came to call themselves Rajputs were — even without the support of their mythology — born fighters. They fitted the Aryan martial Kshatriya caste slot only too naturally. In time, they came to be divided into 36 royal clans.

After the 14th Century, prosperity declined in the area. The Mughals made North India their home in the 16th Century. Winning over Rajasthan was the achievement of Akbar, the Great Mughal, who mixed the right dose of military might with the soft touch of religious tolerance. His trump card was matrimonial alliances with the Hindu Rajputs which turned them from a dangerous enemy into a faithful ally. Jaipur and Jodhpur provided many princesses to the Mughals. By the 17th Century, the Mughal emperors had posted an agent or writer *(nawis)* to the major Rajput courts who informed them of any princely decisions or events affecting imperial interests. When the Mughals weakened, the Rajputs were quick to reassert their sovereignty. In 1757 the British captured Bengal in the east but Rajasthan resisted the English and was among the last to yield. But by the beginning of the 19th Century, all the Maharajas, great and small, surrendered most of their powers to the British, retaining only a limited internal administrative autonomy under the "paramount" power.

Rajputana was Rajasthan's old name, land of the Rajputs, brave and proud. The Maharana of Mewar (Udaipur) was the acknowledged head of their 36 clans.

Preceding pages, Pushkar, Rajasthan; left, Rajasthani beauty.

When India became independent, 23 princely states were consolidated to form the State of Rajasthan, "abode of rajas."

Rajasthan is usually recommended as a must even on a short trip to India. Two days are sufficient to get a feel of Jaipur (which is only 140 miles/230 km from the Taj Mahal), but two weeks in Rajasthan can provide a most memorable holiday.

Jaipur

The "pink city" of Jaipur (the city of *jai* or victory), the capital of Rajasthan, was built in 1728 by Maharaja Sawai Jai Singh II. This royal house had ruled from Amber, seven miles (11 km) away, since the early 10th Century. Jaipur was not always pink. The original city was light gray, edged with white borders and motifs. In honor of the visit in 1883 of Prince Albert, consort to Queen Victoria, it was ordered to be painted the traditional color of welcome, which has been retained since.

The city was designed by Vidyadhar Chakravarty, a young Bengali architect, who succeeded in making a marvelous synthesis of many influences — Hindu, Jain, Mughal (with Persian overtones),

besides his own ideas from eastern India. Jaipur's nine rectangular sectors symbolize the nine divisions of the universe.

The **City Palace,** a part of which remains the residence of the Jaipur family, is definitely worth a visit. Several gateways lead from the crowded streets into the palace, but the Museum entrance is recommended, through the courts of justice to the **Jantar Mantar,** the observatory of Maharaja Jai Singh II. The construction and precision of the observatory were a unique achievement for the year 1716. Jai Singh's Delhi observatory had preceded this and three others followed: in Mathura, Ujjain and Varanasi, when the maharaja travelled over north India as the Governor of Agra.

The **City Palace Museum,** named after Raja Man Singh, is a treat, no matter what the interests of the visitor are — textiles, arms, carpets, paintings, manuscripts. It houses two large urns, possibly the largest silver vessels in India, which were used by Maharaja Madho Singh to carry a six-month supply of holy Ganga water to the coronation of King Edward VII in London.

One of the best known sights in Jaipur is the **Hawa Mahal** or Palace of Winds,

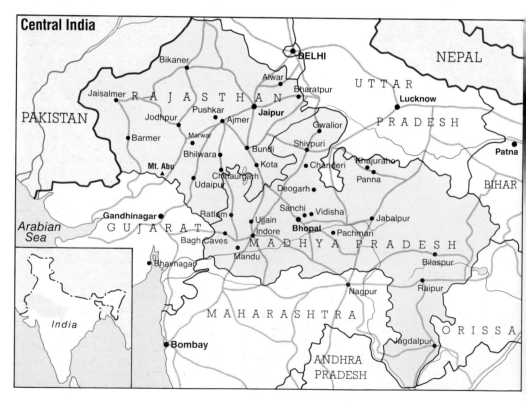

which is, in fact, no palace, but an extraordinary facade of 953 airy windows used by the ladies of the palace to watch the outside world — without being watched.

Forts on Rugged Hills

On the rugged hills that surround Jaipur stand wondrous forts: Amber, Jaigarh, Nahargarh, each one imposing in its own right. **Amber** was once the capital of the Mina tribes believed to be the original inhabitants of this area. Now, painted elephants take visitors up the hill to admire the massive gateways, courts, stairways and pillared pavilions and palaces, that recall the glory and wealth of Amber's association with the Mughals. Raja Man Singh was the Commander-in-Chief of Akbar's army and Mirza Raja Jai Singh was a powerful ally of Jahangir. Of special interest is the **Sheesh Mahal,** the palace of mirrors, where the walls are inlaid with exquisite mirrored motifs that dance to the flame of even a single candle.

Jaigarh Fort was recently opened to the public after being scaled for seven years, following a rumor that an enormous treasure in gold was buried in vaults under deep reservoirs. The vast purity of its austere spaces is admirable. The highlight of the fort is the Jaya Vana — the largest antique cannon in India.

Nahargarh Fort provides a marvelous view of Jaipur city and, en route, of the **Jal Mahal,** the lake palace of Jaipur. The cenotaphs of the Jaipur maharajas at Amber and Gaitor as well as the *chhatris* (memorials) of the maharanis are well-worth a visit.

Five miles (eight km) down the Jaipur–Agra road is the charming garden of the Sisodia queen, and a mile (two km) further are the holy springs of **Galta,** with temples that have a large daily attendance. The **Hanuman Temple,** in particular, is worth a visit on Tuesdays.

Northwest to Alwar

Five major roads lead out of Jaipur. National Highway No. 8 leads north to Delhi. One can branch off right, about 35 miles (60 km) from Jaipur, turning northwest to **Alwar,** picturesque and dotted with historical sites. At **Bairath** or **Viratnagar** are ancient Buddhist rock edicts of Emperor Ashoka, a Buddhist *chaitya* (temple) dating back to the 3rd Century B.C., and a painted garden pavilion built around 1600 A.D.

Founded in 1771, Alwar is one of the most recent of the princely states of Rajasthan. Beginning as distant cousins of Jaipur, they maneuvered their way through the chaos of the 18th Century, changing sides for quick gains, till the British finally acknowledged and rewarded them for their help against the Marathas. But the affairs of Alwar remained troubled, with only a few scattered years of peace, which, however, must have been very prolific, for Alwar has some very fine palaces, built by milking the people dry and using one half of the state exchequer — an extremely high proportion even by feudal standards — for the purpose.

Twenty three miles (37 km) from Alwar is the **Sariska Palace,** once a hunting lodge, now a private hotel set on the outskirts of a wildlife sanctuary where tiger, panther, blue bull, wild boar and deer roam the scrubby thicket and bush. Closer by, five miles (eight km) from Alwar, the charming **Siliserh Palace** commands a wonderful view of a lake full of water fowl. This is a Rajasthan state hotel of moderate comfort.

The **Alwar Museum,** housed in the

Hawa Mahal, Palace of the Winds, Jaipur.

City Palace, has a fine collection of miniature paintings, manuscripts, arms and the famous solid-silver dining table that aroused the curiosity of royal visitors. Adjacent to the museum is a remarkable reservoir with delicate temples, kiosks and symmetrical stairs considered masterpieces of Indo-Islamic architecture.

Shekhavati and Churu

The second northern road (National Highway No. 11) leads to the painted towns of Shekhavati and Churu and further to Bikaner.

En route, the first recommended stop 20 miles (31 km) from Jaipur is **Samod,** a palace hotel set among steep hills. It doubled for Afghanistan in the shooting for *The Far Pavilions.* Its durbar hall is painted with frescos, among the most delicate in Rajasthan. One can stop at this charming spot or drive on through Sikar to Nawalgarh — the first stop in Shekhavati.

Shekhavati was once subordinate to Jaipur. In 1471, Rao Shekhav asserted his independence, giving Shekhavati his name. His successors maintained their independence for nearly 300 years. Shekhavati was fortunately located on the caravan route from the Gujarat ports and from Central India to Delhi. Trade in opium, cotton and spices flourished. The wealthy merchants built palatial *havelis* or mansions for themselves, cenotaphs in memory of their ancestors, and water reservoirs, temples and caravanserais for the welfare of the people. Most of these buildings are covered with frescos painted between 1760 and 1920. The *havelis* were fortified houses which walled in the secluded life of the women who spent most of their days in the *zenana* (ladies' apartments) built around an inner courtyard. The men conducted their business sitting on the white cotton mattresses of their sitting rooms.

Nawalgarh's streets are lined with the richly painted facades of *havelis* and the market bustles with activity. A garden palace on the outskirts provides a cool stopover. From Nawalgarh the road leads on to **Dundlod** and **Mandawa,** the rugged forts of which are now well-stocked hotels of a rare medieval charm.

Fatehpur too offers a wealth of painted *havelis.* A road to Bikaner starts from there, but one can make a detour to roam in the fascinating towns of **Ram-garh** and **Churu,** where the architecture and the art of the region are at their best, before linking up again with the Bikaner road.

Bikaner

Bikaner was founded in 1488, 29 years after Jodhpur. A younger but more intelligent son, Rao Bika, was given an army and asked to seek his own fortune to avoid a war of succession. Thus Bikaner was founded in the heart of the wilderness called Jangaldesh. Perhaps the very bareness of the landscape was the spur to making it up with beauty created by the human hand. The red sandstone carvings at the **Lalbagh Palace** and those in marble are among the finest in delicacy and profusion; the fortress built in the 15th Century contains palaces and temples of great refinement; Bikaner's art of miniature painting is rated high; the **Hall of Audience** has breathtaking frescos, gilded stucco moldings, floral patterns, and carpets of incredibly delicate count.

Outside, the countryside is still rugged, dotted here and there with intricately carved Jain temples of the 16th Century. The men of Bikaner are wiry and handsome and the Bikaner Camel Corps is still a showpiece of the Indian Army's display parade in Delhi on Republic Day.

On the outskirts of Bikaner, the camel farm makes an interesting visit, particularly at sunset when herds of camels return from the dunes.

The **temple of Karni Mata** at Deshnoke (17 miles/28 km from Bikaner) is inhabited by hordes of rats which are revered. They roam around the temple and into its inner shrine with total freedom. It is a unique sight for those who can overcome the queasiness that the sight initially evokes.

Devi Kund (five miles/eight km from Bikaner) is where the cenotaphs of the rulers of Bikaner were built and **Gajner** (20 miles/31 km) has beautiful palaces set around a lake.

Sixty miles (100 km) from Jaipur, on the road to Ajmer, is **Kishangarh,** an interesting city of palaces and lakes. The **City Palace,** the **Phool Mahal** and the **Kalyan Raiji Temple** are beautifully located by the side of a lake. From there one can walk the narrow streets of the old walled city. The largest collection of paintings of the renowned Kishangarh School is at the

Majhela Palace and can be seen there by prior appointment.

Kishangarh is a convenient starting point for visits to the marble cenotaph at **Karkeri,** the **Krishna Temple** of the Nimbarkachari sect at Salemabad, and the fort and palace of **Rupangarh.** A little further away, the salt lake of **Sambhar** is a unique sight along with the marble quarries at **Makrana** from where the marble to build the Taj Mahal was drawn. It continues to be exploited today. Nearby, **Kuchaman** has one of the most beautiful lived-in fortresses of Rajasthan.

Ajmer

About 80 miles (135 km) southwest of Jaipur lies **Ajmer,** the most sacred of all Muslim places of pilgrimage in India. Supposedly founded by Aijpal in 1100 A.D., Ajmer later became a twin Chauhan capital with Delhi. In 1193, its Muslim history began, when Prithviraj Chauhan lost Ajmer to Sultan Mohammad of Ghori. The Persian saint, Khwaja Moinuddin Chisti, who had come with Ghori, settled here where he preached and was later buried.

Palace, Jaipur.

When Akbar captured Ajmer in 1556 he made it his military headquarters and visited the tomb on foot to pray for a son. The boon was granted and the fame of Ajmer was enhanced manifold. Large cauldrons were presented by Akbar that are till today filled with a rice and milk preparation weighing 6,720 kg, which is distributed to the pilgrims and hangers-on at the shrine. Important monuments here are the large gateway built in the 13th Century by Sultan Iltutmish of Delhi, the tomb of the water-carrier who saved Emperor Humayun's life, and the delicate white marble mosque of Shah Jahan.

Ajmer is well-known for a mosque that was hurriedly assembled from building material taken from a Hindu temple and possibly a Sanskrit university dismantled by Muhammad of Ghori. Not far from here is the pleasant sight of **Ana Sagar,** a lake constructed in the early 12th Century. There are cool marble pavilions built by Shah Jahan and a circuit house constructed by the British.

Nine miles (14 km) from Ajmer is **Pushkar,** considered high up in the hierarchy of Hindu places of pilgrimage. It is the site of a temple to Brahma, the Creator, of which there are very few. Here, every year, on the full moon of Novem-

ber, hundreds of thousands of pilgrims gather to bathe in the sacred lake. This is the occasion for one of the largest cattle markets in Rajasthan where the abundance of color, jewelry, turbans and costumes has no equal.

Tonk, Sawai Madhopur, Ranthambhor

About seven miles (12 km) south of Jaipur, the airport road leads to **Sanganer,** a name synonymous with some of the finest block-printing on fabric. It is said that the water of Sanganer makes the colors fast. Traditionally, only coarse cotton was printed for the short, flared skirts of Rajasthani women. A 15th Century Jain temple and a Krishna temple are among spots worth visiting in Sanganer.

Continuing south, the same road winds past **Chaksu** where large numbers gather at the temple every year to pay reverence to Shitala Mata, the Goddess of Smallpox. Although this disease has now been eradicated from India, the goddess continues to have her following.

Some 50 miles (80 km) from Jaipur lies **Tonk,** once ruled by Muslim Nawabs, descendants of Pathan tribesmen from Afghanistan, who had come to India in search of *Zan, Zar, Zamin* — women, gold and land — possibly in that order of preference. Tonk has charming painted mosques and a host of colonial buildings that housed the British resident and. his entourage. Of particular interest is the **Sunehri Kothi** or golden mansion. A fairly small and simple structure from the outside, its interior is studded like a jewel box. An inlay of colored glass, mirrors, gilded stucco and strappings, painted and polished lime floors, stained window panes, all add up to an extraordinary opulence.

From Tonk, the road continues south to Bundi and Kota. But wildlife fans can turn left and continue eastward to **Sawai Madhopur** where the royal Jaipur household used to come for big hunts accompanied by their VIP guests. Queen Elizabeth stayed here in 1962.

Overlooking the wild life sanctuary of Sawai Madhopur (eight miles/13 km from the town) is the formidable fortress of Rao Hamir — **Ranthambhor,** which was conquered from the Chauhan princes by Ala-ud-din Khilji in the 14th Century and then again by Akbar in 1569. Even though in ruins, its palaces, temples and cenotaphs are well-worth a visit for a

City Palace and Lake Palace, Udaipur.

romantic stroll into Rajasthan's valorous past.

Bharatpur, Deeg, Dholpur

The Jaipur–Agra road leads to Bharatpur and on to Dholpur — both Jat states in the predominantly Rajput stronghold of Rajasthan.

The **Bharatpur Palace** houses a museum with exhibits of mixed antiquity, but what makes Bharatpur famous is its 11-sq-mile (29-sq-km) **Keoladeo Ghana sanctuary,** with the largest concentration and variety of birdlife in Asia. A regular visitor is the rare Siberian Crane that migrates to the sanctuary each winter, flying some 4,000 miles (7,000 km). Prior to 1940, this was the favorite shooting ground of the British viceroys, with a record kill of 4,273 birds in a single day. Sunrise or sunset from October to February is the best time to see the birds.

Eighteen miles (30 km) from Bharatpur are the wondrous palaces of **Deeg,** set at the water's edge, with cool channels, fountains and water alleys below, where giant iron balls were made to roll and rumble like monsoon thunder. The rooms are of exquisite beauty.

Mosaic at City Palace, Udaipur

Dholpur, a smaller Jat state, is only 34 miles (55 km) from Bharatpur. Founded in 1805, it is famous for its stone of which the president's palace in New Delhi and the facades of many modern buildings are made. In the wilderness is the first **Garden of Babur,** the founder of the Mughal dynasty. This was recently discovered by Mrs Moyhihan, wife of the former U.S. Ambassador in India. Nearby, the artificial lake of **Mach Kund,** surrounded by dilapidated temples, is a place for meditation.

Bundi, Kota, Jhalawar

Founded in 1342, the ancient kingdom of **Bundi** lies well protected within the ranges of the rugged Aravalli Hills that drop into rocky ravines traversed by four narrow passes. The highlight of Bundi is its stunning palace-fort, the **Chattar Mahal,** which reflects the changing colors of the greenish serpentine of its walls in the **Naval Sagar** lake. These are ribbed with the tracks worn into them by rainwater that has poured over the crenellations through the centuries, giving the structure a stature and dignity that prompted the widely travelled Lt. Col. James Tod to grant it the first rank in Rajasthani architecture. Incredible ramps and stairs zig-zag between the ramparts as overhanging balconies frame perfect views. Besides its architecture, the palace is famous for the **Chitra Shala,** a gallery of very refined frescos painted in the 17th and 18th centuries, unmatched in their harmony of blues, greens and terracotta colors.

The Bundi territory was first claimed by Udaipur and later by Jaipur. It shrank in size when a part of it was given in 1579 as patrimony for a favored younger son. This tract, set in the open plains, grew to be **Kota,** larger than its parent state, bustling with the youth of a commerical city, while Bundi gracefully mellowed into old gold. The secluded position of Bundi saved it, so to say, from the hybridization of the 19th Century, even though the British virtually controlled its affairs from 1818 when Capt. James Tod concluded a treaty between "Boondee" and the East India Company. "Bundi is deliciously behind the times," writes the Maharaja of Baroda.

A rather curious feature of the main Bundi market street is the height from the street at which the shops are built. The reason for their being some two meters high is not obvious unless the visitor stays over for one monsoon to see how the overflow of the town's reservoir, which is atop the hill in the **Taragarh Fort,** is emptied when the sluice gates open. Water gushes out like a cloud burst, flooding the streets. But everyone is forewarned with loud beating of drums and there has never been damage to life or property.

Kota has had to stay awake and alert all through its history because its strategic location on the plains along the Chambal River drew the envy of Udaipur, Jaipur, the Marathas and also the British — to whom it was the first to accede, due to the foresight of Zalim Singh the Regent. Spasmodic spells of peace led to spurts of architecture and a mélange of pillared halls, kiosks, commemorative gateways, carving and painting. Some of the finer frescos and miniature paintings of India belong to the Bundi-Kota school. The **City Palace at Kota** abounds in decorations and ornamentation and a small museum shows treasures hitherto in the private collection of the ruler. The most exquisite is in the hall of private audience, with its walls covered with paintings from the Mughal to British periods.

The ancient and stunning **Baroli Temple Complex,** 25 miles (40 km) from Kota, has exquisite stone carvings from the 9th Century.

For lovers of wildlife, Kota offers the **Dara Wildlife Sanctuary** where tiger, bear, wild boar and spotted deer roam the thick green jungles. The famous hunting paintings from Kota depict this area.

Apart from **Jhalawar's** museum, one should visit the nearby **Jhalra Patan,** the "city of bells" where stand the ruins of one of the finest sun temples in India.

Udaipur

The royal house of Mewar, now better known as **Udaipur,** has two reasons for pride. The first is that it can trace back its recorded history to Bapa Rawal (728 A.D.), whereas Jaipur and Jodhpur lag behind by 200 and 483 years respectively. The second is pride in being Hindu and not losing honor to the Muslims. Jaipur and Jodhpur willingly married their princesses to the Mughal court and shared in the gains of these alliances. Mewar alone resisted such alliances — at least 50 years more than the others. This sense of history and pride persisted dur-

Jodhpur Fort.

ing the British period, earning them the highest gun salute in Rajasthan: 19 guns as against the 17 each of Jaipur, Jodhpur, Bundi, Bikaner, Kota and Karauli. Maharana Fateh Singh of Udaipur had the singular distinction of not attending the Delhi Durbar for King George V in 1911.

Udaipur has a profusion of palaces, lakes, temples and cenotaphs. The **City Palace,** now a museum, is a labyrinth of courtyards richly decorated with inlaid mirror-work, galleries covered with frescos, temples and kiosks from where one can see the **Pichola Lake.** An island on the lake houses the elegant **Jag Nivas,** built in 1746 as the summer residence of the rulers, and now the **Lake Palace Hotel. Jag Mandir,** another island, is worth a visit at sunset. This is where Prince Khurram, who was later to become Emperor Shah Jahan, took refuge in 1624 and lived for a while.

In the old town the **Jagdish Temple,** built in the mid-17th Century, has a remarkable bronze statue of Garuda (a mythical bird) facing his revered Lord Vishnu. The shops and craftsmen's ateliers in the narrow streets of the bazaar justify endless walks. The visitor will marvel at the skill of the artists, their in-

born sense of colors and forms and will be tempted to acquire paintings on paper, ivory or cloth.

The temple of Eklingji, the Shaiva patron deity of the Udaipur royal house, is 15 miles (24 km) by road from Udaipur. On the way are the ruins of the ancient city of **Nagda** where exquisitely carved temples, both Hindu (10th Century) and Jain (15th Century), are a treat for the eyes. **Eklingji Temple** is carved from marble and even today the Maharana of Udaipur who is the *Diwan* of the temple, makes it a point to visit it every Monday.

A remarkable place of worship, **Nathdwara** (30 miles/48 km from Udaipur) is the highly revered temple to Srinathji, a manifestation of Lord Krishna. Non-Hindus are not allowed inside, but images of the Lord painted on cloth are available. These are called *pechwai* and are hung behind the idol. They can sometimes be highly artistic in conception and execution.

Another outing from Udaipur takes one 30 miles southeast to the welcome sight of **Jaisamand,** the largest artificial lake in Asia. This was constructed by Rana Jai Singh at the end of the 17th Century and measures 30 miles in circumference. Not far away is a royal hunting ground turned wildlife sanctuary sheltering panther, wild boar and spotted deer.

From Nathdwara, en route to Kumbalgarh, a pleasant stop is at **Rajsamand,** the cool royal lake at Kankroli. From the dam, one gets a magnificent view of the town. The temple too is interesting.

Kumbalgarh and Ranakpur

In the erstwhile princely state of Mewar there were three almost impregnable forts: **Chittor** (70 miles/112 km from Udaipur), **Kumbalgarh** (40 miles/64 km from Udaipur), and **Mandalgarh** (near Kota). Kumbalgarh is not easily accessible, but the adventurous will be well-rewarded. This fort was built by Rana Kumbha in the 15th Century. It is surrounded by 13 mountain peaks which keep watch over distant horizons. Seven gateways lead up to the palaces.

In a shaded valley, 100 miles (160 km) northwest from Udaipur, lie the superb Jain temples of **Ranakpur** which were built in the mid-15th Century. The **Rishabji Temple** has 1,444 colums, each different from the others. The nearby **Sun

Jodhpur Palace.

Temple is worth a visit, both for its carvings and its unusual plan.

Chittor became the first capital of Mewar in the early 13th Century under the reign of Jaitra Singh (1213-53). There is told the story of the siege of Chittorgarh in 1303 by the Sultan of Delhi, Ala-ud-din Khilji. The sultan had heard of the beauty of Princess Padmini, the wife of Maharana Rawal Ratan Singh, and was determined to bring her back to his harem. Despite the courage of the brave Rajputs who defended Chittor, the citadel was captured by the sultan's force. Rather than face dishonor, the women chose to die by committing *johar*, mass self immolation, led by Rani Padmini. Chanting verses from the Gita, they threw themselves on the funeral pyre.

Chittor was later recaptured by the Rajputs. But, history repeats itself. Two centuries later, in 1535, Chittor was attacked by the Sultan of Gujarat, Bahadur Shah, and 13,000 Rajput women sacrificed themselves in the flames.

Abu is one of the most sacred places of Jain pilgrimage. According to the Jain tradition, Mahavir, the last of the 24 *Tirthankara* (saints) spent a year there.

Mount Abu, situated at an altitude of 4,000 feet (1,220 meters), is a popular summer resort. Many princes built summer bungalows and small palaces around the Nakki Lake there.

The main attractions are the Dilwara Jain temples of which two, the **Adinath** and **Neminath,** display a profusion of carving in white marble. Adinath was built in 1031 and is dedicated to the first Tirthankar. Neminath was erected in 1230 to celebrate the 22nd Tirthankar. The carving is elaborate and exquisite, creating a lacy effect. The 24 elite Chauhan clans, of which the Hara Chauhans of Bundi and Kota are considered supreme, claim descent from the holy fire that springs from the peak of Mount Abu.

Jodhpur

The Rathors of Kanauj (U.P.) moved in 1211 A.D. to Marusthal, the hot and blazing desert land of death in the heart of Rajasthan. Their land came to be called Marwar. Two and a half centuries passed and, in 1459, Rao Jodha founded **Jodhpur** after the old capital of Mandore had proved too vulnerable. Some five centuries later, Maharaja Umaid Singh

Jaisalmer Fort with city in foreground.

144

had completed for himself one of the largest private homes in the world (with 347 rooms) to create employment as a measure of famine relief. This is now a hotel. Awaiting the visitor are the remains, the symbols of seven centuries of history, begun in hardship and austerity, continued in bloodshed and bravery, and culminating in grandiose magnificence and decadence.

The **Fort of Jodhpur** sits on a mighty rock 400 feet (120 meters) tall. A fairly steep climb leads up, winding through seven gateways. The palaces within are carved from a hard sandstone which the sculptors' chisels have carved as if it were soap. An extensive museum displays howdahs, paintings, thrones, banners, doors, weapons and a spectacular 17th Century tent. The city of Jodhpur is an interesting one to walk through, particularly the market near the clock tower.

The old capital of **Mandore**, five miles (eight km) from Jodhpur, now has landscaped gardens surrounding ancient temples and the cenotaphs of the Marwar rulers. The **Hall of Heroes**, with larger-than-life figures painted in gaudy colors, as well as the temple of the black Bhairav and the white Bhairav (destructive mani-

festations of Lord Shiva), where the idols are pasted over with layers of silver paper, are worth visiting.

The **Osian temples** (40 miles/65 km from Jodhpur), both Hindu and Jain, are unique. They date from the 8th to the 12th centuries.

Jaisalmer

The ancient capitals of Rajasthan, Chittor (Udaipur), Amber (Jaipur), Mandore (Jodhpur) and Lodurva (Jaisalmer) have all become monuments. Of the new habitations, **Jaisalmer,** the land of the Bhatti princes, born of the moon, is by far the oldest and dates back to 1156 A.D. The skyline holds kiosks with parapets, balconies and terraces. It is hard to believe that the human hand is capable of executing the intricate stone carvings on these structures — no corner is left unadorned. The beauty of the Jain temples (12th-15th centuries) leaves visitors breathless and photographers usually run out of film.

Down in the city are the renowned *havelis* of Salim Singh, Nathmalji and the Patwas in the same yellow-gold Jaisalmer stone. These were ready to be dismantled and shipped abroad when they were declared National Treasures.

There are remains of a petrified forest at **Aakal**, 17 km from Jaisalmer. All else is sand. Golden turrets, 99 of them, once rose out of the golden Trikuta, the triple-peaked hill which once stood here.

A 10-mile (16-km) drive to the ancient Bhatti capital of **Lodurva** can be fascinating in good weather. The enormous sand dunes make a surrealistic landscape patterned by the wind.

Nagaur

Some 55 miles (90 km) from Jodhpur lies **Khimsar.** (En route, the **Balsamand Lake** and bird sanctuary calls for a brief stop.) The 15th Century **Khimsar Fort** with carved stone grills is now a charming hotel. Should one happen to plan a visit in February or August, it is worth while getting the exact dates for the cattle fairs of Nagaur from the Rajasthan Tourism Development Corporation (100 Jawaharlal Nehru Marg, Jaipur, Rajasthan). In February, Nagaur celebrates the Ramdeoji Fair and in August the Tejaji Cattle Fair, named after local heroes and considered to be among the largest livestock fairs in the world.

Young Rajput.

MADHYA PRADESH, THE INDIAN HEARTLAND

Madhya Pradesh, if literally translated, means "the Middle Land." Is it any surprise that the people of this vast state feel that the whole of India revolves around them?

It is India's largest state, having a land area of approximately 174,000 sq miles (450,000 sq km). The next largest state, Rajasthan, is at least 38,600 sq miles (100,000 sq km) smaller. If India were to have different time zones, Ramanujganj on the eastern border of the state would be 40 minutes ahead of Jhabua on the western border.

Geographically, Madhya Pradesh is one of the most interesting parts of India. The northern part of the state, with Gwalior as its largest city, lies in the Indo-Gangetic plain. Much of the state, however, is upland plateaus and hills, interspersed with the deep valleys of rivers which flow east into the Bay of Bengal and west into the Arabian Sea. The hills are forest-clad. In fact, almost a third of India's forests are located in Madhya Pradesh. They are rich forests, consisting of some of the finest deciduous hardwoods in the world — teak, sal, hardwickia, Indian ebony and rosewood. Bamboo is prolific in the hills and there are magnificent fruit and flowering trees in the forests. The Mahadeo Hills of the Satpura Range are the home of the tiger, panther, Indian bison and the myriad herbivores which make the jungle their home. Kipling's *Jungle Book* was sited in the Mahadeo Hills where the forests, wild life and tribals are today almost exactly as they were in his time.

Gwalior

Gwalior, the northernmost city, is an excellent entry point. It was established in the 8th Century A.D. and named after Saint Gwalipa. The city is dominated by its hill-top fort, one of the most redoutable in the world. Rajput valor and chivalry are redolent in the very stones of the 15th Century palace of Raja Mansingh located in the citadel. The fort also houses the **Teli-ka-Mandir**, an ancient temple. **Gujri Mahal** at the foot of the fort has one of the finest museums of sculpture in the country. Gwalior also has the distinction of being a center of Indian classical music. Miya Tansen, one of the nine jewels of the court of Emperor Akbar the Great, belonged to Gwalior and is buried there. One of the greatest music festivals of India is held each December in Gwalior to commemorate this great singer.

Gwalior is a good take-off point for two of the loveliest places in Madhya Pradesh, Orchha and Shivpuri. **Orchha**, a mere 75 miles (120 km) from Gwalior, is a medieval city frozen in time and space, existing even today as it must have in the 16th and 17th centuries, when it was built. Orchha was founded in the 16th Century by the Bundela king, Rudra Pratap, on the banks of the sparkling **Betwa River.** The countryside undulates gently between riverine plains and rolling forest-clad hills. The builders of Orchha dotted the landscaped with palace and fortress, temple and cenotaph. The architecture is a synthesis of traditional Hindu, hybrid Indo-Saracenic and ornate Mughal. One of the finest sights is the view of the cenotaphs from across the Betwa River: green hills in the background and the architecturally perfect *chhatries* or cenotaphs sharply etched against an azure sky, with the blue Betwa in between. The 20th Century has bypassed Orchha and left it slumbering and at peace in a leisurely bygone age.

About 60 miles (100 km) from Gwalior is **Shivpuri**, the former summer capital of the Scindias of Gwalior. One climbs into the Vindhyan plateau at Shivpuri and the contrast with the Gangetic Plain is immediate and marked. Located at Shivpuri are the two lakes of **Sakhia Sagar** and **Madhav Sagar.** Surrounding them is the **Madhav National Park.** It is the home of a wide variety of deer and antelope species, such as spotted deer, chinkara or Indian gazelle, sambhar, blue bull, black buck, barking deer and four-horned antelope. Also seen in the park are wild dog and sloth bear. Bird life abounds. Peacocks are to be seen in hundreds. In the nearby **Karera Bird Sanctuary** is to be found the Great Indian Bustard, an endangered species that has been rescued by sensitive conservation. The lakes have *muggar,* the Indian crocodile.

Indore and Ujjain

Indore is the western metropolis of Madhya Pradesh. Here, one is well and truly on to the Malwa Plateau, a region of rich black cotton soil of great fertility.

Erotic
sculptures
at
Khajuraho.

Indore is a great industrial center and has the look of a boom town. On its periphery is the city of **Dewas,** made famous by E.M. Foster in *The Hill of Devi.* It is now becoming one of the fastest growing industrial cities in India.

The land of Malwa is sacred and two of the 12 *jyotir lingas* or Shiva icons, are to be found at **Mahakaleshwar Temple** at Ujjain and **Mandhata** at Omkareshwar. For Hindus, these two places enjoy a sanctity equal to that of Banaras. Every 12 years Ujjain has the great fair of *Kumbh,* or *Simhastha* as it is locally called. An interesting legend attends this fair, one of four in the country, the other three being held at Allahabad and Haridwar on the Ganga, and Nasik on the Godavari River.

The sacred river at Ujjain is the **Sipra.** The gods and the *asuras* (demons) churned the ocean for the *kumbh* or pot of *amrit,* or nectar. First emerged a pot of *vish,* or poison. Shiva drank it down in a gulp. So strong was it that his divine neck turned blue, giving him one of the names he is known by — 'Nilkanth,' or the Blue-necked One. Every 12 years, Hindus congregate in millions to celebrate the saving of the earth by Shiva. The congregation at Ujjain at the last Simhastha exceeded 2.5 million.

Ujjain, approximately 35 miles (60 km) from Indore, is not only one of the most sacred cities of the Hindus, but is also a center of both ancient craft and modern industry. Special mention must be made of the art of the *chhipas,* or dyers and printers of **Bherugarh,** a suburb of Ujjain. Using vegetable dyes and hand-carved teak blocks, with designs and patterns which go back centuries, the *chhipas* produce the most exquisite and colorful block-printed cloth for saris, tapestries and hangings, bedsheets and floor coverings.

Mandu — Fortress Town

A tour of Malwa is incomplete without a visit to **Mandu,** the city of joy. A short 55-mile (90 km) drive from Indore, one approaches the capital of the Sultanate of Malwa either from the plains of Dhar or from the mountain pass at Manpur. Nothing in one's experience can prepare the visitor for the first sight of Mandu. There is a chasm, a deep wooded ravine which is crossed by a narrow bridge, and piercing the skyline is the

Stupa with gate, Sanchi.

largest standing fortified city in the world — Mandu, whose walls have a circumference of more than 45 miles (75 km). These walls stand today almost as they did 300 years ago.

One enters through the **Bhangi Gate,** a portal so obviously designed for defence that it would be a foolhardy enemy who dared a frontal assault. Once inside the gates, vistas of a fairyland open to visitors. There are lakes and groves and gardens and palaces galore. The **Jahaz Mahal,** or ship palace, floats serenely on the bosom of its lake, looking like some heavenly ship sailing into eternity. The **Hindola Mahal,** or swing palace, built of massive stone, appears to sway gently in the breeze. There is the **Jama Masjid,** with such perfect acoustics that a whisper from the pulpit is heard clearly in the farthest corner of the huge courtyard. There is the **Nilkanth Temple,** a standing monument to the secularity and love of all religions of the Emperor Akbar.

As one wanders onward through the green vale of Mandu, one comes to **Rewa Kund,** a gem of a lake, said to be filled by the waters of the Narmada River 55 miles (90 km) away and 2,000 feet (600 meters) lower down. Rewa Kund and, in fact, the whole of Mandu, are living monuments to the legend of Sultan Baz Bahadur and his Hindu Queen, Roopmati. Legend has it that she was a commoner whom Baz Bahadur met on the banks of the Narmada River when out hunting. He married her on a promise that he would bring the Narmada to Mandu, and Rewa Kund is the fulfilment of that promise. On its banks he built a palace for himself and, further up, at the very edge of the escarpment, a pavilion for Roopmati, from the terrace of which she could see the Narmada as a silver thread on the horizon. A sheer drop of 2,000 feet from the pavilion terrace ends in the plains of Nimar, through which the Narmada flows.

Bhopal, State Capital

From paradise back to earth, and one turns to the state capital, **Bhopal.** This city, too, is in Malwa and enjoys a moderate climate. It is built, like Rome, on seven hills and round three lovely lakes.

Perhaps it is this which inspired architect Charles Correa to design **Bharat Bhavan,** a multi-arts center without parallel in India. Bhopal has the distinction of being one of the greatest centers of art and culture in the country. A visitor could well spend all his time in the art galleries, museums, theaters, poetry center and library in Bharat Bhavan.

But Bhopal is much more than just natural beauty and human art. Its industries give the city an air of briskness. The city hums with the activity of business and the business of government. After all, as the state capital, government is the principal "industry" of Bhopal.

Bhopal is a modern city, but it is also a very old one. A scant 18 miles (30 km) away is **Bhim-bethka,** where over 500 caves with neolithic rock painting have been discovered. Five periods have been identified, from the prehistoric upper paleolithic down to the early historical and medieval. The oldest cave paintings are at least as old as those of the Pyrenees. When the earth itself was young, Bhopal was already inhabited by man, whose activities pointed to a fair degree of civilization. So ancient is this city that at nearby **Sanchi** are located a great stupa, a dome-shaped monument covering relics of Gautama Buddha, and the remains of a Buddhist monastery. Sanchi is a place of Buddhist pilgrimage.

Near Sanchi are **Vidisha, Udaygiri** and **Gyaraspur,** the cradle of Mauryan civili-

Detail from gate depicting the Buddha as a flaming pillar and showing scenes from his life.

zation and the rocks on which the tide of ancient Grecian conquest broke. The exquisite sculptured *salbhanjika,* or divine attendant of the gods, is preserved here.

Bhopal, as we see it today, was founded in the 10th Century A.D. by Raja Bhoj. The **Bhojpur Temple,** even in its ruined state, bespeaks the greatness of this king, as also do the remains of the magnificent lake, the **Tal** which once covered 230 sq miles (600 sq km) and whose wanton destruction in the 15th Century by Sultan Hoshang Shah of Malwa altered the climate of the region.

South of Bhopal is Kipling country, with the Narmada as the cord which binds the Satpura and Vindhyan Hills together. The **Narmada** is one of the great rivers of India, its water green and foaming as it tumbles from its source at Amarkantak through the gorges and cataracts that it has carved out of the Satpura Hills. The waters of the Narmada are still fairly pure; it has as yet not been fully polluted by man. Its banks are well-defined and rise to high hills, and the hills themselves are densely wooded. This is tiger country.

Ranging from the low hills of Hoshagabad and rising into the Mahadeo Hills at Pachmarhi, Betul and Chhindwara, the forests explode into exuberance at **Kanha,** one of the finest wildlife sanctuaries in the world. In 1983, Prince Philip, Duke of Edinburgh visited Kanha. To reach this 2,700-sq-mile (7,000 sq km) park consisting of 400 sq miles (1,000 sq km) of core area and 2,300 sq miles (6,000 sq km) of forest surround, he drove through 100 miles (160 km) of unbroken forest.

The **Kanha National Park** and its sister sanctuary, **Bandavgarh,** are absolute musts for visitors to the state. These parks have grassy *maidans* or meadows, which are home for deer. The jungles teem with tiger, leopard, bear and wildcat. In some cases, the numbers are prodigious, with spotted deer alone numbering more than 17,000. The number of tigers is about 90. Tiger is king, but not set to rule over gaur, the Indian bison. Where the gaur browses, the tiger makes a wide detour. Kanha is home to that unique species of 12-horned swamp deer, the *barasingha (Duvaceli branderi).* The uniqueness of the Kanha barasingha lies in its being the only swamp deer which has adapted to dwelling on hard ground. It faced extinction till that great naturalist and administrator, M.K.S. Ranjitsinhji,

Worship of ancestor of Gwalior ruling family.

rescued it.

The list of places worth seeing in Madhya Pradesh is unending, but two places deserve special mention: Pachmarhi and Bedaghat. **Pachmarhi** is up in the Satpura Hills. It is a paradise for trekkers, rock climbers and nature lovers. **Bedaghat** is near Jabalpur. Here the Narmada flows through a two-mile-long (five-km) gorge, between towering white marble cliffs. Below the gorge are the **Dhuandhar Falls**, literally "Smoky Falls." A row past **Marble Rocks** on a full-moon night is not to be missed. The silence of the night is broken only by the soft plop of the boatman's oars. The wake trails phosphoresence through the jade waters of the river, which reflect the silver of the moon.

Tribal Territory

From the almost feminine grace of Marble Rocks to the sheer power and grandeur of the **Chitrakoot Falls** on the Indravati River in Bastar is a long journey of over 400 miles (600 km). But then, remote **Bastar** is a world in itself. It is one of the largest districts in India, covering a land area of over 15,400 sq miles (40,000 sq km). Many countries are smaller than Bastar and Switzerland is no larger.

Difficult though it is to reach, Bastar richly repays the visitor for his effort. Here the hills march in serried ranks and the forests are primeval. In the **Kanger Valley** is India's largest national biosphere reserve, in which nature has been left totally undisturbed by man. **Teerathgarh Falls** decorate the hills with a 820-foot (250-meter) lace of white froth, before disappearing into **Kotamsar**, whose limestone rocks produce stalactite and stalagmite caves of a beauty approaching that of the Carlsbad Caverns in the United States.

The sheer inaccessibility of Bastar lends it an enchantment all its own. This is the home of the bisonhorn Madias, whose dances have adorned many a folkdance festival in India and abroad. It is also the home of the hill mynah, which imitates the voice of man better than man himself.

Southern and eastern Madhya Pradesh are jungle-clad and remote, but below the surface lie some of the richest mineral deposits in the world. Here is iron ore of unsurpassed purity; copper and tin so pure that it can be smelted in an ordinary earthenware pot; limestone, dolomite, bauxite and coal in almost unlimited quantities. The sleeping giant is already stirring. Mining, huge power plants, steel mills, aluminium factories and copper smelters are either being set up or already in operation.

A tour of Madhya Pradesh could appropriately end at **Khajuraho**. The period 950 to 1050 A.D., a mere hundred years, saw a flowering of architecture in this small village which has no parallel. Here the Chandelas built 85 temples to the glory of God. Today 22 survive. These temples are designed to lead one's eyes from ground level ever upwards to the ultimate heaven, Kailash. They are ornately carved, with each frieze and sculpture depicting the genius of the men who carved it and the king who inspired them.

Khajuraho has achieved fame for the sensual appeal of the erotic sculptures, but these form only a small part of the wealth of the site. Taken in totality, the sculptures of Khajuraho depict the everyday life of the people and the court in the 10th and 11th centuries. This procession of life itself culminates in the sanctum sanctorum, where one sheds the earthly coil before the deity. Khajuraho is not something that can be described in words;

Gwalior Fort.

it has to be experienced. The annual dance festival in March, when India's leading dancers perform on the podium of the **Khandariya Mahadev Temple,** is a good time to visit Khajuraho.

Rich Variety

Madhya Pradesh is not only places, it is also people. The state embraces at least four agro-climatic zones and thus has a most interesting mix of people and ways of life.

The state is home to about 40 percent of India's tribal population. There are three distinct tribal groups. The most numerous are the Gonds, who once ruled much of the state and after whom **Gondwana,** the central portion came to be known. They inhabited the Satpura and Kymore Ranges and their major branches, the Madias and the Muria Gonds live in Bastar.

Western Madhya Pradesh is inhabited by the Bhils, a colorful group of warriors and huntsmen who held even the Mughal army at bay. Eastern Madhya Pradesh is dominated by the Oraons, now almost wholly Christian.

The tribals of Madhya Pradesh have retained their ethnicity and customs, even in the face of modernization, largely because successive governments have dealt with them with sensitivity. The tribals are great artists. Wood, bamboo and other forest produce are the media in which they work. In Bastar there is the unmatched art of bell-metal casting, as also the most intricate forms of clay sculpture. Bharat Bhavan at Bhopal has a museum of tribal art which gives a representative picture of the crafts of these woodsmen.

But craft comes easily to all the people in Madhya Pradesh, ranging from the exquisite weaving of Chanderi and Maheshwar, to the carpet making of Vidisha, Mandsaur and Sarguja. Carpentry, pottery, textile, printing and dyeing, metal working, woodcarving and fine leather work are some of the skilled crafts of Madhya Pradesh.

Madhya Pradesh is quite easy to reach. One can fly to the state from Delhi, Bombay and Calcutta. Gwalior, Bhopal, Indore, Jabalpur, Raipur and Khajuraho are on the air map. There are excellent train services throughout. Major highways criss-cross the state and road journeys are interesting because the roads

Kandariya Mahadev Temple, Khajuraho.

pass through forests and cultivated areas in succession, skirt quaint villages, up hill and down dale.

Dak Bungalows

Most places have adequate, if simple, hotel facilities. But the real joy of travel is in coming to a remote rest house, or "dak bungalow," maintained by government for its officers on tour or for the weary traveller overtaken by night and in need of shelter.

Dak bungalows generally have two to four bedrooms and baths, austere in furniture, but spotlessly clean and comfortable. Each of them has a *khansama,* or cook-caretaker, who can produce a tasty, hot meal at short notice, cooked as often as not over a fragrant wood-fire. The taste of that first cup of scalding tea drunk at the end of a long drive, sprawled in an easy chair on the veranda of a dak bungalow, will probably be remembered long after the vintage champagne drunk in a smoky drawing room full of chattering socialites is forgotten. The bill at the end of the stay will shock by its very modesty — two dollars for the room and the equivalent of about three dollars for

Marble Rocks on River Narmada, Madhya Pradesh.

all meals, ranging from bed tea to the after dinner coffee. The style will not be of Maxims, but the ambience will be unbeatable.

The Madhyadeshis are only too friendly and the danger is the possibility of the visitor being used as a dummy on whom to practice English conversation. Not to worry, for, paradoxically, the passing of the Raj has made more people English-speaking than ever before. Invitations to visit private homes are readily forthcoming and in the villages the hospitality is overwhelming. Food, milk and tea are pressed on the traveller and the host is hurt by the display of a poor appetite.

The cuisine varies from the wheat- and meat-based food of northern and western Madhya Pradesh to the rice and fish domination in the south and the east. Gwalior and Indore abound in milk and milk-based preparations. Bhopal produces exquisite meat and fish dishes, of which spicy *rogan josh, korma, keema, biryani* and kababs, such as *shami* and *seekh,* are the most famous. They are eaten with thin sheets of unleavened bread called *roomali roti,* literally "handkerchief bread," and leavened, flat loaves called *sheermal.* Equally interesting are the wheat cakes called *bafla,* dunked in rich ghee and eaten with *dal,* a pungent lentil broth, whose tongue-tingling sharpness is moderated by the accompanying *laddoos* or sweet dumplings.

Meals end with fruit — luscious mangoes, juicy melons and water melons, custard apples, bananas, papayas, guavas and oranges. To drink, there are *lassi* or buttermilk, fruit juices, juice from freshly crushed sugarcane, an excellent beer and fine rum from cane. For those with strong heads and a preference for local brews, there is the liquor distilled from the flowers of the mahua tree *(Madhuca indica); sulfi* or the fermented toddy of the sago palm and also date palm toddy — heady drinks for adventurous palates.

The best time to travel in Madhya Pradesh is from the mild autumn of October to the spring of March end. April to mid-July are taboo because of the heat. The monsoon months of July, August and September are interesting because the earth bursts into an exuberance of green and the air is fresh and cool. But no matter what the season, Madhya Pradesh is fascinating. It is almost as if the 'Middle Land' were proclaiming to all and sundry, "Aren't I wonderful."

BIHAR, LAND OF THE BUDDHA

The State of Bihar lies in the eastern Gangetic plain. It was the seat of several of the most famous ancient Indian dynasties and the cradle of Jainism and Buddhism. The name, Bihar, is itself derived from *vihara* (Buddhist monastery).

Patna, the capital of Bihar, is a city of nearly a million lying along the Ganges in a long strip. Under the name of Pataliputra it was the capital of the Magadha empire.

The Maidan, a large square, divides Patna in two. To the west lies **Bankipur,** a cantonment and administrative area, with colonial buildings: **Raj Bhawan,** the governor's residence; the **maharaja's palace,** now the Bihar State Transport Corporation; the **Patna's Women's College,** an early 20th Century neo-Mughal complex; and residential bungalows for senior government officers which were built in the 1920s.

The **Patna Museum** near the **High Court,** houses a collection of Hindu and Buddhist stone sculptures, bronzes and terra-cotta sculptures. Among the exhibits is a 15 m long fossil tree said to be 2,000 million years old and the longest tree fossil in the world. At the entrance of the hall, on the left, is the **Didarganji Yakshi,** a buff-colored Mauryan sandstone statue of a woman, remarkable for her brilliant polish, her firm rounded breasts, her navel, her aggressive belly and hips, considered to be one of the greatest masterpieces of Indian art of all times.

Between the Maidan and the Ganga stands the **Golghar,** a beehive-shaped structure, built in 1786 as a granary. It is 27 m high and 125 m wide at its base, with walls almost 4 m thick. It can hold 150,000 tonnes of wheat. It has hardly ever been used. Two stairways lead to the top, offering a view of Patna and the other bank of the river.

Old Patna spreads to the east of the Maidan, a narrow strip between the Ganga and the railway line that runs parallel to it. In this district of bazaars, a few buildings stand out: the **Khuda Baksh Oriental Library,** with its rare Islamic manuscripts, including some from the Moorish University of Cordoba in Spain; **Padri-ki-Haveli,** or Saint Mary's Church, built in 1775; **Sher Shah Masjid,**

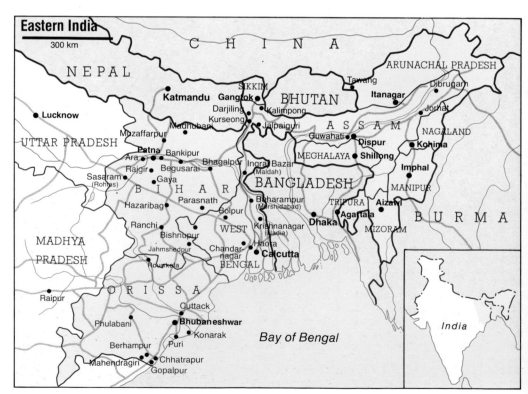

156

and **Patther-ki-Masjid,** mosques erected respectively around 1540 by Sher Shah, and in 1621 by Parwez Shah, son of Jahangir, and Governor of Bihar.

Haramandirji, a gurudwara in old Patna, is one of the holiest places for the Sikhs. Guru Gobind Singh, the tenth and last Sikh Guru, was born, spent part of his childhood and died here. The gurudwara, built in the 19th Century around the room where the Guru was born, stands at the center of Patna's Sikh district. It is a tall building in white marble, housing a museum of the Sikh religion. On the top is a terrace with white marble kiosks from where one can watch the sun going down over the city while loudspeakers broadcast the evening recitation from the Holy Granth.

Near the gurudwara, and visited only by appointment with the owner is **Quila House,** a private residence built on the ruins of Sher Shah's fortress, housing a private collection of jade, Chinese paintings, silver filigree work of the Mughal period, and a bed that once belonged to Napoleon.

At **Gulzarlbagh,** further east near the Mahabir Ghat, is a former East India Company Factory, now a Government Printing Press. Visitors can visit the opium godowns, the former ballroom and the hall where Shah Alam II was crowned Emperor of Delhi (under the protection and patronage of the East India Company) on 12 March 1761. In the same area, to the south, at **Kumhrar,** a park has been created around the remains of **Pataliputra:** the foundations of a *vihara* and of Ashoka's palace, wooden beams from structures in the former city, ramparts, and the pond where Emperor Ashoka is said to have thrown the bodies of his 99 brothers whom he had killed to avoid competition from within his family. Needless to say, this was before his conversion to Buddhism. Nearby, at the beginning of the Patna Bypass Road is a well and a shrine to Sitlamata, the goddess of smallpox, a frightening figure dressed in scarlet.

The **Mahatma Gandhi Bridge,** amongst the longest river bridges in the world, crosses the Ganga to the east of the city. On the north bank, near the confluence of the Ganga and the Gandak, at **Sonepur,** a month long animal fair is held every year in November. Further north, **Vaishali,** 40 km away, is the former capital of the Vajian Confederacy (6th Century B.C.), probably the first republic

in Asia. Mahavira was born in Vaishali. The Second Buddhist Council was held here in 383 B.C. All that now remains is an Ashoka pillar and ruins of Buddhist *stupas.* Nepal is not far away. The road beyond Vaishali reaches the India-Nepal border at Raxaul. Near the border, more to the east, and accessible from Patna through Barauni after a seven-hour drive is **Madhubani,** a village famous for its style of folk painting. Among the artists are some highly talented persons whose works are available for sale at major handicrafts emporia all over the country.

Mughal Monuments

Some of the finest monuments of the Mughal period in Bihar can be seen west of Patna. At Maner, 30 km away, are two mausoleums: **Choti Dargah,** in a small Muslim cemetery, is the grave of Maneri, a Muslim ascetic of the 17th Century. **Bari Dargah,** on the high bank of an artificial pond, was built around 1620 by Ibrahim Khan, Governor of Bihar under Jahangir, as a mausoleum for Shah Daula, his religious preceptor. At **Sasaram** (155 km to the southwest), are some large

monuments of the period when there was an interlude of Suri (Afgan) rule in north India: Emperor **Sher Shah's mausoleum,** built in the 16th Century in the middle of a square; a 300 wide tank, and the mausoleums of Hassan Sur Khan, Sher Shah Suri's father, Alawal Khan, the officer in charge of building Sher Shah's mausoleum and the uncompleted one of Salim Shah, Sher Shah's son.

Buxar, 110 km west is the place where Lord Rama is said to have fought the demon Taraka and received, with Lakshman, higher knowledge from the sage Vishvamitra. Lord Ram is said to have left a footprint here at **Ram Rekha Ghat.** Nearby is the battlefield where, in 1764, the British defeated Mir Kasim, the last independent nawab of Murshidabad and added Bengal and Bihar to their Indian possessions.

South of Patna lies the cradle of Buddhism.

Nalanda

Nalanda, "the place that confers the lotus" *(nalam)* or spiritual knowledge, 90 km from Patna, is the site of the **Sri Mahavihara Arya Bhikshu Sanghasya,** a monastic university that flourished from the 5th Century till 1199, when it was ransacked by the Afghan invader, Bakhtiar Khilji. The university, at the height of its activities, had a vast library, 2,000 teachers and more than 10,000 students from as far as Japan, Sumatra, Java and Korea. Legend has it that it contained 9 million volumes and that it burned for six months after the sack of Nalanda.

Lord Mahavira, the last Jain Tirthankara, and Lord Buddha taught here. Nalanda developed as a center of Buddhist learning.

Excavations over more than 15 hectares have yielded nine levels of occupation, six temples *(chaityas)* and eleven monasteries *(viharas),* all built in red brick. The monasteries are on the eastern side. The main ones are Vihara I founded in the 9th Century by King Balaputradeva of Sumatra, and Viharas 4 and 5, built by king Kumar Gupta in the 1st Century A.D., with later additions by Kings Hashavardan and Devpala. The *viharas* show remains of student cells, lecture halls, bathrooms, kitchens, libraries, storage rooms and wells. To the west are the temples. The most imposing is the **Sariputra Stupa,** built by Ashoka in honor

of Ananda, the Buddha's first disciple, who was born and died at Nalanda. It is a three-level structure, partly covered with stucco figures of Lord Buddha teaching at Bodhgaya, Nalanda, Rajgir, Sarnath and Vaishali, and surrounded by *stupas* erected to the memory of students who died during their studies, that could then last a whole lifetime. Steps lead to a platform on top of the *stupa,* now empty, where a hall originally stood housing a statue of Lord Buddha. Nearby are *Chaityas* 12, 13 and 14, largely ruined, containing remains of sculptures and bas-reliefs.

A new site, **Sarai Mound,** has been excavated to the northeast. At this site half-faded frescos of horses and elephants have been discovered. East of the ruins, is a museum with Buddhist and Hindu stone and terra-cotta statues and figurines.

North of Nalanda, a monument in the shape of a Chinese temple has been built to commemorate the memory of Hsuan Tsang, the Chinese traveller who studied at Nalanda in the 7th Century.

Leaving Nalanda for Rajgir, the road passes a small Chinese temple, the **Nava Nalanda Mahavira Research Centre on Buddhism and Pali Literature,** set up by the Bihar Government, and *Wat Thai Nalanda,* a small Thai temple of recent construction.

Rajgir

Rajgir, or Rajgriha, the "royal palace," 12 km south, was the capital of the Magadha empire in the 6th Century B.C. It is a holy place both for Jains and Buddhists. Lord Mahavira taught here for 14 rainy seasons; Muni Suvrata, the 20th Jain Tirthankara, was born here and all of Lord Mahavira's earliest disciples died here. The Buddha too spent five rainy reasons at Rajgir. He had so impressed King Bimbisara at his first visit to Rajgir that, when he returned from Bodhgaya, having attained enlightenment, accompanied by a thousand disciples, the king built a monastery set in a bamboo park for this new order *(sangha)* of monks. The First Buddhist Council, six months after the Buddha's death, was held at Rajgir.

Contemporary Rajgir, a very small place, is located north of the ancient site that spreads over seven barren hills surrounding a valley. A 50 km long wall with watchtowers built of huge stone blocks used to run round the city. Its remains can be seen on the hills and at the north and south gates, marking the ancient city's limits.

Passing by the remains of the **Agatasatru Fort,** built in the 5th Century B.C., the road reaches a small square lined with shops. On the right is **Venuvana,** the bamboo park where the Buddha and his disciples lived. A small mound, now covered with Muslim graves, marks the site of the *stupa* and *vihara* built by Ajatasatru. In the park are a mini **zoo,** with deer and peacock; a small **Thai temple;** and **Karanda Tank,** where the Buddha used to bathe.

The **Nipponzan Myohoji** is a large Japanese temple and the Centaur Hokke Club caters to the needs of Japanese pilgrims, offering traditional Japanese meals and accommodation. Burmese Buddhists have also built a temple, to the east of the fort, at the foot of Vipula Hill.

Immediately to the south of Venuvana, at the foot of **Vaibhara Hill** are Jain and Hindu temples built around 22 hot springs. Public baths have been set up where one can relax in hot emerald-green waters. Further up, past the **Pippla Cave** and the **Jarasandha-ki-Baithak,** a monastery built out of large blocks of stone,

is the **Saptaparni cave** where the First Buddhist Council was held. Further south, **Manyar Math,** a cylindrical stone structure, is a former temple to Maninaga, a serpent demi-god, referred to in the Mahabharata. Turning left the road passes **Jivakamhavana,** the site of the mango grove presented to the Buddha by Jivaka, Bimbisara's physician, and reaches **Maddakuchchi** from where one has to walk to **Gridhrakuta Hill,** probably the holiest place in Rajgir, where the Buddha delivered most of his sermons. From Maddakuchchi, an aerial ropeway chairlift leads to the top of **Ratna Giri,** a hill at the top of which Japanese Buddhists have built the **Vishwa Shanti** (World Peace) **Stupa,** a huge white structure visible from miles around. Four golden statues, one on each side, recall the Buddha's birth, enlightenment, teachings and death.

Gaya and Bodhgaya

Gaya, 90 km southwest of Rajgir, is an important place of Hindu pilgrimage. Lord Vishnu is said to have conferred upon Gaya the power to cleanse one of one's sins. Thousands of devotees flock here to perform ceremonies to clear their

Paddle steamer on Ganga, Bihar.

dead of the burden of sin they might have carried over to the next world. They take a holy dip in the Phalgu River and lay offerings of *pindas* (sweets) and ritual rice cakes on the ghats along the river, before entering the **Vishnupada Temple** (closed to non-Hindus) built by the Maharani of Indore in 1787 over the footprint Lord Vishnu is believed to have left on a stone. Within the grounds of the temple stands a banyan tree which is said to be the one under which the Buddha spent six years meditating.

The Buddha attained enlightenment in **Bodhgaya,** 12 km south of Gaya, along the Phalgu River. He first meditated in nearby Dungeswari, eating one grain of rice a day for two years, then nothing for four years. Realizing that mortification did not bring enlightenment, the Buddha moved to a cave where voices told him this was not the place where he would receive illumination. He then found a ficus (banyan) tree and sat under it to meditate, vowing not to rise until he attained enlightenment.

King Ashoka had erected a shrine near the *bodhi* tree. This was replaced in the 2nd Century by the present **Mahabodhi Temple** with a 54 m high spire. This was altered in the 11th Century, damaged in the 12th, and restored in the 19th. In the 17th Century, Hindus took over the temple as the Buddha is considered an avatar of Vishnu. The temple is now managed by a joint Buddhist-Hindu committee. Inside the temple is a gilded statue of the Buddha, sitting cross-legged, with his right hand touching the ground in acceptance of enlightenment. Around the temple are votive stupas. Along the western wall is the *"bodhi tree"* or rather its successor. The original is believed to have been destroyed by Emperor Ashoka before his conversion to Buddhism. The replacement was cut down by Ashoka's jealous wife. The next in the line was destroyed by Shasanka, a Hindu king of Bengal. The immediate predecessor of the present *"bodhi"* tree withered in the 19th Century. Under the tree is the **Vajrasana,** the **Diamond Throne,** a stone slab marking the site where the Buddha was sitting when he attained enlightenment. A stone railing runs around the temple on three sides, built in replacement of the original Ashokan one, part of which is in the nearby museum.

Along the north side of the Mahabodhi Temple, the **Chanka Ramana,** a platform built in the 1st Century B.C., marks the place where the Buddha walked in meditation. Carved stone lotuses indicate the spots where lotuses sprung from his feet. South of the temple a statue of the Buddha protected by a cobra stands in the middle of a large lotus pond. Buddhist communities from all over Asia, Tibet, Bhutan, Thailand, Japan, Korea, Burma have built monasteries in Bodhgaya. Each one of these monasteries is a technology center and most of them accept foreign students. The archeological museum at Bodhgaya displays various sculptures, some of them headless and otherwise mutilated during the 12th Century Muslim invasion.

On the way back to Patna, **Pawapuri,** 32 km to the southeast, is a holy place for Jains. It was here that Lord Mahavir attained salvation in 477 B.C. A white marble temple, the **Jalmandir** in the middle of a lotus pond, marks the place where he was cremated. There are five more Jain temples around the pond.

Industrial Centers

Chotanagpur, southern Bihar, is very

Remains of the ancient Nalanda University, Bihar.

different from the north. A large part of the population is tribal, of pre-Dravidian stock, speaking Mon-Khmer languages. The main tribes are the Santal, the Bedia, the Birhor, the No, the Khond, the Munda, the Oraon. Some are still wanderers, living off hunting, wild fruit and root gathering. The majority have settled to cultivate maize and millet, and raise cattle and fowl. About 60 percent of the tribals are Christian. Many now work in the new industrial cities that have sprung up in Bihar since independence.

Ranchi, the former summer capital of Bihar, has lost its cool climate with the felling of most of its trees to make room for a new industrial town. Of the buildings of the colonial period a few remain: the **Eastern Railway Hotel,** the **Lutheran Church** and **Saint Paul's Anglican Church,** and some eccentric villas on Kanke Road, near Ranchi Hill — one called PAR AVION has been built in the shape of a B-52 air craft; the house next door has the shape of a warship. Beyond the bazaar area, on top of Ranchi Hill, overlooking Ranchi Lake, stands a **Shiva Temple** of limited interest compared to the 17th Century fortified **Jagannath Temple** at Jagannathpur near the airport. It is open to non-Hindus.

Jamshedpur (170 km south of Ranchi) is the property of the Tata Iron and Steel Company. The town has grown around the first steel plant in India built in 1912 by the Parsi industrialist, Sir Jamshedji Tata, after whom the city is named. The plant is the most productive of India's steel plants.

Jamshedpur is a well planned city, with adequate housing for labor, green spaces, medical facilities, and the large Jubilee Park laid out round a lake to celebrate the Golden Jubilee of the township and the steel plant.

East of Ranchi, more easily reached from Calcutta, starts "the Indian Ruhr," an industrial zone spreading along the Damodar River into West Bengal. Most of its towns, like **Dhanbad, Chittaranjan** and **Bokaro,** are industrial. To the north west of Dhanbad, however, the **Parasnath Hill** (1,450 m) is an important religious center. Of the 24 Jain Tirthankaras, 20 attained *nirvana* here. On the hill and at the foot of it, are Jain temples of both the Svetambara and Digambara sects, the most interesting ones being the **Samosavan, Bhomia Baba** and **Parasvanath temples.**

Steel works, Jamshedpur, Bihar.

CALCUTTA, A LIVELY CITY

In 1686, Job Charnock, chief of the East India Company's factory in Hoogly, looking for new factory sites, selected a group of three villages — Kalikata, Govindapur and Sutanuti — where Armenian and Portuguese traders had already settled. A factory was established in Kalikata on August 24, 1690. Calcutta was born. A fort was built, named after King William I. With poor defences, surrounded by a maze of narrow lanes, it was easily taken on June 20, 1756, by Siraj-ud-Daula, the Nawab of Bengal. Those English residents who did not escape were crammed into a small room with only one small window. Overnight, 113 of the 146 prisoners died. This is the incident recorded as the tragedy of the Black Hole of Calcutta. Calcutta was retaken on January 2, 1757, by Robert Clive, Governor of Madras. Fort William was rebuilt in its present form in 1773.

Life in the early days had been austere. Company staff lived in thatched mud houses and ate at common tables. There were no distractions and the mortality ran at times at one-third of the expatriate community. The lifestyle evolved rapidly with the development of Calcutta and was distinctly marked by the profile of the European population, most of whom were bachelors in their 20s and 30s. Punch houses made their appearance. Brawls and duels were common. When they were not out, the young "writers," as Company employees were called, would stay home smoking the hookah or watching dances performed by "nautch girls," usually prostitutes. Marriages were few. Writers usually lived with local mistresses, their "sleeping dictionaries."

Things progressively changed. In 1773, Calcutta became the headquarters (potentially, the capital) of the British administration in India. By that time, the European population had swollen from a few hundred to 100,000 through the arrival of new writers, traders, soldiers and what the administration called "cargoes of females." The decline of Calcutta started when the capital of British India was moved to Delhi in 1911. Then with the partition of the Indian subcontinent when India became an independent country and the flow of refugees across the newly created borders, Calcutta had to

Victoria Memorial, Calcutta, with statue of Edward VII in foreground.

Calcutta

make room for a substantial addition to its population. Again in 1971, in the wake of the Bangladesh war, there was a further sudden increase. This, in addition to the rapid growth overburdened the city, and brought urban services to the verge of collapse.

On the eve of its 300th anniversary, Calcutta is the largest city in India, with a population of above 10 million. Recent descriptions of its misery, however, are exaggerated. It is a lively city where something is always happening, be it religious celebrations, concerts, soccer matches, theater or movie festivals, or political demonstrations; and although decaying, the architectural heritage is still there.

Fort William and the Maidan

Calcutta was built around **Fort William.** On the western side of the fort is the **Strand** and the **Hoogly River,** a branch of the holy Ganga, on the eastern side is the Maidan.

The **Maidan** is a huge open park surrounding Fort William. For a long time, to ensure that the fort's guns had a free field of fire in all directions, no buildings were permitted on the Maidan.

Today the main building on the Maidan is the **Victoria Memorial.** It is a massive domed building of white marble from Rajasthan. It was inaugurated in 1921 by the Prince of Wales (later, briefly, Edward VIII). It houses a collection of Victoria memorabilia and also history related objects and documents on Bengal.

In the park in which the memorial stands are statues of Queen Victoria, Lord Curzon and other figures of the Raj. Here, on weekends, people picnic, families meet for matchmaking, and transiting pilgrims bring flowers to the statue of "Maharani Victoria."

Behind the Memorial, on Lower Circular Road, is the **Presidency General Hospital** where, in 1898, Sir Ronald Ross identified the carrier of malaria — the female anopheles mosquito.

The **Racecourse,** opened in 1819, is the largest in the East. In its central oval are the Calcutta Polo Club grounds where the game has been played since 1861.

To the southeast is Cathedral Road starting at **Rabindra Sadan,** a concert hall named after Rabindranath Tagore, which is active all the year round. The nearby **Academy of Fine Arts** has a collection of

Chowringhee, Calcutta, city center.

old textiles, miniatures, Mughal swords, Tagore memorabilia and modern Bengali art. The adjacent **St. Paul's Cathedral** was consecrated in 1847. It is a tall white Gothic building with rows of fans hanging from a wooden ceiling, stalls and pews of heavy wood, and a stained-glass window by Burne-Jones. On the walls are interesting commemorative slabs in memory of British killed during the Mutiny and those who lost their lives in various wars.

Near the Cathedral are the **Birla Planetarium** and the **Nehru Children's Museum.** The latter displays a collection of toys from all over the world and two remarkable dioramas presenting the Rámayana and the Mahabharata in 61 scenes.

At the northern end of the Maidan, the 158-foot (48-meter) high **Ochterlony Monument** was erected to celebrate Sir David Ochterlony's victories in the Nepal wars. In the 19th Century the monument was used by Young Bengal nationalists to hoist the French flag as a sign of rebellion against the British Raj. The monument has been recently renamed **Shaheed Minar** to honor martyred freedom fighters.

Describing the **Maidan** in terms of its monuments does not show how lively it is. In the 19th Century, nationalists had organized a fair, the Hindu Mela, on the Maidan, with concerts of music and dance and also plays and lectures. It was here that Tagore, aged 15, made his first public appearance. Nowadays, the Maidan Mela is a daily 24-hour show. At sunrise, joggers make their appearance; the West Bengal Mounted Police hack their horses; Army units do their morning drills; goats and sheep browse on the course of the Calcutta Golf Club, before being led to slaughter. Later, tramways start plying, bringing people to work. Football or cricket then takes over, as sadhus and bards gather audiences under trees near the **Gandhi Statue** and the **War Memorial.** At night, action concentrates on the square around **Sri Aurobindo's Statue** opposite the Victoria Memorial.

Along the Maidan, **Chowringhee,** once a jungle path leading to the Kali Temple, and the **Esplanade** symbolize Calcutta's past grandeur with late 19th Century buildings such as the **Oberoi Grand** and the **Indian Museum,** opened in 1814. Chowringhee's glory has, however, departed. Most of the facades are

Nakhoda Mosque, Calcutta.

scaling; hawkers, shoe-shine boys, beggars, touts, now crowd the pavement.

Raj Bhavan, or Government House, was built in 1803 by Governor-General Wellesley, who believed that India should be governed "from a palace, not from a counting-house." Towards the river are the **Assembly House,** the old **Town Hall** and the **High Court** built in 1872 on the model of the Gothic belfrey of Ypres in Flanders.

To the west is **St. John's Church,** built in 1784. It is reputed to have the best organ in India. Job Charnock was buried here. In the garden stands a monument to the victims of the "Black Hole" tragedy. Beyond is **Dalhousie Square,** renamed **B.B.D. Bag** in memory of three brothers, Binoy, Badal and Dinesh, who were hanged for having conspired to kill Lord Dalhousie. Facing the tank that once used to be Calcutta's only source of drinking water, stands **Writers Building,** the seat of the West Bengal Government. It was built in the late 19th Century. The first Writers Buildings that stood here housed "writers" of the East India Company, hence its name. Opposite stand **Telephone Bhawan** and **St. Andrew's Kirk,** opened in 1818. The offices of Calcutta's most prestigious companies — tall Victorian buildings, with art nouveau staircases, brass signs, marble steps and floors and wood paneling — are on the old **Clive Row,** now **Netaji Subhas Road.**

These streets are now crowded with hawkers, private cars and taxis moving and double-parked, and pedestrians. Even the Stock Exchange has spilled over onto the street opposite Jardine Henderson's. The present **General Post Office** is on the site of the first Fort William and a plaque near the main entrance marks the location of the notorious "Black Hole of Calcutta."

In India Exchange Lane, near the **Jute Balers Association,** speculators on the jute market operate from booths equipped with telephones, projecting a couple of feet from the walls of the buildings along the street. Buyers in the booths shout their orders to sellers who stand in the street.

The Bazaars

Starting at the northeastern corner of the Maidan, in **Bentinck Street** there is a succession of Chinese shoemakers, Muslim tailors and sweet and tea shops. **Tiretta**

St. Paul's Cathedral, Calcutta.

Market nearby, named after its former owner, a friend of Casanova's who had to flee Venice, sells dry fish, vegetable and meat.

Chinatown is in Tiretta where the Chinese settled at the end of the 18th Century. A whole area in Calcutta once was a Cantonese town, but it has since been greatly reduced after the departure of most of the Chinese in 1962, when Indian and Chinese troops clashed at the frontier. Calcutta still has some 30,000 Chinese citizens, but most of the Chinese buildings have disappeared, except the **Nanking Restaurant** on Blackburn Lane, the **Sea Ip Temple** on Chatawala Gully, a few clubs, and the **Kuomintang Press**, on Metcalfe Street, publishing two dailies in Chinese.

In **Old China Bazaar**, west of Brabourne Road, Parsis have an agiary (fire temple), the Ismallites have a mosque, and the Gujarati Jains a temple, probably one of the most charming in Calcutta, in this area. There are also three synagogues. One of them, Magen David, was built in 1884. Calcutta's Jews came from Iraq in the 19th Century and formed a prosperous community but emigration since the end of the

Second World War has drastically reduced their number to about 200.

Off Old China Bazaar Lane, stands the **Armenian Church of Our Lady of Nazareth.** It was built in 1724. Coming from Isfahan, the Armenians were already here and in Chinsura, upriver on the Hoogly, when Job Charnock founded Calcutta. A grave in the church cemetery is dated 1630. In and around Calcutta, the Armenians have several churches, a school, a club and also one of India's best rugby teams.

Along the Chitpur Road, now called Rabindra Sarani, stands the **Nakhoda Mosque.** It is built in red sandstone with four floors on the model of Akbar's tomb near Agra. It has room for a congregation of ten thousand.

Stately Homes

Joransanko with verandahed houses on Sir Hariram Goenka Street and mansions around Kali Krishna Nagore and Jadulal Mullick streets, has a character all their own. The most eccentric of the mansions is **Tagore's Castle** on Darpanarain Tagore Lane built in 1867 and

Race Course, Calcutta.

reminiscent of Sleeping Beauty's castle at Disneyland. Overbuilt structures have, unfortunately, altered its silhouette.

At the end of Dwarkanath Tagore Lane is **Rabindra Mancha**, an 18th Century house where the poet Rabindranath Tagore was born in 1861, and where he died in 1941. It is now a museum devoted to the poet's life and to the Young Bengal Movement. Adjoining the house is a library and **Rabindra Bharati**, the Tagore Academy.

In **Kumarthuli**, further north, live a community of artisans making clay images of goddesses Durga, Lakshmi or Saraswati for festivals.

In Rajabazar on Badni Das Temple Road are three Jain temples of the Svetambara sect, built at the end of the 19th Century. Their architecture is a mixture of Mughal, baroque, neo-classical and local styles, and their interiors are decorated with mosaics, colored glass, mirrors, colored stones, crystal and marble.

At Chorebagan ('the thieves garden'), the **Marble Palace** on Muktaram Babu Street was built in 1835 by Raja Mullick in Italian marble. The raja's descendants still live here, but most of it can be visited. In dark halls are assembled paintings, clocks, statues, crystal and china. Among them there is said to be a Napoleon by Houdon, one Arnold, one Gainsborough, three Rubens and a statue by Michelangelo. In the yard is the family temple, and a collection of parrots, doves and mynas.

Calcutta University on College Square was founded in 1873. It has, in the past, been the scene of many demonstrations and most of its walls are still covered with political grafitti. In the **University Senate** building is the **Asutosh Museum**, presenting a collection of Pala sculptures, terra cotta, bronzes, *thangkas* (Buddhist religious paintings on cloth) and Bengali folk art. The **Albert Hall coffee shop**, on Bankim Chatterjee Street, is the meeting place for all who matter in the intellectual and student circles of Calcutta.

Behind Chowringhee is where the European community used to live. It is an area of mansions slowly being replaced by modern buildings. **Park Street,** the main thoroughfare, was laid during the first quarter of this century. The **Freemason's Hall** on this street was built in the 19th Century. It houses the Star of the East Lodge, the oldest outside Britain. The **Asiatic Society,** also at the beginning

Contemporary image of Goddess Kali.

168

of Park Street, was founded in 1784. The present building houses a permanent exhibition of oriental manuscripts, prints and paintings that can be visited on request.

The **Raychowdhury Castle** on Albert Road has become the **Radha Govinda Temple of ISKON**, the International Society for Krishna Consciousness.

Another landmark is **La Martinière College** on Lower Circular Road, founded by a Frenchman, Claude Martin, born in Lyons. A former bodyguard to the French Governor of Pondicherry, Martin later joined the service of the East India Company and ended his career as a Major-General. He died in 1800, bequeathing his fortune to set up schools in Lyons, Calcutta and Lucknow, and Rs. 50,000 to the Church of the Sacred Heart at Chandernagore with instructions that the interest earned be distributed every day to the poor, for all time to come.

Park Street used to be called European Burial Road and once ended at the **South Park Street Cemetery,** the oldest extant in Calcutta. It was opened in 1767. Here are buried Major General Charles "Hindoo" Stuart, an Irishman who adopted the Hindu religion; Robert Kyd, founder of the Botanical Gardens; William Makepeace Thackeray's father; Rose Aylmer "who died of eating too many pineapples"; the poet Henry Derozio, founder of the Young Bengal Movement; and Sir William Jones, father of the Asiatic Society.

Nearby, in the suburb of Bhowanipore, is **Netaji Bhawan** on Elgin Road, the house from which Netaji Subhas Bose, the nationalist leader escaped during the Second World War to establish the Indian National Army in Japanese-occupied southeast Asia. It is now a museum.

South Calcutta

South Calcutta is essentially residential, with upper-class localities alternating with middle-class neighborhoods. Warren Hastings' first residence, at Alipore, now an institute of education, is said to be haunted by its former owner. The **National Library,** on Belvedere Road, was once the Winter Viceregal Lodge. The **Agro-Horticultural Society** located behind Belvedere was founded in 1820.

The **Zoological Gardens** were established in 1876. In wintertime thousands of migratory birds from as far off as

Writers Building, Calcutta, headquarters of the West Bengal Government.

tional Library, on Belvedere Road, was once the Winter Viceregal Lodge. The **Agro-Horticultural Society** located behind Belvedere was founded in 1820.

The **Zoological Gardens** were established in 1876. In wintertime thousands of migratory birds from as far off as Siberia stay here on the lake. Among the animals on display at the Calcutta Zoo, are bizarre specimens such as the Tigon, the result of crossing a tiger and an African lioness, and the Litigon obtained by crossing a tigon with a lioness.

Kalighat is a middle-class neighborhood on **Tolly's Nullah,** a canal also called Adiganga, "the real Ganga," because it is believed to be the original bed of the Hoogly. In 1775 a Colonel Tolly drained the silted nulla to bring Ganga water to the Kali Temple.

The present **Kali Temple** was built in 1809. The temple, as such, has, however, been in existence from early times. Thugs used to come here to pray before setting out in search of victims. Human sacrifices are known to have taken place here in the past. Today only goats, and, on occasions, buffaloes, are sacrificed while pilgrims make offerings of milk mixed with Ganga water and *bhang* (Cannabis Indica) to Kali.

There are more temples dedicated to Shiva, Radha and Krishna, and Vishnu further south on Alipore Chetla and Tollygunge roads. Nearby, is the **Tollygunge Club.** Once an indigo plantation was located here. Later the Maharaja of Mysore built his Calcutta mansion on the site. It became the Tollygunge Club in 1895. It offers its facilities (golf, tennis and squash) to visitors on a daily membership basis.

East of Tollygunge, around **Rabindra Sarovar lake,** are rowing clubs and the **Birla Art Academy** on Southern Avenue, a museum, never crowded, with a whole floor of miniatures from all schools, a modern art gallery, and old statues of the Buddhist period. The **Birla Industrial and Technological Museum** displays a life-size model of part of a coal mine.

The **Ramakrishna Mission Institute of Culture** on Gol Park, near the lake, is a branch of the Ramakrishna Mission of Belur Math. It has a school of languages teaching Persian, Sanskrit, Bengali and Hindi, a library, a museum of Indian art and a Universal Prayer Room.

Ghats on the Ganga

From the ghat near the Garden Reach shipyard, a ferry crosses to the **Botanical Gardens** in Howrah. Set up in 1786, it boasted for long the largest banyan tree in the world. The central trunk was, however, struck by lightning in 1919 and was subsequently removed. About 1,500 offshoots remain, forming a circle with a diameter of more than ten meters.

The **Metiaburuz Shiite Mosque** on Garden Reach Road was built and lavishly decorated by the royal family of Oudh in the 19th Century.

The riverside ghats off Strand Road, like any on the Ganga, are most active at dawn and sunset. During festivals thousands of devotees converge on **Babu, Outram** and **Princep Ghats** to immerse clay images of Durga, Kali, Lakshmi or Saraswati into the river. Other communities hold festivals too. On Chaat, the Sun Festival, Biharis dip fruit in the river and Sindhis, on Chetti Chand, immerse statues of the god Jhulelal. On Strand Road, in January, a transit camp is arranged for the thousands of pilgrims on their way to the holy island of Sagardwip. Every morning, the ghats swarm with people taking a holy dip, washing, and praying.

On the riverfront promenade, families take an evening stroll, lovers sit on benches, oblivious of the world, near the **Gwalior Monument,** called the "Pepper Pot" because of its shape, and erected to commemorate a British victory in the Maratha Wars.

At Princep Ghat dinghies are available for hire on an hourly basis for a ride on the river.

Behind Babu Ghat are **Eden Gardens,** a park created in 1877, with a kiosk and a pagoda brought to Calcutta from Prome in Burma by Lord Curzon. Eden Gardens Stadium is the Mecca of Indian Cricket. The world record of attendance at a cricket match was broken here in 1982 when 394,000 fans watched England play an Indian team.

The **Howrah Bridge,** over the Hoogly, now a Calcutta landmark, was built in 1941. It has 8 lanes for traffic, which is not enough for the daily flow of tramways, buses, trucks, trishaws, pedestrians, buffaloes, sheep, goats, taxis and bullockcarts that cross it every day. On hot days its length can increase by one meter. A second Howrah Bridge at Hasting is being built but meanwhile, all Calcutta must get across as best and as patiently as they can.

Lord Curzon, The Viceroy who conceived the Victoria Memorial that stands behind his statue.

170

BENGAL, GANGA'S BOUNTY

West Bengal stretches from the Himalaya to the Bay of Bengal. Before the partition of the subcontinent, the province of Bengal included what is now Bangladesh, with which the Indian Union State of West Bengal shares its language, culture and historical background.

Early mention of Bengal can be found in the Mahabharata and in Ptolemy's geography. Bengal was then a seafaring nation, sending traders to Sri Lanka, Sumatra and Java and being visited by Greeks, Chinese and Persians either by sea or over land.

From the end of the 19th Century onwards Bengal was one of the most prosperous territories of the British Empire. A new Bengali culture developed under the Raj. Temples were built, the Bengali language was enriched by poets and writers such as Bankim Chandra Chatterjee and Rabindranath Tagore. Major religious philosophers like Ramakrishna and Vivekananda appeared. A sense of Bengali and all-India nationalism developed. The attempted partition of Bengal in 1904 by Lord Curzon into a Hindu West and a Muslim East, and the removal of the capital to New Delhi inflamed nationalist feelings.

Early Colonizers

On the right bank of the Hoogly, less than 60 km from Calcutta, along the Grand Trunk Road, are sleepy little towns with palaces, old churches, riverfront promenades and colonial houses and cemeteries — remains of the old Danish, Dutch and French settlements. The Grand Trunk Road is reached by the Bally Bridge crossing the Hoogly at **Dakshineshwar**, where, on the left bank, is the 9th Century **Kali Bhavatarini Temple** complex containing a central temple to Kali, one to Radha-Krishna and twelve small temples to Shiva. The philosopher Ramakrishna lived here: his room is now a museum. Downstream, across the river, is **Belur Math**, headquarters of the Ramakrishna Mission, founded in 1938 by Ramakrishna's disciple, Vivekananda. The main building, the **Sri Ramakrishna Temple**, 75 m long and 35 m high, reflects Ramakrishna's call for harmony between religions. The

gate is Buddhist, the structure above the entrance, South Indian, the windows and balconies, Mughal and Rajput, and the plan, that of a Christian cross.

The first erstwhile foreign settlement north of Calcutta is **Serampore.** The Danish East India Company carried on trade here from the late 17th Century till 1845, when the Danes sold to Britain all their possessions in India. Under the Danes, Serampore became an important cultural center. In 1799, William Carey, an Englishman, and two fellow Baptist missionaries, established a press here and were pioneers of printing in several oriental languages. In 1819 Carey founded the **Serampore College,** incorporated in 1827 as a university by Danish Royal Charter. This was the first modern university in Asia. Still active, the college is now a Baptist theological institute. It stands on the bank of the Hoogly, among other 18th and 19th Century mansions, on a shady tree-lined waterfront promenade. Slightly inland is **Saint Olaf's Church** built in 1747.

A gate bearing the motto of the French Republic, *"Liberté, Egalité, Fraternité,"* marks the entrance to **Chandernagore**, a French *Etablissement* almost continuously from 1673 to 1952. Hardly anybody speaks French there now but a French atmosphere still persists along the shaded Quai Dupleix, now Strand Road, with its public benches exactly like those in Paris parks. The **Eglise du Sacré Coeur** could well be a French village church with its statue of Joan of Arc and a Lourdes grotto.

To the northwest, at **Palpara** and **Narwah** are groups of Shiva temples. The most important is the 18th Century **Nandadulal Temple** at Lal Bagan dedicated to Krishna, a good exemple of flat-roofed Bengali architecture.

The Dutch settled at **Chinsura** further north in 1625 and ceded it to Britain in 1826 against Bencoolen in Sumatra. A Dutch barracks, a church and a cemetery still remain from that period. Chinsura's Armenian community built **Saint John's Church** in 1695 and, once a year, on Saint John's day, in January, the Armenians of Calcutta gather here to hold religious services. To the north, on the riverside, is the **Imambara,** a Shiite mosque with a clock tower donated by Queen Victoria.

The Portuguese founded nearby Bandel de Ugolim, now **Hoogly**, in 1580, and controlled most of the Mughal empire's foreign trade passing through

Bengal, until the arrival of other European nations. In 1632, after a three-month siege, Hoogly was destroyed by the Mughal Emperor Shah Jahan.

The **Church of Our Lady of Bandel** is all that remains of the Portuguese past. Consecrated in 1599 it was rebuilt after it was destroyed by Shah Jahan in 1632, but without the usual exuberance of Portuguese churches. The Bandel church was already a pilgrimage center when it was destroyed. Even today, each Christmas Eve, a mass is celebrated, drawing extra trainloads of Catholics from Calcutta.

Holy Cities

North of Hoogly, at **Bansberia,** are two temples. The small **Vasudeva Temple** built in the 17th Century has sculptured terra-cotta tiles representing ships, Portuguese soldiers and scenes from the Ramayana. **Hangseshwari Temple,** with its 13 towers, was founded in the early 19th Century. Rajah Deb started building it after a dream but died before completion. His widow was to commit sati but was saved at the last moment by the religious reformer, Ram Mohan Roy, founder of the Brahmo Samaj movement. The rani lived on and finished the temple.

Beyond Bansberia, **Tribeni** is a holy place at the confluence of two rivers, the Saraswati and the Jamuna with the Ganga. Twice a year, at Dussera and during the festival of Varuna, the god of water, pilgrims visit the little **Benimadhava Temple** complex and take a bath in the Ganga. On the southern side of the Saraswati is the **Darya Zafar Khan,** Bengal's oldest Muslim building, erected in the 13th Century using material from dismantled Buddhist and Hindu temples.

Nawadwip, 125 km north of Calcutta, also known as **Nadia,** is built on nine formerly distinct islands on the Ganga, called Bhagirathi here. It was the capital of Bengal in the 11th and 12th centuries and is among the holiest of places in West Bengal. Chaitanya Mahaprabhu, said to be an incarnation of Vishnu, taught the Vaishnava philosophy here in the 16th Century. Every year in March, over 500,000 pilgrims come to Nadia for the *padikrama,* a pilgrimage on foot, that takes them along a 50 km loop around places and temples associated with Chaitanya on the nine islands. Chaitanya's birthplace in Mayapur, on **Antardwip,** is

Darjeeling, Bengal.

the usual starting point for the *padi-krama*. Nearby is **Sri Mayapur**, the head-quarters of the International Society for Krishna Consciousness (ISKCON).

At Mayapur, ISKCON is now building a Vedic City, the future "spiritual capital of the world." There is already a temple, a guest house, gardens with lotus-shaped fountains, a museum in the house where the founder of the movement, Swami Prabhupada, lived, and a souvenir shop selling books, tee shirts, clothes, cassettes and discs. From its Calcutta center, ISKCON organizes bus trips to Mayapur at least twice a week with a video pro-gram on the movement and a color movie on Rama and Sita aboard the bus.

Murshidabad and Malda

Murshidabad, some 50 km north of the battlefield of Plassey, became the capital of Bengal in 1705, when the Diwan (Mughal Viceroy) of Bengal, Bihar and Orissa, Murshid Kuli Khan, transferred his capital here from Dacca. Most of the monuments are ruined but **Siraj-ud-Daula's grave,** at **Khusbagh,** across the river, **Murshid Kuli Khan's tomb** inside the **Katra Mosque** and the Jaffraganj cemetery can still be seen. There are also palaces like the **Jaffraganj Deorhi palace,** where Siraj-ud-Daula was assassinated; **Hazarduari,** the Nawab's palace, built in 1837 in Gothic style, now a museum containing old arms, china and special plates used by the nawab that, it was believed, would crack if the food were poisoned. Murshidabad is still well known for its fine silks and ivory carving.

Nearby, at **Baranagar** are 18th Century terra-cotta temples. Further north, 340 km from Calcutta, is **Malda,** formerly called English Bazaar, a foreign settlement dating from 1680, where the Dutch, the French, and then the East India Com-pany carried on trade. **Gaur,** nearby, was the capital of the Pala and Sen dynasties. Under the names of Ramvati and then Lakshmanavati, the city was destroyed by the Afghan rulers of Bengal. Elements from the Hindu monuments were used to build the new capital of **Pandua** where the most important remains are the **Barasona Baroduari Mosque.** completed in 1526; **Feroze Minar,** a 26 m minaret built in 1486; the ruined **Chika Mosque,** with Hindu idols on the doors and lintels; and the now dilapilated **Lattina** and **Adina Mosques.**

The Delta

South of Calcutta start the **Sunder-bans,** 'beautiful forest' in Bengali, formed by the delta of the Ganga and the Brah-maputra, and extending across the entire northern shore of the Bay of Bengal. Two-thirds of this area is in Bangladesh. This Sunderban is a marshy mangrove jungle, the largest estuarine forest in the world. Nature is extremely hostile. The land is saturated with salt, sustaining a poor single crop a year; the man-eating Royal Bengal Tiger can swim and even attacks fishermen in their boats, killing altogether more than 200 persons each year.

There are few roads, Water transport is often the only way of communication. Individual travel is impossible and a per-mit is required to enter this area. The best way to visit it is to join the two-day trip to the Sudhanyakhali and Sajankali Sanctuaries, organized every second and fourth weekend of the month by the West Bengal Tourist Promotion Board. Armed rangers accompany visitors to the watch towers. They are a necessary escort as Bengal tigers hide in ambush and do not flee when they sense the presence of man. The chances of seeing a tiger are slim, but there are many estuarine cro-codiles, the largest in the world, usually seen sleeping on mud flats along the river. Short one-day cruises are also available. All start from Basanti near Canning Port, southwest of Calcutta, which can be reached in two hours by bus or by train from Sealdah Station.

Down the Hoogly

At **Bratacharingam,** 15 km south of Calcutta, on the road to Diamond Har-bor, is **Gurusaday Museum,** a collection of Bengali folk art: terra-cotta temple plaques, clay figurines, wood sculptures, Kalighat folk paintings, scroll painting and *kanthas* (layers of used cotton saris, stitched together and embroidered in a variety of patterns).

On the Hoogly, at the end of Budge-Budge Road, branching off Diamond Harbor Road, is **Achipur** named after Ah-Chi, the first Chinese to migrate to Bengal in modern times (the end of the 18th Century). His red-painted grave facing the river is probably the only Chinese tomb along the Ganga. There is also a Taoist temple. On every Lunar New Year, the Chinese community of Calcutta comes here on pilgrimage, transforming this Bengali village into a Chinese town of more than 20,000 for one day.

Diamond Harbor, 50 km down the Hoogly from Calcutta, a natural harbor, is a former stronghold of the Portuguese pirates. Remains of their fort can still be seen along the riverfront. This small port was a Conradian flavor.

The last island before the ocean is **Sagardwip.** The Ganga flows into the ocean here. The place is so sacred that dying at Sagardwip is believed, by itself, enough to ensure the attainment of nirvana. Every year, in mid-January, a religious festival, Gangasagar Mela, is celebrated here. Over half-a-million pilgrims gather from all over India. They first take a holy dip that washes them clean of all sins and then converge at the **Kapil Muni Temple,** built in memory of Kapila, a philosopher who taught and died on the island.

An independent trip to Sagardwip can take up to two days at festival time as roads are heavily jammed and the boats overloaded with pilgrims. The Tourist Development Corporation offers a two-day boat trip limited to 30 persons with accommodation on board.

On the west coast of the Bay of Bengal 243 km south-east of Calcutta, on the Orissa border, is **Digha,** the only seaside resort with proper hotel accommodation in West Bengal. Rich Calcuttans have built villas here, but the place has since considerably decayed.

Darjeeling

Every year, at the beginning of the monsoon, the Viceroys of India, and after 1911 the Lieutenant Governors of Bengal, would move, lock, stock and barrel, to **Darjeeling,** situated at an altitude of 2,134 m, facing the Himalaya.

The British rapidly developed Darjeeling into a pleasant resort. In the 1840s tea plantation was introduced in the area. Darjeeling "orthodox" tea is now famous and among the most expensive.

Darjeeling is a three-hour drive up a steep and winding road from Bagdogra airport near Siliguri. It first ascends mild slopes covered with tea gardens, then climbs steeply some 1,500 m over a distance of 35 km. Darjeeling can also be reached from New Jalpaiguri railway station by Toy Train. The ride on the two-foot (0.6 m) gauge track takes seven hours through almost the same landscape as the road.

Darjeeling is an abrupt change from the plains and Calcutta. The population is Nepali, Lepcha, Tibetan and Bhutia. There is no pollution, there are no crowds, and the pace of life slow.

At the center of the town is the Mall, Darjeeling's commercial street, lined with souvenir shops. Photo-stores deserve a special mention as they sell prints of old black-and-white pictures from the turn of the century. The Mall leads to **Chaurastha,** a square with a bandstand, a bookshop selling old books on India and Tibet, and antique shops.

On **Observatory Hill** is perhaps the oldest built-up site in Darjeeling. A Red Hat Buddhist monastery, **Dorjeling,** "the place of the thunderbolt" once stood here but was destroyed by the Nepalis in the 19th Century. A Shiva temple and an old-fashioned hotel now occupy the site.

On **Birch Hill** to the north, stands the **Shrubbery,** the residence of the Governor of West Bengal, and further down along Birch Hill Road, the **Himalayan Mountaineering Institute** previously headed by the late Tenzing Norgay, the Sherpa guide who conquered the Everest with Sir Edmund Hillary on May 29, 1953. A

Tea gardens at Darjeeling, Bengal.

museum displays the equipment used on that occasion and for other expeditions.

The nearby Zoological Park specializes in high-altitude wildlife — yaks, Himalayan black bears, pandas, but it also has four Siberian Tigers. Below, the tea estate of Happy Valley is one of the best in Darjeeling. It can be visited every day except on Sundays and Mondays.

Dominating the Mall is the **Planters' Club,** which visitors can join and where they can stay on a daily basis. The club becomes very lively on Sundays when planters from all over the area meet for lunch.

The **Lloyd Botanical Gardens,** were laid out in 1878 on land donated by the owners of Lloyd's Bank. They present a collection of Himalayan and Alpine flora. Nearby is the Tibetan Refugee Self-Help Center with its temple, school, hospital, and a shop selling carpets, textiles and jewelry.

Mount Kanchenjunga can be seen from Observatory Hill, but a much better view of the peak is that from **Tiger Hill,** 10 km south of Darjeeling. Taxis take visitors there to watch the sunrise. On most winter days, the range can be clearly seen, with **Kanchenjunga** (8,598 m) in the middle, flanked by **Kabru** (7,338 m) and **Pandim** (6,691 m). To the right are the Three Sisters, the **Everest** (8,842 m), the **Makalu** (8,482 m) and the **Lhotse** (8,500 m), and to the east, Tibetan peaks. On the way back the taxis stop at Ghoom. The small Tibetan monastery by the roadside is often mistaken for the nearby **Yiga Cholang Yellow Hat Buddhist Temple,** built in 1875 and housing a 5 m statue of Lord Buddha.

Kurseong, Kalimpong, the Dooars

With a plunging view of the plains of Bangladesh below, **Kurseong** (1,458 m), 35 km south of Darjeeling, marks the point where the Toy Train starts running parallel to the road. The train goes so slowly here that one can buy from the hawkers, walking, not even running, along with the train, without leaving one's compartment.

Branching off at Ghoom, a road leads to **Mirik** 40 km southwest of Darjeeling, an artificial lake in a small valley where tourist facilities and mountain river fishing are being introduced. Here the road from Darjeeling runs along the border between India and Nepal.

West of Darjeeling, Dandakphu, a five-hour drive from Darjeeling and situated 130 km from Everest as the crow flies, is a center for trekking. Two to eight-day treks can be arranged, passing through Phalut, Ramam, Molle, Rimbick, Barahatta, Batasia, Tonglu and Manibhangay. Sandakphu deserves a visit by itself as it commands a better view of the main Himalayan range than Tiger Hill does since it is closer and higher.

Kalimpong, east of Darjeeling, is reached after a two-hour drive. Driving among forests and tea gardens, the road descends to about 200 m above sea-level and crosses the one-lane bridge over the Teesta River, near its confluence with the Rangeet at Pashoke, and climbs back to an altitude of 1,243 m, finally reaching Kalimpong 51 km from Darjeeling. The Lepchas have a legend about the meeting of the Rangeet and the Teesta. They say the two rivers are lovers who fled the mountains to hide their love. One came down in a straight line, led by a partridge, the other zigzagged, led by a cobra, and they were united at Pashoke.

Kalimpong has a population of 25,000. It was once the starting point for the land route to Tibet. Twice a week, on Wednesday and Saturday, a market, a

Temple at Vishnupur, Bengal.

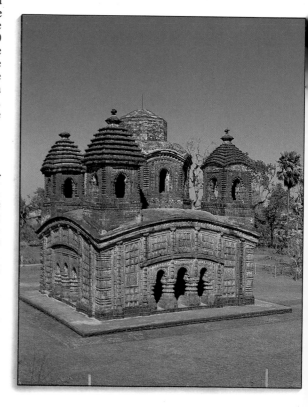

haat, is still held here selling spices, fruit and traditional Tibetan medicines, textiles, wool and musk.

There are two Yellow Hat Buddhist monasteries in Kalimpong. **Tharpa Choling** at Tirpai, the largest one, houses a library of Tibetan manuscripts and *thangkas.* Photography is unfortunately prohibited here as it is located near a military base. **Zang-dog Palrifo Brang Monastery,** on Durpin Dara Hill, is smaller and of more recent construction.

East of Kalimpong, bordering Bhutan, are the **Dooars,** a tea-garden and jungle area little known to tourists. It lies in the valley formed by the lower Teesta River and its tributaries in the foothills of the Himalaya. The Dooars can be reached by meter-gauge railway from New Jalpaiguri and by plane through Cooch Behar or Bagdogra. At **Jaldapara** there is a **Wild Life Sanctuary,** with one-horned rhinos, elephants, deer, gaur and wild boar. The Tourist Lodge at nearby **Madarihat** is a villa on stilts built entirely in timber. Nearby is Phuntsholing, across the border, in Bhutan.

West of Calcutta

The **Tarakeshwar Temple** built around a black stone *lingam* of Tarakeshwar Babu, an avatar of Shiva, 57 km west of Calcutta, has little architectural interest but is one of West Bengal's most active pilgrimage centers. At Shivaratri in February and Kasta-mela in August, bare-footed pilgrims carry Ganga water from Calcutta to the temple in earthen pots decorated with flowers and pour it over the *lingam.*

Further west, **Kamarpukur,** a group of three hamlets surrounded by paddy fields, is religious philosopher Rama-krishna Paramhansdeb's birthplace. There is a temple with a marble statue of Ramakrishna on the spot where he was born, and another next to it devoted to Raghubir, an avatar of Rama, Rama-krishna's family deity.

Vishnupur, still further west (201 km from Calcutta), was the capital of the Malla kings. Under the reign of Veer Hambir and his successors, Rajas Raghu-nath Singh and Veer Singh, in the 17th and 18th centuries, Vishnupur became an important cultural center, developing its distinct style of temple architecture, drawing its inspiration from the curved roofs of Bengali village huts, with facades covered with terra-cotta tiles depicting various scenes from the Ramayana.

The most impressive building in Vishnupur is **Rashmancha,** a flat pyramid-like structure resting on the arches of three circumambulatory galleries. Nearby, opposite the Tourist Lodge, is **Dalmadal,** a huge cannon, almost 4 m long, the boom of which saved the city from the Maratha armies in 1742. There are temples all over the city. The most remarkable ones are **Kalachand Sri Mandir; Shamroy Mandir,** perhaps the finest terra-cotta temple of Bengal, with scenes from the Ramayana and the Mahabharata; **Jore Bangla,** covered with tiles depicting naval battles and hunting scenes; **Madan Mohan;** and **Madan Gopal,** resembling a church more than a temple, with its five towers.

North of Vishnupur, and at about 136 km from Calcutta, is **Shantiniketan.** In 1861 Rabindranath Tagore's father founded an ashram here. The poet spent most of his Nobel Prize money to make it an educational institution in 1902. Then, with the help of the Maharaja of Tripura, he upgraded it to the level of a university in 1921. Here the poet revived the traditional Indian way of teaching in the open air, under a tree, in close contact with nature.

Shantiniketan soon became one of the hubs of intellectual life of India. The University's most famous alumnus is probably the late Indira Gandhi.

At each change of season, and on Shantiniketan foundation day, festivals are held, with dances, songs and plays by Tagore, performed by students of the university.

An annual festival is celebrated near Shantiniketan, at **Kendubilwa,** the birthplace of Jaidev, another great Bengali poet and propagator of Vaishnava philosophy. In mid-January, Bengali bards, known as *bauls,* gather here and hold a four-day non-stop recital of the poet's compositions.

To the north of Shantiniketan are two pilgrimage centers. **Bakreshwar,** 58 km towards the Bihar border, is a place of Shiva and Kali worship, where the space between the goddess's eyebrows is said to have fallen when she was cut in 51 pieces. Bakreshwar is famous as well for its hot sulfurous springs. **Tarapith,** 80 km from Shantiniketan, is a small village dominated by a temple to Tara, an avatar of Kali, whose third eye is said to have landed here. Festivals are held here several times a year, the most important being Tara and Lakshmi Pujas in October.

ANDAMAN AND NICOBAR ISLANDS

The Andaman and Nicobar Islands, home of a number of aboriginal tribes, lie 1,220 km southeast of the coast of Bengal and 1,190 km east of Madras. Their existence was reported as early as in the 9th Century A.D. by Arab merchants sailing past to enter the Straits to Sumatra, 120 km to the south.

The main aboriginal group in the Andamans are the Onges, who live on Little Andaman. Onges, like other Andamanese tribes, are of Negrito stock. They practice food gathering, hunting, honey-collecting and fishing, and are the only tribe on the islands who freely accept contact with the outside world.

In the Nicobars, the only aboriginals are the Shompens with whom little contact exists. The Nicobarese, the largest group, seem to be of mixed Burmese, Malay, Mon and Shan origin. They are cultivators producing fruit, vegetables, copra and coconut oil. They also raise pigs and cows which were first brought in by erstwhile Danish settlers in the 18th Century.

The first westerners to set foot on the islands were the Danes who established a settlement in the Nicobars and then left in 1768 due to poor health conditions. The British surveyed the Andamans in 1789 and established a penal settlement on South Andaman Island but had to abandon it in 1796 because of unhealthy living conditions. The East India Company used the Nicobars in 1816 as a base to launch an attack on Rangoon during the Anglo-Burmese Wars, and reoccupied the Andamans in 1858. Finally, as the Danes in the south had officially renounced all claim to the Nicobars, the British Indian Government annexed both groups of islands in 1872, along with Great and Little Cocos that lie off Burma. The only point of settlement developed by the British was Port Blair, where a penitentiary was built for prisoners serving life terms.

Until World War II, the islands remained untouched by time. In 1942, however, they became the westernmost point reached by the Japanese. Their occupation ended in 1945. During that period, in December 1943, Subhas Bose, the Indian nationalist leader who was

An early photograph of an Andamans tribal group.

then working with the Japanese against the British rulers of India, landed at Port Blair for two days, and there unfurled the *Triranghi Jhanda,* the Indian national tricolor. But he could not, as he had wished, establish an Indian Provisional Government Administration there nor garrison the islands with the Indian National Army that he had raised.

When India became an independent country in 1947, the Andamans and the Nicobars became part of the Indian Union; the Cocos went to Burma.

Port Blair, the capital, on South Andaman, was named after Lt. Reginald Blair who conducted a survey of the area in 1789. Until World War II it had remained essentially a penal settlement.

The **Cellular Jail,** now a museum, where a total of 400 freedom fighters were held during the struggle for independence, is a massive whitewashed 18th Century building that faces the sea.

The zoo on Haddo Promontory has salt-water crocodiles, hornbills and crab-eating monkeys. Other places of interest are the **Anthropological Museum** (exhibiting mini-reproductions of villages of local tribes), a Burmese temple at **Phoenix Bay,** the Ghol Ghar spice stores, and the **Cottage Industries Emporium.**

From Marine Jetty, ferries ply across the harbor to **Aberdeen Market, Vyper Island,** where executions used to take place, or past the **Chattam Saw Mill,** situated on an island off Haddo. Cruises are organized by the Department of Information, Publicity and Tourism, as well as hotels during the day, and at sunset.

The closest beach is **Corbyn's Cove,** 6 km from town. There is a hotel offering various facilities, including windsurfing. There are beaches too at **Wandoor** (25 km) and **Shirya Tapu** at the southern tip of the island. Excursions can also be arranged from Port Blair to the **Botanical Gardens** (14 km), **Burmah Nullah** and the **Wimberlygunj lumbering centers,** in the jungle.

As most of the islands are reserves where tribes are protected from contact with the outside world, only a limited number are open to visitors. Most hotels and tour operators in Port Blair propose one-day picnics, scuba-diving and snorkeling trips to Bird, Grub, Jolly Boy, Red Skin and Snob Islands, as well as an overnight excursion to Cinque Island that includes a small trek through the forest offering much scope for bird watching.

Aboriginals by the beach.

SIKKIM, BUDDHIST STATE

Sikkim is among India's smallest states but it is the highest, with peaks above 21,000 feet meters. Kanchenjunga (28,200 feet/8,500 meters), the second highest summit in the world, is believed to be the abode of a god of the same name, a fiery character, usually depicted with a red face, wearing a crown made of five skulls and riding a snow lion. The legend is that, at the peak, this god has buried five sacred treasures — salt, gems, sacred books, medicines and a suit of impenetrable armor.

Till the 18th Century, the inhabitants of Sikkim were mainly Lepchas, cultivators of Mongol origin who came from Tibet in the 8th Century, followed by Bhotias, also from Tibet, sheep and yak breeders who also carried on a caravan trade between China and India.

The first kings of Sikkim were the Namgyals descended from the Minyaks of Tibet. Khye-Bumsa, a Namgyal prince helped in the construction of the Sa-Kya Monastery in Central Tibet in 1268.

Khye-Bumsa befriended the Lepchas, the original inhabitants, and swore a blood brotherhood with their chief, Thekongtek. When Thekongtek died, the Lepchas turned for leadership to Guru Tashi, Khye-Bumsa's fourth son, who was consecrated king (Chogyal) by three lamas in 1642.

In 1700, the Bhutanese invaded and occupied Sikkim and the young Chogyae, Chador was forced into exile, to return only eight years later, but at the cost of losing Kalimpong and Rhenock.

Chador Namgyal built monasteries at Pemayangtse and Tashiding. He invented the Lepcha alphabet. He was assassinated in 1717 on the orders of his pro-Bhutanese half-sister, Pei Womgmo. His successors had to fight the Bhutanese and the Nepalis with the help of Tibet and China. The early 19th Century saw the penetration of the East India Company into the Himalaya with a view to opening up trade with Tibet. In 1814, in the Anglo-Nepal wars, Sikkim sided with the Company and received, as a reward, in 1816, parts of the Nepali Terai. As a friendly gesture, King Tsugphud Namgyal gave the East India Company the hill of Darjeeling for development as a resort. Relations soured, however, and after a quarrel over the illegal collection of taxes by the British in Sikkim, the British annexed the Terai and established a protectorate over the kingdom. Since the 18th Century there has been a steady migration of Nepalis into Sikkim and they now constitute 75 percent of the population.

When the British rule in India ended on 15 August 1947, the new government of independent India entered into a similar arrangement with the Chogyal as he had with the British and till 1975 the arrangement continued and Sikkim was not wholly merged with the Indian Union. In 1975, however, the Sikkim Parliament, controlled by the Sikkim National Congress, voted in favor of the incorporation of the kingdom into India. The monarchy was abolished and Sikkim became a state of the Indian Union on 26 April 1975.

The capital, **Gangtok,** "the hill made flat," lies at an altitude of 5,400 feet (1,640 meters), facing Kanchenjunga. It is reached easily by road from Darjeeling, Bagdogra airport (70 miles/110 km), or New Siliguri railway station (77 miles/125 km). Access to Sikkim is restricted. Foreigners need an Inner Lines Permit, to be applied four weeks in advance. The eastern part of the state, the Nathu-la and

Preceding pages, Hoogly River, Calcutta. Below, Gangtok, Sikkim.

Jelep-la passes, leading to Tibet, as well as the north are closed to all tourists.

The most important building in Gangtok, in the southern part of the city, is the **Chogyal's Palace,** usually closed to visitors except for the Tsuklakhang Royal Chapel, where festivals and ceremonies are held. The palace itself opens once a year, during the last week of December, for the Pong Labsal festival during which lamas wearing masks perform a dance to Kanchenjunga around a banner-pole.

Most of Gangtok's places of interest are in the southern part of the town. The **Research Institute of Tibetology,** built in 1958 by the last Chogyal to preserve Tibetan culture, houses a library of more than 30,000 books on Buddhism, astrology, medicine and philosophy, as well as a collection of *thanks* (Tibetan religious paintings on cloth). The **Deer Park** is set up on the model of a similar one in Sarnath in homage to the Bodhisattva who got reincarnated as a musk deer. The **Orchid Sanctuary** is where over 250 different types of orchids bloom in April, and May, and in winter, during the months of December and January. Nearby is also a **Tibetan Refugee Craft Centre** and the famous **Hotel Tashi Delek**.

The **Rumtek Monastery,** 14 miles (23 km) west of Gangtok, belongs to the Yellow Hat Karmapa Sect, a reformist branch of Tantric Buddhism, founded in the 15th Century. The monastery, built in the 1960s, is a replica of one in Tibet destroyed at the time of the Chinese takeover.

Further to the west, **Pemayangtse** (6,840 feet/2,085 meters) has a **Red Hat Ningma Monastery,** which the original sect built in 1705. Its walls and ceilings bear frescos of gods and demons. A one-day trek along a Hock leads to **Tashiding Ningma Monastery** (1706) in the north. Another longer trek can be organized from Pemayangtse. As the bridle path approaches Kanchenjunga, the altitude rises to 10,000, then 14,000 feet and terraced rice-paddies and barley fields give way to apple-orchards, then fir trees, and mountain lakes. **Yakshun,** reached after six hours, is a small town where the first Chogyal was crowned in 1642. There is also the **Himalayan Mountaineering Institute.** The next stages are **Bakkhin** (5 hours) and **Dzongri** (6 hours) with a close-up view of Kanchenjunga, Pandim, the Khangla Ridge and the Gorchala Valley.

Lamas at Tibetan monastery, Sikkim

ASSAM, BRAHMA'S GIFT

Assam probably derives its name from Ahoms, the name of the dynasty that ruled there from the 13th to the early 19th Century. Assam today covers the plain of the Brahmaputra River along its whole course south of the hill state of Arunachal Pradesh and the kingdom of Bhutan, till it turns south into Bangladesh.

The origins of the Assamese and their early history are obscure and mixed with legend. The first legendary king of Assam, then called Kamarupa, was Naraksur, a son of Vishnu and Dharitri (Mother Earth). He invited Brahmins from Gaur in Bengal to settle down in his capital Pragjyotishpur, now Guwahati, to spread their teachings and way of life. Naraksur was, however, killed later on by Vishnu for his unreligious behavior. His son, Bhagadatta, was defeated by the Mahabharata hero, Arjuna. This legendary event probably refers in history to the arrival of the Aryans in Assam. From then on, until the 13th Century, Assam was a melting-pot of Aryan, Dravidian and Mongoloid races.

In 1228, the Ahoms, a Buddhist Tai tribe from North Thailand, entered Assam, defeated the Kamrupa ruler and established a kingdom which came to be called Assam, with its capital at Sibsagar. The Ahoms adopted the Hindu Vaishnava religion and the kingdom rapidly became a powerful one. The Mughals sent expeditions to subdue "the rats of Assam," without success, in 1478, 1553 and 1672. Progressively, Assam expanded east, establishing its authority over the Naga kingdom of Cachar, destroying its capital, Dimapur, in 1536. The kingdom was annexed to Assam.

Burmese Invasions

Ahom power started weakening in the 17th Century. Then, in 1792, Burma invaded Assam. The king, Gaurianath Singh, asked the East India Company for assistance. The Burmese were repelled but came back in 1816. After the Anglo-Burmese war of 1824-26, Burma ceded Assam to the East India Company by the

Chital, the swift-footed Indian Spotted Deer.

Treaty of Yandaboo, on January 26, 1826. A revolt, the Khamti rebellion, in 1839, followed by another led by Maniran Barbhander Barua, a former spy for the East India Company, were both crushed.

During World War II Assam played a major role, providing a supply route to China and Burma. The Japanese Kohima offensive of 1944 was an attempt to occupy this strategic area both to cut off supplies to China and to open the way to the Indian plains.

Today, Assam's major problem is the growing imbalance between the Assamese and immigrants — Bengali Hindus displaced by partition of the subcontinent in 1947; Bihari Muslims after the 1971 Bangladesh War, and Bangladeshis infiltrating in, fleeing poverty.

Between 1980 and 1983 there was widespread agitation over this issue and there were attacks on immigrants.

During the disturbances Assam was closed to foreign tourists and a special permit is now required to visit the state. Applications for groups of seven persons are now freely entertained and further liberalization might be expected as the situation is now quiet.

Guwahati

Guwahati, the former capital of the Kamrup kings is Assam's main town with a population of 500,000. The beauty of Guwahati derives from its location on the south bank of the Brahmaputra. On a cliff to the east of the city are **Raj Bhavan,** the governor's residence, and the **Belle Vue Hotel,** commanding a spectacular view of the river both east and west. The municipal area is immediately below, where the Legislative Assembly, the Public Works Department Bungalow and the Chief Justice's residence are located. Behind these buildings, near the Dighali Pukuri tank, is the **State Museum** housing rare stone sculptures from the Kamrupa period.

In and around Guwahati there are several temples. On a small promontory along the river, the **Sulkeswar Janardhan Temple,** consecrated in the 10th Century and rebuilt in the 17th, has a statue of the Lord Buddha facing the river, a rare coexistence with a Hindu deity found in very few temples in India.

Nearby, in the middle of the river on **Peacock Island,** is a small Shiva temple

Sunrise on the Brahmaputra, Assam.

that can be reached by boat from the *ghat* (jetty) next to the High Court. **Navagraha Mandir,** the Temple of the Nine Planets, east of the city, on Chitrachala Hill, is probably the birth site of Guwahati. The temple was an important astrological center, hence Guwahati's earlier name, *Pragjyotishpur,* the City of Eastern Astrology, which is the name that will be given to the new capital now under construction near Dispur, the current capital of Assam. To the south, at the confluence of three mountain streams is the **Vashistha Ashram,** a small temple founded by a sage, now both a pilgrimage center and a picnic spot.

To the West, **Kamakhya Mandir,** Guwahati's most important temple is on the top of Nichala Hill. The legend goes that to stop Lord Shiva's fearful dance of destruction, provoked by the sight of the dead body of his consort, goddess Shakti, the lesser gods stealthily dismembered and scattered her body, far and wide, piece by piece. Shakti's *yoni* (reproductive organ) landed on the top of Nichala Hill, said to be Lord Shiva's *lingam* (phallic symbol). This temple is one of India's main centers of the tantric cult. In former times, 5,000 *devadasis* (temple dancers) were reputedly attached to it and in 1553, it was destroyed by Kalapahar, a Brahmin who had converted to Islam, after being rejected by his caste because of his marriage to a Muslim princess. Its ruins can still be seen around the water tank. The present structure, with its high beehive spire, bas-reliefs of nymphs, and long turtle-back hall, is typical of Assamese religious architecture.

Outside Guwahati, on the north bank, at Hajo, the **Hayagribha Madadeva Mahdap Temple** is believed by the Bhotias to be the place where the Buddha attained nirvana. This temple, located on a hill, was also destroyed by Kalapahar and later rebuilt. It is finely decorated with bas-reliefs of nymphs, elephants and scenes from the Ramayana.

Near Hajo is **Pao Mecca,** a mosque on a hill, to which a pilgrimage is believed to be the equivalent of one-fourth of a *Haj* to Mecca.

Marco Polo, the intrepid explorer of the 13th-14th Century, on first sighting the Indian rhinoceros thought he had, at last, spotted the fabulous unicorn. He was wrong but he might well have been looking at an animal that in our times would be considered as fabulous as the unicorn.

For the Indian rhinoceros *(Rhinoceros unicornis)* is one of nature's last relics from the prehistoric world. Nearing extinction at the turn of the century, it has now been rehabilitated primarily due to efforts in the two game sanctuaries in Assam, Kaziranga and Manas.

The **Kaziranga National Park** on the south bank of the Brahmaputra, 145 miles (233 km) northeast of Guwahati, the main sanctuary for the Indian one-horned rhinoceros, was declared a game sanctuary in 1926. There are now about 1,100 rhinos in the park, over half the world's population of Asian rhinos. At least 20 are killed by poachers each year in spite of stringent protective measures. The horn is removed and sent to Hongkong or Singapore.

Elephants take visitors early in the morning to a few points from where rhinoceros may be viewed. They may also be watched from viewing towers located at various points. The best time of the year to see them is March as the elephant grass has by then dried and lies flat.

To the northwest, 110 miles (176 km) from Guwahati, is the **Manas Wildlife Sanctuary,** set in thick jungle along the Bhutanese border. One-horned rhinoceros, tigers, gaurs, the pygmy hog and the rare golden langur live there but are hardly seen due to the thick foliage. Above all, however, Manas is known as an angler's paradise where the mahaseer, a local variety of carp, abounds.

Further north starts Upper Assam, an oil and tea garden. **Duliajan,** a new well-planned town in the midst of the jungle, is the capital of northeast India's oil country. Assamese oil contributes more than 10 percent of the country's production. Derricks and rigs can be seen standing among tea gardens and paddies. They are an old feature of the Assamese landscape since oil was first struck here in 1867.

Between Jorhat and Duliajan, in and around Sibsagar, on the Assam Trunk Road, is the former capital of the Ahoms. Only a few monuments remain: the water tank, along with Devi, Shiva and Vishnu temples; the Rang Ghar, an original oval-shaped pavilion from where kings watched elephant fights; Charaideo, the necropolis of Ahom Kings; and a palace at Gurgaon. In this area there are still isolated village communities where Shan Thai is still spoken and the Buddhist religion is still practiced.

Rhinoceros unicornis — the famed Greater One-horned Indian Rhinoceros.

NORTHEASTERN STATES

Meghalaya

Meghalaya, "the abode of clouds," south of Assam, was previously part of that state. It became a separate state of the Indian Union in 1972. It is a hilly region, very foggy in winter. It is inhabited by three tribal groups, the Garos in the west, the Khasis in the center, and the Jaintias in the east. They constituted independent little township kingdoms, the Seiyams, which the British annexed one by one to British India in the 19th Century.

The Garos are of Tibetan stock. They were animists and once practiced human sacrifice. In 1848, under a treaty with the British, they agreed to stop displaying skulls in their houses.

The Khasis are Mon-Khmers related to the Shans of Burma. Their religion, Seng Khasi, is simple: God is everywhere and should not be represented or adored in a specific form. There are no churches, just prayer-halls for specific celebrations.

The Khasis love gold and amber, the two basic components of their jewelry. To commemorate their dead, the Khasis erect *mawbynnas,* monoliths of various heights, arranged in groups of three or more that can be seen in most villages. The Pnars, generally known as Jaintias are closely related to the Khasis.

The three tribes have a matrilineal and matrilocal family system. Missionaries in the 19th Century converted most of them to Christianity but the old traditions persist, especially their folk dances. A major dance festival, the Shad Suk Myasiem, the Festival of the Joyful Heart, is held in Shillong in April. In November, the Garo 100-drum festival in Tura celebrates the end of the harvesting season.

Shillong, the capital of Assam until 1972 and of Meghalaya since then, lies 60 miles (100 km) south of Guwahati, a three-hour drive through hills covered with pineapple and betel plantations, and pine forests. It passes along the **Umian Lake,** formed by a recently built dam.

Shillong has been called the 'Scotland of the East' because of its climate and its location at an altitude of 4,900 feet (1,500 meters). The climate is so temperate that its founder is said to have wanted the town to become the breeding ground for potential British soldiers to serve and police the expanding Raj!

Here the British and rich Bengalis built cottages, a golf course and polo grounds. It is a small city with a market, **Bara Bazaar,** selling Nepali silver and Khasi gold jewelry, spices and textiles. Shillong spreads on hills covered with English-style country houses, the largest being **Raj Bhavan,** the summer residence of the Governor of Assam and Meghalaya, and the **Pinewood Hotel.** Nearby are the **Ward Lake** and the **Botanical Garden.**

Cherrapunji, 35 miles (56 km) to the south, is reputedly the world's wettest place with 45 inches (1,150 mm) of rain each year. The most interesting spot however is **Mawphluang,** 15 miles (24 km) further south, a barren and windy plateau covered with monoliths. On the way back, visitors stop at **Shillong Peak** which offers a view of the neighboring hills, and at the **Elephant Waterfall.**

Access to Garo country is difficult. A road from Shillong is being built but, at present, the only way to reach it is to drive to Guwahati and then southwest to Tura. The villages have retained their traditional architecture and some traditional buildings like the bachelors' dormitory at Rongreng.

Arunachal Pradesh

To the north of Assam lies the Union Territory of **Arunachal Pradesh.** In view of its strategic location on the frontier between India and China, the territory is not open to tourism.

The area has 600,000 inhabitants divided into 82 Mongoloid and Tibeto-Burmese tribes, the main ones being the Apatanis, the Khamptis, the Padmas and the Miris. Most are Buddhists. At **Tawang,** at an altitude of 10,000 feet (3,048 meters) is India's largest Buddhist monastery, over 350 years old, where the 6th Dalai Lama was born. Some areas, like the **Chetak Pass** (14,000 feet/4,267 meters), are so remote that an Indian Army expedition recently found a community there that still live in caves and eat their food raw, not having yet discovered fire.

To the east, near the border with China and Burma, the Brahmaputra forms a lake called **Brahmakund,** before entering the plains of Assam. Bathing here is believed to wash away one's sins and Hindus come here by the thousands on Makar Sankranti day in mid-January.

Tribal dancer.

At **Ledo** starts the old road to Mandalay, crossing the Burmese border at the Pangso Pass. Beyond this is the "lake of no return" where retreating British troops in 1942 got lost in quicksand.

Nagaland

Nagaland is inhabited by a variety of Tibeto-Burmese tribes, speaking more than 20 different dialects, the main ones being the Aos, the Angamis and the Konyaks. People in the valleys call them Naga. Nagas were once headhunters, but the practice was abandoned years ago.

The Cacharis, one of the Naga tribes once established a Hindu kingdom at Dimapur from where they used to raid Assam and Burma. The Ahoms of Assam established their authority over Cachar at the end of the 17th Century, but as soon as Burma invaded Assam in 1816, the Naga raids on the plains were resumed. In 1832, the British, while establishing a road link between Assam and Manipur, encountered the Nagas for the first time. For a few years they made attempts to control them, Naga raids being followed by punitive expeditions. In 1879 the British outpost at Kohima came under Naga siege for a whole month. A state of permanent peace was finally reached in 1889.

During the Second World War the Japanese and the Indian National Army launched an attack on Kohima, taking half of the city in 1943. They were at the same time beseiging Imphal. The objective was to reach Dimapur, a vital rail-head for supplies to British Army units in forward areas. Kohima proved to be the furthest point west reached by the Japanese. After being repulsed, they started a long retreat and had to abandon Burma.

In the war against the Japanese, the Nagas were of great help to the allied forces, carrying supplies to the front, evacuating the wounded, and spying behind the enemy lines. After Indian independence, some Nagas grouped in a Naga National Council demanded autonomy but soon extremist elements were asking for independence and the area was disturbed by insurgency. In November 1975, at Shillong, the Government of India and Naga leaders reached an agreement, whereby the Nagas accepted the Indian Constitution, but there are still occasional outbreaks of violence.

Monoliths erected by Khasi tribals in memory of ancestors, Meghalaya.

Kohima has a War Cemetery with Commonwealth Graves, and a memorial with a famous inscription:

"When you go home tell them of us
                              and say
For your tomorrow we gave our today."
Naga villages are usually perched on hills and are surrounded by a stone wall. One, Barra Basti, is a suburb of Kohima.

To the east of Kohima, at Dimapur, are the remains of the former capital of the Cachar Hills which was razed by the Ahoms in 1536.

Manipur

Manipur is another former princely state on the Burmese border. Meitheis, a Tibeto-Burmese tribe related to the Shans, form 60 percent of the population. They live in the valleys and have been Indianized at a stage early enough to allow them to develop *Jagoi*, a Manipuri school of Indian classical dance. There are also 29 other tribes, most of them Tibeto-Burmese and now mostly Christian. They constitute one-third of the population and live in the hilly areas. The largest of these groups are the Lotha, the Konyak and the Nagas.

The Manipuris have a reputation as fierce fighters. They excel in such martial arts as the spear dance *(takhousarol),* sword fight *(thanghaicol)* and wrestling *(mukna).* They are also good riders. Polo, the game that spread over the Mughal Empire in the 16th Century before gaining an international dimension, is said to have originated here.

As a nation of warriors, Manipuris have a history of conflict with their neighbors in Arakan and other border regions of Burma, which they invaded in 1738. In 1819, the Raja of Manipur who previously had paid tribute to the Burmese crown did not attend the coronation ceremonies of Burma's new King Bagyidaw. The Burmese sent out a punitive expedition. The Anglo-Burmese War was caused partly by this incursion.

Burma was defeated, and by the Treaty of Yangdaboo, on 24 February 1826, recognized British sovereignty over Manipur. After years of relative peace, a revolt took place in 1891 during which the British chief commissioner of Assam was killed in an ambush. The rising was rapidly crushed and its leader, Tikenderjit Singh, the maharaja's brother, was hanged on 13 August of that year. There was trouble again in 1930, when a self-styled prophet, Jadonang, announced the imminent departure of the British. He was executed and the priestess of his cult, Rani Gaidiliou, then aged 17, was sentenced to life imprisonment. She was released later by Nehru, when India gained independence.

In 1944, the Indian National Army and the Japanese put Imphal under siege from March to June. They were repulsed and in March 1945, General Slim's 14th Army marched to Mandalay from the Manipur hills.

In 1949 Manipur became Union Territory and a full fledged State of the Indian Union in 1972.

Imphal, the capital, can be reached by road from Kohima after a 80-mile (130-km) drive along the famous road to Mandalay. It has two war cemeteries, a museum displaying tribal artifacts, Kwairamb Bazaar, a women's market, the Rajah's Palace, the Royal Polo Grounds and, nearby at Langthabal, the Raja's Summer Palace. Tribes live in the Ukhrul area, some 35 miles (60 km) to the northeast, a restricted area in view of occasional insurgency there.

Mizoram

Mizoram, the former Lushai Hills District, is bordered by Bangladesh on one side and Burma on the other. Related to the Shan, Mizos are a group of tribes (Lushais, Hmars, Pawis) that came relatively recently to India. They started raiding tea plantations in 1871. The British retaliated and established control over the area in 1872, but peace was not attained until 1892, when the last rebellion was crushed. The British then introduced the Inner Line system. Only missionaries were allowed through. As a result, 95 percent of the population is Christian and literacy has reached 86 percent in some tribes. At the time of Indian independence Mizoram became a Union Territory and there is a possibility, as a result of current discussions with local political groups, that the territory will be granted the status of a full state in the Indian Union.

Tripura

Tripura is the former princely state of Tipperah. The population, mostly of Tibeto-Burmese origin, took up Vaishnava Hinduism early, and was ruled continuously by rajas until Indian independence. Other major ethnic groups in Tripura are the Kukis, related to the Shans of Burma, Chakmas, Moghs, Lusharis and Riangs.

Tripura had been more or less permanently at war with her neighbors when the British, taking advantage of a feud between Maharajah Krishna Manikya and the Nawabs of Bengal, intervened and established a protectorate. They also divided Tripura into a princely state and tribal lands under their direct control.

After independence, Tripura joined the Indian Union in 1949 and became a State in 1972.

Agartala is a small town of 60,000 people, surrounded by hills on three sides, with a palace erected in 1940 by Maharaja Bikram, a philanthropist who helped Rabindranath Tagore finance the Santiniketan University in Bengal. The palace set in "Mughal Gardens" is now the State Assembly House. It is said that the old cannons on display used to be fired in salute once a year, until the 16th Century, when a thousand human sacrifices were held in Agartala. In Udaipur, the ancient capital of Tripura, is a ruined temple, **Tripura Sundari.**

INDIAN TEA

Chinese tradition points to India as the original home of tea. A Brahmin called Dharma went as a missionary to China. Tired, he fell asleep on reaching his destination. On awaking, in anger at such weakness, he tore out his eyebrows. The hair took root and became tea plants, the leaves of which he ate and fell into meditation.

Tea had been spotted in Assam by English travellers as early as in the last years of the 18th Century. When the East India Company's monopoly of importing tea into Britain from China was abolished in 1823, the Honorable Company decided to look into the possibility of growing tea in India.

Expeditions were sent to Assam which confirmed previous reports. In 1826, after the Burmese wars, the Company's troops brought back a tea bush as evidence of the existence of tea in the area. Finally, on Christmas Eve, 1844, the Governor General, Lord Bentinck, officially announced the discovery of tea in India and called for the development of the industry. Production started in Assam in

Tribals from Orissa (famous Bizon Horn hats).

1836, in Bengal in 1839, and in the Nilgiris in the south, in 1863. Tea was introduced into the Darjeeling area in the early 1840s. The bushes were not indigenous. They had been smuggled out of China.

The first Indian teas were of low quality and Chinese experts were brought to Assam to supervise the processing of tea leaves. India soon became a major grower and, by 1900, was supplying Britain with 150 million pounds of tea against 15 million brought from China.

Today, India is the world's largest producer, with an output of 635,000 tonnes against a total world production of 2 million tonnes. India's area under tea (400,000 hectares) is the largest in the world. More than half of Indian tea is grown in Assam, one fourth in West Bengal and about a fifth in the Nilgiris.

There are two sorts of Indian tea. CTC tea, the most common, takes its name from the Crush-Tear-Cool process in which the leaf is broken. It constitutes 75 percent of the total output. It gives a strong liquor of dark color. Most CTC production is for the home market.

"Orthodox" teas have a lighter color (they are said to be "bright") and yield a weaker liquor: one kilo makes 350 cups against 500 for CTC tea. Most of the Orthodox tea is exported, the best varieties being Darjeeling and Assam Golden Flower Orange Pekoe. Sixty percent of the Indian production is sold through auctions, including all export teas. Auction centers exist at Guwahati, in Assam; at Cochin, Coimbatore and Coonoor, in the south; at Siliguri and Calcutta, in West Bengal. The largest center is the one in Calcutta run by the firm of J. Thomas. The center has two auction rooms (one for the home market, the other for exports), and the largest tea tasting room in the world, where purchasing agents can taste all possible varieties of tea available in West Bengal and Assam.

Consumed only by the hill tribes 150 years ago, tea has become the national drink of India. However, on an average, each cup of tea consumed by an Indian is matched by approximately six consumed by an Englishman.

Tea gardens can be easily visited in Darjeeling and in the south, where the whole process of tea preparation can be observed.

Manipuri dancers.

ORISSA, LOVE & DEVOTION

Orissa has an ancient tradition of seafaring. At one time, there were Oriya colonies in Burma and Java. Buddhism became the religion of the kingdom of Kalinga, as Orissa was called, soon after the faith was established. Buddhist universities flourished at Nrusinghanath in central Orissa and Ratnagiri near Cuttack.

In 262 B.C. Maurya Emperor, Ashoka, defeated Kalinga near Bhubaneshwar, slaying 100,000 people and taking 150,000 captive. This scene of bloodshed is said to have turned Ashoka away from violence and led him to adopt Buddhism. After the collapse of the Mauryan empire, two dynasties ruled in Orissa. The temples of Bhubaneshwar, Konarak and Puri were built during that time. The Kesaris reigned from the 2nd to the 12th Century. They brought in Brahmins to re-Hinduize Orissa and built the Jagannath Temple at Puri and the Lingaraj Temple at Bhubaneshwar. The Gangas ruled from the 12th to the 15th Century. They erected the Sun Temple at Konarak. After a period of confusion, came the Mughals in 1508, succeeded in 1751 by the Marathas.

As in other parts of India, western nations first came to Orissa to trade. The Dutch came to Pipli in the 17th Century, and the East India Company at about the same time to Balasore. Bengal, Bihar and Orissa were ceded to the Company in 1765, but it was not until 1803, after a campaign by the Marquis of Wellesley, who took Puri and Cuttack, that British rule was fully established in Orissa.

Orissa is an intensely religious state where fervor is focused on Lord Jagannath, an incarnation of Vishnu. Not surprisingly, Orissan civilization stemmed from its temples, where the most remarkable erotic statuary can be found and where originated Odissi, a style of religious dancing with definite erotic hues. Odissi was performed previously in temples by resident dancers (maharis) devoting their lives to the temple god. Nearly forgotten during the Muslim rule, Odissi has been revived as a performing art.

City of Temples

Bhubaneshwar, capital of Orissa only since 1956, is a city of temples. There were once over a thousand of them; a large number are still standing and active.

An Orissan temple (deul), moving from center to periphery, usually consists of a sanctum, one or several front porches (jagamohanas), usually with pyramidal roofs, a dancing hall (nata mandir) and a hall of offerings (bhoga mandapa). Deuls with semi-cylindrical roofs are called khakhara deul.

A large number of temples in Bhubaneshwar are located around **Bindu Sarovar,** a tank which is believed to receive water from all the holy rivers of India. The **Lingaraj Temple** to the south, built in 1014 A.D. to the glory of Shiva, is certainly the most impressive. A massive wall surrounds a 150-foot (45-meter) high deul with a jagamohana, a nata mandir and a bhoga mandapa, as well as minor temples to Parvati, Gopalini and Bhubaneshwari. All are decorated with a profusion of sculptures of deities, nymphs and amorous couples. Entry is prohibited to non-Hindus.

Vaital Deul is a typical 8th Century khakhara deul with an oblong roof. It is decorated with stone figures of Durga, such as the eight-armed Mahishasuramardini, on the northern wall, piercing the left shoulder of Mahishasura, the buffalo-headed demon, with her trident. Within the sanctum, another avatar of Durga, eight-armed Chamunda or Kapalini, often hidden by a drape, sits on a corpse, with an owl and a jackal on each side. Her face is emaciated, her eyes sunken, and she wears a garland of skulls.

Sisiresvara Temple, next to Vaital, has been damaged but has retained sculptures of lions, elephants, the gods Ganesh and Kartikeya, and the Avilokiteshwara Buddha seated cross-legged and accompanied by a deer and a nag (cobra), showing how strong Buddhist influence was in Orissa. The **Uttaresvara Temple** on the north bank of the lake has undergone extensive restoration. Southeast of the lake, the **Ananta-Vasudeva Temple** is one of the few in Bhubaneshwar belonging to the Vaishnava cult.

East of the lake is another group of temples. **Parasuramesvara** is one of the oldest. Built in the 7th Century, it is still well preserved and is decorated with a four-armed Ganesh, a two-armed Kartikeya mounted on a peacock and killing a snake, amorous couples and rampant lions.

Muktesvara is the gem of Orissan architecture. Entrance to the temple compound is through a sculptured gateway *(torana);* the *jagamohana* has diamond-shaped latticed windows and a richly decorated interior. Temple, *torana,* (gateway) and walls are covered with figures of female warriors, erotic scenes, elephants, maidens, monkeys in various comic scenes, women worshipping *lingas* and *naginis* (half-snakes-half-women). On each side of the *deul* is a grimacing lion face, flanked with smiling dwarfs.

To the east is the **Rajarani Temple.** It is noted for its sculptures of nymphs in extremely sensuous poses, and statues of the *ashta dikpalas,* guardians of the cardinal points of the compass.

Bhubaneshwar has three museums. The **Orissa State Museum** displays Hindu, Buddhist and Jain sculptures, and early Orissan palm manuscripts. The **Handicrafts Museum** has a collection of folk art such as Cuttack silver filigree and *patachitra* painting on cloth. There is also a **Tribal Research Museum.**

West of Bhubaneshwar, on the immediate outskirts, are two hills **Udayagiri** and **Khandagiri** — with a road passing between them. Both were once inhabited by Jain ascetics who lived in cells excavated in the rock. Khandagiri has fewer caves than Udayagiri but a small Jain temple still stands on top of this hill.

On **Dhauligiri,** a hill 8 km south of Bhubaneshwar, there is an example of Emperor Ashoka's edicts, engraved in this case on the sides of a sculptured elephant. To commemorate Ashoka's acceptance of Buddhism, substituting the ideal of *dharmavijaya,* spiritual victory, for *digvijaya,* military conquest. Japanese Buddhists have built a huge white **Peace Pagoda** on top of the hill. Some 10 km south is **Pipli,** a small village specializing in a folk form of appliqué work in vivid colors unique to this area.

Puri, 60 km from Bhubaneshwar, is the holiest place in Orissa and one of the biggest pilgrimage centers in India. The city was in the past a flourishing port identified with ancient Dantpur. Puri is known for its cult of Jagannath, originating some say in the times when the people of Orissa worshipped trees and hence the practice of carving his image in wood. According to the more popular legend, however, the Lord appeared in King Indrodyumna's dream and commanded him to build a temple for him. The king complied, getting the images carved out of a single log of wood found floating in

Below, Sun Temple at Konarak; right, details at that temple.

the sea, as the Lord had enjoined in the dream. The climax of Jagannath worship is the Rath Yatra festival celebrated every year in June-July at the **Jagannath Temple,** since the 10th Century, it is believed.

Known as the "White Pagoda," this temple was built in the 12th Century. It lies in the midst of a huge complex of buildings where more than 5,000 priests and other temple staff live. The main building is 65 m high, surmounted by the mystic wheel or *chakra* and the flag of Vishnu. It is surrounded by a wall 6 m high. Non-Hindus are not permitted to enter the temple or its grounds.

About two weeks before the festival, the images of Jagannath and his brother, Balabhadra, and his sister, Subhadra, are given a ritual bath. Every twelve years, instead of a bath, the images are replaced by new ones carved afresh from a *daru,* a tree ritually selected by the temple priests. The old images are then buried in a secret ceremony performed by the priests without any lay witness.

On the first day of the festival, the deities are placed on *raths,* ceremonial chariots 13 m high, with wheels of more than two meters in diameter. Jagannath's chariot, the tallest of the three, is yellow-striped. Subhadra has a red chariot. Balabhadra's is bright blue. All three are preceded by four wooden horses but are actually drawn by hundreds of devotees from the temple to Gundicha Mandir, a temple 1.5 km away, where they will stay for seven days. The rituals completed, the deities ride back to their own temple.

Although the beach at Puri is one of the best in India, the seas can be very rough there, with giant waves and strong and erratic currents. Caution is not always an adequate safeguard against mishaps and it is advisable to utilize the services of the self-employed *nulia* lifeguards, easily recognizable by their white cone-shaped straw hats.

The Sun Temple

Inland, a few kilometers from Puri, is **Konarak,** a former center of Orissan Buddhism, an active port, now silted, and, in ancient times, a center for sun worship. A temple to the Sun God was built here in the 9th Century. The present **Sun Temple** was erected in the 13th Century. It took 16 years to complete; 1,200 artisans were employed on the task. In its original form the temple consisted of a 70

m high *deul* with a 40 m high *jagamohana*, representing together the Chariot of the Sun, drawn by seven impetuous horses, the chariot having 12 pairs of 8-spoke wheels. The *deul* collapsed in the middle of the 19th Century and one horse is missing. The temple used to stand on the shore, but the sea has since receded three km and the temple no longer serves as a landmark for sailors as it once did. However, despite its dilapidated state the Sun Temple stands out as a masterpiece of Orissan architecture.

Both the *main deul* and the *jagamohana*, and the ruins of the dancing hall and of the **Mayadevi Temple** in the Sun Temple compound, are covered with erotic sculptures of couples in a variety of poses, along with depictions of nymphs, war, hunting and court scenes, musicians, dancers, floral motifs, and elephants. There are also huge animal statues: two lions guard the pyramidal entrance, and on each side of the temple is a colossal war elephant, and a warhorse trampling on fallen warriors.

South of Bhubaneshwar, along the coast, is **Chilka Lake,** a 1,100 sq km shallow inland sea, separated from the bay of Bengal by a thin sandy ridge, spreading over 75 km from north to south. From Barkul, the Orissa Tourist Development Corporation operates a two-hour cruise to **Kalijai Temple,** a small shrine on a rock island, and a four-hour trip to **Nalabar Island.** The lake has an abundance of fish and shellfish. From mid-December to mid-January migratory birds, from as far off as Siberia, spend the winter here.

Further south, 95 km from Bhubaneshwar, is **Golpalpur-on-Sea,** a totally unspoiled beach, probably the best in Eastern Indian.

Some of Orissa's most interesting tribes live in the south of Orissa, in the Koraput area, 300 km from Gopalpur-on-Sea, and 130 km from Visakhapatnam in Andhra Pradesh. Most of them belong to the Austro-Asiatic Munda group. At Sunabeda live Gadabas, a Munda Tribe. Bondas can be found at Balimela, 100 km to the south, where a market is held every Sunday. Koyas live around Kalimela and Malakangiri, and can be seen, along with the other tribes, at the Kudumuluguma Sunday market, 12 km from Koraput. The Bondas are the most fascinating tribe of Orissa. They are of Tibeto-Burmese origin. A settled tribe,

Below, Puri town; right, beach.

198

they cultivate rice, practice shifting cultivation, and breed cows and goats. The women wear rows of silver necklaces, piling up from their shoulders to their chins. Once a year, in June or July, they hold a festival during which they drink *mahwa,* a brew made from the flower of that name, and *handia* made from fermented rice.

Twenty kilometers north from Bhubaneshwar is **Nandanakanan,** a recreation park set in the middle of Chandka Forest. Animals here are kept in natural surroundings. The main attractions are four white tigers, one-horned rhinos, white-browed gibbons and 22 African lions. A section of the park is a **Botanical Garden,** with a rosarium, a two-storied Zen temple and a cactus house.

North of Bhubaneshwar (19 km) is **Cuttack,** the former capital of Orissa, the old Abhinaba Bidanasi Katak. There are few remains; ruins of the blue granite **Barabati Maratha fort,** stormed by the British in 1803; **Kadam Rasal,** a walled compound, with corner towers, containing three 18th Century mosques and a domed building containing footprints of Prophet Muhammad engraved on a circular stone.

Past Cuttack, off the road to Paradeep, there are more Buddhist remains — the former Buddhist monasteries of Lalitagiri and **Ratnagiri** where excavations have uncovered Buddha images, including 1.2 m high heads of the Buddha. Rough tracks, hardly motorable, lead there winding through typical oriya villages.

Further north, **Balasore** is one of the earliest British settlements in India, granted to the East India Company in 1633. Nearby are three shrines. The **Kutopokhari Temple** at Remuna, is a seat of Vaishnava culture and contains an 18-arm, 2 m high granite statue of Durga. **Bhudhara Chandi** at **Sajanagarh,** built in the 16th Century, contains a rare image of Shakti, three-faced, eight-armed and standing on seven boars. On **Devagiri Hill** stands **Panchalingeswar,** a temple with five stone *lingams.*

To the east is the small resort of Chandipur-on-sea, a beach where the sea recedes by more than five kilometers at low tide. Here, in the land of the ancient Sun Temple, the visitor can take a long walk across the beach as he watches the sunrise. At the edge of the sea are fishermen who are willing to take him out for the day in their catamarans.

BOMBAY – BUSY AND BURSTING

The story of Bombay city is a fascinating rags to riches one. From obscure, humble beginnings as a set of seven small islands with tidal creeks and marshes between them, the city has risen to such eminence that, today, it is India's most important commercial and industrial center. Home to the wealthy and the glamorous, Bombay is also India's Hollywood, producing more films each year than any other city in the world.

Like all big cities, Bombay has its seamy side, its slums and its overcrowding, the foothills of poverty on which are built towering skyscrapers. And like all success stories, there have been chapters of intrigue, violence, happiness and calm, and the struggles of the pre-independence years, when Bombay became the political capital of nationalist India.

The Good Bay

Bombay is part of India's beautiful west coast that runs down from Gujarat, through Bombay to Goa, Karnataka and Kerala. South of Bombay, narrow beaches and plains sweep up into the forested hills of the Western Ghats. The city boasts a perfect natural harbor which was developed by the British and, once the Suez Canal opened in the 19th Century, the port of Bombay never knew a dull moment. Today it handles more than 40 percent of India's maritime trade.

Bombay summers are hot and humid, and the winters cool, the sea breeze bringing relief throughout the year. The monsoon that hits the coast between June and September brings down curtains of heavy rain which obscure the view and flood the roads, and when they occasionally part in patches some spectacular sunsets are to be seen over the sea.

Today Bombay's seven islands survive only as names of localities like Colaba, Mahim, Mazgaon, Parel, Worli, Girgaum and Dongri. The tidal swamps have all been reclaimed and, later, even large expanses of the open sea have been filled in, for example, the Churchgate and Nariman Point Reclamations. The name Bombay (Marathi: *Mumbai*) is said to be derived from the name of the local deity, Mumba Devi, whose temple, though re-

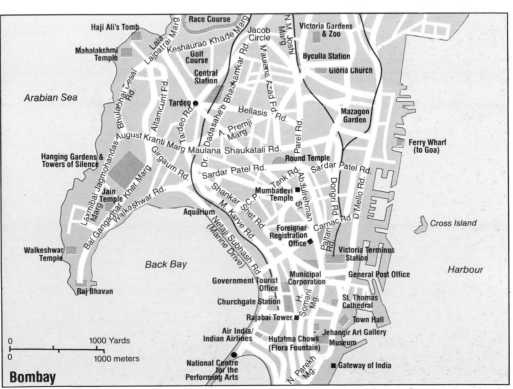

Bombay

built and re-located, still stands. The Portuguese predecessors of the British preferred to think of the name as *Bom Baim*, the Good Bay, an equally apt name for this excellent port. The city now stretches 14 miles (22 km) into the Arabian Sea to its south, west and east. The maximum width of the composite island that now constitutes metropolitan Bombay is no more than three miles (five km). Into this narrow strip are squeezed the majority of Bombay's 9 million people, its major business and commercial establishments, its docks and warehouses, and much of its industry — including almost the whole of its major textile industry which employs some 40–50 thousand workers, men and women.

A Melting Pot

Bombay is the home of people of all Indian creeds and cultures. The Bombay Municipal Corporation provides primary and secondary education in at least 10 languages, including English. Bombay has developed a *lingua franca* entirely peculiar to itself — "Bombay Hindustani," which regular Hindi/Urdu speakers find rather comic. It is often caricatured in Indian films and plays.

Local Muslim nawabs ruled this region for some time, but handed it over to the Portuguese in 1534 in exchange for support against the Mughals. This was the beginning of Bombay's large Christian (largely Roman Catholic) population and its numerous churches, which led to two separate areas in Bombay coming to be known as "Portuguese Church." Till recently, a number of the older churches retained their Portuguese facades, but most of these have been lost to recent modernization. **St. Andrew's** in the suburb of Bandra is a fine example of an original, Portuguese-style facade.

There are also minor remains of Portuguese fortifications both on the main island and the much larger island of Salsette north of the city and now mostly incorporated in Greater Bombay. (Also being developed is a New Bombay on the mainland, a few miles across Bombay harbor.) At Bassein (Vasai is the actual name), from where come a very special type of green banana, there are ruins of a Portuguese walled settlement which include a large church. Bassein is some 30 miles (50 km) from Bombay and is easily accessible by local train and bus.

The Waterfront, with Taj Hotel on the left and the Gateway of India on extreme right.

In 1662 Charles II of England married Catherine of Braganza, a Portuguese princess. As part of the dowry, the British crown received the islands of Bombay. They were leased to the British East India Company in 1668 at the princely rent of $10 per annum. This company of merchant-adventurers had for some time felt the need for an additional west-coast port, to supplement and ultimately to supplant Surat in Gujarat. Far-sighted governors of this period, like Gerald Augiers, began the construction of the city and harbor, inviting the settlement of Gujarati merchants and Parsi, Muslim and Hindu manufacturers and traders to help develop the city. This led to the settlement of these communities in Bombay, and today each of them adds a flavor of its own to the life of the city.

Gujaratis from the state just north of Bombay constitute a very substantial proportion of the city's population, and especially of its business community. Fleeing persecution in Persia, the Parsis migrated to Gujarat and moved to Bombay in large numbers in the 17th Century. Being Zoroastrians, they built Fire Temples and a "Tower of Silence" on Malabar Hill. The latter is an isolated facility for the disposal of the dead by exposure to the elements and vultures. Burial and cremation are ruled out for Zoroastrians since they hold both fire and earth sacred. However, where *dokhura* facilities are not available, modern Parsis permit burial.

Another ancient but miniscule minority Indian community, the Jews, is also based in Bombay. Seven synagogues in the city still serve their dwindling numbers. The house of the Sassoons, Iraqi in origin and no longer Bombay-based since the 1940s, has also left its mark through endowments for educational and other charitable purposes. Bombay still has a Sassoon Dock (now used by the fishing fleet) and a Sassoon Library.

The Hindu population of Bombay is largely Maharashtrian though most non-Maharashtrian Bombayites are also Hindus, with a fair number of Jains among the Gujaratis, and also neo-Buddhists among the ex-untouchables.

The Muslims of Bombay, like the Parsis and Gujaratis, have merged with the rest in the melting pot of urban culture. Yet there are areas in Bombay where their unique contributions to

Detail,
Victoria
Terminus

Indian life can still be observed and enjoyed. On Mohammed Ali Road, one can get *kababs* rolled up in *rotis* (unleavened bread) or hot *jalebi* sweets, at all hours, especially late at night.

The slow transformation of the swampy islands during the 17th and 18th centuries gave way in the 19th Century to rapid changes. In 1858, the East India Company returned the islands to the British crown. In the 1850s came the "Fire Carriage," and by the end of the century Bombay was linked with central and northern India by the Great Indian Peninsular Railway, and, some time later, with eastern India too. During this period, Bombay became a most important "cotton-polis." Raw cotton from Gujarat was shipped to Lancashire, spun and woven into cloth, and brought back to Bombay for sale all over the country. Notwithstanding this, Bombay's cotton textile industry was established in this period, thanks to the grit and persistence of Bombay's entrepreneurs.

The outbreak of the American Civil war in 1861 and the opening of the Suez Canal gave further impetus to cotton exports from India. During the cotton boom, Bombay was given a face-lift. The new-found wealth was poured into the building of impressive commercial and civic buildings in the second half of the 19th Century.

Colonial Architecture

The **Afghan Memorial Church** of St John the Evangelist is in the Colaba area, which is the long arm of South Bombay that stretches into the sea. The church was established in 1847 and consecrated 11 years later as a memorial to those who fell in the First Afghan War. It is a lovely piece of architecture with Gothic arches and stained-glass windows.

The **Old Secretariat and the Public Works Department Secretariat** were designed and built by Colonel Orel Henry St. Clair Wilkins during 1867–74. These buildings are described as High Victorian Gothic in style.

The building of the **University Hall** and **Elphinstone College,** with its central tower and canopied balconies, was funded by Sir Cowasjee Jehangir Readymoney, and along with the Library and Clock Tower (now called **Rajabai Tower**), were completed in 1878.

The **School of Art** was also built at

The celebrated Bombay *dabba-wallas.*

this time. Rudyard Kipling was born and spent his early years here. His father, John Lockwood Kipling, was principal of the school and, under his guidance many local artisans received training and prepared sculptured panels and motifs to adorn the buildings that were then being built in Bombay.

Crawford Market, designed by William Emerson, has bas-reliefs designed by J. L. Kipling. Today, the reliefs are hardly noticed as they stand at some height above the crowd and bustle of this market area. Passing by in a double-decker bus, till recently, gave one a glimpse of them but, with the expansion of a traffic island, this is no longer possible.

Flora Fountain stands in another crowded square at the heart of the Fort area, now called **Hutatma Chauk** (Martyrs' Square). The fountain is a major landmark and was erected in honor of the Governor, Sir Henry Bartle Edward Frere, who built new Bombay in the 1860s. The memorial that has given the square its new name commemorates those who lost their lives in the cause of setting up a separate Maharashtra state in the Indian Union.

The **Fort** (downtown) area in South Bombay derives its name from the fact that the area fell within the former walled city, of which only a small fragment survives as part of the eastern boundary wall of **St. George's Hospital.** Memories of this walled area were preserved in such names as Churchgate, Bazaargate and Rampart Row, all renamed in recent years. Within the Fort was the Castle, the headquarters of the Bombay Government. Till India became independent, government orders were issued as from "Bombay Castle," though the castle itself had long ceased to exist.

The finest High Victorian Gothic structure in Bombay, designed by Frederick William Stevens, is **Victoria Terminus** (V.T.) and the adjoining headquarters building of the **Central Railway,** known originally as the Great Indian Peninsular Railway. It was built over 1878–87. The structure is of yellow sandstone and granite combined with polychromatic stones and blue-gray basalt for decorations in the interior.

The **Municipal Corporation Building** opposite V.T. is another Stevens masterpiece, especially the vast domed central staircase and the cuspated arches in the arcaded stories. The **Western Railway**

A transaction in Bombay's red light district.

Central office building at Churchgate, built in gray-blue basalt with bands of white in the 1890 has towers with oriental domes, which gives the structure an imposing presence.

The foundation stone of the **Prince of Wales Museum** was laid by George V in 1905 during his visit to India as Prince of Wales. George Wittet designed this building with its dome and other oriental features in blue-gray basalt and yellow sandstone. The museum contains some excellent examples of Indian miniature painting of the Mughal and Rajasthan Schools. There are also collections of artifacts of jade and chinaware. The museum is one of the most important in India. Another Wittet building of note is the **General Post Office** near V.T., also oriental in inspiration. Wittet also left his mark in the **Ballard Estate** area, where, however, his office buildings reflect similar 19th Century structures in London.

George Wittet will be remembered most, however, for his **Gateway of India** on the waterfront at Apollo Bunder. It was conceived as a triumphal arch to commemorate the visit of George V and Queen Mary for the Delhi Darbar in 1911.

The honey-colored basalt of the arch, facing the sea, catches the light of the rising and setting sun and changes from shades of gold to orange and pink. It was through this arch that the last of the British troops left India by sea.

While Bombay city boasts no ancient or even medieval monuments, an hour's ride away by motor launch, within the waters of the harbor, is the island of **Gharapuri** or **Elephanta,** site of a magnificent series of rock-cut cave temples with large sculptured interiors. These were excavated in the 7th and 8th centuries. The centerpiece is a massive 18-foot (five-meter) three-headed bust of Shiva, representing his manifestations as Creator, Preserver and Destroyer. The Portuguese called the island Elephanta after a massive elephant sculpture that once stood in one of the excavated courtyards there. It now stands in the garden of the Bombay city zoo.

Some 25 miles (40 km) from the Fort area, near Borivali station of the Western Railway suburban line, is a National Park within which lie the c. 2nd Century Buddhist hill caves of **Kanheri.** Sculpture here too is on a large scale and matches that of the better known Ajanta and Ellora caves

The *Trimurti* at Elephanta Caves on an island in Bombay harbor.

in eastern Maharashtra.

Surrounded as it is on three sides by the sea, life in Bombay draws much of its character from the beaches, seaside promenades and coastline. Beyond the central city are the beaches of **Juhu, Versova, Madh Island, Marve, Manori** and **Gorai**, one-time secluded seaside resorts. Today, Juhu is crowded with residential apartments, its beach swarming with picnickers and hawkers.

Gillian Tindall called her historical study of Bombay *City of Gold* and, certainly, the pursuit of wealth is a major occupation here. But Bombayites do not forget the "temples of their gods" though, perhaps, as often as not, in pursuit of equally material aims. Appropriately, a major shrine near the racecourse is dedicated to Mahalakshmi, goddess of wealth and prosperity.

Notable, however, is the universality of the cosmopolitan Bombayite's faith in the efficacy of offerings at holy shrines, whether of their own religion or of others. Peoples of all faiths queue up patiently in their thousands on fixed days of the week to make their offerings, whether at the tomb of the Muslim saint, Haji Ali, on the tidal island off the shore opposite the racecourse at Mahalakshmi; or for the Wednesday "Novenas" at St. Michael's Church at Mahim; or at the Siddhivinayak Temple at Prabhadevi on Tuesdays. Bandra Fair, in celebration of the feast of St. Mary, is centered on an image of St. Mary at the Mount Mary Shrine and attracts thousands of seekers of succor and favors — with no distinction of caste or creed.

Marine Drive links Malabar Hill to Fort and Colaba. This long gracefully curving road along the buttressed seacoast, viewed from the Hanging Gardens on Malabar Hill or the high-rise buildings at Nariman Point, provides at night a view of the glittering Queen's Necklace, and, by day and night, a panorama of Bombay's skyline. Along Marine Drive runs a wide sidewalk, ideal for the early morning jogger, evening walker and late night stroller. During the monsoons the turbulent waves splash over the parapets.

Chowpatti, at the north end of Marine Drive, is a stretch of sandy beach. In the evenings, it is crowded with people enjoying the cool sea breeze and children playing and stalls selling delicious Bombay *bhelpuri* and other snacks. Chowpatti is famous also for its *kulfi* and ice creams. During the Ganesh Chaturthi festival, processions from the city meet here with images of Ganesh, which are then immersed in the sea. A club nearby offers boating and water sports facilities.

The **Taraporevala Aquarium** is also on Marine Drive. It has a good collection of tropical fish. What is rather disturbing, however, is the fish-and-chips stall just outside the main building.

Feeding the Millions

With more than 3 million people pouring into metropolitan Bombay, especially the southern half of the island, every day by the three local railway lines and by bus, cab and private car, for work and business, there is an enormous demand for soft drinks, snacks and quick lunches which Bombay was geared to meet long before the newfangled fast-food establishments were thought of. Long queues form at food kiosks and restaurants at lunch time for rapid service. *Pau-bhaji* opposite Victoria Terminus and rice *thalis* in vegetarian restaurants are favorite low-cost meals, but everything, from *vada sambar* or *biryani* in little roadside restaurants to Mandarin Chinese and all varieties of western cuisine are available.

However, large numbers of officegoers prefer a warm, home-cooked lunch, and this is made possible by Bombay's unique city-wide organization of *dabbawallas*. These *dhoti* clad, Gandhi-capped men collect *dabbas* ('ever-hot' lunch-boxes) from residences early in the forenoon. Each is identified as to ownership and locations (from and to) by markings decipherable by the *dabbawallas* alone, even the illiterate among them. These are assembled and sorted by destination and carried off by local train. At various stations appropriate batches of *dabbas* are handed to other teams for delivery at offices and other places of work. In the afternoon, the process is reversed.

The heat and rush of the day does not cramp the style of Bombayites. Once the day's work is done, they can be seen walking the gardens, children riding on horses at the old bandstand, and pavement hawkers doing their evening business. Cinema and theater halls are crowded; the sea-faces from Marine Drive to Juhu come alive. The city sleeps late. The streets are never empty. As some people move homewards in cars, others lay out their humble beds on the pavements and try and catch a good night's sleep.

MAHARASHTRA, SERMONS IN STONES

Bombay's pre-eminence may lead you to think that it represents the soul of Maharashtra. But the city is only Maharashtra's avaricious heart; its soul, true to Hindu belief, lies south of it, nearer its navel.

Bombay, because it is the commercial center of the country, contains a cross-section of India's diverse population. But the section of it which is Maharashtrian is very cross; it feels done out of the riches which should rightfully belong to "sons of the soil." This rather muddied offspring theory reasserts itself at times of economic stress. Its principal beneficiary is a local political party, the Shiv Sena, which makes the issue its central plank. The rest of Maharashtra, secure in its parochial cohesiveness, does not bother about the Sena at all.

The Sena is named after the 17th Century Maratha warrior Shivaji, or to give him his full title, Chattrapati Shivaji Maharaj. Shivaji was an anti-imperialist and the empire-builders present hereabouts then were the Mughals. It's no wonder then that there is a Hindu–Muslim communal edge to much of the politics of the area.

In Puné you will find the proprietary pride in Shivaji even more pronounced. There are those who feel that this constant harking back to a glorious past ensures a less than glorious present, that the Maharashtrians' relative lack of initiative and entrepreneurship is partly a result of this habit of lapsing into the past.

But this glorious past — not just from the Shivaji period — has left behind a treasure for the visitor. The best approach is to use five cities (Puné, Kolhapur, Aurangabad, Nagpur and Nasik) as bases for exploratory trips to nearby places of interest. If you *have* to choose only one, choose Aurangabad: the caves of Ajanta and Ellora offer riches comparable to those of the Taj Mahal.

Once called Poona by the British, **Puné** has now reclaimed its original Marathi name. It is 105 miles (170 km) from Bombay, approachable by road, rail or air. The air journey is short (around half an hour) and gives a magical view of Bombay's vast expanse of lights especially at night on the return route from Puné. Unfortunately this evening journey is made in a small propeller plane which, unless

you are an incurable romantic, may make you wish that you had stayed behind with your stomach.

The road journey from Bombay over the Western Ghats is marked by hair-raising bends over steep inclines, in the company of truck-convoys. The roads are good; your driver had better be too.

The best journey is undoubtedly by one of the fast trains, especially *The Deccan Queen* which takes four hours each way through many mountain tunnels and past scenic vistas. The journey is particularly picturesque, if a little wet, during the monsoon when the hills are green and small waterfalls cascade down them.

Puné, once the capital of the Maratha Empire and captured by the British at the Battle of Koregaon in 1818, was developed in the 18th Century along the lines of an archetypal army town. The British passion for order — though passion's not quite the word for such meticulousness —resulted in the usual army cantonment areas, uncluttered and well-served by broad roads, in distinct contrast to the busy and crowded old city.

Puné became the center of many Hindu social reform movements; it also became for a time, during the heyday of Bal Gangadhar Tilak, the epicenter of India's independence movement. Rapid industrialization has changed its character considerably; its clutter now spares no-one; even then a certain old-world charm occasionally asserts itself.

Focus on Indian Arts

Well worth a visit in Puné is the **Raja Kelkar Museum**, a private museum collected with painstaking care by one single individual, Dinkar Kelkar. Its focus is on traditional Indian arts. It has 36 sections which include carved palace and temple doors, 2,000-year-old excavated pottery, traditional Indian lamps, and 17th Century miniature paintings. Of special interest are a collection of brass nutcrackers (some of them explicitly erotic) and brass padlocks (including a scorpion-shaped padlock whose "pincers" lock together). Mr. Kelkar, a benign if loquacious old gentleman, often greets you as if you were his personal guest. His collection is so large that the exhibits have to be shown by rotation.

The **Agha Khan Palace**, with its Italianate arches and spacious well-mannered lawns, was an unlikely place for a prison, but at one time the British interned Mahatma Gandhi and his wife Kasturba here along with other leaders of the Congress Party. Kasturba died in the palace while in detention there and a memorial has been erected in the grounds.

Shinde Chhatri: Mahadji Scindia, one of the Maratha ruling princes, constructed a small black-stone Shiva temple in the 18th Century. His descendant, Madhavrao II, built an annex in Mahadji's memory. But his architectural inspiration was not Indian, like Mahadji's, but Southern European. The contrast in the two styles is a kind of monument to the assimilative powers of Indian culture. Mahadji's *samadhi* (mausoleum) stands across a courtyard. There is a likeness of him in silver, topped by a flame-colored turban. A nearby sign, excessively haughty considering its contents, warns you not to open an umbrella as that would be insulting to Scindia's memory.

Maratha Forts & Temples

Simha Gad, whose literal translation is fortress of the lion, stands on a hilltop 15 miles (25 km) from Pune. Around 300 years ago Shivaji's right-hand-man,

General Tanaji Malsure, with a group of trusted lieutenants, scaled its sheer precipice with the help of ropes and giant lizards especially trained for the purpose. Shivaji won the fortress but lost his general, killed during action. Today, most of the fort's battlements are overgrown with weeds.

Other Shivaji forts within easy reach of Pune are **Rajgadh, Torna, Purander** and **Shivneri.**

Shanwarwada, built in 1736, was once the palace of the Peshwa rulers who succeeded to Shivaji's empire, after having served it as ministers. A massive fire in 1827 destroyed most of the palace, leaving behind only its old fortified walls, large brass-studded gates, 18th Century lotus pools, and the elaborate foundations of the palace.

The 8th Century rock-cut **Temple of Pataleshwar** stands in the middle of Pune. It has been carved into a single boulder of awe-inspiring size. The temple is used by worshippers even today.

There are many other fine temples in Pune, the best known, the **Parvati Temple** on a hilltop on the outskirts of the city. This was once the private shrine of Peshwa rulers. A Muslim shrine, the

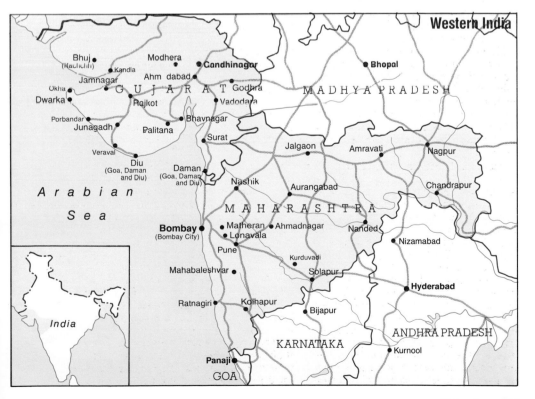

Qamarali Darvesh, contains a celebrated "levitating" stone, which you might be tempted to investigate.

From Puné you can go to hill resorts, called hill stations because the British always "stationed" themselves, even when they were on holiday. Notable amongst these are **Lonavala** (45 miles/70 km from Puné). Three miles (five km) away is an even smaller and quieter hill station called **Khandala. Mahableshwar** (60 miles/100 km) and **Panchgani** (55 miles/90 km) are hill stations which lend themselves to quiet walks amidst unspoilt natural beauty with panoramic views of valleys from several vantage points. Summer temperatures range between 15 and 30 degrees C. Horse-riding is *de rigueur;* horses and ponies of varying spirit are available on hire.

Matheran (72 miles/116 km from Puné), accessible also from Bombay from which it is only 58 miles (94 km), has the added attraction of being inaccessible to automobiles, prohibited by law. You either walk the last 12 miles (20 km) up a steep hill or take a toy-train from Neral. (It's a *slow* toy-train. Journey time: 1½ hours.)

Kolhapur

Kolhapur (245 miles/395 km from Bombay) is one of the most important pilgrimage centers in Maharashtra. In fact, it's often called **Dakshina Kashi** (the Banaras of the South). Not unexpectedly, it has many temples, the one held in highest esteem being the **Mahalaxmi Temple** (also called **Ambabai Temple**), built in the 9th Century. Another temple, to the east of the city, is **Kotiteerth,** a temple of Mahadev in the center of a wide expanse of water.

Kolhapur was also the capital of a former princely state and therefore has some splendid palaces and royal homes. These include an **Old Palace** of the 18th Century and a **New Palace** with an octagonal clock tower and museum. There is also **Shalini Palace,** an example of Indo-Saracenic architecture.

Kolhapur, is also known for its wrestlers (it boasts of a wrestling stadium which can hold 20,000 people). Kolhapur, of course, is *the* place if you are looking for Kolhapur *chappals* (sandals).

A number of interesting places can be reached from Kolhapur. **Panhala,** nine miles (15 km) away, is not only a hill

"The marriage of Shiva," Ellora Caves, Maharashtra.

station but is also of historical interest, being the scene of a famous Shivaji escape. **Sangli**, 30 miles (50 km) away, was also the capital of a former principality. It has a well-known museum and a fine temple. **Ratnagiri**, 80 miles (125 km) from Kolhapur, is the gateway to the beaches of Southern Konkan. Ratnagiri itself has a fine beach but is better known for its succulent Alphonso mangoes, indisputably the best in India. **Ganpatipule**, 95 miles (155 km) from Kolhapur, is an old pilgrimage center, now being developed as a major beach resort. **Pandharpur** (125 miles/200 km) draws pilgrims from all over Maharashtra to its famous **Shrine of Vithal** in July and August each year. **Sholapur** (140 miles/225 km) is now a teeming textile town. It has a formidable fort as well as a temple in the middle of an expanse of water.

Aurangabad

As its name suggests, Aurangabad (230 miles/370 km from Bombay) has a strong Muslim flavor. This dates back from the time of the Mughal Emperor Aurangzeb. Many Mughal monuments and tombs can be seen in and around the city. The mausoleum of Aurangzeb's Begum **(Bibi ka Maqbara)**, may seem familiar. It should be: it was intended to be a replica of the Taj Mahal, but suffers from all the defects of second-hand art.

Aurangabad also has a Buddhist legacy in its caves. Just 1½ miles (three km) behind the Bibi ka Maqbara, there are 12 caves which were excavated between the 3rd and 11th century A.D. The most interesting are caves 3, 6 and 7. Carry a torch with you.

The **Sunehri Mahal** (the golden palace) and **Panchakki**, an old water-mill, were both built by Malik Amber.

At **Daulatabad** (nine miles/15 km from Aurangabad) is a massive hilltop fort, often described as totally impregnable. Many other monuments from the Mughal era survive here.

Ellora

Ellora, 15 miles (25 km) away from Aurangabad, has 34 rock-cut temples representing the Buddhist, Jain and Hindu Brahmanic faiths. Amongst the most important historical monuments in India, these caves were scooped out of the rocks 10 centuries ago.

The term "cave temple" cannot convey the magnitude of the Ellora achievement. The feat could be compared to carving a whole cathedral out of solid rock, interior and exterior.

All the caves are man-made. The artists who flocked to these remote areas from vast distances, literally hammered monuments out of rock. Their technique needed a profound knowledge of rock formations and their structure. The work was usually started from the top of the temple and moved downwards to eliminate the need for scaffolding.

The centerpiece at Ellora is the **Kailash Temple**. Its architects were not modest about their ambitions; Kailash is after all the mythical mountain where the gods live. The total area scooped out is nearly 70,000 sq feet (6,500 sq meters), while the 100-foot-high (30-meter) shrine itself occupies an area of about 18,300 sq feet (1,700 sq meters). In its galleries are recreated various scenes from Shiva myths. One of them represents the eternal struggle between the forces of evil represented by Ravana, the demon king of Sri Lanka, and the forces of good represented by Shiva and Parvati. Ravana violently rocks the throne of Shiva and Parvati, but Shiva and Parvati sit calm and unimpressed.

Although the carvings at Ellora are of three religions, the structures are often similar, probably due to the demands of the rock formations. Within, differences are discernible: the Jain caves are ascetic; the Buddhist caves, inspired by Buddhism's 2nd Century attempt at populism, show an austere richness.

Ajanta

The 30 Buddhist caves of **Ajanta**, 60 miles (100 km) from Aurangabad, not only contain sculptures but remarkably preserved frescos as well. The Ajanta caves are in a secluded site; because of this they were virtually forgotten and discovered accidentally only in the 19th Century. This probably explains why the monuments escaped the depredations of invading armies.

Buddhism was a religion of denial. That's how Gautama Buddha saw it; he was against the worshipping of idols and forbade his followers from making images of himself. He did not even favor the wearing of colorful clothing or any ornamentation which might excite desire.

After the Buddha's death, as Buddhism spread wider, its preachers felt the need for giving a representational form to its teachings. Buddhist monks began to tell stories of Buddha's earlier incarnations; paintings and sculptures of these stories began to proliferate. Thus began the process of Buddhism acquiring some of the sensuousness of Hinduism.

The frescos and sculptures of Ajanta are indeed heady and the westerner, used to the idea of religion being essentially a negation of the senses, will be startled by the voluptuousness of much of the imagery.

The most important caves are the ones numbered 1, 2, 9, 10, 16, 17, 19, 21 and 26.

Nagpur

Nagpur was the capital of the Bhosle branch of the Maratha Empire. Its imperial glory is now revived every winter when today's rulers — cabinet ministers and elected representatives — move there from Bombay to this winter capital of Maharashtra. Nagpur derives additional satisfaction from being located at the geographical center of India. It is also famous for being orange country; the fruit is eaten all over the country.

Ramtek (165 miles/265 km from Nagpur) is so named because Rama, the popular incarnation of Lord Vishnu, stopped here with his wife Sita and brother Laxman when they were banished from Ayodhya.

Wardha, 45 miles (75 km) from Nagpur, is the alighting point for Sevagram and Paunar. The former is the village where Mahatma Gandhi lived in an ashram. This has been well-preserved and is a place of modern pilgrimage. Paunar was made famous by one of Gandhi's disciples, Acharya Vinoba Bhave, who lived and died there.

Nagzira, 70 miles (115 km) from Nagpur, is a game sanctuary in a beautiful setting. The forests of Nagzira have two all-year-round water tanks which provide an ideal habitat for wildlife. Nawegaon National Park, 85 miles (135 km) from Nagpur, is an idyllic forest rich in wildlife. It has an 18th Century artificial lake. The man who made it has been deified as Kolasur Dev and his shrine lies by the lake.

Chandrapur (100 miles/160 km from Nagpur) boasts a fort and several temples. From Chandrapur you can head for Tadoba, undoubtedly Maharashtra's best known sanctuary. In the park is a lake held to be sacred by the tribals. Its sanctity must suit the crocodiles which thrive in it in large numbers.

Chikalda (135 miles/220 km from Nagpur) is the hill station of the region. It is approached through a thick jungle teeming with wildlife.

Nasik is a holy city; it stands on the banks of the river Godavari, venerated by Hindus. Two thousand temples and many bathing ghats testify to its sanctity. An incident in the *Ramayana* features Nasik: when Laxman, Rama's younger brother, tiring of the efforts of the demon Shirpanakha to persuade him to marry her, chopped off her nose, it fell where Nasik now stands.

The Sinhastha Mela, held once every 12 years, is the high point of a pilgrimage to Nasik. The crush of people at this time is best seen from a distance.

In Trimbakeshwar (18 miles/30 km from Nasik), according to legend, a dispute arose between the gods and the demons over the possession of a pot of nectar. In the melée, the nectar spilled. One of the places where some drops fell was Trimbakeshwar. The river Godavari rises here from a hill called Brahmagiri. The Trimbakeshwar Temple is an imposing monument and has beautiful carvings.

Shirdhi (46 miles/75 km from Nasik) is where Sai Baba, the Muslim teacher whose wisdom and miraculous powers made him a saint for people of all religions, including Hindus, lived and died. His followers come in great numbers through the year to pay their respects to his memory.

There are those of you who may want nothing more cultural from Maharashtra than a quiet beach. There are many of these in and around Bombay, but they are not quiet. For that you will have to go further afield. Try Kihim (85 miles/136 km from Bombay or Murud (135 miles/216 km) which has a breathtaking approach, an old palace and an island fort less than a mile offshore. Ganapathipule (230 miles/375 km) has white sand amidst much greenery. It has an old temple of Ganapati on a colossal rock on the shore. The idol inside the temple is said to have been made by nature, not by human artifice. A sea-tossed Ganapati found on white sand and placed in a rock-based temple: nature, religion, monument.

That sort of sums up Maharashtra.

Detail of fresco, Ajanta Caves, Maharashtra.

GOA: WHITE CHURCHES, GOLDEN SANDS

It was almost dusk. Afonso de Albuquerque stood on a grassy hillock overlooking the Mandovi River. To the north stretched miles of fertile green fields edged by an undulating fringe of verdant hills. The wide river lazily slithered away into the horizon. Below him smoke and billowing sails marked the area of battle. It had been a bitter fight, but now the enemy navy lay all but decimated. Albuquerque felt good. This bountiful land was now his — wrested from Yusuf Adilshah, Sultan of Bijapur.

It was Nov. 25, 1510, the feast of St. Catherine. Overwhelmed, Albuquerque knelt and gave thanks and ordered a shrine to be built in the saint's honor. Thus began four centuries of Portuguese influence on this tiny land. The Portuguese came looking for spices; they stayed on to make Goa the capital of their empire in the east.

It is the Iberian aura, the cultural alloy of Latin and Oriental, the coexistence of Hinduism and Christianity that epitomizes the distinct identity of Goa. The Portuguese invested a hitherto predominantly Hindu society with their religion, attitudes and lifestyles, and Goa's ethos and élan are consequences of this encounter. Like the stained-glass windows on the churches that punctuate the hillsides, Goa's fabric is a mosaic of bright and variegated colors — the flamboyant designs of Latin exuberance set against the russet hues of traditional Indian attitudes and lifestyles.

Nature too, has in no mean manner contributed to this symbiotic tapestry. Tucked away snugly between the hills of the Western Ghats and the Arabian Sea, this tiny territory of 1,350 sq miles (3,500 sq km), about halfway down the west coast of the Indian peninsula, is verdant with bottlegreen hills wooded with jackfruit, mango and cashew groves, cut across by rivers and edged by miles of sun-drenched beaches. A warm, languid climate, and a gentle unspoilt people, complete this compelling kaleidoscope.

Cocooned within its natural boundaries and the colonial cloisters of Portuguese rule, this tiny pocket of the Indian subcontinent lay slumbering for several centuries, bypassed by history. While the

Left, Mapusa Cow Market, Goa. right, looking out.

rest of the country progressed towards independence and the 20th Century, Goa remained a Portuguese colony, suspended in a web of nostalgia.

Iberian Legacy

Since Goa's absorption into the Indian Union in 1961, there have been many changes. Yet, sleepy villages and myriads of white churches still characterize this lotus-eater's paradise, where the romance of the past lingers on and the mood is as gentle and unhurried as the undulating countryside. One can drive through peaceful towns with their Spanish-style villas, stop at a small *taverna* (bar) for a drink of *feni* — a locally brewed drink made from cashew or coconut, listen to the sounds of a *mando* (love song) and the strains of a guitar mingling with the sensuous lapping of the waves, or bask for hours on the warm golden sands of lonely, idyllic beaches.

It is easy to slip into Goa's warm, effortless existence. There is a mediterranean atmosphere in the quaint towns with their red-tiled roofs and narrow streets and the charming fishing villages snuggled among coconut groves. Off its sandy coast, fishermen with faces weathered to mahogany by sun, salt and wind, catch mackerel, shark, crab, lobster and shrimp. And on Sundays, and feast days, the local folk, in their Sunday best — the women often in European dress and with lace mantillas on their heads, the men in black suits — file into the baroque-styled churches for service.

Most of Goa's larger towns are situated in the coastal belt where the Portuguese first settled, and their character was formed slowly through the centuries of Christian rule. They are small, certainly by Indian standards, as the mainstream of Goan life flows largely in its villages.

Capital Town Panjim

Panjim (now Panaji), the capital of Goa situated on the southern bank of the Mandovi River, has a population of about 40,000 and, like most other Goan towns, is centered on a church and the square in front of it.

Largo da Igreja (Church Square) is an impressive ensemble: a dazzling white-balustraded stairway in front of the **Church of the Immaculate Conception** heightens the proportions of the baroque

Statue of Louis De Camoes, Old Goa Cathedral.

facade which dominates the square. Built in 1541, its tall, twin towers were the first signs of "home" for the sailors who made the long voyage from Lisbon.

Panjim, in fact, has several squares, the houses lining them rising directly above the wide streets. Most of these villas, painted in pale yellow, green or deep rose, with their embellishments picked out in white or a contrasting color, display French windows opening on to wrought-iron balconies which overlook the street.

Particularly quaint is the old residential area of **Fontainahas** which lies behind the church and where narrow cobbled alleys weave through a miscellany of closely-knit houses with tiled roofs, overhanging balconies and carved pillars, much as one would expect to find in any provincial town in Portugal or Spain.

Down winding streets which echo the sputter of motorcycles and scooters, interspersed among rows of tiny stores, are innumerable cafes which cater to the relaxed temperament of the locals. There is never too little time to stop for a drink or a chat. The pace in this town, as in the rest of Goa, is unhurried. Shops close for siesta and the whole town dozes away the golden hours.

Facing the river, along the broad riverside boulevard, are some of Panjim's public buildings, including the **Secretariat,** built in 1615 by the Portuguese on the site of the Palacio Idalcao (palace of the Sultan of Bijapur, Yusuf Adil Khan, called the Idalcan by the Portuguese), a many-shuttered edifice which was once the viceroy's residence. Beyond **Largo da Palacio** (Palace Square) lies the quay which bursts into feverish activity every morning when the steamer from Bombay spills its contents onto the pier. The ship which plies back and forth from Bombay every day, except for the monsoon months (June to September), provides the most enjoyable means of travel to Goa — slow and relaxed, indicative of the Goan way of life.

The **Campal,** as the riverside boulevard is called, is one of the most picturesque spots in Panjim. If you stand somewhat seaward and look towards the river, you can see in a single glance an astounding chunk of history: in the far distance, the ramparts of the **Aguada Fort** — once one of the main bastions commanding the entrance into the Mandovi — with powder rooms, barracks, a church and a lighthouse, and now used as a prison;

The Strand at Panjim.

218

along the water's edge the white-gabled facade of a church tucked in between the folds of the shoreline; and sailing past on the river a reminder of the present, the slow continuous procession of barges carrying iron ore from mines in the interior to Marmagoa harbor for export.

Margao and Vasco

Margao, the second largest town in Goa and the principal commercial center, is one of the few linked to the rest of India by a railway line. In the heart of one of the most fertile districts, Salcete, Margao is the home of several prominent landowning families who have built themselves town as well as country houses, even while their roots remained in the villages.

A few other towns are sprinkled around the territory: **Vasco da Gama** is slowly developing into an industrial center; **Marmagoa,** Goa's port, is one of India's finest natural harbors; **Mapusa** in the north is an interesting traditional market town. But the true voice of Goan culture is much more audible in the villages and outlying regions. Rich and poor alike live in the villages, visiting the towns for business or trade.

Village houses in Goa are impressive structures. Patterned around a central courtyard or patio, usually overgrown with banana trees, the village house derives its style from a combination of Indian elements and the Italianate form, prevalent in Europe two centuries ago. An open verandah surrounds the patio and leads into airy, spacious rooms, which display carved, rosewood furniture, ornate mirrors, chandeliers and a profusion of blue and white porcelain. Some of the larger homes also maintain private chapels with baroque-styled altars, similar to those in the churches. The houses are built of red laterite stone found all over Goa while window panes are traditionally covered with small rectangles of translucent oyster shell, instead of glass.

Churches and Carnivals

Driving through Goa's villages, one is struck by the deep imprint of four and a half centuries of Latin Catholicism. The Portuguese came not only to conquer, but also to preach: colonization and proselytization went hand in hand. Presiding over every village, commanding the heights at hilltops, hugging the shores of rivers, beside fields and dusty roads, and visible for miles around, sparkling white churches, crosses and small shrines indicate Christian ubiquity; religion is never more than a bend away.

Built mostly in the 16th and 17th centuries, the churches of Goa have been architecturally influenced by the Gothic styles of the Middle Ages and the baroque styles of the Renaissance. With their ornate embellishments, interiors and facades, they are the finest examples of Indo-European architectural fusion in the country.

On the feast day of the patron saint — and every village has one — the whole village is in attendance. The image of the saint, brightly decorated, is carried in procession by priests and laity to the chanting of prayers and litanies, recited or sung, accompanied by a violin or even a brass band. A fair normally provides the finale — refreshments, such as black gram, cashew nuts, coconut and jaggery sweets, fancy goods and even utensils are on display for sale.

Often, music and dance accompany such festivities, the Christian religion having mingled with traditional Indian

Goa

practices of folk worship. Comparable to Rio's Mardi Gras is Carnival in Goa, when for three days towns and villages rock under the wildest spirits. Masqueraders dance in the streets, and *feni* flows freely everywhere.

Sunny Beaches

Strung along Goa's 60-mile (100-km) coastline, like a lace frill on the edge of a colorful skirt, are some of the most beautiful beaches in the world — dazzling stretches of golden sand edging the aquamarine expanse of the Arabian Sea.

An unbroken four-mile (seven-km) crescent of sun-drenched sand marks the twin beaches of **Candolim** and **Calangute,** north of Panjim and the Aguada headland. Despite the concentration of resorts, hotels, beach huts, bars, restaurants, and souvenir stalls, there is an innocence here, a freshness of childhood mornings.

Wake earlier than usual and walk along the crumbly sands towards the gold-speckled silken sheet of an early morning ocean. You may come upon cheerful fisherfolk singing as they heave in their catch. You may be invited to share a steaming cup of tea. You may even be gifted the pick of the day's takings — a fresh, succulent lobster perhaps.

Farther north, past estuaries of the many streams that gurgle through the land, are a series of secluded beaches. **Anjuna,** a haven for the faded flower children from the West; **Vagator** beneath the soaring backdrop of **Chapora Fort;** and the many coves and creeks await discovery by the more intrepid visitor.

A raw beauty characterizes the beaches of the southern coast of Goa. While **Siridao,** near the Zuari estuary, is a shell-collector's haven with its assortment of oyster and mother-of-pearl shells, it is **Colva,** with its broad brow of silver-gray, powder-fine sand that has been the inspiration for many folk tales and songs.

A drive south from Margao through heavily wooded teak plantations and deep green ravines brings the visitor to Betul village where a varied and almost inexhaustible supply of seafood, including some of Goa's largest mussels can be obtained. Accessible only by boat from Betul and with a particular quality of remoteness is the picturesque Betul beach, all but unmarked by the footprints of tourists.

On one of Goa's golden beaches.

Old Golden Goa

No visit to Goa is complete without a visit to Old Goa, the Golden Goa *(Goa Doirada)* of the 16th Century, when it was the "Rome of the Orient."

The best way to come to Old Goa is by boat as the Portuguese did, and through the Viceregal Arch, the ceremonial entry point where Vasco da Gama gazed out from his niche.

From here one can look back to the 16th Century when Goa Doirada boasted a larger population than London or Paris. That was the time when the city reached its apogee, just before the Dutch and the English successfully challenged Portugal's maritime pretensions.

Magnificent churches, sumptuous buildings, stately mansions and broad streets once characterized the three sq miles (eight sq km) of Old Goa (it was called just Goa then). A "noble city full of beautiful buildings and palaces," wrote Albert de Mandelslo, a Dutch traveller who visited Goa in 1639. So magnificent was the city that it was said, *"Quem vin Goa excuse de ver Lisboa"* ("Whoever has seen Goa need not see Lisbon").

Among the many splendid buildings of Old Goa, the **Sé Cathedral** (Cathedral of St. Catherine) remains one of the greatest monuments of the period. Completed in 1619, it is the largest Christian church in Asia, and a grand example of Renaissance architecture. The Cathedral's 260-foot (80-meter) long aisle culminates in a richly carved gilt altarpiece — one of the finest in India. There is a font in the church, possibly a vessel of Hindu origin, which is said to have been used by Goa's patron saint, St. Francis Xavier, who came to Goa in 1542 and converted large numbers of its inhabitants to Christianity. He died in China, while on a similar mission.

Within the compound of the cathedral but facing the opposite direction, is the **Church of St. Francis of Assisi** with a stucco ceiling and a profusion of carvings. Interestingly, the inner sides of the buttressed walls have frescos of intricate floral designs painted in a hybrid style combining Indian and European elements.

A similar style can be detected in the frescoes embellishing the interior of the **Basilica of Bom Jesus**, the focus of interest for many visitors to Goa. The basilica, where the mortal remains of St. Francis Xavier are enshrined, is the best

Flea market at Anjuna Beach, Goa.

specimen of baroque architecture in India. The chapel attracts large numbers of pilgrims. St. Francis's body which was brought to Goa almost 150 years after his death, now lies in an airtight glass coffin, placed inside a silver casket fashioned by a 17th-Century Florentine jeweler.

The tomb which came from Italy, donated by the Grand Duke of Tuscany, is made from alabaster and Florentine marble and inlaid with semi-precious stones and bronze panels depicting scenes from the life of the saint. The interior of the chapel which houses the mausoleum is richly adorned with paintings and wood carvings, and over the south door hangs a picture believed to be the likeness of the saint.

Convents and Chapels

There are many more churches in Old Goa in varying stages of deterioration. The **Church of St. Cajetan**, near the ferry wharf, with its two belfries and cupola in the center was modelled in miniature on the Basilica of St. Peter in Rome by its Italian architect. Also near the river bank stands the **Chapel of St. Catherine** built to mark the site of the bitterest fighting during Albuquerque's conquest of Goa in 1510.

A few minutes' walk up the road from the basilica is **Monte Santo** (Holy Hill) where one haunted tower of the **Church of the Augustinian Monastery** is all that remains of a once splendid vaulted structure. Adjacent to the ruins stands the **Convent of St. Monica**, once one of the largest nunneries in the Portuguese empire.

Past the flying buttresses of the convent, on a grassy mound at the edge of a steep cliff, stands the shell of the **Church of Our Lady of the Rosary,** one of the earliest to be built in Goa. It represents a fusion of European and Indian elements; while the wall frescos reveal Hindu designs, those on the alabaster tomb of Dona Caterina, wife of the 10th viceroy and the first Portuguese woman to hazard the long and arduous voyage to the Indies, demonstrate the impact of the Muslim-Bijapur style.

It is surprising that there is hardly a temple to be seen in the coastal areas. Over the years, the Portuguese zeal for propagating their religion became rigid and intolerant. Conversions were forcibly

"Stately home" — Portuguese-style.

imposed, temples were demolished and churches built in their place; and the practice of any religion other than pure Roman Catholicism was severely punished. Those who were determined to preserve their ancient faith removed their deities from the shrines and fled to the interior, where the arm of the law could not reach them. It is therefore only in the mountainous interior regions to the east that Hindu temples can be seen.

It was not until the 18th Century, when the conquerors' religious zeal had diminished, that Hindu temples were rebuilt in sylvan surroundings, on gentle slopes of verdant hills or in valleys sheltered by thick groves of palm trees. Though influenced by the style of Maratha temple architecture and to some extent by Islamic and Christian elements, the styles in these temples have been synthesized to produce a purely distinctive idiom of Hindu architecture. Several temples have Islamic domes, while the plan of the structure is often similar to Christian architectural patterns.

The **Mangesh Temple** (dedicated to Lord Shiva), and the **Shanta-Durga** (to goddess Parvati) and **Nagesh** Temples in the Ponda neighborhood are among the most frequented in Goa. Ornate, baroque interiors and several storied *deepmals* — elaborate lamp towers — are unique features of these Goan Hindu shrines.

Time Marches On

Considerable changes are shaking the somnolence of Goa — long suspended as it was in a fossilized world of 18-Century Portugal. Reunion with the rest of India has brought water and electricity to the villages, communication with the outside world and the establishment of industries.

While industrialization is necessary and technological advancement and urbanization inevitable, the inflow of migrant labor has aggravated the pressures on domestic resources and brought about the growth of a new culture. Goans fear that the very elements constituting the unique identity of the land are likely to be diluted by the pace of its integration with the rest of the country. Possibly a new identity will emerge. But the image that will, nevertheless, endure will be of a fascinating tapestry of legend and myth, of mists and dreams.

Shri Mangesh Temple, Goa.

GUJARAT, A DELICATE BALANCE

Through the blaring cacophony of bicycles, autorickshaws, cars and bullockcarts, a motorcycle with large milk cans tied astride darts through the streets of Ahmedabad with its rider bedecked in a brilliant red turban, flashing golden earrings and a fierce mustache. He is a *Rabari* from the milk-vending community, who has adopted modern transportation while continuing to wear his traditional dress. He is the essence of Gujarat.

In some parts of India tradition is linked with backwardness, and the acceptance of modern technology necessitates the acceptance of all its cultural accessories and appendages. If you have television in your home, you wear trousers; a bullock-cart is driven only by someone who wears a *dhoti* and a turban. Gujarat, in its vibrant, dynamic and characteristic fashion turns the whole thing topsy turvy and yet lands comfortably on all fours every time.

The archeological finds at Lothal near Dhandhuka in Ahmedabad district and Rozadi in Saurashtra carry the history of Gujarat back to the age of Harappa and Mohenjodaro, 3,500 years ago. In legend, the epics and Puranas tell of how Lord Krishna and his brother Balarama left Mathura and settled at Kusathali or Dwarka on Gujarat's western coast. The name "Gujarat" derives from the Prakrit "Gujjaratta" or "Gurjara Rastra" which means "land of the Gurjaras." The Gurjaras were an immigrant tribe who entered India through the northern passes along with the Hunas, passed through the Punjab and settled in lands that came to be known as Gujarat, a name that became popular only around the 10th Century.

Traders by Tradition

Gujarat has always been a field for conquering and colonizing races. Ethnic and linguistic movements from the northern plains and the western ocean brought with them their own languages, arts and crafts, poetry, thought forms, social practices, historical traditions, religious practices and philosophy. Gujarat therefore has the greatest number of sub-division of communities in India and the Gujarati of today is a product of a widely heterogeneous conglomeration.

Proximity to the sea and the Gujarati's consequent flair for maritime and mercantile pursuits developed a strong spirit of enterprise, practical wisdom and catholicity of taste among them. Continuous seafaring activities produced a well-to-do middle-class which wielded considerable influence. Traders and artisans formed powerful guilds and made business, trade and the acquisition of wealth a strong tradition in Gujarat.

Gujarat spreads itself into the regions of Kaccha (Kutch), Saurashtra and the verdant territories between the rivers Banas and Damanganga. These are fertile lands of wheat, cotton, groundnut and banana plantations kept green by the Banas, Sabarmati, Mali, Tapi and Narmada Rivers on the coastal plains and the Bhadar, Setrunji and Bhogavo on the peninsular plains. A large part of the southern border of Gujarat is covered with hills which are extensions of the Western Ghats lying outside the state.

Ahmedabad's belligerent, swerving autorickshaws, modern Ashram Road with its hotels, shops and cinemas, the heavily populated industrial sections of town, are all manifestations of its character as the great textile and commercial city of Western India. Omnipresent is the Sabarmati River over which four bridges connect the old city with the new. On one side are the crowded streets leading to **Manek Chowk,** where rows of traders dealing in silver jewelry or printed fabrics lean against spotless white bolsterpillows, waiting for customers. On the upper floors of the buildings on this street are exquisitely carved wooden balconies, windows and doorways of old *havelis* (family homes). They are fast being dismantled and sold as antiques or placed in museums. The most beautiful ones stand in **Doshiwada-ni-Pol.** Gujarat wood sculpture is usually part of the decoration of temples and private buildings. Much of it is religious in significance and depicts the deities of old legends.

Mosques, Bazaars, Museums

The reign of Sultan Allauddin Khilji of Delhi witnessed the creation of the first Muslim empire in India and one of his earliest conquests was the wealthy kingdom of Gujarat in 1300. Ahmed Shah I founded Ahmedabad on the site of the ancient city of Karnavati in 1411.

The Indo-Saracen architecture of Ahmedabad blends Hindu and Muslim styles. **Sidi Saiyad's Mosque** near Relief Road is Ahmedabad's most eloquent example of the finest such work in sandstone. Its twin windows of pierced stone with a design of an almost lyrical tree with palm leaves and curving tendrils must be seen. The shaking minarets of **Rajpur Bibi's Mosque** at Gomtipur and **Sidi Bashir's Mosque** at Kalipur are fun. Pressure exerted on the inner walls of the minarets sets them vibrating much to the delight of both the visitor and the tourist guide.

On Sundays, the edge of the Sabarmati River below Ellis Bridge comes alive with the **Khamasa Bazar,** a sprawling market of the most fascinating and sometimes preposterous wares to be found by any collector enterprising enough to wander on the dusty banks. Spread on the ground are "shops" where a visitor might be able to buy an old carved wooden table, old shoes, discarded copper and brass vessels, old lamps, rare books and used bicycle tyres.

There is, of course, no "nightlife" in Ahmedabad, but the substitute it offers is, again, typical of the essence of Gujarat. A 15-minute drive out of Ahmedabad on the main highway to Vadodara (Baroda) is the **Vechaar Utensil Museum** and **Vishalla Restaurant.** Vechaar should be visited in the cool of the evening. It houses a remarkable collection of metalware; utensils of every imaginable shape and size in bronze, brass and other alloys have been collected from every corner of Gujarat. Housed in a building made of mud walls and with a central water tank, the atmosphere is both rustic and evocative of the old Gujarat.

A traditional Gujarati meal at the **Vishalla Restaurant** is delicious and appropriately rounds off the visit to the museum. Vegetarian favorites, baked breads in a variety of cereals, fresh, white butter, jaggery and yogurt are served on large brass dishes by rural waiters to the accompaniment of folk music or puppet shows, in a decor recreating a village ambience. The local potter molds the drinking pots and dishes which are used by the restaurant.

The grace of Ahmedabad's modern architecture and institutions must be seen to understand the Gujarati's appreciation of his own culture and aesthetic sensibilities. The **Indian Institute of Manage-**

Indian Institute of Management, Ahmedabad.

ment in Vastrapur provides a comprehensive education to those aspiring to be modern managers. The buildings, designed by Louis Kahn, are a fascinating display of the sense of drama that can be created by light and shade, angles and arches, and the stark lines of lengthy corridors.

Museums

The **Calico Museum of Textiles** in Shahibag is located in the Sarabhai Foundation which is a public charitable Trust. The Museum is open on all days except Wednesdays and Bank holidays, from 10 a.m. to 12.30 p.m. and 2.30 p.m. to 5 pm. It has an exquisite collection of fabrics and garments from all over India. Rich brocades and fine embroideries from Kashmir, Gujarat and the southern states are laid out with aesthetic simplicity. Free guided tours in English, Gujarati and Hindi are provided twice a day to encourage visitors.

The **Shreyas Folk Museum** in Ambavadi and the **Tribal Museum** on Ashram Road portray the rural heritage of Gujarat.

Hridey Kunj, Mahatma Gandhi's Ashram at Sabarmati is a set of austere yet beautiful buildings nestling amidst mango trees. It was from here that Gandhi experimented in non-violent methods of political struggle. The museum, added later, is stunningly simple and a fitting tribute to the great man. Designed by Charles Correa, a well-known Indian architect, it displays Gandhi's spectacles, spinning wheel, sandals, photographs, and some cloth spun by him as part of the movement for *swadeshi* (self-sufficiency).

Gujarat Vidyapith, a university established by Mahatma Gandhi, has a vast collection of books, a museum, a research center and the **Navjivan Press** which holds the copyright in Gandhi's works. It is located on the busy Ashram Road and visitors can shop for *khadi* (hand-spun) fabrics and other handmade village industry products at the nearby **Khadi Gramudyog Bhandar,** another institution established by Gandhi.

Some 10½ miles (17 km) to the north of Ahmedabad is **Adalaj Vava,** a 15th-Century step-well, an architectural delight with its geometric and floral patterns on the stone pillars and lintels that line the steps that lead down to the rectangular well. The steps are accessible from three sides. Tanks and wells have always been artistically treated in Gujarat and Adalaj

has been created with as much care as any memorable temple. It was built during the most glorious period of the Indo-Saracenic style of architecture.

The **Sun Temple at Modhera** is a three-hour journey by road north of Ahmedabad. It is one of the finest examples of Indian temple architecture. Built in 1026, during the reign of King Bhima of the Solanki dynasty, the temple is dedicated to the Sun God, Surya, and stands on a plinth overlooking a deep stone-stepped tank. Every inch of the edifice is elaborately carved with figures of gods, flowers and animals.

It is a fairly long drive onwards to Bhuj across the Little Rann of Kaccha but a traveller with a spirit of discovery should not leave Kaccha (Kutch) out of his itinerary. From Ahmedabad there are overnight trains and buses but it is more convenient to take a comfortable car right through.

Neglected Kaccha

Kaccha is not on the suggested list of most tourist agencies and many of those who have travelled there so far have chanced upon its existence only after reaching India. It is a large district covering an area of 3,350 sq miles (8,750 sq km) bounded by the Gulf of Kaccha, the Indian Ocean; and the **Rann of Kaccha,** a peculiar tract of territory described by a Lt. Burnes in his memoirs as "a space without a counterpart in the globe." The word *rann* derives from the Sanskrit word *irina,* meaning a waste. The expanse is hard, dry, saline and flat and, as the summer heat intensifies, the salt in the baked and blistered earth shines with mirages of dazzling whiteness.

Bhuj town is partly surrounded by walls built in 1723. In 1865 Rao Pragmalji built an imposing and intricate palace at one of the gates. Its **Aina Mahal** has walls of marble covered with mirrors separated by gilded ornaments with shades of Venetian glass. There are ingenious pumps and siphons to fill the pond which has a fountain spraying water in an intricate variety of patterns. There are fascinating collections of ornaments and paintings, both European and Indian, and exquisite inlaid ivory doors made in 1708.

From Bhuj, half a day and an autorickshaw is what is required for a visit to a street of potters where men mold and fire the local white clay into pots for daily use in the villages. Women paint fine geometric designs on them. Hand block-printing and the techniques of tying and dyeing fabric known as *bandhani* can be seen in tiny shops and workplaces called *karkhanas*.

The **Kutch Museum,** which overlooks the Hamirsar water tank, is the oldest in Gujarat, opened in 1877. It has the largest collection of Kshatrapa (Indo-Scythian) inscriptions, the oldest dated 89 A.D. The silver work of Kaccha is distinctive and the museum has a fine collection of coins and jewelry, apart from gold and enamel work, textiles, woodwork, old utensils, arms and accoutrements and a section on the communities peculiar to Kaccha. These communities live and dress as they have for centuries. The Rabaris, Debariyas, Gracias, Sodhas and others still wear dresses bejewelled with mirrorwork.

Village Handicrafts

Visiting one of these communities involves a two-hour bus or taxi ride from the center of Bhuj to **Hodka** or **Dhordo** in the Rann area known as **Banni.** The villages consist of round mud huts called *bhungas* with a single central support pole, and a thatched or tiled roof, all surrounding a large community courtyard. Women are shy of male visitors but they are warm and hospitable if anyone wishes to see the inside of their houses. They have exquisite personal collections of embroidered quilts and garments, as well as some for sale. Walls, shelves, grain containers and cupboards are fashioned in mud with decorative designs washed with lime paste and embedded with mirrors which throw back hundreds of shimmering reflections when a candle is lit.

For the less intrepid, **Bhujodi,** six miles (10 km) short of Bhuj, just off the main road, displays the life and styles of a weaving community. It is a small village with narrow winding lanes, and a pit-loom in almost every home. Visitors can buy brilliantly woven *dhablas* (blankets), shawls and woolen stoles decorated with *bandhani* designs from the weavers.

The Indian Airlines flight from Bhuj across the Gulf of Kaccha to Jamnagar is an astonishing 13 minutes and certainly saves time.

Jamnagar, the district headquarters, is a walled city with several gateways, typical of traditional towns. The older parts are bursting at the seams but many areas were scientifically planned, as

Jain temples at Palitana, Gujarat.

recently as 1914, and have a systematic layout of facades, squares, circles and broad streets. Textile mill and tie-dyed fabrics both roll out of Jamnagar. Master craftsmen spend months tying intricate traditional designs on saris before dyeing them in a variety of brilliant colors.

The Kotho Bastion of **Lakhota Palace** is located in the middle of a tank and is approached over a stone bridge. It could accommodate a thousand soldiers, and now houses a fine museum.

Jamnagar has a solarium which was built in 1933. With the destruction of two similar solaria in France during the Second World War this is probably now the only one of its kind in the world, and certainly in Asia.

The Five Jewels of Saurashtra

"There are five jewels in Saurashtra, namely rivers, women, horses, the fourth being Somnath and the fifth is the *darshan* of the idol of Hari or Lord Krishna." — *The Puranas.*

Dwarka, 85 miles (137 km) west of Jamnagar was a flourishing port in ancient times and a famed holy spot. It is said that Krishna established Dwarka 5,000 years ago. The **Temple of Dwarkadish** on the northern bank of the Gomti Creek is typical of the architecture of ancient Hindu temples. It has a shrine, a large hall, a roof supported by 60 columns of granite and sandstone, and a conical spire about 160 feet (50 meters) high. The temple has seven floors. Its exterior is profusely carved while the inside is extremely simple. The shrine is elaborately ornamented and has a sculpted figure of Ganesh, the elephant deity, over the entrance. Across the creek of salt water are five sweet-water springs.

Gandhi's Birthplace

For those who have a special interest in the life of Mahatma Gandhi, a visit to **Porbandar,** his birthplace, farther down the coast is a pilgrimage worth planning. It is a quiet coastal town. Gandhi was born here in 1869 in his ancestral home, a quarter of a mile from the sea. With its small rooms at various levels, trellised windows and carved balconies, niches in the walls to place kerosene lamps in, the house has an air of peace and tranquility. The house is open to the public. Nearby is **Kirti Mandir** which has a Gandhian library, some of Gandhi's personal effects, a photographic exhibition on his life and times, and a spinning and prayer hall.

The crowded parts of Porbandar will remind the visitor of the older Ahmedabad and a walk down the long beach will be undisturbed by the usual trappings of a popular seaside resort.

Driving along quiet coastal roads through Chorwad and Verawal you will reach **Somnath,** one of the 12 most sacred Shiva shrines in India. It stands majestically washed by the Arabian Sea. Ransacked repeatedly by northern invaders and rebuilt over and over, successively in gold, silver, wood and finally in stone, it is said to have been built by Soma, the Moon God, in penance and worship of the wrathful Lord Shiva who had laid a curse on him. Much of the temple was destroyed by Mohammed Ghazni in 1026 and parts of the present temple have been reconstructed in the old style. Nearby is a temple marking the spot where Lord Krishna is said to have been accidentally killed by a hunter's arrow. Rhythmic cymbals clash at dusk to mark the time for special prayers.

Three miles (five km) from Junagadh is the only place in the world, apart from Africa, where the lion can be seen in its

The Asiatic Lion, an endangered species.

natural habitat. In the **Gir Forest** began one of the earliest efforts at conservation. In 1900 the Nawab of Junagadh, in whose territory most of the Gir Forest lay, had invited Lord Curzon, viceroy at that time, for a lion shikar. When the viceroy accepted, a newspaper published an anonymous letter which questioned the propriety of an important person doing further damage to an endangered species. Lord Curzon not only cancelled his shikar engagement but also advised the nawab to protect the remaining lions, which the nawab and his successors dutifully did. Now the Gir Forest is one of the largest and most important game preserves in India.

Lions in the Gir

The Gir lion is a majestic animal with a bigger tail tassle, bushier elbow tufts and a smaller mane than its African cousin. Early in the 20th Century there were only a hundred lions left in the Gir; the 1979 census enumerated 205. The forest is one of the few remaining places where a visitor can drive through open scrub country, dry tropical thorn forests and an evergreen corridor along the river-side. The forest harbors a variety of smaller animals and birds. There is also a newly developed crocodile farm in the Gir. Other predators in the Gir are panthers and striped hyena.

Temple City

Palitana in Bhavnagar district almost completes the full circle of Saurashtra. A mile (two km) from town is the **Shatrunjaya Hill,** the most important center of Jain pilgrimage, with an incredible 863 Jain temples atop its twin peaks.

Palitana is a major marketing center for chilies, cereals and pulses and has a bustling market-yard for farmers.

It is worth heading back in the direction of Ahmedabad via **Surendranagar** and **Wadhwan.** The ancestors of the stone carvers of Wadhwan built Dwarka and Somnath. Skilled stone carvers live and work near **Hawa Mahal,** a finely conceived but unfinished palace at the edge of the town. Today some travel on assignments to build temples even in distant Kenya and Uganda.

In the village of **Chitravara** the remarkable technique of dot weaving is used to make wool wraps for women. Traders in Surendranagar town have a vast collection of old embroideries and artefacts from all over Saurashtra.

The "industrial corridor" of Gujarat is due south of Ahmedabad. Tools used by prehistoric man were found in **Vadodara** now booming with an oil refinery, petrochemical complex and other industries. Its **Lakshmi Vilas Palace, Baroda Museum** and **University of Fine Arts** take the bite off the side effects of industrialization.

In its hinterland lies the exclusively tribal belt of Gujarat with its tribal architecture and lifestyle untouched by "progress."

Surat was the first outpost established by the British East India Company and was on one of the old trade routes for silks, embroideries and spices. Despite a dominant Parsi and Muslim influence, its architecture is mostly Portuguese and British. Today it is the center of the diamond-cutting and *zari* (gold thread) industry.

A group of farmers wearing heavy silver jewelry, bright turbans and shawls, stand around a video screen in the town square watching imitation spaghetti westerns. This cultural parallelism is delicately balanced today; of tomorrow, who knows?

Village fair at Gujarat.

MADRAS, CULTURE AND CHANGE

Situated on the east coast, Madras is the fourth largest of the Indian cities, after Calcutta, Bombay and Delhi. It is the most convenient entry point for people wishing to travel in southern India. There are convenient connections by plane, bus and train from Madras to all parts of Tamil Nadu — to the temple cities of Chidambaram, Thanjavur and Rameshwaram, or for day trips to Mahabalipuram and Kanchipuram. Trips to hill resorts like Ootacamund, Kodaikanal and the game sanctuaries can also be conveniently made from Madras. The city is well linked with other parts of India and with Sri Lanka, Burma and the Far East.

Madras city is aligned north to south along the coast, at the northern tip of Tamil Nadu. It has spread far beyond its original site in the north and west to encompass later colonial buildings, the coach factory, cycle and car factories and other industries.

The city has a number of rivers and canals, like the Adyar River and the Cooum, along which are gardens and facilities for boat rides. On the Adyar River are some fine buildings like the Madras Club, the Madras Boat Club, the Chettinad Palace and the Theosophical Society buildings and gardens.

Dosas and Dance Drama

Climatically, Madras goes from hot to hotter and hottest, with relief brought by the northwest monsoon in June-July and the southeast monsoon in December-January. Palm and casuarina trees trim the coastline, sea breezes bring a cool freshness to the land and the beaches are beautiful in the early hours of the day and in the late evenings. The sea here, on the east coast, is not as inviting for the swimmer as the Arabian Sea, but the beach resorts are always humming with picnickers and holiday-makers. At night, lights from fishermen's boats and catamarans can be seen glowing over the dark waters.

Madras is the gateway to Tamil Nadu, and serves as an introduction to Tamil culture, food, customs and people. Excellent vegetarian Brahmin food is available in restaurants like Woodlands and Dasaprakash. They serve delicious, hot *thali* meals with limitless boiled rice, lentil curries and a dozen tiny portions of vegetables. The crisp fried *dosa* and the steamed *idli* are famous rice-powder preparations and have come to be identified with Tamil Nadu worldwide.

The Tamil language is an ancient, beautiful, and poetic one, often spoken at breathtaking speed. The richness of Tamil literature offers endless scope for interpretation in dance and theater and is the very soul of the culture of Tamil Nadu.

The colors and clothing that women wear in Tamil Nadu cannot be compared with that of any others in India, except, perhaps, Rajasthan. The Kanchipuram silk and cotton saris worn at home and for religious and social occasions are characterized by a combination of brilliant contrasting colors — orange with purple, parrot-green with pink. The older generation of Tamil Brahmin women drape their saris in the traditional style, drawing one end between the legs and the other over the shoulder. The men wear *lungis* or *dhotis,* a length of cloth fastened at the waist and hanging down to the ankles sarong-style. A marriage or a religious procession in Madras provides a glittering display of colorful clothes and heavy jewelry.

Madras has a large Christian population of all denominations. The British occupation from the 17th Century onwards has also left an Anglo-Indian population. Though well amalgamated in Indian society, their religion, clothes and culture make them distinct and Madras is home for them too.

Madras today is a curious mixture. While it retains the old legacy of the British East India Company, and is, in some ways, a conservative bastion in social and religious matters, it is also the Hollywood of South India and, simultaneously, a stronghold of traditional Tamil culture. There are churchyards, staid residential areas, and prim gardens side by side with high cinema posters with giant-size cutouts of heros and heroines rising out of them, painted in gaudy colors and dotted with flashy sequins. These occupy prime positions and clutter up the skyline.

"Nothing is impossible" is the motto of the Madras film industry — no plot too unrealistic, no stunt too difficult to engineer, no costume too daring. Legends, myths, historical and social themes, wrapped up in and served with glamor, is the fare. There are heroines who you wouldn't believe could dance and heroines you thought had gone out of style. Everything goes.

But Tamil film stars have always aspired for even greater glory than celluloid could bring them. Politicians, chief ministers of states, members of parliament, social and political leaders, religious gurus and philanthropists spring out of the silver screen into the real world and survive and prosper in it, owing not a little to the popularity and prestige gained through this medium.

British Madras

The British East India Company established one of its earliest seats of power in India in Madras. Unlike Bombay and Calcutta, Madras does not have a natural harbor. The present breakwaters were built in the 19th Century. The construction of **Fort St. George** was begun around 1640. In the city, white and black areas were once clearly demarcated. The Fort was often attacked by Indian and French forces, yet it continued to expand. Today the old buildings in Fort St. George house the Tamil Nadu Government **Sec-**retariat and the **Legislative Assembly.** A charming feature of the East India Company architecture is the use of Madras *chunam,* a glittering white wash of limestone mixed with crushed sea shells. The *chunam*-coated walls of the buildings are a dazzling sight, especially in summer.

Within the Fort, a number of other early buildings still stand, of which **St. Mary's Church** is the most interesting. It is the earliest English building surviving intact in India and the oldest Anglican church in the east. It was consecrated in 1680. The interior of the church is white washed, but there are also elaborate carved wooden panels. It was at this church that Robert Clive, victor of the Battle of Plassey in 1759, which is taken as the beginnings of British rule in India, was married in 1753. Elihu Yale, who later founded the university bearing his name in America, was also associated with this church.

The **Fort St. George Museum** contains some fascinating items belonging to the early days of the East India Company and the colonial period. Coins, weapons, pictures and books form part of the interesting collection. Other buildings of importance in the Fort are the **Old Gov-**

Madras, an early view.

ernment House, the **Banqueting Hall** (now called **Rajaji Hall**) built by Goldingham for the Governor's official entertainments during the Clive period, when British power and prestige in India were in the ascendant. This is reflected in the architectural style of the buildings of this period which draw inspiration from the glory of the classical Greek and Roman period with Doric, Corinthian and Tuscan pillars, entablatures and friezes.

Two beautiful churches in Madras that still have regular services are **St. George's Cathedral** and **St. Andrew's Kirk.** The latter is said to resemble St. Martin-in-the-Fields in London. It was built by James Gibbs. The towering steeples and the strength of the pillars of the facade make it a city landmark. St. George's Cathedral, consecrated in 1816, was designed by Captain James Caldwell and Thomas Fiott de Havillard. The interior here has slim Ionic pillars, plasterwork and stained-glass windows.

The **"ice factory"** on Marina Beach, near the old building of the University was built in 1842. This circular structure was built to store ice imported from America. Later, it was converted into a home for widows.

The **San Thome Church** on the Main Beach Road is associated with the Apostle, St. Thomas. It is believed that he was martyred on what is called **St. Thomas's Mount** in Madras (near the airport) and that his remains were enshrined in this church. The San Thome Church was first built in the 16th Century and has been rebuilt over the years. It is still in regular use and attracts a flow of pilgrims.

Out-of-doors, the interesting places around Madras are the **Guindy Deer** and **Snake Parks.** The former has species of black buck, spotted deer, monkeys and other animals. The Snake Park is perhaps the only major reptilium in India. It was started by an American, Romulus Whittaker, who has done remarkable research and worked towards educating visitors on the types of snakes in India to prevent the thoughtless killing of the reptile. The park is well-worth a visit.

The **Theosophical Society** has its headquarters on the banks of the Adyar River. It boasts a vast library of books on all religions, and in the gardens that lead up to the river and the sea, is a sprawling banyan tree, said to be one of the largest in India.

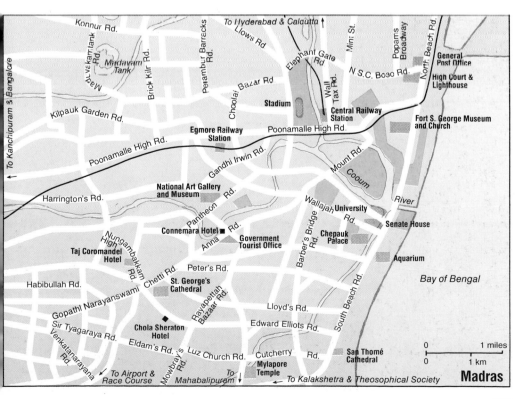

Madras

The **Marina**, almost 13 km long, is a wide sandy beach with a drive along it fringed with palms and casuarinas, running along the whole length of Madras. For the beach walker, the post-monsoon period brings shells, coral and dramatic sunrises. The Marina has an aquarium, located opposite the 19th Century building of the **Presidency College** and the **Senate House** of the University. The University building and its grounds are interesting examples of the adoption of an Indo-Islamic style for Indian public buildings that was in vogue in the second half of the 19th Century. North of the University building and its grounds are town, are other interesting structures such as **Egmore Railway Station,** the **Madras Medical College, Ripon Building** and **Victoria Public Hall.**

One of the most important localities of Madras is **Mylapore,** where the **Kapaleswara Shiva Temple,** the tank, market area and old Brahmin residential houses are situated. Mylapore is a unified complex and is best viewed as such. At the evening bazaar, crowds of women, freshly bathed, adorned with sweet-smelling jasmine flowers in their hair, make their way to the Kapaleswara Temple. Another ancient and important temple is the **Krishna Parathasarathy Temple** on the Triplicane High Road.

The Arts

The **State Government Museum** in Madras has an assorted collection of interesting items. In this complex are the **Museum Theater** and the **Art Gallery.** The museum was established in 1846 and has Departments of Natural History and Art. It houses a rare collection of sculptures from Amaravati in Andhra Pradesh, belonging to the Buddhist period, c. 2nd Century A.D. The white limestone, elegantly sculptured medallions and panels tell the story of the life of the Buddha.

The **Bronze Gallery** of the museum has perhaps the finest collection of Chola bronzes (9-13th centuries A.D.), apart from the Thanjavur Art Gallery and some temple collections. There are small bronzes hardly two inches high and others that are over two feet tall, all perfectly modelled, iconographically sophisticated, and dramatic. The dancing Shivas, Durgas and Ganeshes and the famous Rama, Lakshman and Sita group, are the pride of this museum.

Fort St. George, Madras.

In the world of the performing arts, the Music Academy of Madras is well known. Each year, during the winter, there are music and dance programs by eminent artists. The joy of performing in Madras, artists say, is that audiences are very discerning and this inspires artists, whether of Karnatak music or Bharat Natyam dancing, to give of their best.

Down the coastal road, towards Mahabalipuram, is **Kalakshetra,** an academy of music and dance set up by Rukmini Devi, the doyen of Indian dance. Her efforts to reestablish classical dance in a modern context have given India a good number of leading dancers. The school has young students, both boys and girls, who are trained in the performing arts and related subjects. Artists from all over the world also come to Kalakshetra to share in this experience. Experimentation and innovation are the rule in this school built and run on the lines of the *gurukuls,* where teachers teach and live together in simplicity, amidst natural greenery. Kalakshetra organizes annual dance-drama programs which are well worth seeing.

On the same road, leading from Madras to Mahabalipuram, is **Cholamandalam,** the artists' village. This was created by a group of young modern Indian artists and is an interesting place. There are residential huts, and workshop areas, kilns and furnaces, where the artists work. Cholamandalam artists organize exhibitions, poetry readings and other programs throughout the year.

Almost anything is available in Madras. **Moore Market** near the railway station (recently extensively damaged by fire) once sold secondhand furniture and books. The **Burma Bazaar** towards the port area on North Beach Road is a haven for the trader in smuggled goods — from French perfumes to electronic goods from Japan. Madras, however, is most famous for its silk emporia where silk saris, scarves and material for suiting and dresses are available by the yard at a number of well-known shops. Silks woven in Kanchipuram and other centers are world famous for their quality and vibrant colors. The **Victoria Technical Institute** (VTI) sells handmade items like lace and embroidery, and **Poompuhar,** the Government Handicrafts Emporium, has articles of sandalwood, *papier maché* and bronze. Both these are on Mount Road (Anna Salai as it is now called).

PONDICHERRY

This formerly French-ruled town is now one of India's Union Territories. It lies on the coast, 150 km south of Madras. It first came under French rule in the middle of the 18th Century, but over the years it repeatedly became a battlefield and, on many occasions, even changed hands. The town was finally restored to the French by the British under the Treaty of Paris in 1763. It returned to India only in 1954.

The town was originally divided into two by a canal. One side used to be the *Ville Blanche* (white town) and the other the *Ville Noire* (black town) for the Indian population. The heart of the city used to be the **Government Park,** around which today are the **Raj Nivas** (the official residence of the lieutenant governor) and other official buildings. Near the Railway Station is the Gothic-style **Sacred Heart Church.**

Pondicherry streets, in the old French area, are cobbled like those in old French towns and the seaside pavements and beaches are designed to resemble those at Nice or any other waterfront town of Southern France. The police still wear uniforms patterned on those of the French police.

Some 10 km from the town are the **Sri Aurobindo Ashram** and the new city, still under construction, **Auroville.** The ashram was established by Sri Aurobindo, an important Indian religious philosopher, who had once played an active and revolutionary role in the Indian independence movement. In conformity with his philosophy and teachings, the city of Auroville was designed by a French architect, Roger Auger, as a model universal city, where man can live close to nature and in harmony with his fellow beings. The ashram, its orchards, workshops and activity centers attract a number of foreigners and Indians who share the beliefs of Sri Aurobindo and of the "Mother," who succeeded him and headed the ashram till her death a few years ago. Wealthy patronage and an opportunity to experiment with a different lifestyle attracts many people.

Outside Pondicherry is **Arikamedu,** an important archeological site, where excavations have revealed a Greco-Roman trading center of the early years of the Christian era. The remains indicate a flourishing trade with the Romans in dyed muslins and spices.

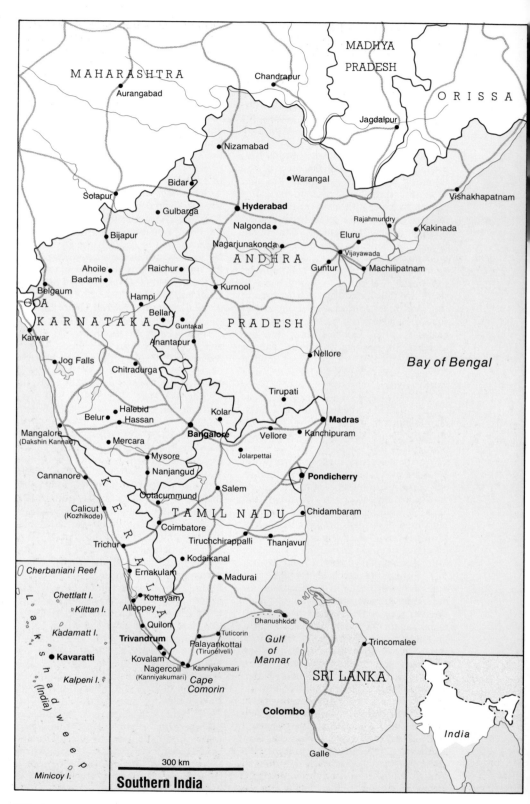

MAHARASHTRA

Aurangabad

Chandrapur

MADHYA PRADESH

ORISSA

Jagdalpur

Nizamabad

Bidar

Warangal

Vishakhapatnam

Solapur

Gulbarga

Hyderabad

Nalgonda

Rajahmundry

Kakinada

Bijapur

Nagarjunakonda

Eluru

ANDHRA

Vijayawada

Ahoile

Raichur

Guntur

Machilipatnam

Badami

Kurnool

Belgaum

Hampi

PRADESH

GOA

KARNATAKA

Bellary

Karwar

Guntakal

Anantapur

Nellore

Jog Falls

Chitradurga

Bay of Bengal

Tirupati

Halebid

Kolar

Belur

Hassan

Madras

Mangalore
(Dakshin Kannad)

Bangalore

Vellore

Kanchipuram

Mercara

Jolarpettai

Cannanore

Mysore

Nanjangud

Pondicherry

Ootacummund

Salem

K
E
R
A
L
A

TAMIL NADU

Chidambaram

Calicut
(Kozhikode)

Coimbatore

Trichur

Tiruchchirappalli

Thanjavur

Kodaikanal

Ernakulam

Madurai

Cherbaniani Reef

Kottayam

Alleppey

Chettlatt I.

Quilon

Dhanushkodi

Kilttan I.

_Gulf
of
Mannar_

Trincomalee

Kadamatt I.

Trivandrum

Tuticorin

L
a
k
s
h
a
d
w
e
e
p

(India)

● **Kavaratti**

Palayankottai
(Tirunelveli)

Kovalam

Kanniyakumari

SRI LANKA

Kalpeni I.

Nagercoil
(Kanniyakumari)

_Cape
Comorin_

Colombo

300 km

Southern India

Galle

Minicoy I.

India

238

TAMIL NADU, A VISUAL LEGACY

The visual legacy of the culture of Tamil Nadu is among the most satisfying spectacles in India. Its numerous ancient temples with their characteristic gateway towers *(gopurams),* hundred-or thousand-pillared pavilions and corridors, their spectacular array of sculptures, bronze images and stucco embellishments; its woodcraft and textile creativity; and the sublimity of its performing arts of dance, music and drama, all form an integral and living part of the Tamil people's life to this day. This deliberately cultivated high level of intellectual and aesthetic sophistication is combined with a sedate and simple personal lifestyle that has characterized the region from the dawn of its history. It arose from its pristine academy, the *Sangam,* and the subsequent rule of three enlightened dynasties — the Pallavas (c.450-900 A.D.), the Pandyas (c.500-950 A.D.), and the imperial Cholas (c.850-1250 A.D.)

Tamil Nadu is no less rich in natural beauty. Three seas meet at the Kanya Kumari Cape (Cape Comorin) where gorgeous sunrises and sunsets are a daily spectacle placed in the thickly wooded vicinity of the Periyar game sanctuary. On the Western Ghats are the remains of the ancient Kannagi Temple, the setting of the final scene of the epic Tamil saga, *Silappadikaram* (The Lay of the Anklet). The spray-filled ravine of the Kuttralam waterfall near Tenkasi, the famed Nilgiris (Blue Mountains) and Palni Hills all have a charm that is entirely their own.

The Land and the People

Tamil Nadu is bounded on the north by the southern limb of the Eastern Ghats, on the west by the lofty backbone of the Sahyadri chain, and by the sea east and south. The land grades steadily from west to east. Two hill stations, **Ootacamund** (Ooty) and **Kodaikanal,** rising to over 8,200 feet (2,500 meters) in the Nilgiri and Palni Hills respectively, have a salubrious climate in contrast to the subtropical humid summers in the plains. The Kaveri, Pennar and Tamraparni rivers underwrite Tamil Nadu's agrarian prosperity. Its ports, beaches and resorts on the Coromandel Coast have welcomed strangers ever since the visits of the ancient Roman galleons in the early decades of the Christian era. Its hillocks of the finest granite made possible an early efflorescence (c.6th-8th Century A.D.) of monolithic rock-cut temple art at nearly a hundred places, under the patronage of the Pallavas, Pandyas, Muttarayars and Atiyamans.

Religion, a Major Concern

Religion is second nature to the Tamils, inextricably mingled with their daily life. The divinities in the Hindu pantheon are innumerable among whom, however, Shiva, Vishnu, Ganesha, Murugan (Subramanya) and Durga stand out. Sometimes, whole towns revolve around a temple, as at Madurai and Srirangam. The traditional marriage customs of the Tamils are a colorful blend of secular practices and religious observance. Following Vedic injunctions concerning various stages of one's life, Tamils attach great sanctity to the sacred thread worn by Brahmins, and the *mangalasutra* (a special necklace) worn by married women.

Death and death anniversary ceremonies held here are more ritually elaborate than those in other communities.

Sculptor at work in Tamil Nadu.

Tamils undertake sacred vows at the temple of their favorite god by shaving off one's hair (for Vishnu), or breaking a specified number of coconuts in front of the shrine (for Ganesha), or carrying the *kavadi* (a bamboo frame decorated with peacock feathers) on one's shoulders and circumambulating the shrine with it (for Murugan).

Pious Tamils wear caste marks or the auspicious *tilaka* of vermilion (on the forehead). Another widespread practice is bathing every day in a river or stream or tank, and certainly *before* worship. As a result, most village houses have no bathroom, as both men and women bathe in the river or pond or temple tank in public, thereby imbibing virtues like discipline, courtesy and decorum.

Temple festivals are usually accompanied by fairs, where holy talismans, trinkets and tinsel ornaments are sold. Mobile eating places spring up; acrobats display their prowess; folk theaters stage (holy) plays; flower, fruit and coconut stalls do brisk business. Dressed in their best, whole families of all communities mingle to receive divine benediction.

In Tamil Nadu, temple worship is offered five times a day — at dawn, early forenoon, noon, eventide and night — with rounds of ceremonial bathing of idols, their decoration with flowers, garments, jewelry and sandal paste, and worship ending with a ceremonial *arti* (circling of an open oil lamp in front of the deity). All this is done to the accompaniment of the *nadasvaram* (a woodwind horn) and *tavil* (drum) and dance by the temple dancer, and the chanting of hymns from the Vedas or the *Prabandhas* of the Tamil saints.

Sacred Places

The most revered temple for the Shiva worshipper is at **Chidambaram** (located near Porto Novo, the early colonial British garrison center in South Arcot district). It is traditionally regarded as the venue of the cosmic dance of Nataraja-Shiva in the presence of Parvati, performed when the Ardra star (Betelguse) is on the ascendant in the month of *Margazhi* (December). Devotees gather in their thousands for this. The god here is visualized as being ethereal *(akasa)*, all-permeating, invisible and soul-filling.

The other sacred centers where *pan-*

Ritual bathing at the seaside, Tamil Nadu.

chabhutas (fivefold elements of matter) are glorified are at **Kanchi (Ekamranatha Temple)** where Shiva is worshipped in the state of earth *(prithvi);* at **Tiruanaikka,** near **Srirangam,** he is revered in the form of water and the idol is permanently immersed under it; at **Arunachalesvara** at **Tiruannamalai,** where he is in the state of fire *(tejas);* and **Kalahasti** (now within the borders of Andhra Pradesh), where he is in the state of air or wind *(vayu).* At **Madurai,** again Lord Shiva festivities are sportive manifestations, many of which are celebrated round the year with great éclat, including the grand float gala in the neighboring spacious temple tank at Vandiyur.

Ancient Vishnu shrines are best seen at **Srirangam, Kanchi, Tirukkoilur, Kumbakonam, Srivilliputtur** and **Alagarkoil,** with the deity depicted in various stances in the sanctum — standing, seated, reclining and rampant.

Murugan temples have six major traditional centers, at **Palani, Tiruchendur, Swamimalai, Tirupparankunram, Tiruttani** and **Kunrakkudi,** and are located mostly on hilltops.

Arjuna's penance, rock carvings at Mahabalipuram.

Temple Craft

Craft too is integrated with religious functions and ceremonies in the temples and the life of the people. In most villages, bronze-casting artisans, florists, jewelers, all live close to the shrine. As the images of gods and goddesses have to be draped after a ceremonial bath every day, hereditary weavers, supplying specific textile requirements for this, are also domiciled within the temple complex. The Saurashtrian (Gujarati) weavers at Madurai and the silk weavers of Kanchipuram had migrated to these temple towns to meet this need.

Casting of images for the temples is a highly specialized and responsible job, as it involves not only knowledge of the art of alloying five different metals *(panchaloha),* namely gold, silver, copper, zinc and lead, but also of the complexities of Hindu iconography. After modeling the image in wax and casting it in metal, the image is finished by hand and polished.

Several notable artisan guilds making bronze images have functioned over the years, each creating images with its own stylistic mannerisms, gradually developed from generation to generation.

Polyglot Culture

Besides Hindus, Buddhists and Jains have lived in Tamil Nadu from the earliest times, though the former disappeared from the scene in the 10th Century A.D., except at Nagapattinam where the Chudamanivarma Vihara (monastery) was patronized by Rajendra Chola I. The Jains became an integral part of Tamil society and many Jain centers are alive even today, as at **Vijayamangalam, Tingalur, Sembattur, Chettipatti** and **Kalugumalai.** The Jains have made original contributions to Tamil literature and grammar and to ethical-moral codes. In the past, they also had rock-cut cave temples, under the patronage of the Pandyan kings. Some of the earliest monasteries of the Digambara Jains were located in natural caves. Some of them, like those at **Mangulam** and **Sittannavasal,** contain inscriptions in the oldest known Tamil script of the 3rd-2nd Century B.C.

Islamic influences were seen mainly from the 12th Century onwards, with their chief concentrations at and around Arcot in north Tamil Nadu, Madurai and Tirunelveli and in the coastal tracts of Thanjavur District. Though coming initially along with the invading Islamic armies of Malik Kafur and others, they have permeated smoothly into Tamil society and the Tamil ethos.

In their speech and graciousness, Tamil Muslims are indistinguishable from the rest of the people. Umru Pulavar made significant contributions to Tamil literature, while one of their *dargahs* (graves of Muslim saints) at Nagore is greatly honored by all people, irrespective of caste or creed. The *Labbais* are religious officials; the *Marakkayars* are seafaring merchants; and the *Rauttars* or militiamen are traders in horses; and other Muslims, mostly *Sunni,* are engaged in lungi- and mat-weaving. Some fine monuments of their architecture are to be found at **Arcot, Valikandapuram** and **Vellore** — in which last place the first rumblings of a "sepoy mutiny" against the colonial British were heard early in the 19th Century.

The Christians also have a long history in Tamil Nadu, starting with Danish, Dutch and, later, British traders and missionaries at Tranquebar, Tuticorin, Sadras, Pulicat and Madras. Bishop Caldwell, G.U. Pope, Ziegenbalg and Father Beschi are highly respected names in the history of Tamil literary growth and printing. Large-scale conversions of the untouchables and fisherfolk took place. Sawyerpuram, Nazareth, Udangudi and San Thome in Madras have fine churches. The legendary mission of St. Thomas, the Apostle, to Madras is a cherished tradition in Tamil Nadu.

Temple Architecture and Art

The greatest creative achievement of the Tamils is, doubtless, their magnificent temple architecture and art. The temple was the hub of the society and, with the village assemblies, served as university or school, hospital, court of small causes, bank, granary and, in general, guardian of moral standards and regulator of social relationships.

Temple styles are characterized by the form, shape and proportions of parts of the building and embellishments used. Throughout India, Hindu temples share a similar basic plan with a central shrine for the main idol, around which are built ambulatory passages, *mandapas* or halls, and subsidiary shrines. Later, were added the *nrittamandapa* (dance hall) and *vahana mandapa,* where tribute is paid to the traditional mount *(vahana)* of the deity

(e.g. Shiva's bull). The ground plan of a temple may be square, rectangular, star-shaped, apsidal or octagonal.

Characteristic of the temples of Tamil Nadu is the rectangular ground plan with the pyramidal form of the *vimana* (the wall and tower over the main shrine) and the *gopuram* (gateway). The tower consists of a series of horizontal bands that grow smaller as they rise to the finial, giving it a pyramidal shape.

Another distinguishing feature is the temple-town complexes. In these the temple lies at the heart of the city, which is enveloped within concentric walls and corridors. In plan, each walled enclosure around the temple had a place for markets, workshops, educational centers and residential quarters.

The temple is invariably enclosed within a *prakara* (walled and often cloistered enclosure), and on the main entrance, or, as at Madurai, facing all four cardinal points of the compass, are set the *gopuradvara* (gateway towers) which rise high above the city as landmarks for travellers. Each temple has its own ablution tank, *nandavana* (flower garden) and temple chariot *(ratha).* On the annual chariot festival day, the *ratha* is drawn

Meenakshi Temple, Madurai.

through the town by hundreds of devotees, with the deity mounted on it.

Temple buildings adhere strictly to ancient manuals that stipulate not only the rituals for the concerned deity but also the various architectural components appropriate to each temple model.

The religion of the early Pallava period was pantheistic. As variations in ritual, metaphysics and symbolism grew more marked, religious sects adopted special gods and temples of their own. This gave an impetus to temple building and image-making and artists, artisans, craftsmen and clergy began to innovate in ritual, art and architecture. Shiva worship in the sanctum, mainly in the aniconic (unfigured) form called for bronze images of the various iconic manifestations of that god as processional and household deities. Vishnu, whose worship got standardized in so far as the deity in the sanctum is concerned, also provided scope as the several forms of his incarnations needed representation.

mostly in sandstone, while those of the Pandyas and Cholas were built in granite. The sculptures in the former were therefore executed in relief on the walls and niches. In the latter, the sculptures were often carved separately and placed in the niches. As temple architecture progressed, and towns and prosperous villages grew, the development of the fine arts became a major temple function. Enclosure walls and gateway towers also multiplied, and themes and episodes from the *Puranas* were narrated in sculptures on the temple walls for education as at Tirucchennampundi, Darasuram and Thanjavur.

Grants were often made to temples for the public reading of epics like the *Ramayana* and *Mahabharata* and the *Puranas* by pandits who also discoursed on them. The listeners saw these legends "illustrated" in the carvings and bronze images of the temple and were thus better able to imbibe their symbolic significance. This tradition continues even today everywhere in Tamil Nadu.

Temple complex, Kanchipuram.

Temples of Sandstone and Granite

Distinct from the rock-cut temples, the Pallava structural temples were built

A Hereditary Skill

Temple building is the hereditary profession of the *sthapati* (stone mason) families.

The "manuals" are conveyed orally and by example from father to son and the tradition has continued, with variations to match cultic changes that took place in every period.

A temple town complex is not only a religious pilgrimage center, but also a seat of learning, attracting scholars, artists, dancers and musicians. Around the temple mushroom markets and commercial craft centers to meet the needs of the devotees and pilgrims. The city streets, even today, are alive with markets, temple processions, street-theater performances and music.

· Pandyan kings coeval with the Pallavas from the 6th to the 10th Century A.D. and competed with the Pallavas in erecting both rock-cut temples and structural ones. When both of them were eliminated politically by the imperial Cholas, the golden age of religious architecture and art was ushered in, which was to witness the building of four of the finest all-stone temples. These are the Brihadiswara temples at Thanjavur and Gangaikonda Cholapuram; Rajarajesvaram at Darasuram; and Kampaharesvara at Tribhuman.

In the later Pandyan period (13th Century A.D.) when the dynasty overwhelmed the imperial Cholas and launched an empire-building· in South India which continued till the 15th Century, several challenging constructions were erected. The massive *kodungai* (cornice) of Ayudayarkoil — a Shiva-Shakti shrine in Ramnad District; the pierced and perforated windows of Tiruvalanjuli, Thanjavur District; the musical pillars of Madurai, Krishnapuram and elsewhere; the massive span of the corridors of Madurai and Rameshvaram, raised high on complex pillar schemes, are all proofs of the tremendous dexterity of the artisans and architects. The quarrying of huge slabs, their dressing, decoration and then their hoisting and mounting at great heights with the simplest of equipment draws our admiration even today.

The Vijayanagar and Nayaka period (c.1500-1700 A.D.) in Tamil Nadu saw the further erection of massive granite constructions, as at Srirangam, Varadaraja Temple at Kanchipuram, and in the Jalakantesvara Temple, Vellore, in the form of *Kalyana* (rejoicing) *mandapas* for the festivities connected with the birth, marriage and exploits of gods in the like- Church, Kanya Kumari.

244

ness of man. All these are veritable museums of sculpture and architecture.

A Temple Tour

A tour of selected temple sites of Tamil Nadu could start from Madras. Taking the coastal road, 34 miles (55 km) south, is **Mamallapuram** (Mahabalipuram) where there are almost 70 monuments, rock-cut monoliths, displaying fine sculpture. Mamallapuram, was the port city of the Pallavas in the 7th Century A.D.

In this picturesque setting, amidst sandy beaches and the sea, can be seen some of the most important temple forms that influenced temple architecture in Tamil Nadu for centuries to follow. The first important group are the five *rathas,* rock-cut monoliths named after the heroes of the Mahabharata epic: Arjuna, Bhima, Dharmaraja, Draupadi, Sahadeva and Nakula. The elevational design of these five models simulates ceremonial chariots. Some of these *rathas* are unfinished, and in them can be seen the carving technique used to form temples out of living rock. They are actually monumental sculptures in the form of temples. Also within this complex is a large sculpture of a lion and of an elephant, and a seated *Nandi* (bull), Lord Shiva's favorite mount.

The other group at Mamallapuram are the cave temples of **Mahishasuramardini,** the **Olalkkanneswara** (God of the Flaming Eye) and others. In these, the hillside has been carved out to form pillared halls and enclosed shrines within which are some magnificent sculptures, some larger-than-life, of gods and goddesses of the Hindu pantheon.

Near the seashore stands the twin temple unit which is particularly important for its place in the early structural temple building forms in South India. Unfortunately, much of the beauty of the sculptures and the form of its elegant towering *shikhara* have been eroded by saline action of the waves and the sea breeze. Today the temples are protected from the fury of the sea.

Kanchipuram

Kanchipuram lies 40 miles (70 km) from Madras, and was the erstwhile capital of the Pallavas and Cholas (7-13th centuries A.D.). These two powerful ruling dynasties gave the city its numerous

Left, Ekampeshwara Temple, Kanchipuram; right, a Tamilian does penance in fulfilment of a vow.

temples and tanks. Kanchipuram today has as many as 150 active temples dedicated to various gods and goddesses. Its streets are broad and designed to accommodate the large processions that take place throughout the year in celebration of festivals dedicated to the many and various deities.

Kanchipuram, one of the seven holiest cities of India, is a well planned one and was an important university center. It is the home of the famed Kanchipuram sari.

Famous amongst the temples of Kanchipuram are the **Kailashanatha** (725 A.D.) and the **Vaikuntaperumal Vishnu Temple** (750 A.D.). Both are built of sandstone and house some of the most elegant sculptures of Shiva, Nataraja (Shiva the dancer), Durga mounted on a lion, and of Vishnu. The Kailashanatha Temple also contains some remnants of mural paintings belonging to the Pallava period.

The **Varadaraja Vishnu Temple** and the **Ekambareshwara Shiva Temple** are large complexes, with *mandapas,* tanks and sculptured halls filled with devotees who still flock here. The Varadaraja Vishnu Temple has an ancient mango tree. Its four branches are said to represent the four Vedas, and each has a different taste. To eat of the fruit is to gain eternal wisdom.

Historically speaking, the next important area with beautiful temples is that of **Thanjavur.** This city is associated with the Chola dynasty who gained supreme power over large areas of south India and beyond to what is now Sri Lanka, Burma and regions further east. It was during this period (9th-13th centuries) that numerous arts such as architecture and sculpture received royal patronage and flourished. The most interesting are the Brihadesvara Temple at Thanjavur; the Gangaikonda Cholapuram and Rajarajesvarma at Darasuram and the Kampaharesvara at Tribhuvanam.

The **Brihadesvara Temple,** built by Raja Chola (985-1014 A.D.), is the tallest ancient monument in India, rising to over 300 feet (95 meters) in 13 floors, in a stark pyramidal form, with the ground floor raised in two levels. Apart from the massive proportions of the temple and sculptures, there are painted murals belonging to the Chola period. These murals are found in the covered ambulatories around the sanctum, and are extremely

Chola bronzes showing marriage of Shiva and Parvati, with Vishnu in attendance.

rich in color and detail.

The city also has an interesting fort and palace. The **Archeological Museum** and the **Tanjore Art Gallery** have some extraordinary examples of Chola bronze sculptures.

Tiruchirappalli (shortened to Trichy) has a unique landmark, a rock fort temple. Not far away is **Srirangam,** with the temple complexes of Sri Ranganathaswamy and the Sri Jambukesvara temple.

The **Madurai Temple** is dedicated to Meenakshi Sundareshvara and is a large temple-town complex of walls, corridors, concentric streets, tanks, shops and, finally, the main shrine. Sculptured pillars, and the figures on the *gopurams* are, to the regret of many, now painted in many hues, and presents a riot of modern colors. The temple has an interesting museum located in its 1000-pillared hall. Elaborate festivals are celebrated each year and thousands come to participate.

Chidambaram is another important temple town on the route south towards Tanjore from Madras. The temple is dedicated to the Cosmic Dancer, Shiva as Nataraja, and the site is said to be the venue of Shiva's legendary dance for his consort, Parvati. The temple complex is large with *gopurams* built by several kings successively (from the 10th to the 16th centuries), and many-pillared *mandapas* and tanks. The life-size sculptures of gods on its wall and the dance panel sequences on the eastern *gopuram* are frozen texts in stone on the art of Indian dancing.

Rameshwaram is an important religious center for Hindus. It is an island in the Gulf of Mannar, beyond which is the narrow gap of ocean between India and Sri Lanka. The **Ramanathaswamy Temple** represents the later period of architecture of Tamil Nadu. Here is to be seen the largest pillared and cloistered corridor in the whole world. Each side of its four-sided circuit runs to nearly 1½ miles (two km) of lofty, massive stonework. In the vicinity of Rameshwaram are beautiful beaches, the Pambam Bridge and the ferry to Sri Lanka across the Palk Strait.

Further south is Kanyakumari (Cape Comorin). Three waters meet here — the Indian Ocean, the Arabian Sea and the Bay of Bengal. Looking out from the very tip of the Indian peninsula, with nothing obstructing the view, the spot attracts many at sunrise and sunset.

Film hoardings, Madurai.

ANDHRA PRADESH

Andhra Pradesh is, geologically, one of the most ancient parts of peninsular India. In historical times, the region got divided into three major segments, namely, the coastal Circars, Telengana and the hinterland Rayalaseema. These are indeed three distinctive geographical tracts, the first being the rich fertile riparian and deltaic parts of the Godavari and the Krishna; the second, the forested and hilly tract of the north, between the Vindhya range and the Godavari River; and the third, the southwestern part of the lower Deccan in the districts of Cuddappah, Kurnool, Chittoor and Anantapur — hilly, plateau land with hot, arid valleys. Telengana is Andhra's core region and Telugu, the name of the language of the Andhras, is derived from its name.

Kingdoms in Andhra have also followed this regional pattern, with the most ancient Vishnukundins and the Vengi Chalukyas and the Matharas in the coastal belt; the Telugu-Chodas and the Vijayanagar kings in Rayalaseema, and the Kakatiyas in Telengana.

The Telugu language has the vocabularial and dictional richness of classical Sanskrit usage, with the result that, despite its basic Dravidian matrix, it is almost overwhelmingly "spoken Sanskrit" in its style and embellishments. The rural traditions are notable for their *padyams* — rolling, sonorous prose narrations of rural life, customs, characteristics and festivities. Telugu is one of the sweetest among the Indian tongues, and has rich epic and Puranic literature, created by a galaxy of poets like Potana, Vemana, Srinatha and Nannayya.

Telugu culture absorbed the best of Vedic Aryan felicities of the north into its Dravidian base and expressed it in art, music and dance. Under the Satavahanas (2nd Century B.C.–2nd Century A.D.) it had played a notable part in shaping and defining the Southern Indian ethos, besides protecting the zone from the onslaughts of medieval Islamic thrusts into the south. Nevertheless, the Telengana region has been continuously exposed to Islam influences since medieval times and Hyderabad, the capital of Andhra Pradesh, was the capital of the Muslim Nizam of Hyderabad till the dawn of in-dependence. It is now the capital of Andhra Pradesh.

The Andhras are excellent craftsmen, making lacquer toys, Anakapalli articles, Nirmal painted pottery, bidri — lead-inlaid black-metal trinkets, and palm-leaf and slate articles, besides the Gadhwal, Pochampad and Dharmavaram silk saris.

Kucchipudi is the classical Andhra dance form. It is essentially a narrative dance enunciation of Puranic legends, branching off in its essential grammar and gestures from the pristine *Bharata Natyam* of Tamil Nadu.

Hyderabad

Hyderabad is essentially a modern city. The Qutb Shahais, who ruled the area in the 16th–17th centuries had their capital city in the nearby fortress city of Golkonda. The capital was shifted to Hyderabad only in 1590. The later off shoot of this dynasty, the Asaf Jahi Nizams, ruled from Hyderabad. Their dominions spread over the whole of Telengana, and Vidarbha and Marathwada of the present-day Maharashtra, and the districts of Bidar and Gulbarga of the present-day Karnataka.

Alone among the Indian princes, the Nizam was given the distinction of being called His Exalted Highness by the British. The last of the clan was Nizam VII, Osman Ali Khan, the owner of fabulous royal jewelry and gems of inestimable value. and unique dimensions, besides several palaces in and around Hyderabad, like the Falaknuma Palace on the Banjara Hills and the main King Kothi Palace in the heart of Hyderabad city, which lies forlorn today.

One of the early generals of the clan, Salar Jung, was noted for his voluminous collections of antiques and rare art treasures which were housed in a showpiece landmark of Hyderabad, the **Salar Jung Museum,** now given the status of a National Museum and housed in a new building. It has a unique collection of miniature paintings and illuminated manuscripts of the Koran and other works, among numerous other interesting exhibits.

The original town of Bhagyanagara, located on the Musi River, has been built into modern Hyderabad, linking it with the adjacent area of its twin city of Secunderabad at the other end of **Hussain Sagar** lake bund which connects the two townships and which has become a

Charminar,
Hyderabad
landmark.

favorite evening promenade.

The last Nizam, though personally extremely conservative, had some able and far-sighted Prime Ministers, notably Sir Akbai Hydari and Sir Mirza Ismail, both statesmen of high calibre. Osman Ali Khan founded the Osmania University, a major center of Urdu, Persian and Arabic studies, in addition to the modern arts and sciences.

Situated on a rocky plateau with access to both the Krishna and Godavari Rivers, Hyderabad has become the rodal point of a transport and communication network and a market for crafts, grains, tobacco and the *anab-shahi* variety of large-sized seedless grapes that thrive in the climate and on the soil of Telengana and, in recent times, has become a money spinner in Rayalaseema also.

City Landmark

The famed **Charminar,** built at the end of the 16th Century, is one of the landmarks of the city. It rises to four stories and has space for a mosque on its topmost floor. Built in typical Qutb-Shahi style, with carefully finished stucco ornamentation and *gul-dasta* style minars, and miniature minarets at the corners and the fringes, it maintains the architectural tradition seen at Golkonda.

The area around Charminar is an interesting bazaar area where some of the best bargains can be struck in goods from silk, metalwork, pearls and bangles, to rare Urdu books and manuscripts.

Adjacent to the Charminar is the impressive **Mecca Mosque,** reputed to be among the largest in the world. Its construction proceeded in stages over almost the whole of the 17th Century.

The twin city, **Hyderabad–Secunderabad,** is among the seven largest cities of India. Secunderabad, till India became independent, remained separated from Hyderabad though adjacent to it, because Secunderabad was a British-Indian cantonment and the seat of the British "Resident" in Hyderabad State. Parts of the town are still typical of that type of British-Indian township — the Secunderabad Club and the old Residency are excellent examples.

By tradition, Hyderabad has always been a cosmopolitan and gracious city, a center of learning and the arts. It has mild cool winters and has now the honor Golconda Fort, Andhra Pradesh.

of being the South Indian seat of the President of India, in the Rashtrapati Nilayam at Bolarum.

Fortress City

Golkonda, now almost part of sprawling Hyderabad, with its grand fortifications, citadel, numerous mosques, tombs, pavilions and *baradaris* and the remarkable tomb cluster of the Qutb Shahi royal cemetery at the foot of the fort is easily visited from Hyderabad. The fortress held out for eight long months when it was besieged by the mighty Mughal Emperor Aurangzeb in 1687 and finally fell only when it was treacherously betrayed. The main citadel is situated on a hill and is surrounded by walls of solid stone. The outer wall, surrounding the whole township, is about 8 miles long and is also strongly fortified. In its heyday, the six-mile long road from Golkonda to Hyderabad was a fabulous bazaar selling jewelry, diamonds, pearls and other gems and trinkets which were world famous.

Going north to south in Andhra Pradesh, there are the coastal districts of the Northern Circars. There, at a wooded site near Gara is the group of temples at **Mukhalingam,** built by Ganga kings. Across the Rishikilya and Vamsadhra Rivers is **Srikurmam,** where there is a unique representation of a zooanthropomorphic incarnation of Vishnu as tortoise-man in the sanctum of the Vishnu Temple. This valley is rich in Buddhist *stupa* sites, as at **Salihundam** and the ancient port of **Kalingapatnam.**

To the south on the Godavari estuary is **Rajamahendrapuram** on the route to **Vengi,** the site of the capital of the Eastern Chalukyas in Eluru District, and also to the delightful group of temples at **Biccavolu** and **Masulipatnam** on the coast.

Further south is **Vijayawada,** an ancient city with a large number of 6-13th Century A.D. rock-cut and structural temples along the banks of the River Krishna, stretching over ten miles. **Amaravati,** the celebrated Buddhist site, with its museums and temples, is 16 miles (20 km) away.

Northeast of Hyderabad, in the Telengana region, is **Warangal,** with its massive and reputedly impregnable fortress, which was under continuous attack from the Delhi Sultans in the 13th and

Worship of the Buddha as a flaming pillar sketch of a bas-relief at Amravati, Andhra Pradesh.

NAGA PEOPLE WORSHIPPING THE TRISUL EMBLEM OF BUDDHA, ON A FIERY PILLAR.

From a bas-relief at Amaravati.

14th centuries. It has four massive *toranas* (gates). Nearby is the spectacular **Hanumankonda Temple** of the Kakatiyas built of blocks of granite. A little further, in **Palampet** on the banks of a lake is **Ramappa Temple,** embellished with attractive sculptures of women dancers.

Across the bridge over the Godavari near Khammam and Kottagudem, is the **temple of the god Bhadrachalam** who is supposed to have descended to earth in human form to ransom Ramadasa, a revered saint, who was being held prisoner by a Qutb Shahi king.

Leaving the Telengana region and turning south towards the Krishna Valley, one reaches **Kurnool,** passing on the way the magnificent group of **Navabrahma Temples** near Alampur. Further south, along the Nallamalai Hills, past the **Ahobilam Hill Temple,** and the Chola temples at **Attirala** on the Pennar River, one reaches **Tirupati,** the great pilgrim center which draws a stream of pilgrims from north, south, east and west to its **shrine of Shri Venkateswara.**

Close to Tirupati is the **Chandagiri Mahal and Fort.** It was here that the last Vijayanagar king, Ranga Raya, approved of the sale to the East India Company of the land on which Fort St. George at Madras was built.

In the opening centuries of the Christian era, the entire coastal belt, and more especially the Krishna River in its deltaic and lower reaches, hummed with activity and sea-going vessels reached as far upstream as Amaravati (or Dhanyakataka), the capital city of the southern wing of the Satavahanas, and beyond up to Nagarjunakonda. Further upstream, the Krishna runs in a long serpentine gorge across the Srisailam Ranges from the upper plateau stretches, after its confluence with the Tungabhadra at Sangamesvaram and the environs of Alampur.

Nagarjunakonda Excavations

This whole area had been subjected to several excavations over the years, especially at **Nagarjunakonda,** near which the great **Nagarjunasagar** multipurpose hydro-electric dam and lake will eventually submerge this whole valley city, the capital of the Ikshvakus (who succeeded the Satavahanas in the lower Deccan in the Krishna basin). In view of the Nagarjunakonda site being submerged, the archeological remains have been moved to an island museum where full-scale model placements of the excavated remains have been set up.

These centers have revealed at Amaravati, Nagarjunakonda, Bhattiprolu, Goli, Ghantasala, Alluru, Ramatirtham, Sankaram and Salihundam, several Buddhist monastic settlements with *stupas* (Buddhist reliquaries), *chaityas* (Buddhist temples), and viharas (monasteries) and records mentioning clergy and scholars participating in these centers and coming from as far afield as Kashmir, Gandhara (now in Afghanistan), China and Kamarupa (now Assam).

Religious, academic and medical services here were on a par with similar activities elsewhere later on, as at Nalanda, Valabhi and Vikramasila. The center functioned in amity with the votaries of Brahmanical Hinduism, as at Nagarjunakonda, where important temples for Shiva, Vishnu and Karttikeya were also erected. These monuments are embellished with sculptures on their green Palnad limestone and the ritual terra-cotta figurines. Crystal reliquaries placed within stone caskets and containing gold, flowers, bone fragments etc., have also been found. Carved *Buddhapadas* (replicas of the feet of the Buddha) also

Shaven-headed in fulfilment of a vow, a devotee prays at Tirupati Temple.

often contained relics in a receptacle cavity cut between the big toes.

Along with Buddhism and Hinduism, Jainism had also flourished in Andhra Pradesh but was mostly confined to the central and southwestern parts of the state, as at Tumbalam in the Cuddappah District, near Adoni.

The Andhra temples are mostly of the *vimana* style similar to the pyramidal storied style seen in Tamil Nadu. These had been notable from the time of the Eastern Chalukyas (7th–11th centuries) ruling from Vengi (Eluru District), after a rich rock-cut art tradition had run its course as at Vijayawada, Mogalraja-puram, Undavalli, Penamaka, Bhairava-konda and Advi-Somanapalli, the last two located in the Nellore and Karim-nagar Districts, while the others are in a chain in the Krishna Delta, around Vijayawada.

The structural temples belonging to the distinctive *Pancharama* group, found variously at Draksharama, Bhimavaram (Samarlakota), Amaravati, Chebrolu and Palakollu, owe their existence to the patronage of Chalukya kings Gunaga-Vijayaditya and Bhima (9th–10th centuries). They have typical *sarvatobhadra*

(facing all directions) shrines or very lofty *lingas* (phallic symbols) rising from the ground floor of the sanctum through to the first floor, where they are worshipped. For this reason the main basal shrine is raised in two *bhumis,* access to the upper one being via a staircase let into the thickness of the side-wall. It was this class of temple that seemingly caught the imagination of the great Tamil king, Raja Raja I Chola, when he was involved in Andhra affairs, which ultimately resulted in a united Chola-Chalukya Empire under the suzerainty of the Cholas under Kulottunga I, Chola, in 1070 A.D. He employed this model for his great temple, the Brihadeshwara at Thanjavur in the Kaveri delta (Tamil Nadu).

The art and architecture of Andhra developed in three main phases: the early historic, the pre-medieval and the medieval, in which last phase Islamic architecture also provides many landmarks. Certainly the richest legacy of Andhra's religious art is that of the Satavahana and Ikshavaku dynasties, when the entire riparian coastal belt turned Buddhist, even before being exposed to the proselytizing zeal of Ashoka Maurya of Magadha.

Consulting an astrologer

The earliest and biggest *stupa* site in Andhra was at **Amaravati**. This was barbarously vandalized by building contractors in search of stone for construction and only remnants were salvaged and carried off to enrich the far-off Government Museum, Madras, and the still more distant Victoria and Albert Museum, London, where whole sections of richly carved veneer slabs of green limestone which once formed parts of the *stupa* are now to be seen.

An earthen structure in its original 4th Century B.C. form, the *stupa* was provided with a granite railing during Ashokan times, which was replaced by limestone workmanship of the most elaborate kind in several stages during Satavahana rule up to the 2nd Century A.D. The *stupa* had a diameter of 49.30 m and a typical *ayaka* platform (7.20 x 2.10 m) for five *ayaka* pillars — a distinctive feature of Andhra stupas — with an estimated dome diameter of 42 m, capped by a *harmika* (railed platform) and triple umbrellas — as can be gathered from the miniature representation of the stupa seen on a railing fragment. The foundation of the stupa has a wheel-shaped plan.

The *chaityas* are apsidal structures and originally contained only a miniature *stupa* inside for circumambulation. The Mahayana *chaityas,* like those at Nagarjunakonda, have standing images of Buddha inside. They are chapels for worship. In front of them are the usual three or four winged monastic residential units, enclosing an open, pillared hall in a quadrangle.

The sculptures of the Buddhist sites of Andhra are in a class by themselves in their classic modulations, rich representations of Jataka tales and Buddha's own life, besides animal studies and floral embellishments.

Among the Brahmanical sculptures, it is of interest to note the evidence of an open, railed shrine recently excavated below the subsequent apsidal temple for Siva at **Gudimallam**. Siva, Skanda and Vishnu temples at Nagarjunakonda have already been mentioned. Perspectives of secular architecture and life are also afforded in the sculptured slab fragments, attesting to organized civic habitation surrounded by walls and provided with ornate gates, besides actual examples at Nagarjunakonda. Bathing ghats, public baths, assembly halls and a unique amphitheatre were all part of the amenities of which the remains can still be seen.

The earliest monuments of the pre-medieval dynasties of Vishnukundins and the Eastern Chalukyas of Vengi were the rock-cut shrines earlier listed. These reveal links with Ajanta and Ellora (in Maharashtra) architecturally and also in terms of sculptural and iconographic usage. Attempts at monolithic carving are also witnessed as at Vijayawada, which also suggest that they are coeval with the Rashtrakuta stages of the Ellora monoliths. Elsewhere, there are structural brick temples like those at **Kapotesvara** at **Chezerla** (4th Century A.D.) and **Pitigayakula.** Additions were made by the early Pallavas of Andhra in the form of *gopura* (gateways) in stone slab work in the 6th Century A.D. It is the temples under the Eastern Chalukyas of Vengi that makes the region once again an important center of structural temples in India. These, besides the *Pancharamas* mentioned earlier, are notably to be seen at **Biccavolu** (East Godavari District); Mahanandi, Satyavolu and Kadamalakalava (all in Kurnool District); and Alampur, Sangamesvara, Panchalingala and Pragaturu in Mehbubnagar District. These temples have a classic affinity to the styles of the Western Chalukyas and the Pallavas, and are rich in iconography. They are built of sandstone and have the usual features like sloping side roofs and a series of tall windows in the front *mandapa* (hall).

Miniature Models

A notable feature of this period is that we find, in close association with some of the temples, miniature temple models, replicas not more than a meter high, with much detail of component parts. Particularly noted for such models are the temples of Satyavolu, Mahanandi and Draksharamam.

It may be said that, while coastal Andhra received its southern temple models and mannerisms mostly from Tamil Nadu, its 'northern' temple forms, were the outcome of borrowings from Karnataka, via the Krishna Valley contact zone between the two states. The fact that the political suzerainty of the Badami Chalukyas extended right up to Kurnool and Mehbubnagar Districts of Andhra, greatly facilitated the spread of the latter forms to Andhra.

A Lambadi woman.

KARNATAKA, TEMPLES AND PALACES

Accounting for a sixteenth of the total landmass of India, Karnataka, with a population of about 38 million, consists of three distinct regions: a narrow fertile coastal strip, comprising the two districts of North and South Kanara along the Arabian Sea; the hilly uplands dominated by the Western Ghats whose peaks stand like stern sentinels barring the entry of monsoon clouds into the Deccan Plateau east of the Ghats where the landscape becomes rock-strewn and bare. No three regions could be more strikingly different from one another.

Coastal Karnataka is about 40 miles (65 km) broad at its widest. A dozen rivers flow through this coastal strip in swift abandon, their banks swollen during the three monsoon months (July –September) of torrential rain. This is when the red soil of Kanara decks itself with brilliant greenery for miles at a stretch.

Malnad, in the foothills of the Ghats, one of the wettest regions in India, is celebrated for its teak and rosewood, its areca and bamboo, its peppervine and cardamon. In the southern region of the Ghats, amidst the profusion of tropical rain forests, roams the Indian elephant, as do the stately gaur and the long-tailed langur, the latter frequently breaking into the silence of the freckled forest with gossipy chatter.

The Deccan plateau is reputed to be one of the oldest land formations on earth — the so-called Gondwana Plate, which we are told, emerged at the very beginning of geological time.

Unlike the rivers of coastal Karnataka, the upland rivers are in no great hurry to rush to the sea. The one exception is the Sharavati which plunges down a yawning chasm in a glorious spectacle of cascading water and flying spray. This is the far-famed **Jog Falls** visited by thousands all the year round but especially in the winter months, when the water flows fullest and the sun paints a whole complex of rainbows.

Karnataka's Inhabitants

As varied as the land are its people. In Karnataka's southern corner, amidst the

The palace at Msyore.

hills and valleys of **Coorg,** live the tall and sinewy Kodagu people whose picturesque costumes are in striking contrast to the simpler lifestyle of the people on the coast.

North of Coorg, in the flatland of what was the former state of Mysore, live the Vokkaligas whose rich farms are watered by the river Kaveri. The language they speak in common with other citizens of the state — Kannada — has a musical cadence and falls softly on the ear, in contrast to the Kannada spoken farther north, which is harsh and guttural. The dividing line between the two regions is the river Tungabhadra, which is also the dividing line between the black and red soils of the state. Incidentally, the word "Kannada" is derived from *kari* (black) and *nadu* (land).

The people of the north are mostly Lingayats, followers of that great scholar-saint, Basava (12th Century), whose masculine vigor in the handling of the Kannada language and whose uncompromising preaching of the equality of all people mark him out as one of Karnataka's notable personalities.

Coastal Karnataka is inhabited, among others, by fisherfolk who have plied their boats for generations and whose forefathers traded with ancient Mesopotamia. Even the Greeks are known to have come to Karnataka's shores in the pre-Christian era. Spoken in this coastal strip are Kannada, the dominant language of the state; Tulu, one of the five Dravidian languages; and Konkani, which belongs to the Indo-Aryan group. Konkani, in its many accents, is spoken by Hindus, Christians and Muslims alike.

The Christians of Kanara are among the oldest converts to the faith, with some of their churches dating back to the 16th Century. The Church of the Most Holy Rosary at Bolar, in Mangalore, was established in 1526.

A Cursory Look at the Past

Karnataka's history is a turbulent one. First in recorded memory is the dynasty of the Chalukyas, who were replaced by the Rashtrakutas, one of whom, the great Amoghavarsha Nripatunga (814–880 A.D.), wrote a magnificent treatise on poetics. The Rashtrakutas were the premier power in the India of their day. It was they who had the massive monolithic Kailash Temple at Ellora in

High Court, Bangalore.

Maharashtra, carved from solid rock.

After the Rashtrakutas came the Chalukyas of Kalyana. There were other princely houses, too, like the Kadambas of Hangal, the Sindas of Sindavadi, and the Silaharas of north Konkan. Later came the Hoysalas and the Rayas of the Vijayanagar Empire.

For several centuries, between the end of the Rashtrakuta rule and the rise of the Vijayanagar kingdom, seers and saint singers of compelling power and truth, rather than warriors, were to dominate the scene. With the downfall of the Vijayanagar kingdom, Karnataka did not emerge on the national scene again till Hyder Ali and his son Tipu Sultan were to galvanize the country with their military prowess and administrative acumen. When the British finally overpowered Tipu in 1799 at the famous Battle of Seringapatam, they dismembered his kingdom with a take-no-more-chances thoroughness. Karnataka thereafter was parcelled out among various political groupings, leaving the core of Tipu's empire to be ruled by a successor of an earlier deposed dynasty, with his capital in Mysore.

But even before the advent of Hyder Ali, other Muslim rulers had established themselves in north Karnataka, in **Bijapur.** The founder of the kingdom of Bijapur, Yusuf Adil Shah, was born in Constantinople in 1443. His successors were to enrich the city with such splendid mosques as to rival anything Islam could raise elsewhere. Outstanding is **Gol Gumbaz,** whose dome is comparable to that of St. Peter's in Rome.

At **Gulbarga** are the remnants of a fort originally built by a Raja Gulchand and later developed by Allauddin Bahmani, founder of the kingdom of that name. The fort covers several hectares and includes the **Jami Mosque** with 37,600 sq feet (35,000 sq meters) of built-up area in the style of the mosque at Cordova in Spain. The interior arches are so designed and the pillars placed that the pulpit can be seen unobstructed from any part of the hall. The acoustics too are perfect.

The capital of modern Karnataka is **Bangalore,** whose beginnings go back to 1537, when a petty chieftain, Kempe Gowda, built a mud fort on a hill. Today, it is a sprawling city, one of the fastest growing in India, covering some 50 sq miles (130 sq km) and attracting

Gol Gumbaz, Bijapur.

industry and commerce. Located here are some of the largest industrial plants in India like Hindustan Aeronautics, Hindustan Machine Tools and Bharat Electronics. Winston Churchill once lived here in one of the earliest clubs set up by the British. Indeed, at one time, Bangalore was a little British island in the south, with a distinct British flavor, and old British connections remain evident in such names as Richmond Town, Cox Town, Fraser Town and Russel Market.

There are many attractive places within 18–25 miles (30–40 km) of Bangalore: the **Nandi Hills** are famous for their salubrious climate, and **Bannarghatta** is an hour's drive from Bangalore and has been made a national park for protected wildlife. Seen here are over a hundred varieties of birds, besides monkeys, bison, wild boar, elephants, panthers, spotted deer and sloth bears.

Fragrance of the Mysore Jasmine

Mysore, capital of the erstwhile princely state of that name, is famous for its jasmine, known locally as Mysore Mallige whose fragrance has been widely celebrated in song. Mysore is just as famous for its silk and sandalwood, its palaces and its leisurely way of life. About eight miles (14 km) from Mysore is the battle-scarred town of **Shrirangapattana,** once Tipu Sultan's capital. It was here that the Tiger of Mysore, as Tipu was called, fought and died. Outside the ruins of the old fort is **Daria Daulat** (Splendor of the Sea), Tipu's summer palace, set in an exquisite garden and still in good shape though it was built in 1784. About 30 miles (48 km) from Mysore is the lovely temple of **Somnathpur** built by the renowned architect, Jakanachari. Around its exterior base are portrayed in sequence the main incidents from the *Ramayana* and *Mahabharata,* India's great epics.

But Somnathpur is only *hors d'ouvre* to the main architectural course — there are still the temples at Halebid, Belur, Badami, Aihole and Pattadakal. It wasn't for nothing that Karnataka has been called the cradle of India's temple architecture. Some are freestanding structures, others have been carved out of granite hills.

First were the cave temples of **Badami** and **Aihole,** carved in the second half of the 6th Century A.D. By the beginning

Left, dancing Shiva, Halebid; right, colossus of Jain saint at Gomateswara, Shravan Belgola.

of the 7th Century, the transition from the rock-cut medium to structural techniques was already underway. **Belur** is a striking example of the latter, as is **Halebid** about 11 miles (17 km) east of Belur. But easily the most remarkable work of art — though not necessarily the most beautiful — is the 57-foot (17½-meter) statue of a Jain saint, Gomateswara, raised on a granite hill, itself 394 feet (120 meters) above ground level. The statue was erected in 983 A.D. and there is nothing comparable to it anywhere else in the world. Of this, the historian Fergusson wrote: "One is astonished at the amount of labour such a work must have entailed and puzzled to know whether it was part of the hill or had been moved to the spot where it now stands."

In north Karnataka is **Hampi**, the site of the capital of the old Vijayanagar Empire. These medieval ruins cover some 10 sq miles (26 sq km). Hampi is eight miles (14 km) from Tungabhadra Dam and on the outskirts of Hospet, a town connected to other cities by an excellent train service. The ruins of Hampi, which are most impressive even today, include the **Virupaksha Temple** where worship continues to be offered as it was when it was first built. Its central hall was raised by the emperor Krishnadevaraya to commemorate his coronation in 1509–10. The Portuguese traveller Paes, who saw Hampi in its heyday, described it as being as large as Rome, with the palaces of its king more spacious than the castles of Lisbon. Hampi was destroyed in 1565, after the Battle of Talikota, in which the Vijayanagar army was defeated by the forces of the Bijapur confederacy.

The Kannada Personality

Karnataka has been described as the crucible in which races, classes, religions and cultures have acted and interacted to produce the Kannada personality — generous, liberal in the understanding of value systems other than its own, and distrustful of fanaticism and flamboyance. One distinguished Kannada writer, V. Sitaramiah, has asserted that "the long-range value preference, the pride and grateful memory of Kannada poets, has been, by and large, for tolerance and the art of peace."

And what are these "arts of peace?" One immediately thinks of the weavers of silk in Mysore, of saris in Irkal, the patient carvers in ivory and sandalwood who have made Karnataka famous, the Yakshagana dancers of Kanara and a whole school of musical articulation that embraces the entire south, but centered at Dharwad. The red clay tiles made in Mangalore on the coast are not only used all over India but have, for decades, been exported to East Africa and elsewhere — east and west.

Savory Delights

Karnataka's culinary genius has peacefully conquered cities all over India and has even established footholds in London, Paris, Frankfurt, Tokyo and New York. If the Kanara coast specializes in a variety of seafood, it is also responsible for the making of the polysyllabic *bisi bele huli anna* (created, as much as made out of lentil, tamarind, chili powder and *dalchini*) and the even more famous *idli* (rice cakes) and *dosai* (a kind of pancake, hot and spicy, often with potato fillings). Lesser known among the gastronomic delights of Karnataka are *uppittu* (made of wheat flour, shredded coconut, green chilis and lemon) and *hoalige* (a flat pancake-like wafer about six inches in diameter, filled with molasses and shredded coconut, or copra and sugar, or a variety of lentils and molasses, and fried lightly in a flat skillet).

One of the pleasures of Karnataka is the variety of its offerings of fruit. There are some 25 varieties of mango alone, from the humble neelam to the royal Bennet Alphonso. In coastal Karnataka, every household has its mini orchard, with mango, banana, chickoo, mangosteen and jackfruit trees, and cashew trees with their delicious nuts. One can get drunk, they say, just on cashew fruit and, indeed, one of the best drinks is a brand of cashew liquor called *feni*. Like vodka, it has to be drunk for its potency.

One has to spend time in Karnataka to savor its many delights. For sheer beauty, there are few places that can excel the string of lakes that constitute the **Sharavati** system or the confluence of the **Hemavati** and the **Kaveri** rivers, just above the **Krishnaraja Sagar**. To the people of Karnataka, the Kaveri is *Mother Kaveri*, the giver of wealth.

The beaches of Karnataka are something else again. From Karwar in the north to Ullal in the south, it is one long stretch of sparkling white. The poet Rabindranath Tagore thought there never was another beach more beautiful than the one at **Karwar,** but he probably had not seen **Thandrabail** or **Suratkal.** Lying there, on a moonlit night, amidst the gathering sounds of the waves scudding scarily against the black basalt that occasionally crops up along the shores, and listening to the whisper of winds as they scurry through the groves of casuarina so casually growing on the rim, or sitting in the shade of a coconut grove, sipping the tender-coconut water, time flows evenly, untroubled.

Folk Drama and Buffalo Races

But nothing can be more memorable than a night spent in a field, the hay mowed, and the stubble still prickly under one's feet, sitting on a straw mat watching *bayalata* (field play), the folk drama of the people. This is not for anyone in a hurry. It calls for a measure of patience, for the drama depicting the exploits of heroes and heroines from India's epics will run from early night till the rising of the sun. It has everything: music, dance, drama, and, of course, there is the easy camaraderie of people who know what it is all about and are willing to share their knowledge with you.

When the fields are flush with water, there is one sight not to be missed: the *kambala* or the buffalo race that is unique to Kanara. Run in a paddy field by pairs of buffaloes, egged on by strong-muscled ryots in a highly charged atmosphere, the *kambala* is an annual event.

Here is a man crouching behind the buffaloes on a stout wooden shaft yoked to the animals. Not a muscle moves. Only the wind is playing on his locks of hair. Suddenly the scene explodes, the man springs up, his hand cocked, his whip held high, and the huge animals lunge forward, bellowing, their hooves churning the muddy waters and sending their wet spray into the hot air, their eyes wide, wild and white — man and beast engaged in one spurt of activity and with one aim — victory!

This is Karnataka where every day brings adventure and joy. As they say in Karnataka: *Banni, bega banni!* or Come, come soon!

Remains of Hampi, capital of Vijayanagar Empire in the 16th Century..

KERALA, LAND OF CONTRASTS

Long ago a demon called Darikan sought invincibility by undergoing an arduous penance. His dedication forced Brahma, the Lord of Creation, to grant him his wish. Revelling in his immortality, Darikan proceeded on a wave of destruction so terrible that the whole world trembled and even the gods felt threatened. Quivering with apprehension they prostrated before Lord Shiva and beseeched Him to save the Universe.

As the great and all-powerful God knew Darikan had contemptuously rejected Brahma's offer of immunity from women, He summoned up His divine energy to create, from His third eye, a goddess. Called Bhadrakali, this warrior-goddess rode forth, fully armed, to do battle with the mighty demon in a war which only ended when Darikan paid for his arrogance with his life. When the victorious Bhadrakali returned to Lord Shiva He requested her to select a place on earth and reside there as the protector of Mankind.

The goddess did not hesitate; she immediately left her Father's heavenly abode and came to the land now known as Kerala, a land of paradox and contrast that nestles in the southwestern corner of India. The collection of experiences gathered on a journey through Kerala will breed many disparate thoughts, for the images the traveller absorbs and the impressions he forms, will depend on who he meets, what he sees, why he looks, when he comes, how he responds — and on himself.

Some of the contrasts of Kerala can be found in the state capital of **Trivandrum**, former seat of the Maharajahs of Travancore. Although the temple of **Sree Padmanabhaswamy** that they built to honor their deity, Lord Vishnu, still physically dominates the bustling city, its secular and political importance is enough to warrant an international airport. The crowds, bazars and activities of the new, and growing, urban India can also be seen in the busy, sprawling towns of Cochin, Quilon, Kottayam, Trichur, Calicut and Cannanore.

All these urban centers are linked by trains and buses which pass through a different Kerala — a Kerala of great natural

Temple elephants, Trichur, Kerala.

262

beauty bordered by a shoreline where fishermen land their catch to more ancient and timeless rhythms. Whilst the wealth of the sea satisfies the tastes of fish-loving Keralites, the land that it laps against is tilled to yield an equally generous harvest.

Coconuts and Coffee

Much of the landscape and wealth of Kerala is dominated by tall, elegant coconut palms. No part of this tree is wasted and a flourishing coir industry exists because of its plentiful presence. Coffee plantations spread across the foothills of the Western Ghats, tea grows at higher altitudes and, in southern Kerala, acres of rubber trees stand in lines of military precision. When Columbus sailed from Spain he sought a route to the land of spices — Kerala. The Malabar coast grows the world's best pepper, known as Black Gold, which got half of Europe involved in power struggles to command supplies of this small, pungent berry. The fragrant cardamom and the sweet cashew nut are other important cash crops and no compound is without a few banana trees. The flatter, fertile land supports two or three annual harvests of rice, an essential ingredient in a Keralite's diet.

Rural Kerala is a traditional land with beautiful old houses blending into the contours of the land; with the scholarly and religious dedication of the great 9th-Century Hindu teacher, Adi Shankaracharya, born at Kaladi; with the necessary stamina to master temple arts such as Kathakali; with the austere spiritual magnificence of temples such as those at Ettumanoor, Irinjalakuda and Trichur, and with the stark, white elegance of traditional Kerala dress. In traditional Kerala there is no abuse, waste or vulgarity; there is, instead, along with respect, appreciation and restraint, a deep understanding and reverence for the land which supplies all needs.

Modern Values

Today there is also another, newer, Kerala where many of these old values are ridiculed or ignored. Houses are concrete structures built in defiance of the climate and environment; towns like Chavakad have become "little Dubais," brash and vulgar with the new wealth of thousands of migrant workers to the Gulf states.

The Kerala of today is a mixed land of

Kovalam Beach, Kerala.

calm and noise, honesty and corruption, beauty and ugliness, tradition and progress, faith and atheism, learning and ignorance. There is also the Kerala with not only Hindus, Muslims, Christians and Jews but many different castes and communities — all with their own customs and traditions and styles of dress, food jewelry and marriage.

Many of these different factors come together: for instance, a Marxist politician might prostrate before a Hindu shrine; a Muslim contribute to a temple festival; or a Christian make a Hindu pilgrimage; and buses display the religious icons of three faiths. However, confusing it may be for outsiders, Malayalis, the people of Kerala, find nothing contradictory in either their behavior or their nature. A high-caste Namboodiri brahmin, trained in the priestly *Vedas,* but teaching college mathematics, was amused that his existence could be considered schizophrenic: "Why do you mention *two* levels? — I live on at least six."

Originally, worship in Kerala revolved around the great mysteries of Nature, a natural respect for one's ancestors and a strong attraction towards the concept of a Mother Goddess. Bhadrakali is the presiding deity in most of the villages of her chosen land and the *thattakkam,* Kerala's equivalent of a parish, is always under the divine jurisdiction of a goddess.

Over the centuries, the early strains of religious beliefs flowed into the mainstream of Hindu philosophy, so that now the most evolved and austere of Hindu ritual flourishes alongside an ancient and darker Dravidian style of worship. God is conceived in the most formless, fathomless way by the same people who find the divine in a snake, a tree or a stone. Ghosts, demons and evil spirits are a reality in India's most literate state — the same state that saw, in 1957, the world's first freely elected Communist government. The temple of Chottanikkara, near Cochin, attracts a growing number of pilgrims/patients who seek release from evil spirits, and the long iron nails driven into the huge tree near the sanctum of the goddess testify to their successful exorcism.

Maybe these contrasting elements explain the genuine religious tolerance found in Kerala, a state remarkably free from the communal violence which still haunts other parts of India. According to

Below, preparing for "snake boat" races during Onam festival; and, right, a more plebian vessel on the Kerala backwaters.

popular belief, the oldest of the Christian denominations, the Syrian Christians, was established by the apostle St. Thomas in 50 A.D. The followers of the Prophet Muhammad also came early to Kerala, and although the exterior of the mosque at Kodungallur is a brash, modern concrete structure, its interior is still the cool and serene original of India's oldest mosque. This mosque was built on land given by Kodungallur's Hindu ruler; a gesture echoed by the Rajah of Cochin when he welcomed the Jews, followers of a faith unaccustomed to tolerance elsewhere. Although recent emigration to Israel has reduced the community to a handful, their magnificent synagogue at Cochin still stands.

Christians, Muslims and Jews all found a welcome in Kerala, as did the early Phoenician, Greek and Roman traders. However, when the Zamorin of Calicut greeted Portugal's Vasco da Gama in 1498 he unwittingly received the first European greedy for Indian wealth. Over the centuries, Kerala witnessed and played its part in the colonizing struggles of the Portuguese, the French, the Dutch and, finally, the British.

The Raj left a deep and lasting impression on Kerala's social institutions and legal procedures but the Malayali never surrendered his individual identity or passionate awareness of his own culture. There is little colonial architecture and even though the famous Mattancherry Palace at Cochin was built by the Portuguese and repaired by the Dutch (renaming it the Dutch Palace), its architectural style is of Kerala.

Cultural Contributions

Kerala's contribution to the cultural wealth of India has been enormous. Although the stunning palaces of Padmanabhapuram and Krishnapuram have decorative, flowing carvings and intricate, earth-colored murals, similar to those in the temples at Vaikom and Tripprayyar, gods and men usually dwell in more austere and restrained houses.

Any list of Indian writers, poets and musicians features Malayalis prominently: people like the diplomat turned writer K.P.S. Menon, the poet Vallathol Narayana Menon (also famous as the man who revived Kathakali and founded the Kalamandalam School near Shoranur), and the great singer of Karnatak

music, the late Chembai Vaidyanatha Bhagavatar.

The major cultural contribution of this small state, which covers a mere 15,000 sq miles (38,850 sq km) is probably its theater — some of the world's greatest. There is the highly classical art of Koodiyattam, the lyrically sensuous dance of Mohiniattam, the religious fervor of Krishnanattam and, above all, the spectacular magnificence of Kathakali. Deep within all these highly developed and refined art forms beats the generating spirit which gives them their existence: an extraordinarily rich folk theater, a theater which evolved out of the religious beliefs of its participants and, despite its highly dramatic presentation, is less a theatrical performance than an act of worship. The spectacular *theyyams* of Malabar demonstrate this concept when the fantastically costumed god-actors dance before small shrines, possessed with the spirit and power of their ancient Dravidian deities.

Only during the monsoon months of June to August is it difficult to find some ritual, ceremony or festival taking place. Although the non-Hindu is not usually permitted to enter a temple and witness the most sacred rites, temple festivals are accessible and visible to all. In central Kerala the use of elephants brings a fairy-tale quality to these festivals; there can be few sights to beat that of the 30 great caparisoned tuskers assembled before the Vadakkunathan temple on the day of the Trichur Pooram.

Although legend declares that the land of Kerala was formed when Parsurama, an incarnation of Lord Vishnu, threw his mighty battle-ax into the Arabian Sea, the fertile land that emerged was only established as the state of Kerala in 1956, with the integration of three Malayalam speaking areas — Malabar and the two former princely states of Cochin and Travancore. Between the ancient creation myth and modern political fact is a land of lush, physical beauty which contains a rich and unique storehouse of legend, romance, history, culture and tradition.

The Open Air

Among Kerala's excellent beaches, the best known is Kovalam, 16 km south of Trivandrum, where facilities at all levels are available. But for the tourist amenities in the vicinity of the beach itself, in the

Kathakali dancers.

countryside around and the fishing settlements in the area, life goes on very much as in the rest of rural Kerala.

The **Periyar Game Sanctuary**, 80 km from Kottayam, surrounds the **Periyar Lake** formed by a dam across the Periyar River. In its 775 sq km area, a variety of wildlife, from elephants, bison, leopards and tigers to monkeys, may be seen, either from lodges or viewing huts or from a launch cruising down the lake which meanders through the jungle-covered hills that surround it.

Lakshadweep

Scattered some 200–400 km west of the Kerala coast lie the islands of the Union (centrally administered) Territory of Lakshadweep, a name anglicized earlier to Laccadive Islands. It is an archipelago of 27 coral islands and of open reefs. Of the islands only 10 are inhabited by some 40,000 people, though some of the others serve as fishing stations. The people are like those of the Kerala mainland and, like them, speak Malayalam.

Coconut farming and fishing are the main occupations, the latter rapidly gaining in importance with the mechaniza-tion of fishing operations. There is also some dairy and poultry farming.

The headquarters of the Administration of Lakshadweep is on Kavaratti Island and the smallest of the inhabited islands is Bitra (0.1 sq km) with a population of 181 persons.

Facilities for communication with the mainland and between the islands have been greatly improved in recent years. Tourist facilities are also being developed by way of luxury cruises round the islands and, Bangaram, one of the uninhabited islands, provides facilities for water sports in the fair (non-monsoon) season.

Potentially, the archipelago could offer good facilities for cruising in the crystal-clear waters of the lagoons, for watching coral and numerous varieties of fish from glass-bottom boats, for deep-sea fishing, and bathing on uncrowded, even lonely, beaches.

However, till facilities are fully developed, it is essential that the intending visitor should ascertain the current situation and availability of accommodation, etc., from *Secretary to the Administrator, Lakshadweep, Harbour Road, Cochin 3, Kerala.*

Chinese-style fishing nets, Cochin, said to have come to Kerala with traders from the Kublai Khan court.

A FESTIVAL A DAY

On almost every day of the year, there is a festival in some part of India — Inevitable perhaps, given the thousands of deities, saints, prophets and gurus named by six major religions who must be worshipped, propitiated, offered thanks or simply remembered.

No dichotomy exists between the sacred and the secular. The vitality of deep religious belief is enhanced by an exuberant celebration of life. Color and pageant merge with ritual, spontaneous enjoyment with worship. And festivals become important social events: occasions to meet and exchange news, to contract marriages and shop for little luxuries, to feast on traditional delicacies, and to share in the exhilaration of a community gathering.

Naturally, a large number of Indian festivals stem from Hinduism. A myriad cults and subcults, an enormous body of legend and historical events, bring an extensive range of significance and association to most major Hindu religious occasions.

Dussera commemorates both the victory of the warrior-goddess Durga (consort of Shiva) over the buffalo-demon, Mahiasura, and that of Rama a god-king (an incarnation of Vishnu), over Ravana, the ten-headed king of Lanka, who had abducted Rama's wife, Sita. Worship of the goddess is the older tradition, particularly significant in this case as it represents the female deity's supremacy over the male gods who were unable to destroy the demon.

Navratri is a nine-day festival, when the goddess is venerated as the supreme mother. Images installed in homes are worshipped every day and *kathas* (stories) are told. In Gujarat, women dance the *garba* with swaying steps and rhythmic clapping around an earthen lamp, while, in the south, girls sing and dance around a pitcher crowned with a coconut symbolizing the goddess.

In Bengal, the main festivals are *Kali Puja* and *Durga Puja*. During this time rituals at the Mahakali Temple in Calcutta and other Kali-Durga temples attract large crowds.

In Durga Puja praises to the *devi* are sung and much cultural activity is initiated. On the 10th day, buffaloes representing Mahisasura are ritually slaughtered and offered to the goddess. Household and communal images of Durga are then taken out in procession and immersed.

Durga worship also has social implications. As goddess of war, she is a particular favorite of the Kshatriyas, the warrior caste, once constituting the ruling elite and aristocracy. After the sacrifice on the 10th day, it was customary to embark on the season's military campaigns. Today this is symbolically re-enacted in the magnificent Dussera processions of Mysore and Jaipur. The erstwhile ruler, seated in state on an elephant, rides in glittering procession from the center of the city to a point just outside its gate. Trumpets blare and war drums boom. Richly caparisoned elephants, soldiers in ceremonial uniforms and nobles in traditional attire are in attendance.

Meanwhile preparations are being completed for the evening's spectacle commemorating Rama's victory symbolizing the triumph of good over evil in his ten-day battle against Ravana. Over nine evenings the epic story (the *Ramalila*) has been narrated or presented in dramatic form. On the 10th night comes the climax: colorful effigies of Ravana, complete with curling mustaches and princely ornaments, his son and his brother, are burnt, setting off a fusillade of crackers — and good is established for another year.

Continuing the story of Rama, *Diwali* or Dipawali (literally a row of lights) is celebrated 20 days after Dussera. It commemorates the hero-king's return from voluntary exile undertaken to fulfil a father's rash vow. Twinkling oil lamps *(divas)*, replaced latterly by candles or even electric bulbs, light up every home, symbolizing the lifting of spiritual darkness. Fireworks explode in a riot of noise and color. Ritual devolves on the worship of Laxmi (consort of Vishnu), goddess of wealth and prosperity, of whom Sita was an incarnation. The beginning of a new financial year, Diwali is particularly significant for traders and businessmen. Old books are closed, new accounts opened and there is a general emphasis on a fresh beginning.

Festival of Holi

Laxmi is a fastidious goddess, averse to dirt and squalor. Houses are spring-cleaned to ensure her favor. City homes are whitewashed, while in villages walls are freshly plastered with insulating and antiseptic cowdung paste. Decorative designs are painted on floors and

Preceding pages, Krishna plays Holi (Kangra School, c.1780); *Garba Ras,* Gujarati folk dance. Child dressed to play the part of Ram during the Dussera festival, left.

walls. New clothes are bought, families gather and sweets are distributed.

On the day after the full moon in early March, the whole country goes wild in a celebration of the festival of *Holi*. People throng the streets, smearing each other with brightly hued powder *(gulal)* or squirting colored water on all within reach. Marijuana-based *bhang* or *thandai*, traditionally eaten or drunk during Holi, adds to the relaxation of the usual restraints of propriety and a general atmosphere of hilarity prevails.

Originally a fertility festival, later legends have ascribed varied origins to Holi. One speaks of a king so arrogant that he demanded that his people worship him. Only his young son, Praladh, dared refuse. Attempts to kill the prince failed. Finally his father's sister

memoration of Kama's destruction and resurrection by Shiva. To rouse in the ascetic god a passion for the maiden Uma, Kama loosened his flowery shaft at him. Enraged at this disturbance of his meditation, Shiva reduced Kama to ashes, but later succumbed to Uma's charms. Subsequently, on Rati's pleading, he relented and restored Kama to his beloved. Holi songs of the south dwell on Rati's distress.

Honoring the Gods

The day after Holi, the sleepy town of Anantpur in Punjab comes to life with boisterous Sikh war games. Mock battles, tent-pegging, archery and fencing, organized by the blue-and-saffron-clad Nihangs is the major at-

Holika, said to be immune to burning, sat with the boy in a huge fire. So potent was Praladh's devotion, that he emerged unscathed while Holika burnt to death. Huge bonfires are lit on the eve of Holi in symbolic commemoration, and the grain of the harvest is thrown into the flames.

The playing of Holi is closely associated with the Radha-Krishna story. In Vraj, legendary homeland of the pastoral god, the festival is spread over 16 days. Apart from the usual fun with *gulal* and colored water, there are colorful processions with much music, song and uninhibited dance, and boisterous scenes in and around the temples.

Kama, god of love, and his consort, Rati (passion), are also worshipped on Holi in com-

traction of the day.

Vishnu is invoked in his human incarnations as Rama and Krishna on their birth anniversaries in the festivals of *Ramanaumi* and *Janamasthami* respectively. Thousands of pilgrims converge on the temples of Ayodhya and Pondicherry, which are closely connected with the events of the *Ramayana,* to participate in Ramanaumi festivities. Colorful processions are held carrying images of Rama, Sita, the epitome of self-sacrificing Indian womanhood, his loyal brother Laxman and Hanuman, Rama's monkey general.

Janamasthami is particularly extravagantly recalled in the temples around Vrindavan. The *Rasalila* is performed to recreate incidents in Krishna's life. Midnight birth ceremonials center on the ritual bathing of the image of the divine infant. It is placed in a silver cradle and toys are offered for its diversion and songs of intense personal devotion and love are sung. Similar ceremonies take place at all Krishna temples, especially those of Rajasthan and Gujarat.

The anniversary of Krishna's birth is known as *Govinda* in Maharashtra. Devotion is expressed in exuberant enactments of the god's childhood endeavors to reach pots of curds and butter placed out of his reach. *Matkas* (earthen pots) containing his favorite foods are suspended between buildings high above the street. Groups of young men form human pyramids, rising six and even seven tiers, till one is able to reach and break the *matka*. As

images. Different areas vie with one another to produce the biggest, most impressive idols. Elaborate arrangements for lighting, decoration, devotional singing and cultural activity are organized for the two to 10 days during which Ganesh is fervently worshipped. In the days of the freedom movement, when British laws often prohibited political gatherings, the nationalist leader, Tilak, used this and other festivals to arouse feelings of nationalism. On *Ganesh Chaturthi,* the last of the days dedicated to Ganesh, thousands of processions converge on Chowpatty beach, bringing their images with them for immersion. Drums beat and devotees dance and sing nostalgically, calling upon the god to return early next year.

The night of Shiva, *Shivaratri,* occurs on a moonless night in February or March. This is

the contents include coins there is an added incentive.

The God of Wisdom

Ganesha, elephant-headed son of Parvati and leader of Shiva's attendants, is widely venerated as the vivacious and munificent god of wisdom. The festival in his honor reaches its peak in Bombay. Preparations begin months in advance. Domestic figurines are installed and so are spectacular community

Left, festival participants at Madurai; and right, durga image immersion at Calcutta.

the night on which the great god of destruction, performed the *tandav,* the dance of primordial creation, preservation and destruction. A fast nd a night-long vigil are considered particularly meritorious on Shivaratri. Temple bells ring, sacred texts are chanted, traditional offerings of bilwa leaves and milk are offered to the *lingum,* the phallic symbol of the god. Major Shiva temples all over the country are inundated with devotees. Large *melas* (fairs) spring up near the temple sites to cater to the needs of worshippers.

Merry Melas

Secular asides to major festivals, *melas* or fairs are also held during more localized religious occasions and are important regional events. People come from miles around to buy and to sell, for fun and relaxation. One of the best-known festival fairs is held at Pushkar in Rajasthan on the eighth day after Diwali. Religious activity centers on bathing in the lake, one of the most sacred places of the Hindus. On the secular side, the fair has become the annual market for livestock from all over Rajasthan. Horses, camels, cows, bullocks, even sheep and goats, all decorated with elaborate halters, exchange hands. Bullock-cart and camel races add to the excitement. Wandering minstrels, puppeteers and entertainers of every kind mingle with crowds decked in traditional rural finery. And little shops sell handcrafted rural wares.

Similar fairs are held at other hallowed sites.

each divine day is equivalent to 12 earth years the cycle was established. One *ardh* (half) *kumbha* occurs every six years.

The extensive riverbed draws crowds unparalleled anywhere else in the world. Heads are representatives of all Hindu sects participate. The prospect of their *darshan,* of the benedictory act of *seeing* them, is an added attraction.

Celebrating the Seasons

Some Hindu festivals are connected with the annual cycle of the seasons. Nationwide festivities mark the beginning of the northward journey of the sun. *Pongal* or *Sankranti* in the south marks the withdrawal of the southeast monsoon as well as the reaping of the harvest.

There is the Bhakteshwar fair near Agra, where the Yamuna flows from south to north; the Garh Mukteshwar mela 60 km from Delhi and dozens of others. At Sonpur in Bihar, brisk buying and selling of elephants enhances local color.

The greatest and most important of Hindu fairs, the *Kumbha Mela,* is held every sixth and 12th year at Prayag (Allahabad). The city's supreme sanctity as the confluence *(sangam)* of the Ganga, Yamuna and the mythical Saraswati, is accentuated by the story behind the gathering. After wresting the jar *(kumbha)* of immortal nectar from the *asuras* (demons), a god in the form of a rook flew with it to paradise. Prayag was one of the places where he rested. The journey took 12 days. Since

Festivities are spread over several days. A general spring cleaning and the burning of accumulated junk on household bonfires before the festival symbolizes the destruction of evil. Beautiful *kilars* (decorative designs) are traced on floors with moistened rice flour. On Pongal day, the new rice of the harvest is ritualistically cooked till it boils over to joyous cries acclaiming the bounty of the gods.

The next day, *Mattu Pongal* or *Jellikattu* is dedicated to the cattle. Bathed, decorated and sumptuously fed, they are paraded through the village. Bulls are stampeded down

Sikhs celebrate Baishaki — doing the *bhangra dance.*

narrow lanes and the fun begins. They are faced by daring young men who leap at their horns to wrest the money tied in bundles around them and for the garlands of rupee notes often strung around their necks.

Meanwhile the people of Ahmedabad have their eyes fixed to the sky. It is *Makar Sankranti,* the kite festival. The entire city participates actively or vicariously in the skills of kite fighting. From dawn to dusk the sky glitters with fluttering color. As night falls, little oil lamps attached to kites multiply the stars.

Other harvest festivals include the Assamese *Ranguli Bihu.* Rituals are performed for the welfare of the herds and for a good harvest and young men collect orchids for the maidens of their choice. In the evening Bihu drums throb, love songs are sung, and graceful folk dances are frankly sensual.

Temple Festivals

Each Hindu temple has an annual festival in honor of the particular deity it enshrines. These are especially elaborate and colorful in the southern and eastern parts of the country, where more ancient shrines have survived the iconoclastic destruction that occurred elsewhere. Continuity was thus maintained in the prominence of the local deity, and the form and location of its worship. Spread over several days, these festivals are important regional events. People from neighboring towns and villages gather to pay homage to the god or goddess, with whom they have had close cultural, racial and religious ties for centuries.

The marriage of the local goddess Meenakshi to Lord Sundareswara (Shiva) is celebrated for several days every year at the magnificent Meenakshi Temple in Madurai. Appropriate rituals leading to the nuptials culminate in a spectacular procession. The goddess and her divine husband riding a golden bull (Shiva's mount) are carried through the city in elaborately carved temple chariots.

Another spectacular Madurai festival is the *Floating Festival,* commemorating the birth of Tirumala Nayak, a 17th-Century king. Elaborately decked images are taken in procession to a tank outside the city and installed there in an ornamented barge illuminated by thousands of lamps.

The *Pooram* festival at Trichur in Kerala honors Lord Vatakunnathan (Shiva) in the temple dedicated to the god. Friendly rivalry between two groups culminates in a parasol display. Richly caparisoned elephants carry the ceremonial umbrellas with much rhythmic fanning with yak-tail and peacock-feather whisks. They flank the elephant carrying the temple image and go round the temple to the sound of traditional musical instruments.

Farther east, at Puri in Orissa, a major temple festival celebrates Lord Jagannath. Considered a living manifestation of Krishna, the unfinished and crude image is invested with tremendous sanctity and draws huge crowds for the annual festivities. The high point is the drawing of the temple deities through the city to their country residence. Temple images of the god and his brother and sister are placed on giant chariots *(raths)* which are then drawn by pilgrims. An atmosphere of almost hysterical devotion prevails. In earlier years devotees were known to have thrown themselves under the wheels of the *rath* in the hope of obtaining instant salvation.

Onam, an unusual and important Kerala festival, reveres the memory of a local demon king, Mahabali, who was ousted from his kingdom by Vishnu. So attached was the king to his country and subjects, that he was granted permission to return once a year. Houses are cleaned, floral decorations constructed to welcome the beloved ruler. Songs are sung of the happy days of his reign, various sports are arranged for his amusement. Snake boats manned by around a hundred oarsmen each rowing to the rhythm of cymbals and drums race in thrilling contests at Aranmula, Champakulam and Kottayam. Competitions of *thallu,* a local martial art, are also organized. In Trichur a colorful procession with resplendently caparisoned elephants is taken out.

Associated with Shiva as well as Vishnu, snakes are considered immortal by orthodox Hindus and are worshipped on *Naga Panchami.* Milk and flowers are offered to live cobras and at snake shrines, while snake charmers demand their tithe. Hundreds of snakes are released by trappers at Shiva temples in Varanasi and Ujjain. Worshippers pour milk over themselves to ensure lifelong immunity to snake-bite.

Tribal Festivals

Celebrating the sun god and local deities, most tribal festivals retain much of the ancient racial traditions. The harvest, hunting expeditions, marriage and other social events are welcome opportunities for an unsophisticated expression of joy. Quantities of local brew are imbibed and feasting is followed by dancing, some of which is quite intricate and highly skilled. The focus in most festivals is on a medium, who, possessed by the spirits of the dead, enthralls the people with pronouncements both spiritual and material.

Non-Hindu Festivals

India's immense religious and cultural diversity is evident in the large number of non-Hindu festivals, celebrated with tremendous fervor, enthusiasm and the external manifestations peculiar to each. Islamic festal events occurring throughout the year range from major festivals to localized *urs* held at tombs of various Muslim saints. Visits to mosques, much feasting, visiting, and the donning of new clothes, mark all Muslim festivals. But there is little to actually see except at Muharram, which is not a festival in the celebratory sense as it mourns the murder at Karbala of Imam Hussain, grandson of the prophet. Despite their connotation of grief, the memorial processions are colorful and dramatic.

Profusely decorated and vividly hued *taziahs*, bamboo and paper replicas of the martyr's tomb, embellished with gilt and mica, with domes that revolve in the breeze, are carried through city streets with the green *alam* or standard of Hussain. A frenzied beating of drums and the wail of wind instruments mingle with songs of praise and lamentation. Wrestlers and dancers enact scenes depicting the battle of Karbala and at each step young men beat their breasts crying "Hussain! Hussain!" in collective sorrow. Processions are particularly splendid in Agra, Lucknow, Delhi and Hyderabad, while at Baragaon, near Jaunpur, commemorative ceremonial is particularly extravagant.

Buddha Jayanti, the birth anniversary of the Buddha, is widely celebrated. But this and other Buddhist festivals have less visual interest than the lamaistic festivals of the Himalayan states. Celebrations commemorating the birth of Padmasambhava at the Hemis Gompa in Ladakh and in Towang in Arunachal Pradesh are alive with folk vitality. Ritual dances represent the ancient shamanistic evil spirits in conflict with the powerful deities that developed in Mahayana Buddhism to subdue them. Grotesque masks worn by the dancers symbolize the power and fearsome ability of the deities as well as the malignancy of the demons. Bright robes and swirling emphatic movements create a tremendous impact.

Jainism, with its preoccupation with the sad reality of life and emphasis on salvation does not lend itself to outward spectacle and gaiety. Religious events such as the birth of Mahavira, its founder, are largely observed in quiet prayer. *Deep Diwali,* however, marking Mahavira's liberation from the cycle of life, is celebrated 10 days after Diwali. Illuminations are said to be an endeavor to mitigate the darkness caused by the passing of the "light of the world" and are particularly splendid at Mount Girnar near Junagadh.

Celebrated every 15 years at Shravana Belgola in Karnataka, the ceremonial anointing of the colossal image of Gomateshwara, a prince turned ascetic, is also a major Jain communal event. Scaffolding is erected for the ceremony and the image is "bathed" in 16 traditional precious substances which include gems, gold and silver.

The festivals of the Parsis too are not outwardly demonstrative. *Pateti,* their *New Year* and *Jamshedji Navroz,* two major festivals, occasion visits to the fire temple and prayer. Secular manifestations involve the usual socializing, feasting and the wearing of new clothes.

Christian festivals in India follow the same basic patterns as elsewhere, with a few interesting differences, particularly among the Syrian Christians. Obviously influenced by local Hindu tradition, elephants, umbrellas and traditional music are important accessories.

Catholic Goa comes to life with the *Carnival* preceding the Lental period of penance. Similar to Mardi Gras, it is a boisterous event. A carnival parade, full of color and movement, presided over by Momo, king of the underworld, is accompanied by much drinking, song and dance.

Left, an Independence Day parade; and, right, effigy of Ravana — destined to go up in flames at the end of the festival.

In India, dance and music are all pervading, bringing color and joy to numerous festivals and ceremonies, and reaffirming the faith of the people in their heritage. The tradition of the performing arts in India has its roots in age-old texts — the *Vedas,* in which ritual manifested itself through music, dance and drama.

The *Natyashastra,* an ancient treatise on dramaturgy, explains that when written texts became the sole prerogative of an educated few, the gods appealed to Brahma, the Creator, to promulgate a fifth Veda, in the form of audiovisual art, that would be accessible to all, irrespective of caste or formal education. Thus the *Natya Veda* was conceived, drawing for content and teaching from the other four *vedas* and presenting the quintessence of all the arts, whether literature, sculpture, music, painting or dance.

In India, religion, philosophy and myth cannot be divorced from their art forms. Dance and music are tied inextricably to ceremony of any kind. Weddings, births, coronations, entering a new house or town, welcoming a guest, religious processions, harvest time — any or all of these are occasions for song and dance.

Indian music and dance demand a spirit of devotion and of total surrender. For the physical is transitory and easily transmuted, while a sincere practice of the arts can achieve the highest spiritual experience.

Classical Dance Forms

Spontaneity, intuition and the joy of life are the soul of dance and music and the quest of every artist. Her endeavor is to search for the ultimate in perfection of body and mind through these art forms. Rukmini Devi, a pioneer and one of the most renowned figures in the world of performing art in India, has said: "The keynote of good art is when its message does not merely appeal to the senses and through them to a purely external enjoyment, but to the soul of the artiste and of the perceiver."

India offers not one, but several well-defined classical dance forms. Each of these has been nurtured in a different part of the country and has taken on the hue and texture of its region. Each represents an entire culture, the ethos of a people and a personalized artistic signature. Chief among them and at present the most popular classical styles of

dance seen on the stage are Bharata Natyam of Tamil Nadu, Odissi of Orissa, Kathakali of Kerala, Kuchipudi of Andhra Pradesh, Kathak of Lucknow and Jaipur and Manipuri of Manipur. But these are not all. Several other forms of traditional dance that fall into the category of semi-classical, folk, drama, and martial arts, contribute to the panorama of dance in India. Today the major styles are performed all over the country and not exclusively by people from the regions of their origin. Together, these styles offer a large variety in costume, in richness of literary content, in beauty of musical mode and instrumental accompaniment, and in variation of theme and creative scope.

The Fundamentals

Indian dance is based upon the concepts of *nritta* and *nrittya,* of *raga* and *tala,* of *hastas* and *nayaka-nayika bhav,* and of the *guru-shishya parampara* (guru–disciple tradition) — the common foundation of all its major forms resting on the authority of ancient and revered texts, numerous temple sculptures and frescoes, and in the myth and legend of the land.

Nritta is pure dance. It is abstract movement that signifies beauty. It is performed in union with rhythm and expresses human ecstasy very simply. *Nrittya* on the other hand is expressional, the enactment of a theme. Here, the dancer is aided by *sahitya* or verse; by *hastas* which are gestures of the hands, each representing a word, a phrase or an idea; and by *abhinaya,* or facial expression. In combining these with music, a "language" is established, so that the viewer sees words fly off the tips of the dancer's fingers, each moment reflected in her eyes and in her smile. This capacity for expression is a unique feature of Indian dance.

Raga is the musical mode of an item, a melodic base with rules governing its elaboration and yet allowing for improvisation. The *raga* decides the mood of a situation and governs its emotional impact. *Tala,* on the other hand, is the heartbeat of a song, a time cycle that weaves itself through the music, reining it in, conserving its strength yet lending it mood and character.

For generations, all this, and more, has been invested in the hands of *gurus,* the traditional preceptors. They were the receptacles of knowledge and transferred it orally, demanding, in return, a high degree of faith and loyalty from the student. Ideally, the guru represents for the *shishya* (student) the personification of his art form. This one-to-one relationship, of God and devotee, of parent and child, of master and disciple, derives from the *guru–shishya parampara* and is a central concept of Indian culture.

Myth and Legend for a Theme

Indian dance forms take their themes from India's rich mythology related to the Hindu battlefield of Kurukshetra. Krishna's childhood is described in the *Puranas* and he figures also in the *Mahabharata,* an epic of enormous proportions that provides an endless variety of moral themes, characters and incidents for expositions in dance form.

Each style draws liberally on stories that depict the life, folklore, ethics, and beliefs of the people of India. Like Hindu philosophy, they explore life and nature and man's interaction with them. Much of the thematic content of Indian dance thus reflects, on the spiritual level, man's interaction with God, and

pantheon and from a variety of folk legends. Vishnu, the Protector, in his 10 incarnations, is perhaps the most popular deity depicted in classical Indian dance. His consort is Lakshmi, goddess of beauty and wealth. She reappears as Sita and Radha, as consort to two of his later incarnations. Rama, Vishnu's seventh incarnation, is celebrated, along with his consort Sita, in the epic, *Ramayana,* a rich source of themes and anecdotes for presentation in Indian dance. Another popular incarnation is the colorful Krishna, beloved of Radha, and charioteer and counselor to Arjuna on the

on the human level, his relationship with other men or women.

Nayaka–nayika bhav, the "hero-heroine" concept in Indian dance provides inexhaustible scope for the representation of the man–woman theme, presenting a variety of shades as it changes with the age, experience, physical attributes and moods of the people portrayed.

Bharata Natyam and Kathakali

Bharata Natyam is Tamil Nadu's most celebrated art form, a tradition that demands of the dancer a detachment from wordly ties, a sublimation of the self to the deity and her

Flutist accompanied by *tablas* and *tanpura.*

art. Such *devadasis,* "servants of God," carried a temple tradition forward, till patronage shifted to the hands of the landed aristocracy who marked them with the stigma of courtesanship.

Bharata Natyam is a dynamic, earthy and extremely precise dance style. It is built upon a balanced distribution of body weight and firm positions of the lower limbs, allowing the hands to cut into a line, to flow around the body, or to take positions that enhance the basic form. *Padams,* poems on the hero–heroine theme, are a special feature of expressional dance that allows the dancer great scope for the enactment of a theme. The tempo of these love songs is slow and each phrase is crystallized into a specific mood and aspect of love.

Odissi and Kathak

The ambience of Orissa, the philosophy of Lord Jagannath and the sculpture of the 13th-Century Sun Temple of Konarak, are reflected in its dance form — Odissi. Perhaps the most lyrical style of dance in India, Odissi follows unique body norms; the iconography of a whole culture is echoed in its structure. The *tribhanga,* a three-bend posture, interlinking a people's philosophy with the physical, is a series of triangles which are not only physically difficult to execute, but which also call for immense restraint and finesse on the part of the artist. The numerous postures of the style reflect specific moods and adorn the carved panels of the Konarak Sun Temple.

Popular devotion to Sri Krishna is embodied

Kathakali is the most developed dance drama art of India. In Kerala, the drums roll, beckoning an audience to a spectacle most magnificent. Here, the actors depict characters from the *Puranas* and from the *Mahabharata* — superhuman beings, demons and ordinary men and women. The dancers, all males, adorn themselves in huge skirts and headdress, wearing what must surely be the most intricate make-up known to any dance style anywhere in the world. Dialogue is combined with dance to bring myth and legend to life in the temple courtyards of Kerala. So strong is the identification of the dancers with the characters they play, so absolute is their conviction, that they seem to surpass themselves and display an incredible level of histrionic skill.

in Jayadeva's unique Sanskrit love poem, *Geet Govind,* and its verses are interpreted by every representative of Orissa's culture, whether he be a singer, dancer or devotee.

Waves of influence of various cultures have traversed India's northern plains, giving Kathak its Hindu-Muslim texture, and its exciting and entertaining quality. The *kathak* or storyteller of yore was a versatile actor-musician-dancer who addressed himself directly to his audience, throwing a web of verse and verve over them. Involved and complicated footwork and rapid pirouettes are the dominant and most endearing features of this style. Long strings of bells are tied around the ankles of the dancer and a whole gamut of rhythmic patterns are woven into a chosen time cycle.

Balance, poise and control are strong requisites for this exacting art. Traditionally the nautch dance of the courts, Kathak reflects a simplicity and vigor that is visually most attractive.

Manipuri

Protected for years in a valley of exceeding beauty, Manipuri is the art expression of every man, woman and child of Manipur. The musical forms of that culture reflect the worship of Vishnu. It is around episodes from his life that the faith of the people is entwined. The *sankirtan* and the *raas* are revered musical traditions enacted appropriately at different times of the year by the community as a whole.

Manipuri is not aggressive. It is tender and

almost reticent on the one hand, and extremely vigorous on the other. A continuity of movement and a restraint of power are underlying features of the style.

Music, the Soul of Dance

All these dance styles depend upon music for their sustenance, for music is the soul of dance. *Nada* (sound) is believed to be the very process of creation and ancient verses from the

Left, *garba ras,* folk dance from Gujarat. Above, left, male Kuchipudi dancer; and, right, Bharata Natyam.

holy scriptures were chanted in a special manner, peculiar to India. This tradition continues and is a form of meditation, of concentration and of worship.

Indian music has its traditional origins in the *Sama Veda,* an age-old text. It is believed that a musical scale, aesthetics in music, basic rhythm, and a system of notation, all go back to this ancient exposition of their principles.

Indian classical music is broadly divided into two systems, commonly described as the Hindustani and Karnatak systems. Hindustani music is practiced in North India and Karnatak music in South India. As in the case of the dance styles, their heritage and philosophy is a common one; their base and general structure is the same. Their *ragas* however, are usually different, and they have unique methods of articulation and treatment, even when they present the same *raga*. While Karnatak music remained untouched by foreign influences, the same cannot be said of Hindustani music, which surely felt the influence of Persian and Central Asian music after invasions and migrations from those areas.

Raga and Tala

Indian music, as mentioned earlier, is built on a subtle combination of *raga* and *tala*. *Raga* is an aesthetic and emotional rendering of a scale of notes. It is a melodic mode having rigid conditions that govern its elaboration; yet it is capable of infinite improvisation. *Ragas* have specific moods and flavors and a given *raga* may be sung only during a particular season of the year, or at a specific time of the day or night.

Ragas have an inbuilt harmony and are, in fact, not a rendering of mere notes, but a rendering of *swaras,* which are notes that have the frequency of the human voice. This is why pride of place in Indian music was often given to vocalists rather than'to instrumentalists. However, this attitude is no longer as common as it used to be, thanks to the amazing skill of great contemporary instrumentalists. An instrumentalist's constant endeavor is nevertheless to match the inflexions of the human voice with his instrument and in this achievement lies his greatness. The instrument he uses

into minute pulses, the crisscross patterns, the regular and off-beat emphasis of time, the running together of two contrary cycles meeting creatively at a point, offer a regularity that calms the mind and an excitement that heightens mood.

North Indian Music

North India offers a variety of forms of music like the *dhruvapada, khyal, thumari, tappa* and *ghazal.* Each of these has a specific history of development and the lay listener may not be able to identify the particular form. Such identification requires some familiarity with the school from which the particular vocalist or instrumentalist hails, or an

thus becomes an extension of himself. A *raga* leaves one unmoved if the spirit of the artist does not come through in the mood being attempted.

Tala, on the other hand, binds music together. It is a time cycle that remains fixed throughout a particular rendering. Romantically, it is believed to be the divine fusion of the masculine and feminine forms of dance. The *tala* repeats itself in cyclic regularity, offering amazing dimensions for improvisation between beats. One witnesses the virtuosity of percussionists who render extremely complex variations within these cycles. *Tala* is the pulse of Indian music. To listen to the interplay of *tala* with musical phrases is a fascinating experience. The division of time

understanding of the structure of these forms.

The *dhruvapada* is a strictly classical and slow form. The *khyal* incorporates into this rigidity the romanticism of yet another form, the *thumari.* This is why, for a casual listener, it is perhaps simpler to appreciate a *khyal* than a *dhruvapada,* without exactly knowing why, since all these forms follow the same basic tenets of the *raga-tala* system. The *khyal* is perhaps the most widely performed form of classical music in North India. The *thumari* is used quite extensively to accompany Kathak.

Kathakali dancer depicting Hanuman, the monkey god.

This is because it incorporates in itself a high degree of emotional and aesthetic content, speaking, as it were, from the heart. The *tappa* is a lighter form of classical music that is brisk and replete with a variety of phrases, which makes it difficult to render without adequate virtuosity.

North Indian music has a wide range of ancient and beautiful instruments, each having a tonal quality quite unique. Some of the more well-known are the *sitar,* the *sarod,* the *rudravina,* the *santoor,* the flute, the *shehnai* and the *saarangi.* Among the percussion instruments are the *tabla* and *pakhawaj.* The *tabla* is used in accompaniment of most music recitals. The *pakhawaj* has a deeper tone than the *tabla.*

A word often heard in relation to North Indian music is *gharana,* literally meaning "house." This word is used to denote the house of a specific school of music. The nomenclature arose in the days when artists were retained in the courts of particular princes, thereby confining the area of their performances and their training of disciples. Some of the better known among these *gharanas* are those of Gwalior, Agra, Delhi and Jaipur.

South Indian Sounds

South Indian music, Karnatak music as it is called, differs from the Hindustani in its stricter adherence to structure, thereby shifting the emphasis away from improvisation within that structure. The musician of the South adheres very firmly to his composition and even more firmly to the *tala* cycle. *Ragas* in the South mostly have Sanskrit names, unlike in the North, where their names often come from specific regions or from the dialects of regions.

A certain rigidity marks recitals of Karnatak music, and *bhakti* or devotion, is its mainstay. Karnatak music is therefore deeply spiritual. It was blessed with a plethora of greatly devoted composers and musicians. The literary content of the *kritis,* or songs, are in the form of offerings. The immortal Trinity of Karnatak music are Thyagaraja, Shyama Sastry, and Dikshitar, whose compositions are widely sung. Every great musician maintains the purity of the original structure of these compositions, but embellishes them with ornamentation peculiar to his skill or to the scope of his instrument.

The flute, the violin, the *veena,* the *nadaswaram* and the *gottuvadyam* are among the most well-known South Indian instruments. The *mridangam, ghatam* and *ganjira* are the most loved and widely heard percussion instruments.

Viewing a Concert the Correct Way

Watching an Indian music concert heightens the pleasure of listening to it. This is because the Indian musician tries to "speak" to his audience. Perhaps unconsciously, he uses his hands and fingers to express himself. These actions help to spell out his thoughts, and bring into focus the intricate pattern of his creative process. A small venue, with a restricted gathering of interested people, is the ideal setting for an Indian dance or music recital. Informality tends to a deeper appreciation of the artist's endeavor. At close proximity, one is able to share some of the emotional involvement of the artist in the presentation. A closer rapport enhances mood and intensifies the *rasa,* the flavor, experienced both by the artist and the audience collectively.

It is wrong to believe that the classical arts of India are rigidly bound by rules, regulations and ancient traditions. The *Shastras,* the holy texts, merely laid down the framework and the boundaries of these art forms. Practice, research, experience and intuition make for a continuity in the arts, giving them a living tradition. Truly gifted artists soar into this world of creativity where no conflict exists between the past and the present, and where the pursuit of happiness is a subordination of the self. Technique and talent do not lift one from the temporal. The god of dance, Nataraja, brought body and soul together, thereby unifying the heavens and the earth.

No account of what India has to offer by way of music and dance can be complete without a mention of at least some of the other classical, semi-classical, folk, martial art, and drama traditions. Kuchipudi of Andhra Pradesh and the Bhagavata Mela Nataka of Tamil Nadu are solo and group dance drama forms performed originally by men only. Mohini Attam, a sensuous female dance form; Theyyam, a ritualistic art-form; and Kalaripayatu, a superb martial art form, are the treasure of Kerala. Manipur's martial art and wrestling techniques; the strong Chhaw traditions from Seraikella, Mayurbhanj and Purulia; and a host of folk and tribal forms are performed seasonally in the villages scattered over the country.

These spontaneous expressions of rural culture vary in costume, language, instruments, style and zest from one another. Every village has its own festive days, its own peculiar customs, its own favored lyrics, and its own sense of music and dance. To witness and listen to these art forms in their own environment is a special pleasure.

Classical Indian sculpture does not seem as though it were cut and chiselled as much as it seems to grow forth from the rock, organically, like a ripe fruit to be plucked. There does seem to be, too, a remarkable affinity between the figures of tree goddesses and the branches of trees which they embrace — as though the vital sap of energy of life flowed from vegetation into their veins. The *yakshis* embody the trees, as much as the celestial goddesses embody the flow of rivers Ganga and Yamuna. Divinity exists, it is expressed through the elements, the rivers, the mountains, the trees.

Divinity exists as much in a stone. The most obvious instances of this belief are to be seen in the elemental shapes of stones that are enshrined, daubed red and orange and silver, and worshipped with flowers, under the shade of a tree or beside a river. Offerings are made to the *salagrama,* the stone that represents the god Vishnu, to the *tulsi* plant in the garden by the housewife, to the *lingam* which represents Lord Shiva, to the *peepal* tree outside almost every village that represents the local guardian deity.

The inherent continuity of beliefs is remarkable and observed even in the earlier archeological excavations from the Indus Valley of the 2nd and 3rd millennium B.C. Tiny terra-cotta seals introduce *peepal* leaves surrounded with a railing, as though marked sacred. In another seal a horned deity in the yogic posture is enthroned, surrounded by four animals which have earned him the name of *Pashupati,* the Lord of animals. This archaic deity is an early form of the god Shiva, in aspects that are worshipped to the present day.

The mother goddess is molded in clay with pellets building up to an elaborate headdress, necklaces and girdle, to accentuate her breasts and hips — in her role as the earth mother. Through the centuries to the 3rd Century B.C., when other material evidence is mostly lacking, the earth mother continued to be molded and worshipped in terra-cotta — as much as she is today in every village *mata,* in the forms of Durga or Lakshmi being ritually immersed each year in the river, so that earth returns to earth.

Two outstanding objects from the first cities of India depict its cosmopolitan culture. The superb head of a priest in limestone, with its accentuated mongoloid cheekbones and slit eyes is in sharp contrast to the sensuous tribal features of a bronze dancing girl. Although worked on a miniature scale, the figure shows tremendous sophistication in rendering a young tribal girl with slender angular limbs and a pouting face, poised in a moment, as it were, between two dance movements.

Official and Popular Buddhist Art

Much of Indian art is religious in purpose; but we would be mistaken to believe that it is all religious in content. The next chapter of great Indian sculpture opens in the 3rd Century B.C., with the Emperor Ashoka adopting Buddhism as the official religion of the Mauryan Empire. The legend goes that in his zeal to embrace the new religion, he constructed 84,000 stupas (dome-shaped monuments). His edicts were inscribed upon rock and pillar, from Girnar in Gujarat to Tiruchirapalli in the far south, in Tamil Nadu. The lion capital at Sarnath, now the official emblem of the Indian Republic, gleams in polished sandstone, representing the hieratic art and the political aspirations of the empire. Originally surmounted by the *dharmachakra,* the sacred wheel of the law that refers to the Buddha's sermon, these pillars were actually worshipped, as we witness in later reliefs at Sanchi. Thus, homage was paid by the populace both to the Buddha and to the empire.

A more persuasive, natural art was that in terra-cotta — not only of the mother goddess, but of urban ladies from Tamluk in Bengal or Pataliputra in Bihar, replete with elaborate headgear and, of course, that indispensable item, jewelry. There are also terra-cotta plaques depicting *mithunas* or couples, seated in a loveseat with the group strewn with flowers; or of a young boy writing the alphabet with his chalk on a board. These are evidence of the urban sophistication of the times.

Buddhism did not remain the preserve of the orthodox. To acquire new members of the laity, it had to yield and accept more popular cults and legends. The goddess Sri is beckoned, rising from lotus petals and watered by elephants, as the auspicious omen of wealth and fertility. *Yakshas, yakshis* and *nagas,* the familiar tree spirits and water spirits, are now established as the guardian deities on railposts which encircle the *stupas.* Their names are inscribed, and although divine, they appear sometimes in the form of local tribal men and women. From Barhut we encounter the unexpected, sensuous face of a Koli girl, with tattoo marks on the face and flowers braided through her hair.

The foundations of the Great Stupa at Sanchi were first built by the Emperor Ashoka, along with his edict and pillar that now lies in the site museum. Monasteries were set up here as a retreat from the hectic city life of Vaishali, seven miles (11 km) away. Here, on an open hill rising above the city sounds, in touch with the sun and sky and the elements, there is tranquillity. Even today the visitor senses that he is on a pilgrimage, as he takes the ritual path of circumambulation around the stupa — following the course of the sun through the heavens, with the four gateways *(toranas)* to the east, west, north and south marking out the four directions.

These gateways were carved in the 1st Century A.D. with reliefs depicting the Buddha as

tain reluctance to represent him except through symbols: the *Bodhi-tree* with which he so closely associated himself, the *dharmachakra* which he used by way of analogy in explaining the righteous path, the *stupa* which enshrined his mortal remains. Later, interest shifts to the story of his life. In sculptures of northwest India and Gandhara (now in Afghanistan), these scenes acquired a heightened degree of pathos and realism, believed to have been borrowed from Roman reliefs.

A cult image of the Buddha became essential for acts of ritual worship. How else was he to be represented but in the form of man? And if he was to be rendered in human form, and he was divine, how was his divinity to be expressed? These were basic questions that seem to have obsessed the sculptors at Mathura and

a prince, his moment of enlightenment at Bodhgaya, his sermon at the deer park, miracles, and conversion of the serpent king, the gods in paradise and the acolytes at the *ashram.* Mirrored through these reliefs that shimmer with light as the sun moves around the *stupa,* there is experienced a tremendous joy in nature and an affinity with all creatures of the earth.

In the 1st Century A.D. the position changed radically in art — to focus almost entirely on the human figure. The Buddha, meaning 'the Enlightened One,' came to represent one of the highest aspirations of human thought and art. Originally, at Sanchi, there was a cer-

Miniature of the Basholi school.

Gandhara, when they evolved the anthropomorphic image of Shakyamuni, the royal prince of the Sakya clan who became the savior of mankind.

To emphasize the Buddha's divinity, certain *lakshanas* or signs were described upon his person: the *urna* between the eyes, the *ushnisha* rising from the head, the *dharmachakra* incised upon the palms of his hands and the soles of his feet, the halo that spelt illumination, the lion throne that implied his royal ancestry. When he sat, it was in the yogic pose of meditation, when he spoke it was with a gesture of the hand that said "do-not-fear." These early images of the Buddha are awe-inspiring, in terms of sheer size and physical presence. It has been shown by the great scholar Coomaraswamy that they were inspired by the colossal cult images of the 1st and 2nd centuries B.C. such as the Parkham Yaksha near Mathura, and the Besnagar Yaksha, towering to a height of 14 feet.

By the 5th Century, a different sensibility is evident. The Buddha is yielding, meditative, with a body so subtle in modelling that it seems insubstantial, with a face that glows with illumination. In the seated Buddha, the body seems to melt away and our eyes are focused upon the exquisite hands unfolding, the gesture of teaching, and on the eyes that are half-closed in introspection. This then becomes the ultimate definition of the divine.

Saviors of Mankind

Buddhism was not the only religion to conceive icons of the deity *(pratima)* for worship. At Mathura, said to be the birthplace of Lord Krishna and the center of the Vaishnava sect, there are powerful images of Balarama, the brother of Krishna; of Surya, the haloed sun god wearing a tunic and boots (as did the Kushan invaders and kings); of Kartikeya designated the lord of war; and of the goddess Mahisha Mardini in her magnificent moment of triumph as, with remarkable composure, she slays the demon buffalo and thus redeems all mankind.

The early centuries A.D. witnessed a tremendous resurgence of Hinduism; more especially when it became the official religion of the Gupta Empire in the 4th, 5th and 6th centuries. The images were then militant. At this point the gods were designated as the great heroes, the saviors of mankind. How else was Hinduism to compete with the reformed sects and win over the faithful?

The most singular monument to this victory is heralded in the colossal image of Lord Vishnu, at the Udaigiri caves just a few miles from the Buddhist monasteries at Sanchi. Here we witness the gods and the sages rejoicing as Vishnu, in his incarnation of the bear Varaha, rescues the tiny, exquisite image of mother earth from the depths of the ocean, to place her securely upon his broad shoulders. An inscription refers to the Gupta emperor, Chandragupta, whose empire extends "from sea to sea" — thus creating a political allegory, to present his ambitions materialized in the image of Lord Vishnu as the great savior.

At the National Museum in Delhi a superb bust of Lord Vishnu from the 5th Century A.D. counterposes a sense of poise that could rival any image of the meditating Buddha. Another bust in the same museum depicts Lord Shiva in his terrifying aspect, his third eye burst open on the forehead, two arms flung wide open holding the *damaru* or drum of destruction as he dances. Yet a profoundly different dimension of the same deity is revealed in the *mukhalingam* from Khoh (Uttar Pradesh) where he is conceived as the supreme *maha-yogi*. The head of Shiva in his ascetic form is superimposed upon his symbol of the phallus — to render an image of ineffable calm, of serenity.

Fusion of the Arts

The link between literature and the visual arts becomes crucial to our understanding of these images. An aesthetic sensibility had evolved that was shared between dance, drama, literature and art.

The celebrated beginning to the ancient text of the *Vishnudharmottaram* describes the predicament of the king who wished to learn the art of painting *(chitra kala)*. He was informed that to paint, to render figures in plastic volume, he must first learn to sculpt. To attempt sculpture, to understand gesture and movement, he must apply himself first to the principles of dance. And to dance he must have recourse to the appreciation of rhythm, of *tala* of instrumental and then vocal music. And music, of course, seeks its inspiration from poetry. Thus the king learnt that to be skilled in one of the arts, he must be informed about all of them.

Nowhere is this fusion of the arts better illustrated than at the caves at Ajanta. Instances of such cave "temples" have survived from the 3rd and 2nd centuries B.C. as a retreat for Buddhist and Jain monks, especially during the monsoon months. At Ajanta itself the earliest *chaitya* hall for a congregation dates back to the 2nd Century B.C. with a simple unadorned stupa set into the apse, to serve as the symbolic image; but with fragments of paintings surviving illustrating the *Saddhanta Jataka*. Gradually, the pillars of the later columnar halls, the capitals, the entire surface of walls in the interior came to be decorated with sculpted and painted figures.

The experience of entering these caves is dramatic. Usually, light enters them from only one source at the entrance, through the giant rose window above the door. As the eyes get used to the darkness, the figures loom larger than life-size, they become palpable and infused with life — "As though breathing" to quote from the *Vishnudharmottaram*. Add to this the sensation of color, defining the figures that are now suffused with a kind of languid flow of movement. Add to this the acoustics of a closed hall, with the sound resonating around the stupa and up to the high ceilings, and the flicker of oil lamps offered in prayer.

The viewer is transported into another state of consciousness where sound and light and color and palpable form are fused into one inseparable reality. Even the ceilings are painted, in magical circles that seem to float upwards and are adorned with a thousand flowers. The experience, then is one of a total wrap-around mystery that transports the pilgrims into another world.

These images are not representations of a clinical reality — not any more than are the figures of the *Dark Princess* or of the *Bodhisattya Padmapani,* looming out of the darkness as a water-lily blooms out of the water. Not any more than the deer and geese and flowers and creepers, the pavilions and processions through gateways are part of the everyday experience of the monks who painted

them. They grow out of the imagination; and yet, occasionally, there is a sudden, unexpected thrill of a portrait, of an old monk that pulls us back to observations from life. It becomes apparent that monasticism in India, although enjoined to celibacy, did not resemble the Christian monasticism of medieval Europe. The monks were free to paint whatever they willed, dreamed or experienced.

Emboldened by drama and poetry, the visual metaphor becomes even more explicit. At the National Museum, Delhi, a life-size image of Ganga, the divine river goddess,

Chola bronze showing Nataraj, Shiva performing the cosmic dance.

depicts her swaying on the aquatic animal, the *makara,* the wet folds of her garment flowing as a river in spate. Profiled, both the river goddesses, Ganga and Yamuna, flank the doorway to the terra-cotta temple at Ahichchatra (Uttar Pradesh), and lead the pilgrim into the shrine.

As much as the iconography of the gods was now defined, so too the temples evolved to a precise locationing of the sculptures. *Dwarapalas* or door guardians flank the entrance, as do the river goddesses. The *dikpalas* or guardians are stationed at the different directions. The front lintel above the doorway carries the *navagrahas* or nine planets, and often a small relief of the deity who is enshrined in the sanctum within. The projecting walls on the south, west and north sides of the temple may carry an epic relief of the major deity performing a miracle, slaying the demon Gajasura, or grandly recumbent on the serpent Ananta on the ocean bed.

The temple is in essence the cosmic mountain. As the Greek gods lived on Mount Olympus, so too do the gods in India live on Mount Kailash, in the Himalaya. The greatest temples, such as the Kailashanath at Khajuraho, and the Kailash of Ellora testify to this belief.

Both at the caves of Ellora and Elephanta in the Deccan, we see an attempt to "reconstruct" the image of Shiva's home in the Himalaya that is more than a thousand miles away. Giant reliefs enact the legend of his marriage to Parvati, the "daughter of the mountain," of their conjugal bliss as they play chess on Mount Kailash, undisturbed by Ravana shaking the mountain, of the descent to earth of the river Ganga through the locks of Shiva's flowing hair, of his vanquishing demons and dancing the fearful *tandava* dance, and finally of his being stilled into deep meditation. These are some manifestations of the same deity, who is both destroyer and savior, the lord of dance *(Nataraja)* and the lord of meditation *(Mahayogi).*

The most profound aspect of this deity, and one of the greatest aspirations of Indian art is found at the Shiva temple at Elephanta. Set deep into the recesses, looming up from the darkness to fill the full height of the cave is *Maheshamurti.* In this image the seemingly irreconcilable aspect of Shiva as Aghora, the malevolent being with terrifying eyes and tusked teeth, is fused with his tender, feminine aspect of man-woman, *Ardhanarisvara.* These two faces being profiled, meet in a frontal image that is composed, calm and beatific, unmoving as the *Mahayogi.* This is an image which transcends the limitations of the material and the scope of the human imagination, to achieve a grandeur that remains with us, undiminished by the centuries.

The most spectacular case of "mountain building" is surely the great temple of Kailash at Ellora. At the insistence of a Rashtrakuta king, the temple was excavated a hundred feet downwards into the mountain rock, scooping out 3 million cubic feet of stone before it was completed a century later. An inscription declares the delight of the final architect who exclaims, "Wonderful! O how could I have ever done it!"

It must have taken infinite patience and manpower to work out the detailed plan on two stories. In addition, there are free-standing pillars of victory (kirti-stambha) in the spacious courtyard, ancillary shrines surrounding the courtyard that are dedicated to the

ers and *pechwai* painters (who paint on cloth) also produce the paintings which serve as popular mementos and souvenirs. At the classic 10th Century temple of Thanjavur known as the Brihadesvara, mural paintings have recently been discovered in the inner sanctum. At the Virupaksha Temple in Vijayanagar, magnificent 16th Century wall hangings have been preserved.

Although these murals are in a fragmentary condition today, it is possible to suggest that they inspired the narrative style of manuscript paintings. Here, our earliest records are to be found in religious institutions — the Jain and Buddhist libraries *(bhandars)* where such manuscripts have been carefully "bound" in wooden covers wrapped in cloth and preserved since the 10th and 11th centuries. Since paper

mother goddesses *(matrikas)* and other deities, long galleries filled with images, and a stupendous relief, at the entrance porch, of the goddess of fertility, Gajalakshmi, seated upon beds of lotuses in full bloom. These militant sculptures are carved from living rock — asserting the triumph of the Brahmanical faith in India.

In medieval India the temple grew in importance and power, in its cohesive role as the center of religious, political and social activity. To this day, many temples maintain their own craftsmen: chariot-makers, lamp-makers, sculptors, painters, weavers and bronze-image-makers — as well as the cooks and scribes who were in the daily service of the pilgrims. At Nathdwara in Rajasthan, the mural paint-

was not introduced into India until the 14th Century, these writings were inscribed on palm leaf or on parchment, with illustrations that related specifically to the texts of the Jain *Kalpa Sutra* or the stories of the *Balagopala Stuti.* Curiously, no manuscripts of that time have survived of the Hindu epics such as the *Ramayana* and the *Mahabharata.* They appear only with the tremendous surge of vernacular literature in the 16th Century.

As opposed to images in stone and in bronze that were installed for worship, paintings were commissioned for both religious and secular reasons. Manuscripts were often commissioned as an act of piety by merchants.

Detail of sculpture from Khajuraho.

Remarkable attention was given to details of the interiors of homes, to door hangings, to fine jewelry and patterns of cloth that were actually exported from the west coast of India.

Much of the art was inspired by the dance dramas (natakas) that formed part of the entertainment of medieval India. In paintings from Malwa, passages from the epics of the *Mahabharata* and the *Ramayana* are dramatized against a red ground with the figures of the heroes profiled, with Hanuman leaping across the great blue divide of the ocean, and his army of monkeys poised to attack the kingdom of Lanka. The narrative element of the pictures is all-important, depicted with brilliant colors, clarity and linear movements, as though they were moving across a stage.

A great religious fervor was awakened in medieval India. The *Ramayana* was rewritten in the vernacular by Tulsidasa. Ecstatic poems on Lord Krishna were composed, by the blind singer Surdas, the princess Meerabai and a host of other mystics. Most of all, it is the *Gita Govinda* of Jayadeva which transports us into romance, immortalizing the passion of Krishna and his beloved Radha. Their secret meetings beside the river Yamuna, Krishna's dalliance, Radha alone pining with blossoming trees that wound her like arrows, and their ultimate reunion became favorite themes in painting. Here the lotus, the peacock and the sky thundering with clouds, are all symbolic in contributing to the essential mood of the text.

Another set of mood paintings are the *Ragamalas,* where modes of music are personified in pictorial situations. The colors here are inflamed with pure passion, undiluted. In *Raga Bhairavi,* for example, a brutal, brilliant red serves as the background, to a captivating woman seated before the *Shiva lingam,* performing a *puja.* A remarkable affinity is shared between her and the dark peacock on the roof, set off by the white flower garlands draped on the lingam.

In Rajput paintings from the state of Bundi, lovers are shown in different seasons watching the lightning and clouds gathering in the monsoon skies, or bathing in the river in the hot months of the summer. These are the *Baramasa* paintings, depicting the activities of the 12 months of the year. These paintings are permeated with a feeling to awaken us to the natural beauty of the landscape.

Krishna becomes the archetypal love, so much so that every prince or lover is portrayed as *Shyama,* the blue god, with lotus eyes and a skin as dark as the clouds.

In Islam the proscription against idolatry and the making of images resulted in the refinement of the decorative arts. Yet it was the art of the book that was held to be the noblest form of expression, combining as it does the talents of the calligraphist, the illuminator in gold, the illustrator and the bookbinder. Calligraphy acquired a semi-mystical place in the arts, being reproduced on paper and vellum, on leather, metal and canvas, on tile and ceramic, and on the walls and arches of the great monuments.

Book Illustration

In India, in the three sultanate courts, book production was encouraged. The Mughals again were a very literary dynasty, with Babar, the founder, having written his memoirs as the first guidebook to Hindustan. Here, with the eye of the naturalist, he describes the different species of fruits and trees and animals of Hind. Almost a hundred years later, his great grandson Jahangir, also wrote his memoirs of the Tuzuk, where he boasts of the fact that he can improve on the passages of Babar. He can summon his master painter of animals, Mansur, titled the Wonder of the Age, to paint with great accuracy and remarkable detail and so illustrate his descriptions of exotic animals such as the zebra and the turkey cock.

Curiously, it was the Emperor Akbar who is reputed to have remained illiterate throughout his life, who became the greatest patron of painting. Perhaps his predilections were developed by the fact that pictures compensated for his not being able to read the text, which he would have read out aloud to him. To commemorate the Mughal dynasty, histories of the reign were commissioned — the *Babur Nama,* the *Timur Nama* and the *Akbar Nama* — as official chronicles. Each of these was illustrated, not once, but several times. To develop an understanding of other religions, Akbar had the Hindu epics translated into Persian, and illustrated.

Thus a new studio of artists had to be recruited from all over India. The fusion of the Islamic and the Hindu elements resulted in a new style that was bold and dynamic, bursting with energy. There is tremendous curiosity for the anecdotal, as well as an inbred realism in depicting people from the court and the village. Singers, sufis, dervishes, horse-trainers, falconers, musketeers, carpenters, and stone masons appear to be rendered with as much interest as are the courtiers, the ambassadors and the princes.

This becomes then, the ultimate contribution of Mughal painting: in rendering the details of life and in introducing a quality of portraiture that remains unsurpassed even today.

"The natives there show very much ingenuity in their curious manufactures, as in their silk stuffs, which they most artificially weave, some very neatly mingled either with silver or gold or both ... They make likewise excellent carpets of their cotton wool, in mingled colors, some of them 3 yards broad and of great length. Some other richer carpets they make all of silk, so artificially mixed as that they lively represent those flowers and figures made in them. Their skill is likewise exquisite in making of cabinets, boxes, trunks and standishes, curiously wrought within and without, inlaid with elephants' teeth or mother of pearl, ebony, tortoise-shell or wire, and curious they are in cutting of all manner of stones, diamonds as well as others."

What the English explorer Terry saw in his *Voyage to the East Indies* in 1655 A.D. holds equally for India today. A feast of colors, textures, techniques and motifs awaits the traveller. Every village in each state of India has its own unique skills and exquisite objects, made often by the same families in a continuing tradition for centuries.

Indian crafts can be broadly divided into two streams — those created for their personal use and adornment by men and women whose primary livelihood is agriculture or animal husbandry, which only incidentally find markets elsewhere; and those made by professional craftsmen on commission for a particular market or buyer.

Some states and regions predominate in one kind of craft and others in another. In the hill states and Gujarat, every village surface, utensil and garment is vibrantly alive with color and ornamentation spontaneously created for their own pleasure, while the equally skilled and varied hands of Uttar Pradesh and Kashmir make almost entirely market-oriented shawls, silverware, carpets, ivories and brocades. Is it history, geography, economics or the weather that impels the directions creativity takes? If it is the dry, brown parched landscape of the Bani desert that causes the contrasting exuberance of Kutchi craft, and the green fertility of Kerala that evokes the austere simplicity of its architecture, bronze *varpus* and white cotton weaves, how does one explain the flowering lushness of Kashmiri craft motif?

The craftsman in India traditionally has had the status of an artist, tracing his descent from Vishwakarma, "Lord of the Many Arts, Master of a Thousand Handicrafts, Carpenter to the Gods, Architect of Their Celestial Mansion, Designer of All Ornaments, the First of All Craftsmen." Products of his skill can be traced back 5,000 years and the same skills endure today. The fine muslins used as shrouds for royal Egyptian mummies draped Mughal emperors 3,000 years later, and were given poetic names like "running water" *(abrawan),* "evening dew" *(shabnam),* and "woven air" *(bafthava),* by their court poets. Now they are commissioned as scarves by Yves St. Laurent and Zandra Rhodes! Weavers in Bengal tell the story of the Emperor Aurangzeb rebuking his daughter, Princess Zebunissa, for appearing in public wearing nothing. She showed him that her muslin drapes were wound seven times round her body!

For the novice tourist, the first overwhelming impact is of Kashmiri crafts — papier mâché, crewel embroidery and carpets, all vibrant with the flowing imagery and color of the foliage, flora and fauna of Kashmir's enchanted landscape. The glint of metal comes next. Brass, copper, silver and gold — hammered, beaten or cast, engraved, enameled or repoussé — have been used through the centuries all over India in shapes consecrated by tradition to temple ritual or court ceremonial, or simply to bring water from the village well. Each metal has its ascribed attribute: according to an ancient text, the *Kalika Purana,* gold "removes the excesses of the three humors and promotes strength of vision," and silver is "favorable and inimicable to bile, but calculated to increase the secretion of wind and phlegm," bronze is "agreeable and intellectual," but brass "wind generating, irritating," iron "beneficial in overcoming dropsy, jaundice and anaemia"!

Metals Made to do Wonders

Techniques and traditional craft forms worth looking out for are the engraved and enameled *meenakari* brassware of Rajasthan and Uttar Pradesh, with its main centers in Jaipur and Moradabad, known as *siakalam, chikan* and *marori* work. The designs are chased on tinned brass, then filled in with black or colored lacquer applied with a hot tool and finally polished. The colored patterns, generally flowing arabesques of flowers and foliage, stand out on the glittering metal.

Applique artist, Orissa.

In Jaipur and Udaipur, you will also find exquisitely enameled silver and gold ornaments and *objets d'art,* with precious stones embedded amongst the brilliant blues, greens and deep reds, fired in furnaces sunk deep into the ground. Less well-known but stunningly subtle in its dramatic black and white is *bidri,* the silver damascene work originating in the old Hyderabad State. The designs, stylized floral motifs or geometric trellis designs from Mughal architecture, are engraved and set in silver leaf on boxes, bowls and vases made of an alloy of copper, zinc and lead treated with a solution of copper sulphate and saltpeter which turns it jet black.

The more common form of damascene wirework — the base of brass or bronze, with gold and silver wire ornamentation — which is a favorite technique all over India, from the Tanjore plates of the South, with mythological figures encrusted in high relief in white metal on copper, to the brass and copper utensils of the hill states in the northeast.

Cire-perdue, or the lost-wax technique of casting brass, bronze and bell metal objects, is also used all over India. Made in this way are the life-size bronzes of Hindu deities made at Swamimalai in Tamil Nadu; the austerely elegant ritual vessels of Kerala; and the delightful *dhokra* toy animals of Madhya Pradesh and Bengal. Styles differ, but the technique remains the same; the object is molded in clay, coated with wax, and then encased in more clay. The molten metal is poured in through a small hole in the outer layer, melting the wax which runs out, with the

travelled to India via Iran and Afghanistan from its original home in Damascus, was patronized by the Emperor Akbar. His warriors went to war with Quranic verses inscribed in golden *koftagiri* calligraphic arabesques on their sword hilts. In Udaipur, Alwar and Jodhpur, you can still see beautiful daggers and shields made by descendants of the royal armorers who now occasionally turn their hands to more domestically utilitarian objects — nutcrackers, scissors, and betelnut cutters.

When two metals are used in conjunction — gold and silver, or copper and brass — either by inlaying or embossing, or welding them together, the resulting contrast of color and texture is known as *Ganga-Jamuna* (the confluence of India's two great rivers). This

metal taking its place and hardening. The clay coating is then removed and the object polished, chased and finished on a lathe.

Stoneware and Woodwork

Everyone's image of India is the Taj — almost a cliché if it weren't so magically enchanting. Its exquisite marble mosaics and inlays and delicate trellises are still reproduced in Agra today in beautiful boxes, tabletops, plates and bowls, the translucent white

Left, detail of *zari* (gold embroidery) on palanquin cover, Jodhpur. Right, potter at work, Gujarat.

marble or alabaster inlaid in Mughal flower designs in mother-of-pearl, lapiz and cornelian.

Other stoneware to look out for is the statuary of Mamallapuram (Mahabalipuram), which echoes the vibrant, powerful themes of South Indian temple art; the green serpentine or rust Gaya stone; rock crystal and alabaster boxes, bowls and animal figures of Jaipur, Banaras and Bihar; the black chlorite utensils of Orissa; and the wonderful red and buff sandstone pillars, balconies and windows of domestic and temple architecture all over Rajasthan and Gujarat, whose stone lattice-work is often described as "frozen lace."

Similar themes and patterns are echoed in wood. India was once called "the land that has no furniture," but wood was always extensively used, not only in architecture and sculpture but also for ceremonial carriages and palanquins, dowry chests, screens and myriad smaller articles, ornamental or utilitarian. Sandalwood was considered the most auspicious and in both South and North India, finely carved statuettes, fans, frames and boxes are made of this delicate, aromatic wood. Walnut in Kashmir; black wood, mahogany, redwood and ebony in the south and east; teak everywhere, are carved and ornamented in a variety of ways, though the ancient *Shilpashastras* sagely prohibited the use of wood from trees struck by lightning or withered by disease; those in which birds had built nests; or those growing near burial or cremation grounds; or those trampled by elephants!

The *sadeli* marquetry work of Surat in Gujarat; the *tarkashi* brass wire inlay of Rajasthan and Uttar Pradesh; ivory and mother-of-pearl inlay in the south; the brass sheet inlay *pattara* dowry chests and doors of Saurashtra; the *kamangiri* figurative painted woodwork of Jodhpur and Jaipur; the brilliantly hued lacquer work of Sankheda, Nirmal and Sawantwadi; the lattice lace of *jali* screens from Saharanpur; the flowers and foliage carved into the satin finish of Kashmiri walnut; the gesso and goldleaf of Bikaner, are all worth looking for. (Bikaneri gold gesso-work is also done on lampshades and scent bottles made of the translucent inner hide of the camel!) Kondapalli in Andhra, Udaipur and Sankheda all make delightful, painted wooden toys.

Ceramics and terra-cotta are not the most durable of souvenirs for the tourist to take home but no visitor to India should miss the sight of the village potter turning his wheel with his big toe and producing, with a few flicks of his thumb, a shape identical to that his forefather threw in Mohenjodaro 5,000 years ago. Not turned on a wheel but molded is the famous Blue Pottery of Jaipur. Made of ground felspar mixed with gum rather than clay and painted a pure, opaque white with turquoise and cobalt blue floral and figurative designs, it is reminiscent both of Persian encaustic tiles and Chinese porcelain and yet is richly, eclectically Indian in feel. Other lovely shapes and glazes are the blue and green cutwork pottery of Khurja, the black ware of Chinhat and Azamgarh in Uttar Pradesh, and the huge terracotta horses of Tamil Nadu and Bengal.

Color Language

Color in India is one's most enduring impression and, as Kamladevi Chattopadhya, one of the foremost names in the local art scene, has said, every color has its tradition, emotional content and rich significance. "Red, the color of marriage and love; orange, saffron the color of the ochre earth and the *yogi* who renounces that earth; yellow, the color of spring, young mango blossoms, of swarms of bees, of southern winds and the passionate cry of mating birds. Blue...the color of indigo also the color of Krishna, the cowherd child god ... he that is of the color that is in the newly formed cloud, dormant with that darkness that is rain. Even the great gods had their color — Brahman was red, Shiva was white and Vishnu was blue."

Different Kinds of Textiles

The richness of color and motif in Indian textiles is overwhelming. Its use can be subtle or dramatic. The *Vishnudharmottaram* speaks of five white tones — ivory, jasmine, the August moon, August clouds after rain, and mother-of-pearl. A *tanchoi* brocade from Banaras will play on the contrast of one delicately differing shade against another in shadow and sun, while a South Indian temple sari might have a body of shocking Indian pink and a border of parrot green with stylized elephants, tigers and peacocks running riot in gold on its trailing *pallav*!

Woven, waxed, embroidered, appliquéd, brocaded, block-printed, painted, tie-dyed, tinselled; running the whole gamut from simple to splendid, a few rupees to a fortune, there is something for every season and ceremony — symbolic or merely spectacular.

Often seen abroad are block-printed cottons and Saurashtrian mirrorwork, Indian silks and brocades, Kashmiri carpets and shawls. (The celebrated "ring shawl" is made from the fleece the wild Himalayan ibex sheds on rocks and bushes and is so fine that a meter-length passes through a man's signet ring.) Textiles have been among India's major exports since the Pharaohs, and the ancient Greeks and Romans. Fascinating lesser known techniques are the tie-and-dye *bandhani* saris and scarves of Rajasthan and Gujarat, in which fine cotton or silk is knotted into minute patterns with waxed string and dyed in successive deepening shades of different colors. The knots are untied later to produce delicate spotted designs, each dot often no bigger than a matchhead, all over the body of the fabric. In *laheria bandhani* the cloth is tied to make fine diagonal stripes of contrasting color. When the Prince Regent's passion for snuff in the late 18th Century made snuff-taking a European fashion and colored handkerchiefs to hide the ensuing stains a painful necessity, it

handle with which the melted beeswax is painted on to cloth before it is dyed, is another beautiful and subtle textile, similar in technique to Indonesian *batik,* but with very different coloring and designs. There are two main centers in coastal South India: Machlipatnam specializing in the delicate, all-over floral trellis designs that were the origin of chintz *(Chhint);* Kalahasti in bold, black-outlined, heavily stylized mythological panels where calligraphy and pageantry, goddesses and warriors, riot together in baroque curliques. Both styles use indigo and myrobalam vegetable dyes on handspun fabric with deep blue, ochre and dun as the predominant colors.

Marco Polo said in the 13th Century: "embroidery is here (India) produced with

was the *Bandhani* or Bandanna spotted kerchief that came to the rescue of the Regency Buck!

Allied to the *bandhani* technique is *ikat.* In the case of the *patola, pochampalli, telia rumal* and *mashru* weaves of Gujarat, Andhra and Orissa, the warp and weft threads are separately tie-dyed before being woven into intricate, stylized designs of flowering shrubs, birds, elephants and fish set in geometric squares and stripes. Both *bandhani* and *patola* are associated with marriage, and no bride's trousseau is complete without one or the other.

Kalamkari, literally "the art of the pen," a wax-resist technique taking its name from the bunch of steel wires attached to a wooden

more delicacy than anywhere in the world." Among a myriad of stitches, two differing but equally exciting techniques are the *phulkari* (flower-craft) of Punjab and the *chikan* work of Uttar Pradesh. In its bold surface satin stitch in vivid satin floss oranges, pinks and flames, the *phulkari* reflects the vigor and vibrant energy of the Punjabi peasant; while the *chikan* work's typical delicate white on white floral net and shadow work shows the subtlety and refinement of the Mughal court, where, legend has it, Noorjehan, Queen Consort to the Emperor Jahangir, first devised the craft.

Delightful too are the *kantha* quilts of West Bengal. *Kantha* literally means rag, and is done on old saris laid one on top of the other and quilted in white asymmetrical circles and swirls. Colored threads are then extracted from the borders of the saris and used to embroider folk motifs of animals, humans and trees all over the quilt, either in a spiral formation, starting with a central lotus or in squared-off panels, each with a different design. A *kantha* is a family enterprise and many women work together on each.

All over India, embroidery, unlike weaving, is a female occupation. Secluded by custom or religion from the public eye, women get together and sew either for pin money or their daughters' dowry chests. Designs and stitches are handed down from generation to generation as are the wooden pattern blocks. In Kutch, villages less than a couple of miles

crewel, *Kani* and *Kashida* of Kashmir are all done by men. Making the various coiled and twisted gold and silver wires, spangles, sequins and braid is a craft in itself.

Images of Indian crafts are inescapably accompanied by images of their makers. It may be an 80-year-old ivory carver in the shadow of the Jama Masjid, his white beard curved over an ivory that's already taken him seven years, calmly speculating whether he'd live the further two he'd need to finish it; or apple-cheeked Kashmiri boys in skullcaps weaving carpets to the singsong drone of the pattern-reader's chant; a Rajasthani cobbler embroidering gold peacocks on shoes whose turned up toes echo the ends of his moustache; a papier-mâché painter chasing a squirrel for new hairs for his brush; or even

apart will each have their own distinctive stitches, patterns and colors — each community and caste distinguishable from the others.

The exceptions in this female-dominated field are Uttar Pradesh and Kashmir, two states whose crafts have traditionally been practiced by skilled professionals for patrons, originally the Imperial Court and local nobility, but are now for exporters and the tourist trade. The gold and silver sequin and *zardoshi* embroidery of Uttar Pradesh, and the

Kashinath Meenakar, deaf and with throat cancer, deeply eloquent with eyes and hands, demonstrating the vivid blue enamel on a tiny golden cup.

So many of these images are of old men. Despite the vitality and variety of Indian craft, some skill dies every year. Mill prints and plastic are elbowing out traditional crafts in the village and greedy middlemen, ignorant of tradition, with their eye on foreign markets, are debasing them in the town. Craftsmen, generally illiterate, keep no records of what their forefathers made. The skills are in their fingertips but if you paint Mickey Mouse to order on a papier-mâché box often enough instead of a Mughal rose, eventually the memory of the rose will fade away.

Left, *Ikat* saree being woven, Andhra Pradesh; and, right, carving in soapstone.

Amitabh Bachchan, Indian cinema's superstar, lay seriously ill in Bombay's Breach Candy Hospital. He had been injured while shooting an "action" scene for a film (euphemism for violent fisticuffs). What had seemed to be a minor injury, developed major complications and now the leading surgeons in the land struggled to save his life.

It all seemed like a re-enactment of the cinematic melodrama Bachchan had acted in every day of his film career. But no script writer, even in the extravagant world of India's fantasy films, would have dared write of Indian movies, called it a day at the peak of his career...but not to retire to a quiet life. When Rajiv Gandhi succeeded his mother as Prime Minister, he persuaded Bachchan to join politics. You could say that Bachchan exchanged one set of lights for another. If you were cynical you could add that he had stopped acting only in front of the cameras.

Such is an Indian film star's appeal — and particularly Bachchan's charisma — that his opponent, H.N. Bahuguna, one of the opposition parties' most experienced politicians, was ousted at the polls.

such a scenario: Breach Candy Hospital besieged by hysterical crowds from sunrise to nightfall, morning and evening bulletins on the patient's health which became national headlines, queues stretching miles at temples as devotees prayed to their favorite deities to restore this other god's health. One young man walked 300 miles *backwards* as his offering to the gods. Even India's Prime Minister, then Mrs Indira Gandhi, came to visit.

Perhaps, like the heroes he portrays on screen, Bachchan made one supreme effort to defeat his adversary. Perhaps, collective national prayers were answered. In any case, Amitabh Bachchan lived. But, alas, not to fight another day. The doctors decreed that he should retire so Bachchan, Angry Young Man

The road to politics via the movies is not new as Ronald Reagan has shown. But Reagan had retired from films and served a fairly long political apprenticeship before becoming Governor of California, whereas Bachchan, M.G. Ramachandran (Chief Minister of Tamil Nadu) and N.T. Rama Rao (Chief Minister of Andhra Pradesh) became politicians at the apex of their cinematic popularity and with no political experience at all. They won their elections because the mass adulation they received blurred the distinction between image and reality. Amitabh, MGR and NTR (to give

Poster of film starring one of the super-heros of the Indian screen.

them their popular names) had *become,* in the popular imagination, their screen personae of champion of the underdog or mythological god. In fact, NTR campaigned for his election in a motorized chariot, in an echo of the vehicles used by the gods he portrayed on screen.

Super Reality

Indian films are so far removed from reality that this confusion of identities seems at first glance, difficult to understand. But in fact, Indian cinema suggests a super reality that its audience can look up to. All films are morality tales which uphold traditional virtues: the intrinsic goodness of poverty, the pre-eminence of familial loyalty, the importance of chastity and faith in God. These are values associated with temple, church or mosque and therefore close to the heart of a religious, poor and not highly literate audience.

These "virtues," on the other hand, are not what one might call the stuff of entertainment. Indian cinema solves this problem by concentrating on the *antithesis* of these values. Thus films will generally feature characters whose wealth is displayed with ostentatious garishness, who frequent cabaret shows of startling vulgarity and whose attempts at violating feminine purity are shown in graphic detail. These are the bad guys. They get their comeuppance at the hands of the Bachchans who overcome picturesque poverty (and impossible standards of goodness) to beat the villians, more often than not, literally.

There is of course catharsis involved in all this and that's why critics of Indian cinema often accuse it of pandering to the establishment: the disadvantaged who make up the bulk of the audience get their wish-fulfilment at the movies and accept the inequalities of real life with greater equanimity. Supporters of Indian cinema, on the other hand, see virtue in this: movies help to keep the lid closed tight and prevent a blow-up in Indian society.

The supporters also say that almost all Indian films drum in the message of religious harmony, of vital importance in India's frequently strife-torn multi-religious society. *Amar, Akbar, Anthony:* directed by filmland's most successful filmmaker Manmohan Desai, is the story of three brothers, separated by accident in their childhood from their parents and each other. Each child drifts away to be adopted by a family belonging to one of India's three dominant religious groups, Hindu, Muslim and Christian (hence the title of the film). The long arm of coincidence — often stretched beyond yogic proportions by Indian scriptwriters — brings the three brothers together as adults. "We are like brothers," they proclaim in many a song, unaware how near the truth they are.

The end of the film sees them defeat the villains in a long-drawn-out fight which leaves them "drained." Urgent blood transfusion is needed; their blood is of the same type (they are like *blood* brothers!); the type is rare. But a donor is found. It's an old lady, and as she lies in a hospital bed, connected by rubber tubes to the three men into whose veins her blood flows directly, we discover that she is one of the lost parents. The film fades on that image of Mother India.

Nine Emotions — One Film

The biology may be weak, but the symbolism is strong and it pervades through Indian cinema. Also coursing through its veins is an adherence to traditional Indian theatrical forms which lay strong emphasis on the *nav ras* (nine emotions), plots and sub-plots as well as song and dance.

The *nav ras* theory means that a single film runs through the entire gamut of feelings, from farcical comedy to wrenching tragedy. The sub-plots make a film's seemingly excessive length (about 150 minutes) an absolute necessity: each film isn't dealing with one story, but three or four.

Then of course there are the songs and dances. *All* films must have them, although the number of songs have dropped from an average of 30 to just about six per film over the years. All actors and actresses are expected to dance, though mercifully, given some of their voices, they aren't expected to sing. They mime to pre-recorded songs sung by "play-back" singers, behind-the-scene professionals who lend their voices to the prettier faces on screen. The stars of the play-back world for many years have been Kishore Kumar for male voices and Lata Mangeshkar for female. In fact, Mangeshkar has dominated her field for so long that she figures in the *Guinness Book of Records* for the highest number of recordings made by any one in the world. With a total of 25,000 recordings and a fee reputedly in the region of Rs. 30,000/- (US$3,000) per song, the jingle of small change must make sweet music in the Mangeshkar household.

Obviously, the play-back voice and the on-screen face do not match quite often. That's part of the suspension of disbelief that an Indian film demands in great measure from its audience. But that's nothing like the suspension of sound economic sense that the film industry demands of its producers. Only 25 percent of films recover their investment, but it's the 5 percent that are big box-office successes — plus cinema's glamorous image — which act as siren songs. Producers, most of them one-time, fall by the wayside, only to be replaced by others happy to embrace such star-spangled bankruptcy. That's why the Indian film industry is a 2,000 million dollar industry employing 300,000 people full-time and several

thousand more on a casual basis. And that's why it produces so many films every year. (1984 figure: 833 feature films). The films are in many of India's myriad languages and dialects but mostly in Hindi (generally made in Bombay; 1984 figure, 165), Telugu (Hyderabad, 170) Tamil (Madras, 148) and Malayalam (Trivandrum, 121). No other country in the world produces even half that number.

The star system is often to blame for Indian cinema's financial doldrums. Actors' fees not only use up 40 percent of a film's budget (Bachchan's fee was reported $300,000 per film) but producers' excessive reliance on a few bankable names means that a few stars like Jeetendra, Rekha and Sridevi are so much in

demand that they work in a number of films simultaneously to a system of dates and shifts. "Dates" are the days of a month when the star will act in your film; "shift" indicates the hours in that day (a day consists of three shifts) in which he or she will be available to you. At the peak of his career Shashi Kapoor (seen internationally in *Heat and Dust*) was signed on for 140 films at one time and called himself good-humoredly the Taxi Star of India: you could take him anywhere as long as you paid the fare. No wonder films take such a long time to make. Two years is considered zipping around; four years is not uncommon.

It was not just disenchantment with this system gone haywire but also with the industry's values and its essential vulgarity that led to a breakaway group of filmmakers, often referred to as the New Wave. Unlike the French *Nouvelle Vogue,* this was not a cohesive group united by a single ideology; the New Wave's members often did not speak the same language. The one language they did share was cinema and through it they were determined to portray the *reality* of India. Almost all of these filmmakers also wanted to get away from the star system (although ironically, many New Wave actors and actresses have now become stars of the larger film industry).

The initial inspiration was Satyajit Ray's who brought India into the International film scene with *Pather Panchali* (The Song of the Road, 1955) and the rest of his Apu trilogy, *Aparajito* (The Unvanquished, 1956) and *Apursansar* (The World of Apu, 1959). Later, aided by the government-funded Film Finance Corporation (now the National Film Development Corporation) other directors began to emulate his example. Mrinal Sen, also from Ray's Calcutta, was notably successful — both critically and commercially with *Bhuvan Shome,* financed by the FFC. This success was the spur the movement needed and soon outstanding movies were being made in regional languages, not just in Calcutta, but also in Bangalore, Trivandrum and Madras.

In 1974, Shyam Benegal burst on the scene with a dazzling first film called *Ankur* (The Seedling), followed quickly by *Nishant* (Night's End) and *Manthan* (The Churning). Although not formally called a trilogy, the three films were linked by the common theme of exploitation and oppression in rural India. Benegal's success was important because his films were financed, not by the FFC but by private producers, thus encouraging other financiers to put in money into similar films. (Actor Shashi Kapoor has turned producer and has backed five movies, including two by Benegal.) His success was significant too because he worked in Hindi, the language of Bombay-Babylon, the richest film center in the country.

Ankur, Nishant and *Manthan* shattered a well-nurtured myth of the Indian film industry: Hindi is the national language, crossing regional boundaries not only of language but culture. So, the myth had held, to draw audiences from disparate centers, the Hindi film must appeal to their lowest common denominator. The statement is still occasionally heard, but it is now made with much less conviction.

Ray, Sen and Benegal continue to work steadily at the rate of one film each per year. Joining them in the movement is a whole host of talented directors struggling with tight budgets and an unhelpful distribution system

krishnan's *Mukhamukham* which skilfully explores the breakdown of a Marxist political leader). However disparate their subjects, these films are distinguished by their passionate intensity.

The world — or at least that part of it which is India — is not so easily changed. Like the two Indias — the rich and the poor — which live together in uneasy co-existence, the Indian box-office cinema and the New Wave live warily with each other, one envious of the other's popularity, the other resentful of the critical acclaim and prizes denied to it. More and more of the three and a half million people who go into Indian cinema houses every day, now go to see New Wave films, but their number is still miniscule.

Most would go to see films like Ramesh

to change the face of Indian cinema.

Initially the focus was almost entirely on rural India, where 70 percent of India still lives and where development takes time to catch up, but the emphasis has now moved to contemporary problems in the cities, areas spiritually and physically much closer to the film-makers themselves. Themes vary from police corruption (Govind Nihalini's *Ardha Satya*), the absurdities of the legal system (Saeed Mirza's *Mohan Joshi Hazir Ho*), student unrest (Ketan Mehta's *Holi*), or even the psychological ravages of an individual (Adoor Gopala-

Left, popular movie actress Shabanah Azmi; and, right, cops and crooks — pot-boiler being shot on Madras beach.

Sippy's movie, Sholay, which became one of the biggest box-office successes in Indian history. A phrase was coined to describe it, "Curry Western," a tribute to its inspiration, the Italian Spaghetti Western which was itself a derivative of the Hollywood Western. *Sholay* invented a country of good-hearted desperados fighting a gang of vicious bandits. Critics aimed their intellectual six-shooters at its appalling violence and its make-believe world but even as they pressed the trigger they couldn't but admit that, infuriatingly, the film was entertaining. For an audience which wants to forget the hurly-burly of life around it, films like *Sholay* are the perfect answer. There were, at the last count, over 800 ways of shutting out the world!

An Inspired Use Of Spices

Food is a serious business to most Indians. A gift of the gods, it is treated with respect and is subject to innumerable prescriptions. Based on pragmatic medical precepts evolved over hundreds of years of experimentation and observation, most are aimed at nourishing the body and pleasing the mind and eye. Governing the ingredients in each meal are the time of the year and minute classifications on heating or cooling foods, age, and even personality. There were injunctions also on the six *rasas* or flavors that must be included in every meal — sweet, salty, bitter, astringent,

and digestives. "Heating" condiments for the winter are also used. Immense care is taken to ensure that spices enhance rather than dominate the basic flavor, and that they do not diminish nutritive value. Thousands of different dishes have been developed using various combinations of the dozen-odd basic condiments.

Other important ingredients are milk and milk products, particularly, ghee and *dahi* (curd). To the orthodox, a meal is pure only if cooked in ghee — an emphasis that derives not just from its distinctive fullness and

sour and pungent. Each believed to have its particular physical benefit was prescribed in a specified ratio to the others. Since food was believed to influence behavior as well as physical wellbeing, these canons were taken very seriously, becoming, through time, part of the "subcontinental subconsciousness."

Despite the universality of these attitudes, there can be no generalization on Indian food. The cuisines of India are as diverse as the country's culture, its racial structure, and the varied geographic conditions that determine climate, crop patterns and occupations.

Characteristic of all Indian cooking is the inspired use of spices. Far from being used only for flavor, they are appetite stimulators

unique flavor but from its acclaimed preservative qualities. With rising prices, vegetable oils have replaced ghee in most homes and restaurants.

Dahi is part of almost any Indian menu. Served to mitigate the chili "hotness" of some dishes, it is often mixed with vegetable or fruit and is lightly spiced to create the *raitas* of the north and the *pachadis* of the south. An important ingredient in several recipes, *dahi* is also churned and salted or sweetened to taste and served in summer as a cooling drink called *lassi*.

Dals (split lentils) too, are common to most parts of the country. Regional preferences and availability dictate the type used. This, together with the wide range of ingredients, has resulted in a bewildering variety, ranging from the thick tamarind-flavored *sambhars* of the south and the sweetish *dals* of Gujarat to the delicious *maaki dal* of North India topped with fresh cream or butter.

Vegetables naturally vary with region and season. The style of cooking is determined by the cereal or main dish with which they are served. Deep-fried vegetable crisps are perfect accessories to the *sambhar* and rice of Tamil Nadu. The thick *avial* stew of Kerala cooked in coconut oil, or the *kaottu* in a coconut and gram sauce, are perfect for rice-based meals.

it is served with *sambhar, rasam* (a thin peppery soup), vegetables, both dry and in a sauce, and *pachadi.* Coconut is lavishly used in cooked foods as well as chutneys. Made of fermented rice and *dal* batter, the *dosa, vada* and *idli* are inexpensive South Indian snacks popular all over the country.

The semolina-based *upma,* cooked with curry leaves and garnished with nuts and copra, is another favorite. Other in-between bites found everywhere are the *samosa,* a three-cornered flour patty with potatoes, and *pakoras* or *bhajiyas* — vegetables coated in a

Sarson ka sag, mustard greens, eaten with *maki ki roti* (maize bread) is a particular favorite in the Punjab, while the delicately flavored *chorchori* of Bengal complements the Bengali's rice and fish.

Vegetarian Variety

India presents a vast range of vegetarian cooking. The largely non-greasy, roasted and steamed food of the south is very light. Rice is the basis of every meal. Saturated with ghee,

Left, *pilau,* one of innumerable variations; and, right, the ever-popular pork *vindaloo* from Goa.

gram batter and deep-fried. All are inexpensive and safe, provided they are eaten hot.

In Gujarat, another region famous for its vegetarian food, gram flour, a rich source of protein, is used in the making of breads and as a component of various dishes. *Kadi,* made from *dahi* and gram with a subtle combination of spices is delightful. An interesting difference is the use of *gur* or jaggery to add a hint of sweetness to piquant sauces. *Aam rasa,* the puréed pulp of mangoes eaten with *puris* is a summer treat.

Although Bengali food is never actually sweetened, it is customary to serve a sweet along with the other food as a foil to the chilis or for a change in flavor. In keeping with religious mandates, Gujarati (especially Jain) and Bengali vegetarian food are often cooked without the ubiquitous garlic, ginger, onions, and the "heating" or stimulating spices, thus preserving the delicate flavor of the vegetable.

Possibly the purest form of North Indian vegetarian food is the Banarsi. Lightly spiced, many of its specialties are based on *paneer* (cottage cheese). A perfect protein substitute, it is cooked in innumerable ways, with spinach *(palak paneer),* in a gravy with peas *(paneer mutter)* or lotus seeds *(paneer phulmakhana).* Then there is a whole range of deep-fried or stuffed breads, made of various combinations of refined and wholemeal flour; the golden puffs called *puris,* the *parathas, baturas* and so on. Most widely eaten is the simple *chapatti,* baked on a griddle in homes all over India.

and crushed nuts. An amazing variety of types and subtypes evolved: the rich *kormas* and *nargisi koftas* (meatballs shaped around a hard-boiled egg) of Lucknow; the *pasindas* or mutton steaks cooked in an almond sauce; the *biriyani,* a layered rice and meat concoction famous in Hyderabad; and a variety of *kababs* that literally melt in the mouth. Laden with nuts, dried fruits and saffron, Kashmiri Muslim food is a gourmet's joy. *Haleem,* mutton pounded with wheat; *gaustaba,* incredibly light meatballs; and *rogan josh,* are well-known Kashmiri specialties.

Although rice is not the staple cereal of the north, it is an important accessory. Indeed, a good *pilau* (rice cooked in stock, with meat, vegetable or nuts) is considered the supreme test of a good cook. Innumerable variations

Mughal Menus

Muslim influence is most evident in the cooking of meats. Their major contribution was the *tandoor,* the conical earthen oven from which emerged a delectable array of *kababs* and *rotis.* This was the origin of the famous *tandoori* cooking, synonymous with the north, but available all over the country — the *tandoori* chicken, *seekh, boti* and *barra kababs,* and recently, *tandoori* fish. Among the *rotis* are the elongated *nan,* the *tandoori roti,* or its richer equivalent, the *tandoori paratha.*

The fastidious Mughals transformed local recipes, developing the superb Mughlai cuisine, with its luscious sauces of *dahi,* cream

have been evolved, but the most commonly available is the plain *muttar* or *chicken pilau* — rich, heavy and sustaining.

Vinegar lends a different taste to the meat dishes of Goa. The pork *sorpotel, vindaloo,* the Goan sausages and the chicken *shakuti* or *cafreal* are inimitable.

Fish too is prepared in dozens of different ways: the mustard-flavored *macher jhol* and *malai* or cream prawns of Bengal, the chili-hot curries of Andhra, and the coconut and curry-leaf flavored specialties of the south, as well as the west coast and, of course, the memorable fish and shellfish curries of Goa. Dried fish cooked with vegetables or *dals* adds interest to the simpler fare of Maharashtra.

There are also the interesting dishes of the Parsis. *Dhansak,* meat cooked with five different *dals* and an unusual blend of spices, and *patrani machi,* lightly spiced fish steamed in banana leaves, are just two examples.

Chutneys and pickles — sweet, sour or hot, or all three, whip the appetite and add relish to a meal. Every conceivable ingredient can be used: mint, coriander, mango, ginger, lime, and different kinds of vegetables. Some are extravagantly spiced, while others may contain only salt.

Papads, roasted or fried savory crisps, are also popular meal adjuncts. Made of previously rolled and dried lentil or rice dough, or of vegetable tubers, they provide the crunchiness considered essential to every repast.

nuts. Crisp golden *jelabis,* dripping with syrup, made even in the tiniest bazars all over the country, are breakfast and tea-time favorites.

Kheer, the Indian equivalent of rice pudding; *shahi tukra,* an exotic variation on bread pudding; *phirni,* made of powdered rice and served in earthenware bowls; and *kulfi,* a rich nutty icecream; are common northern desserts.

Sweets from the south include Mysore *pak* and the creamy *payasum,* while the Gujaratis are partial to *shrikhand* made of drained, sweetened and spiced *dahi. Halvas,* another genre of traditional desserts, are created from ingredients as diverse as carrots, semolina, *dals,* eggs, or even wholemeal flour.

And finally, there is the satisfying ritual of the after-dinner pan, a must for any true con-

Savory Sweetmeats

Often too sweet for the non-Indian palate, the huge array of Indian confections and desserts is largely milk-based. Bengal is particularly well-known for its confections. These include the *rasagulla, sandesh, rasamalai* and the steaming hot *gulab-jamuns.* Typical of the north are the *barfis* (milk cakes), some of pure milk, others of coconut or various types of

Left, *samosas,* one of India's favorite savory snacks. Above right, spices and condiments on sale; and left, the ubiquitous pan-wella.

noisseur of Indian food. Lauded for its digestive and medicinal properties, it is a fragrant combination of betel leaf, areca nut, catechu, cardamom, cloves and a choice of a whole host of other exotic ingredients of varying flavors, effects and strengths — an acquired taste perhaps, but quite an addiction thereafter.

Rising costs and the constraints of time inherent in urbanization have led to an inevitable decline of the traditional Indian meal, now to be enjoyed only on very special occasions. In compensation, food from all over the country is now available in larger restaurants everywhere, which are less authentic perhaps, but certainly most welcome.

CALL OF THE JUNGLE

The range and diversity of India's national heritage undoubtably matches the grandeur and magnificence of her civilization. Throughout the Indian subcontinent numerous sanctuaries have been established, some small and obscure but with a definite purpose such as the Keibul Lanjoo National Park in Manipur to preserve the last refuge of the world's rarest deer — the Sanghai or Manipur brow-antlered deer *(Cervis eldi eldi).*

The present century has not been kind to either India or her heritage. The sheer size of her ever-increasing population has led to fire,

vested in Senior Forest Officers.

Of all the countries in the world, India is unique in the richness and variety of its wildlife. There are almost 350 mammal species, 1,200 species of birds in nearly 2,100 forms and, at a conservative estimate, at least 30,000 known species of insects. There is also a bewildering array of fish, amphibians and reptiles.

Some species are found throughout the country, but it is a sad irony that many species are fast disappearing in the land that produced three of the world's greatest and most

the ax, plow and now the bulldozer and chainsaw, being used to turn vast areas of the once-great jungles to barren, dusty tracks of wasteland. The great forests have shrunk and the vast herds of black buck, sometimes 50,000 strong 50 years ago, have diminished to small groups: "The predators have become the hunted." The cheetah has become extinct in India and the tiger is gravely endangered.

But all is not lost; India's wildlife has, since the early 70s, been protected by both central and state government legislation supported by considerably increased awareness of people such as the late Prime Minister, Mrs. Indira Gandhi. The uncontrolled hunting of the 50s and 60s is now over and poaching is inhibited by strong laws and the magisterial powers now

compassionate religions: Hinduism, Buddhism and Jainism. In 1982, 66 species of mammals, 38 species of birds and 18 species of reptiles and amphibians, plus all three crocodilians found in India, were listed as rare and threatened under the Wildlife Protection Act. At the beginning of the century there were 40,000 tigers in the country and by 1972 the first comprehensive census gave a figure of only 1,827. The Asiatic lion, approximately 250 of them, is now confined to a small pocket in the Gir forest of Gujarat. The hungul or Kashmir stag is confined to two or three valleys in the mountains to the East of Srinagar. The "dry" sub-species of swamp deer is confined to a single pocket in the Kanha National Park. At certain times of the year it is possible to see all these threatened animals in their natural habitat.

"In-Depth" Wildlife Tours

India's wildlife sanctuaries and national parks as tourist destinations have received little publicity and attention outside the country. This has been chiefly due to the extreme remoteness and inaccessibility of some of the areas and the lack of suitable facilities. It is only recently that the Government of India has increased its efforts to open up these areas for

previously visited the African game reserves and parks and it is, therefore, necessary to make a quick comparison between the two, stressing the differences. Whereas the wide open African plains have led to the evolution of large herds of animals that can easily be observed either on the plains or near waterholes, the difference in vegetation and terrain is such that in India animals are often solitary or in small herds, elusive and shy and, therefore, always taking advantage of the cover afforded by the vegetation. Although the vegetation and terrain varies throughout

tourists, thus revealing what incredible richness and variety India has to offer. Even so, an "in-depth" wildlife tour of India remains an enterprise more suited to the wildlife enthusiast seeking an adventure than the leisurely tourist interested mainly in the cultural heritage of India. There are, though, some parks within close vicinity of cultural sites and, which, as such, provide an ideal option for tourists.

A visitor to India on an "in-depth" tour of sanctuaries and national parks may well have

Preceding pages, egrets in flight at Bharatpur. Left, Sambar hind at Bandavgarh, Madhya Pradesh; and, right, tiger at Ranthambhor, Rajasthan.

India, the norm is thick forest cover or dense grassland with only the occasional opening for streams and rivers or near waterholes. Accordingly, game viewing means penetrating this cover, singling out animals, tracking them and literally hunting them (with a camera!).

The sighting of animals is always a thrill as it can never be predicted. The chances of seeing a tiger, a rhinoceros or a herd of wild elephant is always present and yet never a certainty.

Project Tiger

One of the world's most successful conservation projects is undoubtedly Project Tiger launched in April 1973 with a grant of US $1 million from the World Wildlife Fund matched by a similar amount from the Indian Government for the first five years of the project. Initially, there were nine areas designated as Project Tiger reserves and this has now been increased to 15, covering a total of 24,712 sq km. The largest reserve is the excellent but obscure one at Nagarjunasagar in Andhra Pradesh: an area of dry mixed deciduous forest and rugged hills in the middle reaches of the Krishna River.

In the heart of Central India, the magnificent Kanha National Park (five hours driving from Jabalpur, six from Nagpur) has become internationally known as perhaps the most magnificent park for seeing Asian wildlife. Other parks, such as Bandhavgarh National Park (five hours from Khajuraho), perhaps offer better chances to see tigers but few areas in India match the diversity of Kanha's faunal population and varied habitat.

The nine original Tiger Reserves selected for the Project are widely separated and are quite dissimilar in their terrain, vegetation and even much of their wildlife species, although adequate prey breeds had to be available along with water, cover and protection.

Kanha National Park is a success not solely because of its lead as the largest of the original tiger reserves. Twenty-five years ago it was realized that the quantity of the small local herd of swamp deer had fallen to the appallingly all-time low of 130. With careful management and vigilant protection, there is now a viable population of 350.

India's first national park was the small Hailey National Park established in 1935 in the undulating Himalayan foothills. During the 50s, in honor of the famous sportsman/ naturalist Jim Corbett, the now enlarged area was renamed the Corbett National Park. Easily accessible from Delhi (a six-hour drive), this very attractive park of valleys, grassland and sal forest, with a backdrop of the Himalayan ranges, is characterized as "a land of roar, trumpet and song."

The diversity of cover and food in Corbett supports a great variety of mammals and over 585 species of birds have been recorded. The wild elephant population is on the increase and both tiger and leopard are regularly seen.

Another of India's success stories also began long before wildlife conservation became as topical as it is today. In Assam, wedged between the Brahmaputra River and the Mikir Hills of Eastern India, in Kaziranga National Park (four hours from Guwahati), the local population of the greater one-horned rhinoceros has now reached saturation point and small groups are being relocated in other suitable areas. In 1960, there were only 80 rhinos within the Kaziranga Sanctuary — now

there are over 850. Also in Kaziranga is a sub-species of the swamp deer found in Kanha. A third sub-species (and the largest population) of swamp deer is at Dudhwa National Park in northeastern Uttar Pradesh.

An exception to the general rule about the remoteness of wildlife areas is the magnificent bird sanctuary at Bharatpur (three hours from Delhi). Originally a duck-shooting preserve the reserve ensures a vast breeding area for native water-birds. During the winter months (November-March), migratory birds arrive in vast numbers, including the rare Siberian crane.

Three hours south of Bharatpur by train is the smallest of the Project Tiger reserves at Ranthambhor. Set at the junction of the Vindhya and Aravalli Hills and covered in scrub forest, the area is interesting both as a wildlife reserve and as a place of historical importance.

While the parks of northern and central India are certainly the better known, there are some remarkable areas in South India also. At the junction of Karnataka, Kerala and Tamil Nadu, four sanctuaries come together: Madumalai in Tamil Nadu, Bandipur Tiger Reserve and Nagahole National Park in Karnataka, and Wynad in Kerala. Easily accessible from Mysore, each of these sanctuaries has accommodation, although the most comfortable is definitely the Kabini Lodge at Karapur, Nagahole. This exclusively sited camp and lodge on the banks of the Kabini Reservoir, dividing Nagahole and Bandipur, arranges field trips into the parks. The jungle is denser than that of the north, with teak, rosewood and even sandalwood trees making these forests both valuable and vulnerable to the depredations of the local population. The viewing in Nargahole of gaur and wild elephant is excellent, with a fair chance to see tiger, leopard and numerous other species.

Farther south, on the Kerala-Tamil Nadu border, is another beautiful tiger reserve at Periyar. The central lake was created at the turn of the century to irrigate the plains to the west and the Maharaja of Travancore declared the area a sanctuary at that time. Grasslands cover many of the gently undulating hills while deciduous forest surrounds the lake and river, providing excellent cover to numerous wild animals. The elephant population of Periyar is the largest of any of India's protected areas and is easily seen in a variety of circumstances: feeding in herds or as individuals along the lake or even swimming with only the dome of their heads above the water.

The egret was once hunted for their plumes used to decorate turbans and ladies' hats — hence the term *aigrette*.

TRAVEL TIPS

GETTING THERE

BY AIR

The majority of visitors arrive in India by air. Bombay and Delhi airports are the major entry points with fewer international flights using Calcutta and Madras. Other "international" airports are Patna and Varanasi with daily flights to/from Kathmandu (Nepal), Hyderabad and Trivandrum with flights to/from the Gulf region, Dabolin (Goa) with charters to/from Germany, France and UK. There are occasional flights from Bangalore to Singapore. Trivandrum also has flights to/from Male (Maldives) and Colombo.

Delhi and Bombay are well served with flights from most parts of the world. Most long haul flights unfortunately arrive between midnight and six a.m.; apparently to suit the night landing regulations of European and Far Eastern cities.

The four major airports are constantly improving and all have baggage facilities. Porters and licensed taxis are available. Delhi, Bombay, Calcutta and Madras all have duty free shops in both the arrival and departure halls.

BY SEA

A few cruise ships such as Cunard's QE II, do call but India is not a regular cruise destination. Some freighters offer passage to India and excellent accommodation is available. The American President Line, British India Steam Navigation Company, Eastern Shipping, Lloyd Triestino and the Shipping Corporation of India have regular sailings to and from: Bombay, Calcutta and Madras.

BY ROAD

The "hippy trail" which winds through Turkey, Iran, Afghanistan and Pakistan is not a route that is often used by tourists, but when peace returns to this fascinating area, it might again become popular with the more adventurous traveler. A few companies in England and Germany do however still operate a few departures.

The land border with Pakistan is only open at Wagi (Attari Road) west of Amritsar. Please bear in mind that you will need to apply for a permit if you want to travel through the Punjab. The land border with Nepal is only open for non Indian or Nepalese nationals at Birganj/Raxhal, Bairwa and Kakarbitta/Naxalbari.

AIRLINES

Aeroflot
Bombay: 7 Bradbourne Stadium, Vir Nariman Road Tel: 221682, 221743
Calcutta: 58 Jawaharlal Nehru Road, Tel: 443765, 449831 APT: 572611/395
New Delhi: BMC House, N-1 Connaught Place, Middle Circle Tel: 331-2843, 3310426 APT: 392331
Madras: c/o Air India Tel: 847799

Air Canada
Bombay: Hotel Oberoi Towers. Tel: 202-7632, 202-7512
Calcutta: 35-A Chowringhee Road Tel: 248371/4
New Delhi: 341-D, Ashoka Hotel, Chanakyapuri Tel: 604755, 600121
Madras: 733 Mount Road, Tel: 89832, 87957

Air France
Bombay: Taj Mahal Hotel. Tel: 202-4818, 202-5021 APT: 6320700
Calcutta: 41 Chowringhee Road Tel: 240011/2
Delhi: 6 Scindia House, Connaught Circus Tel: 331-0407, 331-0424 APT: 545-2294, 545-2099
Madras: 769 Anna Salai Tel: 88337, 82469

Air India
Bombay: Air India Bldg, Nariman Point Tel: 202-4142, 202-3747 APT: 6329666
Calcutta: 50 Chowringhee Road Tel: 442356 APT: 572031
Delhi: Connaught Circus Tel: 331-1225 APT: 545-2055, 545-2050
Madras: 19 Marshalls St, Egmore Tel: 847799, 848899 APT: 431656

Air Lanka
Bombay: Mittal Tower, Nariman Point Tel: 223588, 223599 APT: 6322829
Madras: Connemara Hotel, Mount Road Tel: 87432, 89701 APT: 433131
Trivandrum: Geetabali Bldg, Ganpatti Tel: 63261

Air Mauritius
Bombay: M 7-8 Oberoi Towers, Nariman Point Tel: 202-4723, 202-4525

Air Tanzania
Bombay: c/o Ethiopian Airlines, Taj Mahal Hotel Tel: 202-4525

Alitalia
Bombay: Vir Nariman Road, Churchgate, Tel: 222144, 222177 APT: 6329082, 6328083
Calcutta: 2/3 Chitrakoot, 230A Acharga Bose Rd Tel: 447394
Delhi Suryakiran, 19 K.G. Marg Tel: 331-1019/20 APT 393140
Madras: 738 Anna Salai Road Tel: 810936

Alyemda
Bombay: Oberoi Towers, Nariman Point Tel: 202-4229

Bangladesh Biman
Bombay: 199 J Tata Road, Churchgate Tel: 221339, 220676, 224580 APT: 6320700
Calcutta: 1 Park Street, Tel: 247603, 212862/4
Delhi: c/o Jet Air Tel: 331-0306, 331-3331

British Airways
Bombay: 202 Vir Nariman Road Tel: 220888, APT: 6329061
Calcutta: 41 Chowringhee Road, Tel: 293430

Delhi: 1A, Connaught Circus, Tel: 332-7428 APT: 545-2077/8
Madras: Fagun Mansions, 26 Cinc Road Tel: 474272

Burma Airways
Calcutta: 8/2 Esplanade East, Tel: 231624 APT: 572611 ext 397

Cathay Pacific
Bombay: Taj Mahal Hotel, Tel: 202-9112, 202-9113 APT: 6321580
Calcutta: 1 Middleton St, Tel: 447238
Delhi: Hotel Janpath, Tel: 351286
Madras: Connemara Hotel, Tel: 86241, 89373

Czechlosovak Airlines (Ceskoslovenske Aerolinie)
Bombay: 308 Raheja Chambers, 213 Nariman Point, Tel: 220736, 220765 APT: 6329660
Delhi: 104 Ansal Bhawan K.G. Marg Tel: 331-1833

Druk Air
Calcutta: 38 Tivoli Court, 1A Balygunge Circular Road: Tel: 447718 APT: 572611

Egypt Air
Bombay: 7J Tata Road, Churchgate Tel: 221415, 221562 APT: 6320700
Delhi: Hotel Ambassador, Sujan Singh Park, Tel: 697232

Emirates
Bombay: Mittal Chambars, Nariman Point, Tel: 2871645
Delhi: Kunchenjunga, Barakhauba Rd, Tel: 3316044 APT: 392851

Ethiopian Airlines
Bombay: Taj Mahal Hotel, Apollo Bandar, Tel: 202-4525
Delhi: Hotel Janpath, Tel: 351235, 350070

Garuda Indonesian
Bombay: Tulsiani Chambars, Nariman Point Tel: 243075
Madras: 769 Mount Road, Tel: 86356

Gulf Air
Bombay: Air India Building, Nariman Point, Tel: 202-1441

Calcutta: 30A Chitrakoot Building, Tel: 444697
Delhi: Hotel Janpath, Tel: 344295
Madras: Haridevi Chambars, 68 Pantheon Rd, Egmore, Tel: 811740

Iran Air
Bombay: Sundar Mahal, Marine Drive, Tel: 253524, 297070 APT: 6320700
Delhi: Ashok Hotel, Chanayakapuri, Tel: 600121

Iraqi Airways
Bombay: Mayfair Building, 79 Nariman Road, Tel: 221217
Delhi: Ansal Bhawan, K.G. Marg, Tel: 3318632 APT: 392621

Japan Airlines
Delhi: Chandralok Building, 36 Janpath, Tel: 343130. APT: 5452082

Kenya Airways
Bombay: 199 Churchgate Reclamation, Tel: 220064, APT: 6322577

KLM
Bombay: Khetan Bhawan, 198 J. Tata Rd, Tel: 221013
Calcutta: 1 Middleton St, Tel: 447238
Delhi: Prakash Deep, Tolstoy Marg, Tel: 3315841, APT: 392192
Madras: Connemara Hotel, Tel: 86356

Korean Air
Delhi: 40/2 Pearelal Building, Janpath, Tel: 350561

Kuwait Airways
Bombay: Chateau Windsor, Vir Nariman Road, Tel: 298351
Delhi: Hansalaya, Barakhamba Road, Tel: 3314221/3 APT: 391993
Madras: Embassy Towers, 55 Montieth Road, Egmore, Tel: 83337/9

Lot
Bombay: Nariman Bhawan, Nariman Point, Tel: 221431
Delhi: G-55 Connaught Circus, Tel: 3326958

Lufthansa
Bombay: Express Tower, Nariman Point, Tel: 2023430, 2020887 APT: 6321485

Calcutta: 30 A/B Jawaharlal Nehru Road, Tel: 248611/3
Delhi: 56 Janpath, Tel: 3327609 APT: 5452063/4
Madras: 167, Mount Road, Tel: 81483/5

Maldives Airways
Bombay: 7 Bradbourne Stadium, Churchgate, Tel: 202-9020

Malaysian Airlines System
Delhi: Hotel Imperial, Janpath, Tel: 3324789, 33247582
Madras: 189 Mount Road, Tel: 868970, 868625 APT: 431656

PIA
Bombay: Hotel Oberoi Towers, Nariman Point, Tel: 202-1480 APT: 6320700
Delhi: 26 Kasturba Gandhi Marg, Tel: 331-3161/2 APT: 5452093/4

Pan Am
Bombay: Taj Mahal Hotel, Tel: 2029020, Tel: 6329660
Delhi: Chandralok Building, 36 Janpath, Tel: 3313161 APT: 5452093/4
Madras: 164 Anna Road, Tel: 811209

Qantas
Bombay: Hotel Oberoi Towers, Nariman Point, Tel: 2020343 APT: 6327864
Dehli: Hotel Janpath, Tel: 351434

Royal Nepal Airlines
Calcutta: 41 Chowringhee, Tel: 298534
Delhi: 44 Janpath, Tel: 3320817 APT: 393876

Royal Jordanian
Calcutta: Chitrakoot Building, 230A A.J.C. Bose Road, Tel: 447783
Delhi: G-56 Connaught Circus, Tel: 331-9890, 3327418

Sabena
Bombay: Nirmal Building, Nariman Point, Tel: 2023817 APT: 6320700
Delhi: Himalaya House, K.G. Marg, Tel: 3312701
Madras: Regency House, 250 Mount Road, Tel: 451786

Saudia
Bombay: Express Towers, Nariman

Point, Tel: 2020049 APT: 6329991
Delhi: Hansalaya, 15 Barakantba Rd,
Tel: 3310466 APT: 391357

Singapore Airlines
Bombay: Air India Bldg, Nariman Point
Tel: 2023316 APT: 6327024
Calcutta: 18-D Part Street, Tel: 299293
Delhi: G-11 Connaught Circus Tel:
3320145 APT: 394200
Madras: 16 Anna Salai Tel: 82871 APT:
433860

Swissair
Bombay: Makar Chambar VI, 220 Nari-
man Point Tel: 222559 APT: 632682
Calcutta: Everest, 46-C Chowringhee
Road Tel: 444643
Delhi: 56 Janpath Tel: 3325511
Madras: 40 Mount Road Tel: 82583

Syrian Arab Airlines
Bombay: 7 Brabourne Stadium, Churchgate, Tel: 22604 APT: 6320700
Delhi: 13/90 Connaught Place, Tel:
343218, 391058

Thai
Bombay: Cuffe Parade, Colaba, Tel:
214180
Calcutta: 18G Park Street, Tel: 249696
APT: 573937
Delhi: 12A Connaught Place, Tel:
3323608 APT: 392526

Turkish Airlines
Bombay: Maker Chambars V, Nariman
Point, Tel: 2046491 APT: 6320700
Delhi: 56 Janpath, Tel: 3326661 APT:
5452021

Yemen Airways
Bombay: Mittal Towers, Nariman Point,
Tel: 223145

Yugoslav Airlines
Calcutta-Oberoi Grand, J.N. Road,
Tel: 292323

Zambai Airways
Bombay: 87E Stadium House, Vir Nariman Road, Tel: 241251 APT: 6329666
Delhi: Janpath Hotel, Tel: 312029,
350070

TRAVEL ESSENTIALS

VISAS

All visitors to India require a valid visa.
These are available from Embassies or High
Commissions in most major capitals. Any
visitor visiting more than once (i.e combining a visit to India with side trips to Nepal,
Sri Lanka, Bhutan or Bangladesh) on a particular tour is advised to obtain a multiple
entry visa.

Indian tourist visas are valid for three
months and can be extended for a further
three months. Applications should be made
to the Foreigners Registration Offices in
major cities or the Superintendent of Police
in district Head Quarters.

Business visitors can obtain multiple entry visas valid for 90 days stay within a one
year period. Not all Indian missions issue
this visa.

RESTRICTED AREA
AND INNER LINE PERMITS

Many parts of India fall within the pur-
view of Restricted Area. The Inner Line
varies but is usually between 50-100 km of
the border with China and Burma. The border with Pakistan is open only at Wagi (west
of Amritsar). It is safe to assume that a visit
to anywhere within 50 km of Pakistan in
Rajasthan (except Jaisalmer town) requires
special permission. Apart from border areas,
special permits are required for visits to
Assam, Arunachal Pradesh, Nagaland,
Manipur, Mizoram, Tripura and Meghalaya
in the north east; the Lakshadweep Islands;
the Andaman and Nicobar Islands; Sikkim
and the hill area of West Bengal; parts of
Kashmir and Himachal Pradesh and Bastar
district in Madhya Pradesh.

Restricted Area and Inner Line permits can be applied for through Indian missions abroad. In New Delhi, applications are made through the Ministry of Home Affairs (Foreigners Wing), Lok Nayak Bhawan, Khan Market. Allow a minimum of six weeks!!

MONEY MATTERS

All encashments of travelers checks and exchange of foreign currency must either be recorded on the currency declaration form or receipts kept, as hotel bills, airline tickets etc, can be paid for in local currency only against proof of legal conversion. These will also be necessary for reconversion of any balance of Indian currency left unspent on departure. Visitors leaving after a stay of 90 days or more will have to produce proofs of encashment of travelers checks or exchange of currency for income tax exemption, and to show that they have been self-supporting.

Indian currency is based on the decimal system, with 100 paise to the rupee. Coins are in denominations of 5, 10, 20, 25 and 50 paise. One and two rupee coins are also in use. Notes are in one, two , five, ten, twenty, fifty, hundred and the rarer five hundred rupee denominations. Indian rupees may not be brought in or taken out of the country. Exchange rates fluctuate against all currencies.

Major credit cards are accepted in the larger hotels, restaurants and shops. Although travelers checks and cash can get you a better (and illegal) rate of exchange in small establishments, it is best to deal with banks and licensed money changers. Since encashing travelers checks could take time, it is advisable to change amounts adequate to cover a few days' needs at a time.

HEALTH

Only visitors arriving from Africa and South America are required to have an International Health Certificate with record of a valid yellow fever inoculation (validity is for 10 years). Remember that immunity is effective only 10 days after vaccination.

No other vaccination certificate is required, but for personal protection, the whole range of inoculations is recommended—cholera, typhoid, and tetanus. Do consult your doctor for advice on gama globulin shots to boost immunity to hepatitis and for suggestions on anti-malarial pills.

A personal medical kit to take care of minor ailments is useful to have along. Antienetic and anti-diarrhoea medication, a broad spectrum antibiotic, aspirin and something for throat infections and allergies would be a good idea. Also include band aids, an antiseptic cream, an insect repellant and water purification tablets. Salt pills to combat heat exhaustion are particularly necessary if your visit is in summer. A locally available powder (Vijay Electrolyte) containing salts and dextrose is an ideal additive to water especially when traveling in the summer months or suffering from diarrhoea.

Never drink unboiled or unfiltered water. When in doubt, stick to a soda, mineral water, or aerated drinks of standard brands. In smaller towns, avoid factory ice as this is often made with unboiled water. All food should be cooked and eaten hot. Avoid salads and always peel fruits.

WHAT TO WEAR

Plan your wardrobe according to your itinerary and the season of your visit. In winter a sweater, preferably two, one light and one heavy, as well as a jacket or an anorak are necessary, especially in the north where daily temperature differentials can be quite wide. Lighter clothing would be adequate in the south and along the coast. Cottons are the ideal fibre to wear in summer. Avoid synthetics. Casuals in natural fibres are inexpensive in India, so bring only essentials and leave plenty of room in your suitcase for acquisitions. Comfortable footwear, sneakers for winter and sandals for summer, make walking on uneven surfaces easier.

For their own convenience women should avoid sleeveless blouses, mini skirts or potentially provocative dress.

WHAT TO BRING

Unless you enjoy paying excess baggage charges on your way home it is best to arrive light. The shopping possibilities are more often limited by space rather than cost.

The golden rule of traveling light applies. Traveling in South India or the north during summer is "shirtsleeve weather" and it is best to wear cotton. In the north during winter sweaters and jackets are required. Cotton shirts, blouses and skirts are easily available throughout the country. Good trousers or dresses can be made up within 24/48 hours by almost any tailor.

If traveling away from the major cities or big hotels it is worth taking along a medical kit, a padlock, and a sewing kit among other items. Sun cream or sun block (vital in the mountains) is not readily available so they should be brought. A hat is a sensible precaution. A bath plug is also useful in smaller hotels which often seem to have basins without them!

CUSTOMS

Most international airports have red and green channels. Tourists seldom have any trouble. Occasionally, customs officials ask to see one suitcase at random and make a quick check. Prohibited articles include certain dangerous drugs, live plants, gold and silver bullion and coins not in current use. Firearms require possession licenses (valid for 6 months), issued by Indian Embassies or Consulates abroad, or on arrival in India, by a District Magistrate. For further details, check with the issuing authority.

Duty-free imports include 200 cigarettes (or 50 cigars), 0.95 liters of alcohol, a camera with 5 rolls of film and a reasonable amount of personal effects, including binoculars, a portable typewriter, sound recording instruments and so on. Professional equipment and high value articles must be declared or listed on arrival on the TBRE form with a written undertaking to re-export them. Both the list and the articles must be produced on departure. As this is sometimes a lengthy process, allow extra time, both on arrival and at departure. For unaccompanied baggage or baggage misplaced by the airline, make sure you get a landing certificate from customs on arrival.

To avoid last-minute departure problems, remember that the export of antiques (over 100 years old), all animal products, and jewelry valued at over Rs. 2,000/- (in the case of gold) and Rs. 10,000/- (in the case of articles not made of gold), are banned. When in doubt about the age of semi-antiques, contact the office of the Archeological Survey of India in Delhi, Bombay, Calcutta, Madras or Srinagar.

Currency Declaration forms for amounts in excess of US$1,000/- must be completed at customs on arrival.

ON DEPARTURE

Do remember to reconfirm your reservations for departure well in advance to avoid any last-minute difficulties. Security checks can be intensive and time consuming so allow 2 hours for check-in. An airport/seaport tax of Rs. 100/- per person (Rs. 50/- for flights to Nepal, Bhutan, Bangladesh, Pakistan, The Maldives and Sri Lanka) is charged on departure and must be paid prior to check in. Do ensure that your out bound carrier is endorsed on the tax receipt. For visitors with entry permits, exit endorsements are necessary from the office where they were registered. Should a stay exceed 90 days, an income tax exemption certificate must be obtained from the Foreign Section of the Income Tax Department in Delhi, Bombay, Calcutta or Madras.

GETTING ACQUAINTED

GOVERNMENT & ECONOMY

The Indian Union is a federation comprising 24 States and 7 Union Territories. Each State, and some Union Territories, has its own Legislative Assembly and Government, headed by a Chief Minister. The Central (federal) government is headed by a Prime Minister and Council of Ministers (Cabinet) responsible to the two houses of Parliament: the Lok Sabha (the Council of the People) which is directly elected by the people on the basis of adult franchise; and the Rajya Sabha (the Council of States), and indirectly elected body, which functions somewhat like those of the British House of Lords. The President and Vice-President are elected by an electoral college consisting of Members of Parliament and members of the State Legislatures.

Elections are held every five years but can, in certain situations be called earlier. India has had eight general elections since it became an independent country in 1947.

With a well developed, democratic political and administrative structure, a large skilled labor force and an adequate communications system, India has made considerable progress since independence. Despite the agrarian bias of its economy, industry has grown enormously, placing India among the 20 top industrial nations of the world. Her relatively low level of exports is partly due to the large volume of domestic consumption. The per capital national income although meagre in comparison with the rest of the world, is a considerable improvement over 1947. In the matter of production of food grains particularly, the advance has been spectacular—once a chronically deficit area, India can now export.

TIME ZONES

Despite its size, India has a uniform time zone all over the country. Indian Standard Time is 5 1/2 hours ahead of Greenwich Mean Time and 9 1/2 hours ahead of the U.S. E.S.T. (Eastern Standard Time).

Specific international time differences are as follows:

Delhi/India 12 noon today
Bonn 7.30 am. today
Paris 7.30 am. today
London 6.30 am. today
New York 1.30 am. today
San Francisco 10.30 pm. yesterday
Hawaii 8.30 pm. yesterday
Sydney 4.30 pm. today
Tokyo 3.30 pm. today

CLIMATE

When talking about a country of such tremendous size and geographical diversity as India, it is difficult to make a general statement concerning the climate. It ranges from the eternal snows of the Himalayas and the temperate conditions along the coasts, to the continental climate of inland areas. Besides that, there are many regional and seasonal variations.

October to March is the cool season and therefore the best time of the year to visit Peninsular India. On the whole, the weather is beautifully predictable in winter, with blue skies and bright sunshine in most areas. Some parts of the south and the east however, see a brief spell of rain from the North East Monsoon, while snow and sleet combine to make the extreme north very cold and often inaccessible.

Summer, from April to June, is hot and dry for most of the country, and humid along the coasts. Kashmir and the hill stations of Himachal and Uttar Pradesh are particularly lovely at this time of the year. The South West Monsoon begins to set in along the western coast towards the end of the May, bringing welcome respite from the heat, and varying amounts of rain, as they move across the rest of the country through June and July and withdraw by late September. North Eastern India has particularly heavy rain during this season, and is one of the world's wettest regions.

CULTURE & CUSTOMS

Removing one's shoes before entering temples, mosques or gurdwaras is essential. Overshoes are provided in some places at a nominal cost and stockinged fee are usually permissible. Avoid taking leather goods of any kind into temples as these could be taken exception to. Photography is prohibited inside most places of worship. Do obtain permission before using a camera. Visitors are usually welcome to look around at their leisure and can sometimes stay during religious rituals. For places of worship, modest clothing, rather than brief skirts and skimpy tops or shorts, are appropriate. A small contribution to the donation box is customary.

The namaste, the greeting with folded hands, is the Indian form of greeting and its use will be appreciated though men, especially in the cities, will not hesitate and will even offer to shake hands with you if you a man. A handshake would even be appreciated as a gesture of special friendliness. Most Indian woman would hesitate to shake hands with men, whether Indian or foreign, and no offence is meant. Most would also be somewhat taken aback at the easy informality of interaction between the sexes common in the West.

In private homes, visitors are received as honored guests and your unfamiliarity with Indian ways will be accepted and understood. Should you be tempted to eat with your fingers, remember to use only your right hand.

TIPPING

There is no harm expressing your appreciation with a small tip. Depending on services rendered and the type of establishment, this could range from Rs. 2/- to Rs. 10/-. In restaurants the tip is customarily 10 to 15 per cent of the bill. Leading hotels add a 10 per cent service surcharge and tipping in such places is therefore optional. Although tipping taxis and three wheelers is not an established norm, it would not be taken amiss. Here again 10 per cent of the fare or leaving the change if substantial would be adequate. Porters at railway stations would expect around Rs.2/- a bag. At airports a rupee per bag in addition to the fee charged by the airport authority, though not essential, would be welcome.

If you have been a house guest, please check with your host whether he has any objections to your tipping any of his domestic helpers (e.g a chauffeur who may have driven you around) before doing so.

WEIGHTS & MEASURES

The metric system is uniformly used all over India for weight and for measure. Precious metals, especially gold, are often sold by the traditional tola, which is is equivalent to 11.5grams. Gems are weighted in carats (0.2grams). Financial outlays and population are often expressed in lakhs (one hundred thousand) and crores (one hundred lakhs or ten million).

ELECTRICITY

India is on a 220-V, 50 cycle system. Most larger hotels provide step-down transformers to provide voltage suited to your electrical appliances. Check with the bell boy or at the information desk.

BUSINESS HOURS

Central Government offices now work a 5-day week, from 9 a.m. to 6 p.m., Monday through Friday. This is a recently introduced change and has not yet been implemented in all states.

Post Offices are open from 10 a.m. to 4.30 p.m. on weekdays, and only till 12 noon on Saturdays. Here again, in most larger cities, the Central Post Office works till 6.30 p.m. on weekdays, and 4.30 p.m. on Saturdays. On Sundays, they are open only till 12 noon. Major telegraph offices are open 24 hours.

Shops are usually open from 10 a.m. to 7 p.m. Some close for lunch. Although Sunday is the official holiday, different localities in major cities have staggered days off so that there are always some shopping areas open. Most restaurants are open till 11 p.m. with some nightclubs and discotheques closing very much later. Hotel coffee shops are often open round the clock.

BANKING

Business hours of all foreign banks and nationalised Indian banks (of which the State Bank is the largest) are from 10 a.m. to 2 p.m. Monday through Friday, and from 10 a.m. to 12 noon on Saturdays. Some banks operate evening branches, while others remain open on Sundays, closing on another day of the week. All banks close on national holidays and on June 30 and December 31. Outward remittance, which goes through the Reserve Bank of India, is a difficult and lengthy process, and at best avoided. However, should you require additional money while you are in India, have it remitted through a draft or mail transfer. Do remember to keep all receipts.

HOLIDAYS

Most business and banks close for the following holidays: 1989

Republic Day	January 26
Holi	March 22
Good Friday	March 24
Mahavir Jayanti	April 18
Idu'l Fitr (Romzan Id)	May 7
Buddha Purnima	May 20
Idu'z Zuha (Bakrid)	July 14
Muharram	August 13
Independence Day	August 15
Janmashtami	August 24
Mahatma Gandhi's Birthday	October 2
Dussehra (Vijaya Dashami)	October 10
Diwali	October 29/30
Guru Nanak's Birthday	November 13
Christmas	December 25

RELIGIOUS SERVICES

There are few towns in India, even among those of medium size, that are without a church and a mosque, though you may not always get one of your particular denomination. There are gurdwaras in major towns all over the country and Hindu temples everywhere. There are a number of synagogues in Bombay, two in Calcutta, and one each in New Delhi and Pune. Your hotel will give you more information as to the kind of religious institution you are seeking.

SECURITY & CRIME

India is no worse than any other country with regard to theft and in fact considerably safer than most. However, the usual precaution of locking bags, not leaving money or jewelery in hotel rooms and holding onto cameras apply.

If anything is stolen and reported to the police a copy of the FIR (First Information Report) should be kept to support any insurance claim.

COMMUNICATIONS

MEDIA

With a large number of English dailies and hundreds of newspapers in Indian languages, the press in India provides a wide and critical coverage of national and international events. Among the better known national English language dailies are the *Times of India*, *The Indian Express*, *The Hindu*, *The Statesman*, *The Telegraph*, *The Hindustan Times* and *The Indian Post*. There are also two Sunday papers *The Sunday Observer* and *The Sunday Mail*. The major news magazines include *India Today*, *Sunday*, *The Illustrated Weekly*. There are also several excellent general interest magazines such as *The India Magazine* and *Sanctuary* magazine, which specializes in South Asian natural history and *The India Magazine*.

There are several women's magazines, financial journals (and dailies), city weeklies and special interest journals.

RADIO AND TELEVISION

Both radio and television are government-run and controlled. Both are huge networks with programmes in English, Hindi and regional languages. The local timings vary with the location of the relay stations.

All India Radio (AIR) broadcasts on the shortwave, medium wave and in Delhi, Bombay and Madras on FM (UHF). The frequencies vary from place to place.

Doordarshan is the government television company with two channels in Delhi, Bombay, Madras, Calcutta, Bangalore and a few other centers. The English news is broadcast at 0750 hours and 2130 hours every day. A 'teletext' service is also being developed.

POSTAL SERVICES

The internal mail service is good in most areas. The rates for inland letters is 60 paise for the first 10 grams and 40 paise for each additional 10 grams. Inland letter forms cost 35 paise each and a plain postcard 15 paise. Picture postcards and postcards with printed matter require 40 paise stamps.

For foreign destinations, airmail letters require Rs. 6.50 for the first 10 grams. Aerogrammes cost Rs. 5.

It is advisable to personally affix stamps to letters or post cards and hand them over to the post office counter for immediate franking rather than to slot them into a letter box.

Sending a registered parcel overseas is usually a complicated and time consuming process. Most parcels should be stitched into cheap cotton cloth and then sealed (there are often people sitting outside major post offices offering this service). Two customs forms also need to be completed. Once the parcel has been weighed and stamps affixed, make sure they are franked and a receipt of registration is issued to you. Note that important or valuable material should always be registered.

Many shops offer to despatch goods, but not all of them are reliable. It is usually only safe when handled by one of the government run emporiums.

Air freighting purchases is possible but can be equally time consuming. No matter how you send your package, you will need the cash memo or bill and receipt, encashment certificate, passport and onward airline ticket. There are many airfreight agents throughout India and most travel agents will be able to provide assistance.

COURIER SERVICES

Most of the major international courier networks have agency agreements with Indian companies. DHL, Skypak, IML all work under their own brand name while Federal Express operates as Blue Dart! All of these companies have their offices in the major towns. In addition to linking into the international networks, they also operate extensive networks within the country.

In most towns this will but make sure your name is clearly written. Most towns have only one main post office but there is often confusion between Delhi and New Delhi. New Delhi's main post office is near Connaught Circus while Delhi's main post office is between the Red Fort and Kashmere Gate in "Old" Delhi.

TELEPHONE & TELEX

Overloaded exchanges have traditionally made making a call a frustrating business. However in the major cities with the introduction of electronic exchanges, the phones are getting better. Long-distance calls to most parts of India can now be made direct or booked through the operator. A demand service (not person to person) is available between some towns and to the United Kingdom. Lightning calls are the quickest but cost eight times as much as regular calls.

International calls can now be dialed to most parts of the world or booked through the operator. Delays do still take place. If staying in a hotel ask the operator to book for you, if possible, to avoid frayed nerves.

Telex services, both domestic and international are good and reasonably priced.

A limited number of fascimile transmission machines operate in the major cities. Most large hotels offer a fax service in their business centers.

GETTING AROUND

ORIENTATION

Apart from this book there are a few others giving useful information about the country as a whole or its regions. The Insight Guide to Rajasthan is the most comprehensive book on that state. Other books cover sections of the Himalayas.

The Insight Guide to Indian Wildlife has the most detailed listing available on national parks, sanctuaries and reserves along with details of the facilities at each. For more information, refer to the detailed bibliography given in the appendix.

The best maps available are the five sheets published by Nelles Verlag GmbH in West Germany and available throughout India. Unfortunately the best maps of the Himalayas are only available outside India.

FROM THE AIRPORT

Once through customs the arriving passenger is often besieged by porters, taxi drivers and others. Choose one porter and stick to him. There is a system of paying porters a fixed amount per piece of baggage before leaving the terminal — a tip of about Rs. 5/-once the bags are aboard the taxi or bus, is sufficient. If a travel agent or a friend is meeting you they may be waiting for you outside the building. If taking a taxi or bus into town it is advisable to change money in the arrival hall.

In both Delhi and Bombay, a system of prepayment for taxis into the city is operated by the traffic police. This saves considerable anguish when the occasional unscrupulous driver takes a long route or tries to overcharge. Elsewhere, enquire at the information desk for the going rate for a journey to your destination before getting into the taxi: also make sure the meter is "down" before you start the journey. It is acceptable to share taxis even if the destination is not the same (although in the same area). In some cities, taxis have fare charts which when applied to the amount on the meter give the correct fare. There is often a night surcharge of 20% between 2300 and 0600 hours and a rate of Rs. 1/- to Rs. 2/- per piece of baggage.

Some major hotels operate courtesy buses and a public service known as EATS (Ex Serviceman's Transport Service) operates an airport bus service in Delhi, Bombay and Calcutta with stops at hotels and major points enroute to the city center.

DOMESTIC TRAVEL

Indian Airlines (not to be confused with the international carrier, Air India), covers one of the world's largest domestic networks. It carries an average of 30 000 passengers every day to 62 destinations within the country and to Afghanistan, Bangladesh, the Maldives, Nepal, Pakistan, Sri Lanka and Thailand. On the routes operated by Airbus aircraft, an Executive class is available. All Boeing and other aircraft are a single (economy) class.

BY AIR

The previously lengthy and time consuming reservations system has now been theoretically improved by the introduction of computers. Instantaneous responses to reservations requests for multi-sector itineraries are now possible through CRT units installed at the major stations which are connected by automatic teleprinter circuits to other stations. The system is also linked to the international circuit and this has reduced delays in obtaining confirmations. When travelling during peak season (September to March), make reservations well in advance as flights are usually heavily booked.

With time-consuming check-in and security procedures, you must be at the airport a good hour before departure time. Coach services from some city terminal are available and reliable. In-flight service is adequate. Snacks and meals are served by pleasant English-speaking air hostesses. Alcohol is only available on inter-country flights. Incidentally, an airport tax of Rs. 50/ is levied on all flights to neighboring countries, as against the Rs. 100/- for travel to other countries.

Indian Airlines has a good safety record. Its fares are often lower than those charged for comparable distances elsewhere. The free baggage allowance per adult is 20 kg and 30 kg in Business class.

Cancellation charges on tickets purchased locally are extremely high, but none are applicable for domestic sectors issued on international tickets.

The US$400 Discover India fare valid for 21 days of travel all over the country is particularly attractive. Travel must, however, be in a roughly circular direction. You are permitted to return to a city only to make a connection. Change of flights and even re-routing are allowed at no extra charge. This ticket must be purchased abroad, or paid for in India using foreign currency. Other concessional fares include a youth discount of 25 per cent for students and travelers under 30. A 30% discount on the US dollar tariff is applicable on a South India excursion when the gateway is Madras, Trivandrum or Tiruchrapalli. Groups of 10 or more are eligible for discounts up to 50 per cent, however, this is subject to certain conditions. For details, contact your travel agent or an Air India office abroad, or write to the Traffic Manager, Indian Airlines House, Parliament Street, New Delhi.

Air India carries domestic passengers on their linking flights between Bombay and Delhi, Calcutta, Madras and Bangalore. These flights leave from the International Terminals in the respective cities.

A third government carrier is the recently established "feeder" or third level airline Vayudoot. Vayudoot has an especially strong network in the North East but also links small towns throughout the country with major cities. Most flights are operated by 19 seater Dorniar 28s or HS748s (Avros).

Vayudoot also operates a charter service. More information can be obtained from:

The Commercial Department
Vayudoot
Safdarjung Airport
New Delhi-110-003
Telephone: 699272
Bombay: 6121405
Calcutta: 576582
Hyderabad: 72855

BY RAIL

Carrying about 10 million people every day to over 7000 stations, the Indian Railways are the largest system in Asia and the second largest in the world. Rail travel is safe and comfortable, but can be confusing. Of the many different categories of accommodation available, those recommended are air-conditioned first class (the most expensive and comparable with the best anywhere); two-tier air-conditioned sleeper, and air-conditioned chair car (both second class). Travel by non-air-conditioned first and second class can become dusty and uncomfortable and is best avoided, especially during the hot dry months. Advance reservation is strongly recommended.

Trains are slow compared to those in the West, so if you are in a hurry, stay with the expresses; fares are generally low. The Indrail Pass, to be paid for in foreign currency, offers particularly good value for those on an extended tour of India. Prices range from US$190 for air-conditioned first class for 7 days and US$690 for 90 days in the same class, to US$95 and US$345 for the air-conditioned (2nd class) chair car for the same periods. The Passes can be bought only in India through leading travel agents or Railway Central Reservations Offices in Delhi, Bombay, Calcutta, Madras, Secunderabad and Hyderabad.

Tourist Guide Offices at railway reservation centers are helpful in planning itineraries and obtaining reservations. Railway time-tables available at Indian Tourist Offices abroad, also contain much useful information. For the enthusiast, the more detailed *All India Railway Time-Table* or the concise but comprehensive *Trains at a Glance* can be bought at railway stations.

Remember to check which station your train departs from and do allow at least an hour to find your seat/berth. Lists of passengers with the compartment and seat/berth numbers allotted to them are displayed on platforms, and on each compartment an hour before departure. The Station Superintendent and the conductor attached to the train are available for assistance.

Food can usually be ordered through the coach attendant and, on some trains, the fare covers food as well. Snacks, tea, coffee and soft drinks (colas etc) are also usually available. Refreshment rooms are provided at big stations and stalls at others. Bed rolls are available on payment on certain routes in the first and second class, provided this request is made at the time of reservation. Bedding is provided in the air-conditioned first class.

Retiring rooms (for short-term occupation only) are available at most railway stations, but these are usually heavily booked and should be reserved well in advance. All first class waiting rooms have couches for passengers using their own bedding.

Trains are usually overcrowded so to ensure that you get a seat, do remember to reserve your seat well in advance.

BY BUS

Almost every part of the country is connected by an extensive and well-developed bus system: The railway stations are natural hubs for both local and regional services. Some of the more rural routes are serviced by noisy dilapidated vehicles but an increasing number of deluxe and air-conditioned expresses ply the trunk routes. Unfortunately many of the trunk routes are now operated by the recent phenomenon, video coaches—if you have never been to an Indian cinema, a night bus journey is an introduction to the low-brow popular brand of Hindi or regional film.

There are many parts of the country where the bus service is the only means of public transport—the Himalayas in particular. Buses are also more convenient than trains on sectors such as Delhi-Jaipur; Jaipur-Agra and Bombay-Goa.

On many routes, even local ones, reservations can be made. Most baggage is carried on the roof so all bags should be locked and watched at intermediate stops.

Most cities have a bus service. Bombay's

is excellent whereas Delhi's is inadequate and consequently crowded. In cities the best mode of transport is the taxi or three wheeled "auto-rickshaws".

BY TAXI

Chauffeur-driven cars can be rented through major agencies and most hotels. No self-drive hire system is available, which, given traffic and road conditions, is just as well. Taxis are both air-conditioned and non-air conditioned. Charges vary, ranging from Rs.325 for 8 hours and 80 km to Rs 450 for an air-conditioned car. For out of town travel, there is a per km charge, usually between Rs. 2.30 to Rs.3.00 per km in the plains, with an overnight charge of Rs 100. Package tours, sold by travel agencies and hotels, include all assistance, guides, hotel accommodation and so on in addition to the taxi charges.

The local yellow-topped black-bodied taxis are metered, but, with constant hikes in fuel prices, charges may often be higher than indicated. If so, this will be prominently stated in the taxi and the driver will have a card showing the excess over the meter reading that can be legitimately charged. The fare for three-wheelers that ply in almost every Indian city are roughly half those of taxis. They are also metered. Do not forget to ensure that the meter is flagged down to the minimum fare.

MOTORING

A network of metalled roads connects all important cities and towns. The trunk roads are generally good, but secondary roads are more often bad, especially during the monsoons, which play havoc with the roads and the bridges.

Full information regarding road conditions, driving licences, "Triptyque" and "Carnet" can be obtained from the automobile associations listed below, which periodically issue regional motoring maps, general information regarding roads, and detailed route charts.

Automobile Association of Upper India, Lilaram Building, 14F Connaught Circus, New Delhi-110 001.
Tel: 331-4071, 331-2323/4/5.

Western India Automobile Association, Lalji Narainji Memorial Building, 76 Veer Nariman Road, Bombay - 400 020.
Tel: 291085, 291192.

Automobile Association of Eastern India, 13 Promothosh Barna Sarani, Calcutta - 700 019. Tel: 474804.

Automobile Association of Southern India, 187 Anna Salai, Madras- 600 006.
Tel: 86121-2-3.

U.P. Automobile Association, 32A Mahatma Gandhi Marg, Allahabad. Tel: 2445.

Do remember that in India you drive on the left of the road. A third party insurance policy is essential, and it must be with a company registered in India or one abroad that has a guarantor in India.

WHERE TO STAY

HOTELS

There are four main hotel chains each of which has a central reservations system. Bookings can be made either through another member of the same chain or through a travel agency.

The Ashok Group
The hotel wing of The Indian Tourism Development Corporation (ITDC) wholly owned by the government of India. Many ITDC hotels can be booked through Golden Tulip World-Wide Hotels (KLM).

Oberoi Hotels
Privately owned and India's most international hotel chain. Bookings worldwide through LOEWS Reservation or through The Oberoi, Dr. Zakir Hussain Marg, New Delhi 110008. Telex: 3829/63222 OBDL IN, Tel: 699571.

The Taj Group of Hotels
The Indian Hotels company is part of the Tata industrial group and has some of India's most magnificent hotel properties. Booking through UTFL International worldwide and The Leading Hotels of a World and Superaps International London for selected properties. Sales Headquarters located at The Taj Mahal Hotel, Apollo Bundar, Bombay 400039, telex 112442/3837/3791/6176/6175 TAJB IN, Tel: 202-3366, 202-2524.

The Welcom Group
India's newest hotel chain is part of ITC (India Tobacco Company). Some properties are booked through Sheraton Hotels worldwide or through Welcomgroup group

Headquarters, Maurya Sheraton, New Delhi: 110021, Telex: 031-65217. WELC IN Tel: 301-0101, 301-0136.

In the lists that follow, any properties with ITDC, Oberoi, Taj Group or Welcomgroup after it can be booked through the above addresses respectively or directly.

NEW DELHI/DELHI

Deluxe

Ashok (ITDC)
80-B Chanakyapuri
New Delhi 110021
Tel: 600121, 600412
Telex: 031-65207, 65647.

Centaur
Delhi Airport,
New Delhi 110037
Tel: 391411
Telex: 031-5477 CHDR IN,
031-62744 CHDA IN

Hyatt Regency
Bhikaji Cama Place
Ring Road, New Delhi 110066
Tel: 609911
Telex: 031-62779, 031-63069 HYT IN

Le Meridien
Windsor Place
New Delhi 110001
Tel: 383960, 389379
Telex: 031-63076 HOME IN

The Oberoi
Dr. Zakir Hussain Marg
New Delhi 110003.
Tel: 699871, 363030
Telex: 031-62133, 3829,
63222 OBDL IN Fax: 694484.

The Taj Mahal Hotel
Number One Mansingh Road
New Delhi 110011
Tel: 3016162
Telex: 031-4758, 66874,
61898 TAJD IN

Welcomgroup Maurya Sheraton
Diplomatic Enclave
New Delhi 110021.

Tel: 301-0101
Telex: 031-65217 WELC IN

4-5 Star

Clandges
12 Avranzab Road
New Delhi 110001
Tel: 301-0211
Telex: 031-62898/65526 CLAR IN

Imperial
Janpath
New Delhi 110001
Tel: 332-8511
Telex 031-62603

Kaniska (ITDC)
19 Ashok Road
New Delhi 110001
Tel: 343400
Telex: 031-63788/62736

Oberoi Maidens
7-Sham Nath Marg
Delhi 110054
Tel: 252 5464
Telex 031-66303/66801 OMDL IN

Park Hotel
15 Parliament St
New Delhi 110001
Tel: 326715
Telex: 031-65231 PARK IN

Quterb Hotel (ITDC)
Off Sri Aurobindo Marg
New Delhi 110016
Tel: 660060
Telex: 031-0637, 62537

Samrit (ITDC)
Chanakyapuri, New Delhi 110008
Tel: 603030
Telex: 031-5296/5241

Siddharth
3 Rajendra Place
New Delhi 110008
Tel: 671250
Telex: 031-61293 SIOHIN

Sofitel Surya
New Friends Colony
New Delhi 110065

Tel: 635070
Telex: 031-66700

Vasant Continental
Vasant Vihas
New Delhi 1100
Tel: 678800
Telex: 031-66723

Medium and Budget Hotels

In addition to the following, New Delhi also has a large number of reasonably priced guest houses with air-conditioned rooms, room service etc.

Ashok Yahri Niwas (ITDC)
19 Ashok Road
New Delhi 110001
Tel: 344511
(Budget)

Diplomat
9 Sadar Patel Marg
New Delhi 110021
Tel: 301-1070
Telex: 031- 2532

Haw Plaza
15 Barakambar Road
New Delhi 110001
Tel: 331-0861
Telex: 031-4695

Jakaso Inn
50 Sundar Nagar
New Delhi
Tel: 690308

Lodhi Hotel (ITDC)
Lala Lajpat Rai Marg
New Delhi 110003
Tel: 362422
Telex: 031-2268

Marina
G-59 Connaught Circus
New Delhi 110001
Tel: 352419
Telex: 031-66224

Nirula's
L Block, Connaught Circus
New Delhi 110001
Tel: 352419 Telex: 031-66224

Sartaj
A-3 Green Park
New Delhi
Tel: 663277
Telex: 031-61709

Youth Hostels

YMCA International Guest House
Parliament Street
New Delhi 110001
Tel: 311561

YMCA Tourist Hostel
Jai Singh Road
New Delhi 110001

All hotels hereafter are listed by town alphabetically.

Agra, Uttar Pradesh

Deluxe and 5-Star

Welcomgroup Mughal Sheraton
Taj Ganj, Agra 282001.
Tel: 64701 Telex: 0565-210 ITCO IN

Taj View (Taj)
Taj Ganj, Fatehabad Road, Agra 282001
Tel: 64171 Telex: 0565-202 TAJU IN

4-Star

Agra Ashok (ITDC)
The Mall, Agra 282001
Tel: 76223

Clarks Shira
54 Taj Road, Agra 282001
Tel: 72421 Telex: 0565-211 SHRZ IN

Welcomgroup Mumtaz
Fatehabad Road, Agra 282001
Tel: 64771-6 Telex: 0565-222 MMTZ IN

Others

Amar
Fatehabad Road, Agra 282001
Tel: 65696-8 Telex: 0565-341 AMAR IN

Grand Hotel (2 star)
137 Station Road, Agra Cant, Agra
Tel: 74014

Lauries Hotel
M. G. Road, Agra 282001
Tel: 72536, 77047

Ahmedabad, Gujarat

Cama Hotel (4 star)
Khanpur, Ahmedabad 380001
Tel: 25281 Telex: 0121-377 CAMA IN

Hotel Karnavati
(Swee-Cinema Premises)
Ashram Road, Ahmedabad 380019
Tel: 402161, 402170
Telex: 0121-519 CSCO IN

Hotel Natraj (4 star)
Near ITO, Ashram Road,
Ahmedabad 380019
Tel: 448747 Telex: 0121-685 SHIN IN

ALLAHABAD, Uttar Pradesh

Presidency Hotel (2 star)
19-D Sarojini Naidu Marg
Allahabad 211001, Tel: 4460, 4097

Alleppey, Kerala

Prince Hotel (3 star)
A. S. Road, Alleppey, Kerala 688007
Tel: 3752-58 Telex: 0883-202 JONS IN

Amritsar, Punjab

Airlines (2 star)
Cooper Road, Amritsar, Punjab
Tel: 44545

Amritsar International Hotel (3 star)
City Center, Amritsar, Punjab 143001
Tel: 34146, 52864/5
Telex: 0384-300 MOHN IN

Ritz Hotel (3 star)
45 The Mall, Amritsar 143001
Tel: 44109, 34143
Telex: 0384-242 RITZ IN

Aurangabad, Maharashtra

Ajanta Ambassador (5 star),
hikalthana, Aurangabad 431210
Tel: 82211, 82451
Telex: 0745-211 AMBA IN

Ashok Travellers Lodge (ITDC)
Ajanta Caves, Dist Aurangabad 431117
Tel: 26 (situated at Ajanta, 106 km from
Aurangabad airport)

Aurangabad Ashok (ITDC-2 star)
Dr Rajendra Prasad Marg
Aurangabad 431001
Tel:4520-29 Telex: 0745-229

Welcomgroup Rama International
R-3 Chikalthana, Aurangabad 431210
Tel: 8340, 8241-4, 8455-7
Telex : 0745-212 RAMA IN

Balrampur, Uttar Pradesh

Traveotel Maya (2 star)
Balrampur, Dist Gonda,
Tel: 129

Bangalore, Karnataka

5 star

Ashok (ITDC)
Kumara Kruna, High Grounds
Bangalore 560001
Tel: 79411
Telex: 0845-433

Taj Residency (Taj)
14 Mahatma Gandhi Road
Bangalore 560001
Tel: 568888, Fax: 0812-575009
Telex: 0845-8367 TBLR IN

**Welcomgroup Windsor Manor
Sheraton**
25 Saukey Road, Bangalore 860052
Tel: 79431/28031
Telex: 0845-820 WIND IN

West End Hotel (Taj)
Race Course Road, Bangalore 560001
Tel: 292281, 74191, Fax: 0812-27610
Telex: 0845-337 WEND IN

Others

Hotel Bangalore International (3 star)
2 A/B Crescent Road
High Grounds Bangalore 560001
Tel: 258011-7
Telex: 0845-2340 HOSI IN

Nilgiris Nest (2 star)
St. Marks Road, Bangalore 560001
Tel: 568185, 578672
Telex: 0845-251 SHIL IN

Bareilly, Uttar Pradesh

Cival and Military Hotel
Station Road, Bareilly
Tel: 75879

Hotel Oberoi Avand
46 Cival Lines, Bareilly
Tel: 75728, 73717, 77448
Cable: OBIHOTEL

Baroda (Vadodara), Gujarat

Express Hotel (4 star)
R. C. Dutt Road, Vadodara 390005
Tel: 323131, 321960 Telex: 0175-311

Hotel Utsav (2 star)
Navrang Cinema Compound
Prof Manekrao Road, Vadodara 390001

Hotel Sarita (1 star)
Mahida-Niras, Mandwa-Chandad
Dist Baroda 391005
Tel: Chandod 24
(55 km from Baroda airport)

Welcomgroup Vadodara (4 star)
R.C. Dutt Road, Baroda 390005
Tel: 64311 Telex: 0175-525

Bhagalpur, Bihar

Hotel Niher (2 star)
Shiva Market, Bhagalpur 812001
Tel: 888 Telex: 0245-202 HONI IN

Bharatpur, Rajasthan

Bharatpur Forest Lodge (ITDC)
Bharatpur Bird Sanctuary
Bharatpur 321001
Tel: 2322, 2864, 2260

Golbagh Palace Hotel
Agra Road, Bharatpur 321001
Tel: 3349

Sivas Tourist Bungalow (ITDC)
Fatehpur, Sikri Road,

Bharatpur 321001
Tel: 2169

Bhavnagar, Gujarat

Hotel Apollo (2 star)
Opp. Central Bus Station, Bhavnagar
Tel: 25249-7 Telex: 0162-225 APLO IN

Welcomgroup Nilambagh Palace
Bhavnagar 364002
Tel: 24340, 24422, 29323
Telex: 0162-253 WGNP IN

Bhopal, Madhya Pradesh

Hotel Ramsons International (2 star)
Hamidia Road, Bhopal
Tel: 72298, 72299, 73331
Telex: 0705-354

Jehan Numa Palace Hotel (3 star)
Shamla Hill, Bhopal 462013
Tel: 76080, 76190
Telex: 0705-343 JNPH IN

Bhubaneswar, Orissa

Kalinga Ashok (ITDC-2 star)
Gautam Nagar
Bhubaneswar 751014
Tel: 53318 Telex: 0675-282

Kanorak Bhubaneswar
86/A-1 Gautam Nagar
Bhubangesnar 751014
Tel: 754330 Telex: 0675-343 KNEK IN

Oberoi Bhubaneswar
Nagapalli, Bhubaneswar 751013
Tel: 56116 Telex: 0675-348 HOB IN

Bijapur, Karnataka

Ashok Travelers Lodge (ITDC)
Station Road, Bijapur 586101

Hotel Mayura Adil Shahi
Anand Mahal Road, Bijapur 556101
Tel: 934, 401

Bikaner, Rajasthan

Hotel Lallgarh Palace
Bikaner, 334001, Tel: 3263

Dholamaru Tourist Bungalow (ITDC)
Major Puran Singh Circle
Bikaner 334001
Tel: 8002

Bokaro, Bihar

Blue Diamond (3 star)
Western Ave, Bokaro Street City
Dist Dhanbad, 827001
Tel: 6445/6, 7247
Telex: 0628-204 HBD IN

Hotel Limcas (2 star)
Sector 1, City Center,
Bokaro Steel City, Dist. Dhanbad
Tel: 7375/6, 7387

Bodhgaya, Bihar

Ashok Travellers Lodge (ITDC)
Bodhgaya 824231
Tel: 25 Cable: TOURISM

Bombay, Maharastra

Deluxe / 5 Star

Centaur Hotel
Santa Cruz Airport
Bombay 400099
Tel: 612-6660
Telex: 011-71171 CHTL IN

Holiday Inn
Balraj Sahani Marg, Juhu
Bombay 400049
Tel: 571425, 571435
Telex: 011-71266 HINN IN,
011-71432 HOL IN

Hotel President (Taj)
90 Cuffe Parade
Colaba, Bombay 400005
Tel: 495-0808
Telex 011-4135, 5769, 3124 PRES IN
Fax: 022-495-1201

Oberoi Towers
Nariman Point, Bombay 400021
Tel: 202-4343
Telex: 022-4153, 4154, OBBY IN
Fax: 204-3282

The Taj Mahal Hotel & The Taj Mahal

Inter-continental
Apollo Bundar, Bombay 400039
Tel: 202-3366
Telex: 011-2442, 3837, 6175,
6276 TAJB IN Fax: 022-287-2711

Welcomgroup Sea Rock
Land's End, Bandra, Bombay 400050
Tel: 642-545
Telex: 011-71230, 71140 ROCK IN

4 & 3 star

The Ambassador (4 star)
Veer Nariman Road
Churchgate Ext, Bombay 400020
Tel: 204-1131
Telex: 011-2918

Bombay International
29 Marine Drive, Bombay 400020
Tel: 202-6060
Telex: 011-3428 BINT IN

Centaur Hotel Juhu Beach
Juhu Tara Road, Juhu, Bombay 400049
Tel: 614-3040
Telex: 011-78181

Fariyas Hotel
25 Off Arthur Bundar Rd
Colaba, Bomby 400005
Tel: 204-2911
Telex: 011-3272 ABAN

Grand Hotel
17 Sprott Road, Ballard Estate
Bombay 400038
Tel: 268211

Hotel Natraj
135 Netaji Subhash Road (Marine Drive),
Bombay 400020
Tel: 204-4164
Telex: 011-2302

Others

Astoria Hotel (2 star)
4 J. T. Road, Churchgate
Bombay 400020
Tel: 221814/7 Cable CASABLANCA

Hotel Diplomat
24/26 Mereweather Road, Colaba

Bombay 400039
Tel: 202-1661

Calcutta, West Bengal

Deluxe & 5 Star

Airport Ashok (ITDC)
Calcutta Airport
Calcutta 700052
Tel: 575111
Telex: 021-2271

Oberoi Grand
15 Jawaharlal Nehru Marg
Calcutta 700013
Tel: 292323
Telex: 021-7248, 7854, OBCL IN

Taj Bengal (Taj)
84 B Belveder Road, Alipore
Calcutta 700027
Tel: 494923, 492729
Telex: 021 2612, 2185 TJCA IN

4 & 3 star

Hindustan International
235/1A, J.C. Bose Road
Calcutta 700020
Tel: 442394
Telex: 021-7164, 2321

Park Hotel
17 Park St
Calcutta 700016
Tel: 297941, 297336
Telex: 021-7159, 3177

Great Eastern Hotel
1, 2 & 3 Old Court Home St
Calcutta 700069
Tel: 282311, 282331
Telex: 021-7571

Fairlawn Hotel
13/4 Sudder St
Calcutta 700016
Tel: 244460, 241835 Cable: FAIROTEL

New Kenilworth Hotel
1 & 2 Little Russel St
Calcutta 700071
Tel: 448394
Telex: 021-3395 NKAY IN

Rutt Deen Hotel
21-B London St
Calcutta 700016
Tel: 443884, 445210
Telex: 021-2266

Others

Lindsay Guest House
8B Lindsay St
Calcutta 700087
Tel: 248639

Lytton Hotel
14 Sudder St
Calcutta 700016
Tel: 291875/79
Telex: 021-3562 NYLO IN

Chamba, Himachal Pradesh

Hotel Akhand Chandi
College Road, Chamba
Tel: 171

Chandigarh

Hotel Pankaj (2 star)
Sector 22, Chandigarh
Tel: 41906, 25083
Telex: 0395-367

Hotel Piccadilly (4 star)
Himalaya Marg
Sector 22 B, Chandigarh
Tel: 32223-7
Telex: 0395-256 PICC IN

Hotel President (3 star)
Madhya Marg
Sector 26, Chandigarh
Tel: 40840
Telex: 0395-490 HYG IN

Chorwad, Gujarat

Palace Beach Resort
Chorwad, 362250
Tel: 56, 97, 98
(40 km from Keshod Airport)

Cochin, Kerala

Casino Hotel (3 star)
Willingdon Island, Cochin 682003

Tel: 6821
Telex: 0885-6314 SAFE IN

Grand Hotel (2 star)
M. G. Road, Ernakulam
Cochin 682011
Tel: 33211

International Hotel (2 star)
M. G. Road, Ernakulam
Cochin
Tel: 353911
Telex: 0885-6698 INHO IN

Malabar Hotel (Taj-4 star)
Willingdon Island
Cochin 682009
Tel: 6811
Telex: 0885-6661 MLBR IN

Coimbatore, Tamil Nadu

Sri Annapoorna (3 star)
47 East Arokiasamy Row
R,S. Puram, Coimbatore 641004
Tel: 37621 Telex: 0855-447

Sri Aarvee Hotels (3 star)
308/9 Bharathiar Row
Siohapvour, Coimbatore 641004
Tel: 23201/6
Telex: 0855-460 ARVE IN

Chingleput (Tamil Nadu)

Fisherman's Cove (Taj-5 star)
Covelong Beach
Chingleput Dist, 603112
Tel: 04114-268
Telex: 041-7194 TAJM IN
(32 km south of Madras)

Cuttack, Orissa

Hotel Ashoka
Ice Factory Road
College Sq, Cuttack 753003
Tel: 25708, 25709 Cable: HOTASH

Coonoor, Tamil Nadu

Hampton Manor
Church Road, Coonoor
643101 Nilgiris
Tel: 244, 961

The Ritz
Coonoor , 643101 Nilgiris
Tel: 6242

Dalhouse, Himachal Pradesh

Aroma-n-Claire (2 star)
Court Road, The Mall
Dalhouse 176304
Tel: 99 Cable: AROMAHOTEL

Daman

Hotel Gurukripa
Sea Face Road
Daman 396210 via Vapi
Tel: 446/7

Darjeeling, West Bengal

Bellevue Hotel (2 star),
The Mall
Darjeeling 734101
Tel: 3431/2

Windjammer Hotel (3 star)
Observatory Hill
Darjeeling 734101
Tel: 2397,2541

Dehra Dun, Uttar Pradesh

Hotel Maohuban (3 star)
97 Rajpur Road
Dehra Dun 248001
Tel: 24094/7, 26041
Telex: 0585-268, HMB IN

Hotel Meedas Grand (2 star)
28 Rajpur Road
Dehra Dun 248001
Tel: 27171/2
Telex: 0585-288 HMG IN

Dhanbad, Bihar

Hotel Skylark (2 star)
Bank Mose
Dhanbad 826001
Tel: 4416/8 Telex: 0629-236

Gangtok, Sikkim

Hotel Nor-Khill (3 star)
Stadium Road

Gangtok 737101
Tel: 2386, 2720

Hotel Tashi Delek (3 star)
Mahatma Gandhi Marg
Gangtok 737101
Tel: 2991, 2038

Goa

Deluxe & 5 Star

Aguada Hermitage (Taj)
Sinquerim
Bardez, 403515
Tel: 4401/7
Telex: 0194-206 TAJ IN

Fort Aguada Beach Resort
Sinquerim
Bardez 403515
Tel: 4401/7
Telex: 0196-234 TAJ IN

Majorda Beach Resort
Majorda
Salcete 403713
Tel: 20751, 20303
Telex: 0191-234 MBR

Oberoi Bogmalo Beach
Bogmalo
Dabolim Airport, 403806
Tel: 2191, 2183
Telex: 019-297 OBGA IN

Cidade de Goa
Vainguinim Beach
Dona Paula 403111
Tel: 3301/8
Telex 0194-257 DONA IN

3 & 2 star

Hotel Baia Do Sol (2 star)
Baga, Calangute
Tel: Baga 84/6 Panjim 5207, 3345
Telex: 0494-303 SOL IN

Hotel Fidalgo (3 star)
18H Tune Road, Panjim 403001
Tel: 6291/9 Telex: 0194-213 REST IN

Hotel Mandou (3 star)
D. B. Bandodkar Marg

Panjim 403001
Tel: 6270/9
Telex:0194-226 SHOME IN

Taj Holiday Village (Taj)
Sinquerim
Bardez 403515
Tel: 4414/7
Telex: 0194-206 TAJ IN

Gopalpur-on-Sea, Orrisa

Oberoi Palm Beach
Gopalpur-on-Sea
Dist Ganjam 761026
Tel: 23
Telex: 0673-261

Gulmarg, Kashmir

Hotel Highland Park (3 star)
Gulmarg 193403
Tel: 7, 30, 91
Telex: 0375-320 HHPT IN

Nedous Hotel (2 star)
Gulmarg 193403
Tel: 28

Woodlands
Gulmarg 193403
Tel: 68

Gwalior, Madhya Pradesh

Motel Tansen
6-A Gandhi Marg
Gwalior 470002
Tel: 21568

Welcomgroup Usha Kiran Palace
Jagendraganj, Lashkar
Gwalior 474009
Tel: 2345

Guwahati, Assam

Hotel Bellevue
M. G. Road
Guwahati 780001
Tel: 28291/2

Hotel Nandan
G. S. Road
Guwahati 781008

Tel: 32621-9
Telex: 0235-267 NNDN IN

Hassan, Karnataka

Hotel Hassan Ashok (ITDC)
Bangalore-Mangalore Road
Hassan 573201
Tel: 8731/7

Hubli, Karnataka

Hubli Woodlands (1 star)
Keshwapur
Hubli 580023
Tel: 62246

Hyderabad, Andra Pradesh

5 star

Hotel Banjara (Taj)
Banjara Hills
Hyderabad 500034
Tel: 222222
Telex: 0155-6947 BANJ IN

Krishna Oberoi
Road No 1, Banjara Hills
Hyderabad, 500034
Tel: 222121
Telex: 0425-6931 OBH IN

4 & 3 star

Hotel Ashoka (3 star)
6-1-70 Lakidikapool
Hyderabad 500004
Tel: 220077

Ritz Hotel (4 star)
Hillfort Palace
Hyderabad 500463
Tel: 233571
Telex: 0425-6215

Hotel Sampura International (4 star)
Mukran Jahi Road
Hyderabad 500001
Tel: 40165/6

Others

Rock Castle Hotel (2 star)
Road No 6, Banjara Hills

Hyderabad 500034
Tel: 33541/3

Indore, Madhya Pradesh

Hotel Kanchen
Kanchen Baugh
Indore 452001
Tel: 33394/7

Lantern Hotel (3 star)
28 Yashwant Niwas Road, Indore
Tel: 35327

Jabalpur, Madhya Pradesh

Jackson's Hotel (2 star)
Cival LinesJabalpur
Tel: 21320 Telex: 0765-207

Jaipur, Rajasthan

Deluxe

Rambagh Palace Hotel (Taj),
Bhawani Singh Road
Jaipur 302005
Tel. 75141
Telex: 0365-254 RBAG IN

5 & 4 star

Clarks Amar (4 star)
Jawaharlal Nehru Marg
Jaipur 302017
Tel: 822612
Telex: 0365-276

The Jai Mahal Palace (Taj-5 star)
Jacob Road, Cival Lines
Jaipur 302006
Tel: 73215/6
Telex: 0365-250 JMPH IN

Hotel Mansingh (5 star)
Sansar Chandra Road
Jaipur 302001
Tel: 78771 Telex: 0365-344

Others

Bissau Palace
o/s Chandpole Gate
Jaipur 302006
Tel: 74191, 67728

Jaipur Ashok (ITDC-3 star)
Jaisingh Circle, Bani Park
Jaipur 302006
Tel: 75121/6
Telex: 0365-262

Khasa Kothi (3 star)
MI Road, Jaipur
Tel: 75151
Telex: 0365-451

Meru Palace (3 star)
Ramsingh Road, Jaipur 302004
Tel: 61212
Telex: 0365-259 KEPL IN

Jaisalmer, Rajasthan

Narayan Niwas Palace
Near Malka Prol, Jaisalmer
Tel: 108

Jammu (Jammu & Kashmir)

Asia Jammu Tawi (4 star)
Nehru Market
Jammu 180001
Tel: 43930, 43932
Telex: 0377-224 ASIA IN

Hotel Jammu Ashok (ITDC)
Opposite Amar Mahal
Jammu Tawi 180001
Tel: 43127, 43864
Telex: 0377-227

Jhansi, Uttar Pradesh

Jhansi Hotel
Shaskri Marg, Jhansi
Tel: 1360

Hotel Veeragann
(UP Tourism)

Jodhpur, Rajasthan

Ajit Bhawan
Near Circuit House
Jodhpur 342006
Tel: 20409

Hotel Ratanada Ashok (ITDC)
Residency Road
Jodhpur 342001

Tel: 25910
Telex: 0552-233 POLO IN

Welcomgroup Umaid Bhawan Palace
Jodhpur 342006
Tel: 22516, 22316
Telex: 0552-202 UBP IN

Kangra, Himachal Pradesh

Palace Motel
Paragarh, Kangra 176081
Tel: Baijnath 34

Kanpur, Uttar Pradesh

Hotel Meghdoot (3 star)
17/B-3 The Mall
Kanpur 208001
Tel: 51141
Telex: 0325-282 MGDT IN

Kargil, Kashmir (Ladakh)

Welcomgroup Highlands
Baroo, Kargil
Ladakh 194105, Tel: 41

Kasauli, Himachal Pradesh

Alasia Hotel
Kasauli 173204, Tel: 8

Khajuraho, Madhya Pradesh

Chandela (Taj 5 star)
Khajuraho
Dist Chhatrapur 471606
Tel: 55

Jass Obero (5 star)
Khajuraho
Dist. Chhatrapur 471606
Tel: 85/8

Khajuraho Ashok (ITDC 3 star)
Khajuraho 417606
Tel: 24

Khimsar, Rajasthan

Welcomgroup Royal Castle
P. O. Khimsar
Dist Nagaur
Tel: 28

Kodaikanal, Tamil Nadu

Carlton Hotel (3 star)
Lake Road
Kodaikanal 624101
Tel: 560 to 576
Telex: 0445-285 CARL IN

Kota, Rajasthan

Brijraj Bhawan Palace Hotel
Cival Lines
Kota 324001
Tel: 23071

Hotel Navrang
Cival Lines
Kota 324001
Tel: 26852/3

Chambal Tourist Bungalow (RTDC)
Nayapura, Kota
Tel: 26527

Kottayam, Kerala

Anjali Hotel (2 star)
K. K. Road
Kottayam 686001
Tel: 3661 Telex: 0888-212

Kovalam, Kerala

Kovalam Ashok Beach Resort (ITDC)
Kovalam, Vizhinjam
Trivandrum 695522
Tel: 68010 Telex: 0884-216

Kulu, Himachal Pradesh

Span Resorts (3 star)
Kulu-Manali Road, Dist Kulu
Tel: Katrain 38, 40

Leh, Ladakh, Kashmir

The Ladakh Sarai
Stok, Ladakh.
(Book through Mountain Travel, Delhi
Tel: 771055, 523057)

Lonavla, Maharastra

Fariyas Resort (3 star)
Tungarli, Lonavla

Tel: 2701-5
Telex: 011-3272

Lucknow, Uttar Pradesh

Clarks Avadh (4 star)
8 Mahatma Gandhi Marg
Lucknow 226001
Tel: 40130
Telex: 0555-243

Carlton Hotel (3 star)
Shahnajaf Road
Lucknow 226001
Tel: 44021
Telex: 0555-217

Madras, Tamil Nadu

Deluxe & 5 star

Taj Coromandel Hotel (Taj)
17 Nungambakkam High Road
Madras 600034
Tel: 474849
Telex: 041-7194 TAJM IN
Fax: 044-470070

Welcomgroup Adayar Park
132 TTK Road
Madras 600018
Tel: 452525
Telex: 041-6868 WELC IN

Welcomgroup Chola Sheraton
10 Cathedral Road
Madras 600086
Tel: 473347
Telex: 041-7200 WELC IN

4 star

Connemara Hotel (Taj)
Binny Road
Madras 600002
Tel: 860123
Telex: 041-8197/488 CH IN

3 & 2 star

Hotel Ashoka (3 star)
33 Pantheon Road, Egmore
Madras 600088
Tel: 568977
Telex: 041-7510 ASOK IN

Hotel Dasa Prakash
100 Poonamalse High Road
Madras 600084
Tel: 661111
Telex: 041-7837

Hotel Imperial
14 Whanness Rd, Egmore
Madras 60008
Tel: 566176

Savara Hotel
69 Dr Radhakrishnan Road
Madras 60004
Tel: 474700 Telex: 041-6896

Madurai, Tamil Nadu

Hotel Madurai Ashok (ITDC)
Alagarkoil Road
Madurai 625002
Tel: 42531
Telex: 0445-297

Padyan Hotel (3 star)
Race Course, Tallakulam
Madurai 625002
Tel: 42471
Telex: 0445-214 COSY IN

Mahabalipuram, Tamil Nadu

Silversands Beach Resort (3 star)
Kovelong Road
Mahabalipuram 6030104
Tel: (04113)-228
Telex: 041-8082 SANDS IN

Mandawa, Rajasthan

Hotel Castle Mandawa
Mandawa, Dist Jhunjhunu
Shekhavati 337004
Tel: 24 Cable: CASTLEMANDAWA
(Jaipur Tel: 75358, 65901)

Mangalore, Karnataka

Hotel Srinavas (3 star)
Ganapatti High School Road
Mangalore 575001
Tel: 22381 Telex: 0832-328 SIRI IN

Moti Mahal (3 star)
Falnir Road

Mangalore 575001
Tel: 22211
Telex: 0832-314 MOTI IN

Welcomgroup Manjarun (4 star)
Bundas Road
Mangalore 575001
Tel: 25455
Telex: 0832-316 WELH IN,
0842-253 KWVD IN

Mount Abu, Rajasthan

Hotel Samrat International
Near Bus Stand
Mount Abu
Tel: 73,53

Mussoorie, Uttar Pradesh

Savoy Hotel
Library, Mussoorie 248 179
Tel: 2510, 2628

Mysore, Karnataka

Lalitta Mahal Palace Hotel (ITDC)
Mysore 570011
Tel: 27650
Telex: 0846-217

Hotel Metropole (3 star)
5 Jhansilakshmibai Road
Mysore 570005
Tel: 20681
Telex: 0846-214 RITZ IN

Hotel Rajendra Vilas Palace
Chamundi Hills
Mysore 570010
Tel: 22050
Telex: 0846-231

Nagpur, Maharashra

Hotel Jargsons
30 Back Central Avenue
Nagpur 440018
Tel: 48611-19
Telex: 0715-369 JAGS IN

Hotel Radhika
Panchshesl Sq, Wardha Road
Nagpur 440012
Tel: 22011-16 Telex: 0715-459 RDKA IN

Nanital, Uttar Pradesh

Sharvani Hilltop Inn
Sharvani Lodge, Mallittal
Nanital 263001
Tel: 2504, 2498

Grand Hotel
The Mall
Nanital 263001
Tel: 2406

Ootacamund (OOTY), Nilgiris, Tamil Nadu

Hotel Dasaprakash
Ootacamund
Nilgiris 643001
Tel: 2434

Savoy Hotel (Taj-3 star)
Ootacamund
Nilgiris 643001
Tel: 2572, 2463
Telex: 0853-240 SAHO IN

Pahalgam, Kashmir

Hotel Woodstock
Pahalgam 192126
Tel: 27 Cable: WOODSTOCK

Pahalgam Hotel (3 star)
Pahalgam, 192126
Tel: 26, 52, 78

Palghat, Kerala

Hotel Indraprastta (3 star)
English Church Road
Palghat 678001
Tel: 4641
Telex: 0852-230 HIND IN

Patna, Bihar

Hotel Chanakya (3 star)
Birchand Patel Marg
Patna 800001
Tel: 23141

Hotel Pataliputra Ashok (ITDC 3 star)
Birchand Patel Marg, Patna 800001
Tel: 26270, 23487
Telex: 022-311

Welcomgroup Maurya-Patna (5 star)
South Gandhi Maidan
Patna 800001
Tel: 22061
Telex: 022-214 MAUR IN

Port Blair, Andaman Islands

Andaman Beach Resort
Corbyn's Cove
Port Blair 744101
Tel: 3381, 2599

Welcomgroup Bay Island
Marine Hill
Port Blair 744101
Tel: 2881, 3380
Telex: 069-5207 BAY IN

Pune (Poona), Maharastra

Hotel Blue Diamond (4 star)
11 Koregaon Road
Pune 411001
Tel: 63775
Telex: 0145-369

Hotel Amir (3 star)
15 Connaught Roa
 Pune 411001
Tel: 61840
Telex: 0145-292 AMIR IN

Rajkot, Gujarat

Hotel Tulsi
Kanta Shee Vikas Gruh Road
Rajkot 360002
Tel: 31795
Telex: 0169-339

Ranchi, Bihar

Hotel Arya (3 star)
H. B. Road, Lalpur
Ranch 834101
Tel: 20477
Telex: 0625-253

Hotel Yuuraj (2 star)
Doranda
Ranch 834002
Tel: 24805
Telex: 0625-229 HYRE IN

Sariska, Rajasthan

Hotel Sariska Palace
Sariska, Dist Alwar 301022
Tel: Sariska 22

Shilong, Meghalaya

Hotel Pinewood Ashok (ITDC)
Shilong 793001
Tel: 23116
Telex: 0237-222

Shimla, Himachal Pradesh

Oberoi Clarkes (3 star)
The Mall, Shimla 171001
Tel: 6091
Telex: 0391-206 OBCL IN

Asia The Dawn
Mahavir Ghati
Shimla 171001
Tel: 5858
Telex: 0391-205 ASIA IN

Siliguri, West Bengal

Hotel Sinclairs (3 star)
Pradhan Nagar
Siliguri 734403
Tel: 22674

Srinagar, Kashmir

4 star

Hotel Broadway
Maulana Azad Road
Srinagar
Tel: 79101, 79201
Telex: 0375-212 BWAY IN

Oberoi Palace
Gupkar Road
Srinagar 190001
Tel: 75617, 75618
Telex: 03715-201 LXSR IN

Others

Hotel Boulevard (2 star)
The Boulevard, Srinagar 190001
Tel: 77089

Nedou's Hotel
Maulana Azad Road, Srinagar
Tel:7301

Hotel Pamposh (3 star)
Residency Roa, Srinagar
Tel: 75601

Hotel Zabaruan
The Boulevard, Srinagar
Tel: 71441

Trichur, Kerala

Hotel Elite International
Chembotil Lane, Trichur 680001
Tel: 21033
Telex: 0087-202 ELIT IN

Tiruchrapalli, Tamil Nadu

Hotel Sangam (3 star)
Collector's Office Road
Tiruchrapalli 620001
Tel: 25202, 25292
Telex: 0455-221

Hotel Aristo
2 Dindigul Road
Tiruchirpalli 620001
Tel: 26565
Telex: 0455-265 ARIS IN

Trivandrum, Kerala

Hotel Horizon (3 star)
Aristo Road, Thampanoor,
Trivandrum 695014
Tel: 66888
Telex: 0435-346 HRZN IN

Mascot Hotel (3 star)
Palayan, Trivandrum 695033
Tel: 68990
Telex: 0435-229 KTDC - IN

Udaipur, Rajasthan

5 star

Lake Palace Hotel (Taj)
Pichola Lake, Udaipur 313001
Tel: 23241
Telex: 033-203 LPAL IN

Shivnivas Palace
City Palace
Udaipur 313001
Tel: 28239
Telex: 033-226 IPAL IN

Others

Hotel Shikarbadi (4 star)
Goverdhanvilas
Udaipur 313001
Tel: 25321
Telex: 033-227 BADI IN

Hotel Anand Bhawan
Fatehsagar Road
Udaipur 313001
Tel: 23256, 23257

Hotel Hill Top
5 Ambavaa Garh
Fatehsagar, Udaipur 31300
Tel: 23151, 23708

Udipi, Karnataka

Summer Sands Beach Resort
Chotamangalore
Ullal-574159
Tel: 6400/7

Varanasi (Benares), Uttar Pradesh

5 star

Hotel Clarks Varanasi
The Mall
Varanasi 221002
Tel: 42401
Telex: 0545-204 CLAK IN

Taj Ganges (Taj)
Nadesar Palace Grounds
Varanasi 221002
Tel: 42480, 42495
Telex: 0545-219 TAGA IN

Others

Hotel Varanasi Ashok (ITDC)
The Mall
Varanasi 221002
Tel: 42550
Telex: 0545-205

Pallavi International (3 star)
Hathwa Place
Chetgaunj
Varanasi 221001
Tel: 54894, 66483

Visakhapatnam, Andra Pradesh

Park Hotel (4 star)
Beach Road
Visakhapatnam530023
Tel: 63081
Telex: 0495-230

Dolphin Hotel (4 star)
Dabagardens
Visakhapatnam 530020
Tel: 64811
Telex: 0495-316

SHOPPING

WHAT TO BUY

Leave plenty of space in your baggage for the shopping you are bound to do in India. The assortment of wares is staggering, and so are the comparatively low prices.

Places selling handicrafts (of all kinds) are an inevitable first stop for the shopper. These handicrafts are themselves statements of the diversity that is India, and are at the same time products of its remarkably varied and attractive artistic traditions. Nowhere else could such variety exist. Interesting as souvenirs, many are also valuable investments.

Carpets from Kashmir, at the upper end of the price range, crafted in the Persian tradition, are available in different sizes and counts. Unless you know a lot about carpets, shop at a government emporia. Less expensive but lovely, rugs and druggets from all over the country are attractive accessories for your home. Then there is the huge assortment of precious and semi-precious gemstones, jewelry set both in gold and silver, traditional as well as modern, chunky or dainty, all at prices that are irresistible.

Textiles for which India is justly famous, present a bewildering array of textures, weaves, prints, designs and colors, which would make unusual and attractive dresses, cushion covers or bed spreads. Shawls, rich evening stoles and silk scarves make excellent gifts. Remember that many hotel tailors offer 24-hour tailoring.

Carved figurines of ivory or sandalwood and elaborately worked wooden panels from the south make memorable souvenirs. Objects in brass, copper and gun metal, inlaid, enamelled, worked or simply beaten, offer a wide choice.

Exquisite marble inlay work and papier-mache items with intricate designs are painstakingly crafted in traditions that have existed for centuries. Reproductions of miniature paintings on ivory, paper or cloth must be chosen carefully. Look at several before you decide. Leather wallets, shoes and bags, if less exotic, are also good buys. handprinted pottery, and cane goods ranging from table mats to furniture, are excellent value. The incredible array of ready-made clothes, both the cheap cotton casuals, and the more sophisticated boutique clothes, could be interesting additions to your wardrobe. Antiques and semi-antiques of every kind are tempting, but bear in mind laws governing the export of antiques and beware of fakes.

USEFUL ADDRESSES

TOURIST INFORMATION

Government of India Tourist Offices in major cities both in India and abroad are valuable sources of information. Pick up a selection of their wide range of brochures on popular destinations. They are primarily information and advice centers and are not equipped to make reservations. They are however, able to assist in itinerary planning and have a list of Government Approved Travel Agencies. Should you want to meet the local people, tourist offices also have lists of families who would be happy to have you visit. They can also help put you in touch with people in your line of business.

Information on paying-guest facilities is also available at tourist offices. Guides proficient in English and other world languages can also be arranged. Charges range from Rs, 50 to Rs 70 for a half day to Rs.50 to Rs. 100 for a full day's sightseeing. Information on current cultural events is also available at tourist offices.

The governments of the various States of the Indian Union also run tourist offices in all the big cities. The levels of efficiency vary in these offices, but most are useful stops for detailed information.

SHOPPING AREAS

With the amazing variety of goods offered, shopping can be bewildering, so do look around before you start buying. For safe shopping, government emporia and shops on the approved list of the Department of Tourism are recommended.

The Central Cottage Industries and the various State Emporia have branches in major cities. They help make the diversity of Indian wares accessible at central points. If you prefer to wander in the bazaars and bargain, visit these first to get a feel of quality and prices. Be wary of shops to which guides or taxi drivers seem over-eager to take you. You will pay more in these shops to cover their commission. Exports of skins furs and ivory are either banned or strictly regulated. Remember to get a certificate of legitimate sale and permission for export.

GOVERMENT OF INDIA TOURIST OFFICES IN INDIA

New Delhi
88 Janpath
Tel: 320005/8

Agra
191 The Mall
Tel: 72377

Aurangabad
Krishna Villas
Station Road
Tel: 4817

Bangalore
KFC Building
48 Church Street
Tel: 579517

Bhubaneswar
B-21 Kalpana Area
Tel: 54203

Bombay
123 M Karve Road
Tel: 293144, 291585

Calcutta
4 Shakespeare Sarani
"Embassy"
Tel: 441402, 441475

Cochin
Willingdon Island
Tel: 6045

Guwahati
B K Kakati Road
Ulubari, Tel: 31381

Hyderabad
3-6-369/A-30+31
Sandozi Building
2nd Floor
Himayat Nagar
Tel: 66877

Imphal
Jail Road
Tel: 21131

Jaipur
State Hotel
Khasa Kothi
Tel: 72200

Khajuraho
Near Western
Group Temples
Tel: 47

Madras
154 Anna Salai
Tel: 88685, 88686

Nahariagun
Sector C
Arunachal Pradesh
Tel: 328

Goa
Communidade Building
Church Square
Panaji
Tel: 3412

Patna
Tourist Bhawan
Bir Chand Patel Path
Tel: 26721

Port Blair
VIP Road
Jungli Ghat
P.O. Port Blair-744103
Tel: 3006

Shillong
GS Road
Police Bazar
Tel: 25632

Trivandrum
Trivandrum Airport

Varanasi
15B The Mall
Tel: 43189

OVERSEAS

• **Australia**
  Sydney
  Level 5
  65 Elizabeth Street
  Sydney, NSW 2000
  Tel: (02)-232-1600

• **Austria**
  Vienna
  Operning l/E/1
  1010 Vienna
  Tel: 5871462

• **Canada**
  Toronto
  60 Bloor Street West Suite No. 1003
  Toronto
  Ontario M4W 3B8

Tel: 416962, 3787/88

- **France**
  Paris
  8 Boulevard de la Madeleine
  75009 Paris 9
  Tel: 4265-83-86

- **Italy**
  Milan
  Via Albricci 9
  20122 Milan
  Tel: 804952

- **Japan**
  Tokyo
  Pearl Building
  9-18, Ginza
  7 Chome Chuo-ku
  Tokyo 104
  Tel: (03) 571-5062/63

- **Malaysia**
  Kuala Lumpur
  Lot No. 203
  Wisma HLA
  Jalan Raja Chulan
  50200 Kuala Lumpur
  Tel: 2425285

- **Singapore**
  Singapore
  05-01, 5th Floor Podium
  Block, Ming Court Hotel
  Tanglin Road
  Singapore 1024
  Tel: 2355737/2353804

- **Spain**
  Madrid
  C/o Embassy of India
  31-32, PIO XII, Madrid
  Tel: 4570209

- **Sweden**
  Stockholm
  Sveavagen 9-11,flr
  S-111 57 Stockholm
  Tel: 08-215081/08/101187

- **Switzerland**
  Geneva
  1-3 Rue Chantepoulet
  1201 Geneva
  Tel: 022-321813/315660

- **Thailand**
  Bangkok
  Singapore Airlines Building
  3rd Floor
  62/5 Thaniya Road (Silom)
  Bangkok 10500
  Tel: 2352585, 2356670

- **UAE**
  Dubai
  P. O. Box 12856 DNATA
  Dubai
  Tel: 236870

- **United Kingdom**
  London
  7 Cork Street
  London WIX 2AB
  Tel: 01-437-3677/78

- **USA**
  Chicago
  230 North Michigan Avenue
  Chicago ILL 60601
  Tel: 312-236-6899/7869/7870

  Los Angeles
  3550 Wilshire Blvd
  Suite Apartment 204
  Los Angeles CA 90010
  Tel: (213) 380-8855

  New York
  30 Rockefeller Plaza
  Suite 15
  North Mezzanine
  New York NY 10020
  Tel: 212-586-4901/2/3

- **West Germany**
  Frankfurt
  Kaiserstrasse 77-111
  6000 Frankfurt Main-1
  Tel: 235423/24

PHOTOGRAPHY

Film in India is expensive and not always available. Some of the Japanese print films are becoming more common but quality reversal film such as Kodachrome 25 and 64 is rarely available. Bring more film than you think you will need. Surplus film can be given away as presents and are always greatly appreciated.

There are few places where prompt and reliable camera servicing can be done, so equipment should be checked before arriving in India. If your equipment is new , it is advisable to shoot a test roll before leaving home to ensure that you are familiar with the equipment and check that everything is working as expected.

Carrying an extra camera body not only gives flexibility in using alternative lenses or film types, but also acts as a back up in case of mechanical or electrical failure.

Protect both your camera and film from excessive exposure to heat, dust and humidity. Do not leave it in direct sun or a locked car (which can get incredibly hot) as heat affects film.

It is best to hand carry film in a plastic bag which at airports can be handed to the security officers for inspection rather than go through the X-ray machines. Processing of print film is available even in small towns and the service is usually quick. The quality varies from acceptable to poor so unless you need prints in a hurry, it is best to take film 'home' for processing.

Ektachrome and Fujichrome slide film can also be processed in Delhi and Bombay. There are some extremely good laboratories. Although most shops offer to do E-6-process, the quality varies. For advice, consult a local professional photographer.

The magic hours of two hours after dawn and before sunset are the the best period for photographs. The haze and dust during the dry months demand extra care. Most people are good-natured about being photographed but in some areas they now realise they can demand a fee. Photography is prohibited in some tribal areas and inside most temples. For security reasons, photography at airports, bridges, railway stations and defence installations is prohibited. Photography from the air is also prohibited.

Special permission is required from the Archeological Survey of India (behind the National Museum, Janpath, New Delhi) for the use of a tripod and artificial lights at monuments or museums under their control.

ART/PHOTO CREDITS

INDEX

H

Haily National Park, 310
Halebid, 260
haleem, 304
Hall of Audience, 138
Hampi, 260, *261*
Handicraft Museum, Orissa, 196
handicrafts, 227, 293-5
 embroidery, 295-6
 in brass, 293, 294
 in gold and silver, 294
 in stone and wood, 294-5
Hangseshwari Temple, 173
Haramandirji, 157
Harappa, 25-6
Hardwar, 113
Hari Parbat, 122
Harwan, 121
Haryana,
 see, Punjab and Haryana
Hawa Mahal, Jaipur, *13*, 136, *137*
Hayagribha Madadeva Mahdap
 Temple, 186
Hazratbal, 122
health and emergencies, 322
health precautions, 315
Hemavati River, 260
Hemis, 127
high commissions, 336-8
hijruh, 84
Hill of Devi, E.M. Foster, 148
hill resorts, 113, 125
Himachal Pradesh, 20, 114-9
 background and physical
  features, 114-5
 folk song and dances, 115
 Kangra District, 117-8
 Lahaul and Spiti, 117
 Mandi, 118
 trekking, 119
 winter sports, 118-9
Himalaya, 20, *114*, *155*
Himalayan landscape, 7
Himalayan Mountaineering
 Institute, 183
Hinayana, 81
Hindi, 68
Hindola Mahal, 149
Hindu deities, *74*
Hindu divinities, 239
Hindu festivals, 273-7
Hinduism, 73-9, 285
 during the Gupta Age, 29
 festivals, 74
 ideas and practices, 78
 in comparison to Buddhism, 82
 in modern India, 78-9
 in the Middle Ages, 78
 mythology, 76-8
 Vedic Age, 74-6
Hindus, 120
Hindustan, 116
history,
 see, ancient history
 see, British rule
 see, modern history
 see, religion
 see, sultanates
hoalige, 260
Holi, 273-4
Hoogly, 164, 172, 174
Hospital, Presency General, 164
hot springs, 117
houseboats, *120*, 122
Hridey Kunj, 226
Humayun's Mausoleum, 101

Hussain Sagar, 249
Hutatma Chauk, 208
Hyderabad, 19, 249-50
Hyderabad-Secunderabad, 250

I

Iberian, 217
ice-skating, 118
idli, 303
ikat, 296
Imambara, 172
Imphal, 191
independence, 53
Independence Day parade, *278*
India Gate, 101
Indian Institute of Management,
 225
Indian Union, 93
India today, 54-9
 "dangerous decade", 55
 democratic roots, 55-6
 development through time, 54
 economic enigma, 58
 federal polity, 56-7
 industrial policy, 58-9
Indian Institute of Management,
 225-6
Indore, 147-8
Indus River, 128
industrial centers, 161
Indus Valley, 25
industrial plants, 259
industrial policy, 58
industrialization, 41-2, 45, 59
industries, 41-2
invasions, 38
iron, 27
iron-ore, 18
irrigation, 30
Islam, 183, 184, 291
 in India, 184
 Muhammad and his creed, 83-4
Islamic influence, 241
Islamic rule,
 in Utta Pradesh, 107

J

Jagannath Temple, 197
Jahanpanah, 98
Jahaz-Mahal, 101, 149
Jaigarh Fort, 137
Jainism, 73, 82-3
Jain temples, 161
Jaipur, 136-7
 City Palace, 136
 City Palace Museum, 136
 Hawa Mahal, 136
 Jantar Mantar, 136
Jaisalamer, 18, 145
Jaisalmer Fort, *144*
Jal Mahal, 137
Jami Masjid, *79*, 103, 123
Jammu and Kashmir, 120-6
 craftsmen, 123-4
 hill resorts, 124-5
 Jammu, 120-1
 Kashmir Valley, 121
 Ladakh, 125
 Leh town, 126
 monasteries, 125-6
 mosques, 123
 Mughul Gardens, 122
 Nagin Lake and Hari Parbat, 122

 religion, 121
 Shey, Thikse and Hemis, 126-7
 Srinagar city, 121-2
Jamnager, 227
Jamshedji Navroz, 278
Jamshedpur, 18, 161
Janamsthmi, festival, 274
Jantar Mantar, 102
Jaransanko, 167
jasmine, 259
jati, 66
Jawalamukhi, 118
jelabis, 305
jewelry,
 in silver, 224
Jews, 87, 207
Jhalawar, 141
Jhelum River, 122
Jodhpur, 144-5
jiva, 83
Jnana, 76
Jodhpur, 18
Jodhpur Palace, *142*
Jog Falls, 256
Jugal Kishore, 110
juley, greeting, 127

K

kababs, 304
Kaccha, 18
Kadam Rasal, 199
kadambas, 258
kadi, 303
Kailasa Temple, 257
Kailashanath, 289
Kailash Temple, 213
Kaivalya, 82
Kalachand Sri Mandir, 177
Kalahasti, 241
Kalakshetra, 237
kalamkari, 296
Kalimpong, 176
Kali Temple, 170
Kalka, 114
Kalijal Temple, 198
Kalpa, 116
Kamakhya Mandir, 186
kamangiri, figurative painted
 woodwork, 295
kambala, 261
Kanchenjunga, 182
Kanchi, 241
Kanchipuram, 245-6
Kanger Valley, 151
Kangra District, 117
Kanha,
 wildlife sanctuary, 150
Kanha National Park, 308
 tiger reserve, 310
Kani, 297
Kannada, 65, 257
 origin, 257
kantha quilts, 296-7
kara, (steel bangle), 86
Kareri Lakes, 118
Kargil, 125
Karma, 76
Karnal, 130
Karnataka, 19, 256-61
 architecture, 259
 beaches, 260-1
 folk drama and buffalo
  races, 261
 geographical position, 256
 history, 257-8